SHIRLEY TEMPLE
American Princess

Books by Anne Edwards

BIOGRAPHY

Sonya: The Life of Countess Tolstoy
Vivien Leigh: A Biography
Judy Garland: A Biography
Road to Tara: The Life of Margaret Mitchell
Matriarch: Queen Mary and the House of Windsor
A Remarkable Woman:
A Biography of Katharine Hepburn
Early Reagan
Shirley Temple: American Princess

NOVELS

The Survivors
Miklos Alexandrovitch Is Missing
Shadow of a Lion
Haunted Summer
The Hesitant Heart
Child of Night

AUTOBIOGRAPHY

The Inn and Us (with Stephen Citron)

CHILDREN'S BOOKS

P. T. Barnum
The Great Houdini
The Bible for Young Readers

SHIRLEY TEMPLE
American Princess

ANNE EDWARDS

COLLINS
8 Grafton Street London W1
1988

William Collins Sons & Co. Ltd
London · Glasgow · Sydney
Auckland · Toronto · Johannesburg

BRITISH LIBRARY CATALOGUING IN PUBLICATION DATA

Edwards, Anne
Shirley Temple: American Princess.
1. Cinema films. Acting. Temple, Shirley, 1928 –
I. Title
791. 43'028'0924

ISBN 0–00–217988–1

First published 1988
Copyright © 1988 by Anne Edwards

Printed and bound in Great Britain by
T. J. Press (Padstow) Ltd, Padstow, Cornwall

ACKNOWLEDGEMENTS

THIS BOOK DEPENDS IMMEASURABLY on those people who have been a part of Shirley Temple Black's life and career, and who shared their memories so generously with me. Their fine recall and insight have enabled me to reconstruct the first sixty years of a woman who, I suspect, is one of the world's best-loved citizens. I hope I have given a truthful picture of her life and the forces that shaped it. That is a biographer's goal.

I owe a great debt to Mrs. Black's life-long friend Nancy Majors Voorheis, and to John Agar, as well as to Marcia Mae Jones, Sybil Jason, Diana Serra Cary, Dick Moore, Jackie Cooper and Delmar Watson, who grew up on the sound stages of Hollywood with her. I am especially grateful, also, for the tremendous help of Alice Faye, Alex Gottlieb, Graham Greene, June Lang, Joseph LaShelle, George Montgomery, Laraine Day, Ginger Rogers, Gloria Stuart, Robert Young and Richard Zanuck, who figured strongly in her movie years.

The great joy of writing this book has been in researching the richness and variety of Shirley Temple Black's experiences and accomplishments. Many people interviewed were so articulate and knowledgeable about her post-Hollywood years that their insight has made a considerable contribution to the story. These include former President Gerald R. Ford; Congressmen Dante B. Fascell and Paul McCloskey; members of Ambassador Black's immediate staff in Ghana: Craig Baxter, Kenneth Bache, Ralph H. Graner, John (Jack) Linehan and William Rosner; and Sylvia Lowry and Evelyn Nielson of the National Multiple Sclerosis Society.

No biography can hope to create a solid, in-depth and accurate book without the aid of dedicated archivists and historians. I have been most fortunate to have had the assistance of: Leith Adams and Ned Comstock of the University of Southern California; Rose Sue Berstein and Amin Abdelsamad, United States Mission to the United Nations, New York, NY; Roger Bonilla, Palo Alto Main Library, Palo Alto, CA; Emily Boyles, San Francisco Public Library, San Francisco; Columbia University Oral History Department, New York, NY; Anne Caiger and Brigette Kueppers, University of California at Los Angeles, CA; Ernest Conant, Kern County Historical Society, Bakersfield, CA; Debbie Cromwell, New Milford Public Library, New Milford, CT; Alan Hall, Jay Smith and Penny Vogel, San Mateo Public Library, San Mateo, CA; Robert C. Herr, Librarian, State of Hawaii Department of Education, Honolulu, Hawaii; June E. Hetz, Fairview, PA; Richard L. Holzhausen, Gerald R. Ford Library, Ann Arbor, MI; Phyllis W. Johnson, genealogist, Arlington, Virginia; Kristine L. Krueger, Los Angeles, CA; Peg Major, Editor, *Santa Clara Magazine*, Santa Clara University, Santa Clara, CA; Harry Medved and Mark Locher, Screen Actors Guild, Hollywood; Anthony Slide and Lisa Mosher, Academy of Motion Picture Arts and Sciences, Beverly Hills; Christine Munck, *Redbook* magazine, New York, NY; Margaret Olson, Mercer County Historical Society, Mercer, PA; Deidre Patty, San Mateo Historical Museum, San Mateo, CA; Jennifer Pawlowski, Tulsa City-County Library System, Tulsa, OK; Nancy T. Peluso, Senior Librarian, Connecticut State Library, Hartford; Pat Perilli, British Film Institute, London; Sandra K. Peterson, Documents Librarian, Yale University Library, New Haven; Miriam Phelps, Research Librarian, *Publishers Weekly*, New York, NY; Marian Powers, *Time* magazine, New York City; Grace Reiner, Writers Guild of America West, Los Angeles; Charles Silver, the Museum of Modern Art, New York, NY; Barbara M. Soper, Librarian, Buffalo and Erie County Public Library, Buffalo, NY; Suzanne Sutton, Reference Coordinator, Palm Springs Public Library, Palm Springs, CA; Myrna Williamson, the State Historical Society of Wisconsin, Madison, WI.; and Susan Gorman, Linda Zucca, Joey LaRoche and Teri Donley, Sherman, Connecticut.

I would also like to thank Carol Aramaki, Dole Packaged Foods Company, Honolulu, Hawaii; Michael J. Binkow, Fox,

Inc., Los Angeles, CA; Melanie S. Illian, Director of Public Relations, Hotel Inter-Continental, New York, NY; David L. Jensen, Ampex Corporation, Redwood City, CA; Robert S. Poliner, State Chairman, Connecticut Republicans, East Hartford, CT; Jocelyn Clapp, Bettman Archives, New York, NY; Deborah Cohen, Time/Life, Inc., New York, NY; Maxine Fleckner Ducey, University of Wisconsin, Madison, WI; Robert Gough, BBC Hulton Picture Library, London, England; and Jan-Christopher Horak and Kathleen MacRae, George Eastman House, Rochester, NY.

No author could have been more fortunate in the amount and quality of editorial enthusiasm and advice received. I am most grateful to Harvey Ginsberg at William Morrow, and to Carol O'Brien of Collins Publishers, London. I also want to extend my appreciation to Franklin Mount and Bernard Schleifer at Morrow, and to my cross-Atlantic agents, Mitchell Douglas of International Creative Management, New York, his assistant, Jerry Thomas, and Hilary Rubenstein of A. P. Watt, London.

There remains the necessity of acknowledging the private help that enabled me to get through the writing of this book. My secretary/assistant, Barbara Howland, who has now been with me for the span of six books and deserves a special medal; my friend, daughter-in-law and indefatigable researcher, Polly Brown Edwards; and my husband, Stephen Citron, whose participation and support of me and my work cannot be categorized. We are a sharing couple, and my writing—and his as well—are all part of this process.

CONTENTS

ACKNOWLEDGMENTS   5

INTRODUCTION   11

With Gertrude   13

On Her Own   203

Appendices

    Chronology: Shirley Temple Black   355
    Trial Transcript of the High Court of Justice   359
    Review of *Wee Willie Winkie* in *Night and Day,*
       October 28, 1937   363
    Movie Chronology: Shirley Temple   365
    Television Credits: Shirley Temple   393

NOTES   395

BIBLIOGRAPHY   417

INDEX   425

INTRODUCTION

To most of the world, Hollywood from 1934 to 1939 was the Enchanted City, where dwelt numerous queens who came and went, but only one princess—Shirley Temple. True, her position rested on publicity, not ancestry, but she was as well known and beloved in her own country as Britain's little princesses, Elizabeth and Margaret Rose, were in theirs. Hers was the most recognizable face in a world that included Franklin Roosevelt, Winston Churchill, Wallis Simpson, Clark Gable, Greta Garbo and three kings—George V, Edward VIII and George VI. Throughout her seventh to tenth years, wherever movies were exhibited, she was the top box-office star.

Her childhood was lived amid unprecedented adulation. Her ebullient spirit and child's innocence helped America come through the Depression, and reminded a world on the brink of war that there had been more innocent times. Obediently, the cherubic face had refused to age or change much. But the girl who bore it grew into adolescence and then womanhood and, like Peter Pan, was not permitted to grow up—at least by her public.

Then, on a particularly balmy August day in 1967, Shirley Temple Black, age thirty-nine, a housewife and mother, confronted a bevy of newsmen at a press conference in a San Mateo, California, motel dining room and explained why she should be elected to Congress. Her audience was not exactly disrespectful, but even for the most hardened reporter among them there was an unwillingness to let go of the fantasies that prevailed. And so Shirley Temple Black found herself "in mortal combat" with her own "larger-than-life child of the past."

A frown masked the fabled dimples. The golden ringlets had been replaced by a severe, darker hairdo more reminiscent of a Victorian matron than a sixties political candidate. The small, onetime petulant mouth was set grimly. The figure in the neat, burnt-orange executive-type suit, once so childishly guileless, was full-bosomed and wide-hipped. Yet, with its own defiance, the child's face that had given Shirley Temple such celebrity refused to be camouflaged.

"Little Shirley Temple is not running for anything," she said sharply, in a low, resonant voice that had disconcertingly lost its youthful timbre. "If someone insists on pinning me with a label, make it read Shirley Temple Black, Republican independent."

Memories of a dimpled, curly-topped child sitting on the knee of that most famous of all Democrats, Franklin Delano Roosevelt, danced tantalizingly before the eyes of the estimable Fourth Estate. Not only was Shirley Temple declaring her candidacy for Congress, she was entering the highly competitive arena of eleven male candidates, which included three other Republicans and eight Democrats. By the end of that press conference, no one in the room doubted either her dedication or her tough-mindedness. The question in the minds of many of those attending was when and how this amazing transformation from America's little princess to hard-edged political advocate had taken place.

What follows is not only a biography of an American phenomenon. It is the story of a child who was raised to rule, and then, when she reached womanhood, had crown, scepter and power seized from her possession.

With Gertrude

 SOME PEOPLE are able to make themselves believe their own fantasies. George Francis Temple understood that his wife was one of them. In 1927, Gertrude was convinced that she was not just an ordinary housewife, married to a bank clerk, and the mother of two sons, Jack, age twelve, and Sonny, age eight, but a woman who would one day find worldwide love and adulation. George considered her a dreamer and blamed the matinee movies she attended, the crooning love songs she played on their gramophone, and the radio dramas she listened to religiously. Nonetheless, he humored and indulged these romantic pursuits. Whatever else she might be, Gertrude was attractive, a loving wife, a good mother and a careful manager. George also knew that Gertrude had married him at the age of seventeen to escape a difficult home situation, but that she had not been able to abandon her youthful dreams.

Gertrude Amelia Krieger was born in Chicago, Illinois, July 15, 1893. Her father, Otto Julius Krieger, was born in Germany in 1864; and his wife, Maude Elizabeth McGrath, in St. Joseph, Michigan, in 1875. Shortly after Gertrude's birth, the family moved to Elgin, Illinois, also the site of the Elgin Watch Company, where Otto was employed as an experienced technician. Following the birth of Gertrude's younger brother Ralph, the Kriegers returned to Chicago, where Otto opened a small jewelry and watch-repair store at 2049 Adams Street, establishing living quarters for his family above the store. But the Chicago winters proved too harsh for Otto, who had developed lung congestion, and in 1903 he sold his business, and the Kriegers boarded a train to relocate in booming Los Angeles, California, where the sun shone most of the time.

As she journeyed west with her family, the ten-year-old Gertrude's first dreams were born. Being the eldest in her family, and a girl, had hastened her maturity. She had always been a courteous, reliable child, and so, during her father's illness and. the difficulties of selling a business and moving a family, the Kriegers had expected her to help in the care of her brother, Ralph, who was four years her junior. Gertrude possessed an exotic beauty. Olive-skinned, dark-haired, with large, wide-set amber-brown eyes and a smile slow to come but dazzling when displayed, she was her father's favorite. But Krieger's authoritarian personality had turned Gertrude into a shy, fairly reticent girl, and except for her closeness to her family, a loner. Her consuming passion was her love of books. To entertain Ralph, she would read to him by the hour, often repeating the same story three or four times, embellishing the romance and adventure each time, pretending she was the characters about whom she was reading.

The idea of going to California—that legendary land of perpetual summer, of orange groves in sight of snowy peaks, of explorers who came in pygmy galleons by sea looking for fabled El Dorado and the gold rushers centuries later who proved the legend true—was intriguing. Fired by the tales she read and her own dreamy nature, Gertrude anticipated great adventure when she reached her destination. The train journey fired her imagination as the vehicle crossed the vast, spreading plains and climbed up thick-forested slopes, traveled across narrow bridges that spanned wild-currented rivers and paused in bleak towns where tough-skinned, wizened old Indians performed war dances for pennies.

Upon their arrival, the Kriegers went directly from the low white stucco, red-tile-roofed buildings that formed Los Angeles Union Passenger Terminal to the home of a fellow Chicagoan. An enterprising man, Mr. Krieger soon moved his family into the second floor of a frame building at 2022 Bonita, and opened a jewelry and watch-repair shop below. Gertrude's life in Los Angeles did not differ significantly from her life in Chicago, apart from the dry and temperate climate. She was enrolled in school and was obliged to help care for Ralph in her free time while her mother joined Mr. Krieger in the store. Gertrude's romantic adventure had been reduced to taking a round-trip Angel's Flight, a miniature cable railway that traversed 315 feet up and down the steep slope of nearby Bunker Hill. For the two-cent fare, she used the money she earned tending neighbors' children along with her brother.

Soon after the family had set down roots in Los Angeles, Otto Krieger's health declined further, and in 1908, when Gertrude was fifteen years old, he died. For a time, Maude tried to keep her husband's business afloat, but watch repairing had always been the mainstay of the business. Krieger's Jewelry Shop was forced to close, and Gertrude, resentment festering, left Polytechnic High School to help her mother support the family. Still mesmerized by stories she read in books, Gertrude had nurtured ambitions of becoming an actress or a ballet dancer.

These were dark days for the Kriegers. Both mother and daughter took what odd jobs they could find: Maude did sewing at home, and Gertrude became a file clerk. Ralph, only eleven when his father died, still required some supervision. Gertrude was a withdrawn young woman, but her dark good looks set her apart, and when she was encouraged to speak, her natural intelligence and a radiant smile would surface. When George Francis Temple, age twenty-one and five years her senior, met her, he was immediately captivated. Here was just the wife he had been looking for: pretty, hard-working, conservative, well-mannered, unspoiled and intelligent. George was employed by the Southern California Edison Company as a clerk, but he had ambitions for which a supportive wife would be an asset. He wasted no time in proposing marriage. Maude thought Gertrude was too young. The couple waited until late summer, 1910, when Gertrude had celebrated her seventeenth birthday and George his twenty-second, by which time he was earning enough to support his new wife and her family.

George Francis Temple was born in Fairview, Pennsylvania, in May 1888, of Dutch, German and English descent.* His ancestors had come to America before the Revolutionary War

*George Temple later wrote to Mrs. Robert Hetz of Fairview, Pa. (March 19, 1976): "My daughter [Shirley Temple Black] tells everyone that I am Penn. Dutch. I personally think that we are more English. We consider General Amberson as one of the famous people connected with our family. I have some old land grants showing that we owned land in Fort Pitt, which is now Pittsburgh, Pa."

from England and the western region of Germany to seek economic and religious freedom, settling first in the area of Lancaster. George's father, Dr. Francis Temple, had been born in Crawford County, Pennsylvania, in 1850, and graduated the medical department of the University of Pennsylvania at Philadelphia in 1884. He began his practice in Mercer, Pennsylvania, where he had married Cynthia Yaeger in 1876. Their first two children, Grace and Herbert, were born in Mercer, where Dr. Temple and his family lived with his elderly aunt, Nancy Flake. Upon her death, Dr. Temple inherited a small amount of money and moved his family north to Fairview, near the shores of Lake Erie, where two more sons, George and Francis, Jr., were born.

Dr. Temple was a flamboyant man, and stories about him soon made him legend in the county. George was later to write another old-time Fairview resident: "Our home in Fairview, as I well remember, was a two story house and the doctor's office was on the first floor . . . I also remember the shooting incident. My father had purchased a revolver, in case of burglars, and one night he awoke and saw a figure passing through the bedroom, took the pistol from beneath his pillow, and shot at the figure, which just happened to be my mother, the bullet just missing her head. I also remember when he was chopping wood out behind the house one day, and mother placed her finger on the chopping block and said, 'Chop this off.' He did just that and the finger fell in the snow. He picked up the finger, and took mother Temple in the house, and sewed the finger back on again. And there were many times that she showed us the scars and told us to never goad a person into doing anything like this, as people will call your bluff."

Dr. Temple was on the staff of the County Coroner, and his many activities, "driving through storms [to tend the sick], performing operations on kitchen tables," may have taken too much from him, for on June 18, 1896, at the age of thirty-nine, he died of pneumonia. Mrs. Temple and the children moved back to Mercer, where they lived with her family until 1900, when she bought a house in Erie, Pennsylvania. George's only sister, Grace, soon contracted tuberculosis, and Mrs. Temple sold their home in 1903 and set out for the sunnier climes of Los Angeles, California. The family resettled in a house at 2519

Powell Street, where Grace's health improved. Herbert, who was five years older than George, became the man—and the protector—of the family and saw that his two younger brothers received a fair education (although neither George nor Francis attended college).

A dapper young man, short of stature but trim, broad-shouldered and quick-stepping, George compensated for Gertrude's aloofness with his affable personality and sense of humor. He tended to tease Gertrude, to her embarrassment, but they made a handsome couple, about equal in height, his lighter hair and hazel-brown eyes complementing her darker good looks. Their first home was a five-room apartment at 1907 West Forty-first Place, which they shared with Mrs. Krieger and Ralph. Marriage had not won Gertrude the independence for which she had longed. Since George refused to have his wife work, she once again was taking care of her family and their home, and all too soon, an ailing mother and a baby. On January 3, 1915, John (Jack) Stanley Temple was born. George was delighted to have a son. Small boys were hardly a novelty to Gertrude and she nurtured a wish for a daughter in the future.

His many responsibilities kept George safe from the war. They also gave him the opportunity to advance while others in the company went off in 1917 to fight overseas with the Allies against the Kaiser's German forces. George Francis Temple, Jr., (thereafter known as Sonny) was born on January 24, 1919. The Temples moved to 263 Kenilworth Street in the more suburban area of Eagle Rock. George was no longer just a clerk, but an accountant (so designated on Sonny's birth certificate), with the Southern California Edison Company. Gertrude's life had spun around full circle as she cared for her two small boys and still sublimated her fantasies of being "in the theater" by enacting the characters in the storybooks she read aloud to her sons. But about this time a new art form—the "flickers"—had entered her life.

Movies were being made practically in Gertrude's backyard as motion-picture companies opened their studios in Los Angeles, Santa Monica, Glendale and, finally, in Hollywood. The trek to the Pacific by film hopefuls began in 1912, when Pearl White, saucer eyes fixed upon the camera, golden curls askew as she landed rudderless sky balloons and jumped from the rooftops of tall buildings, became the heroine of thriller serials. Any girl could get a job if she would ride along in the cab of a runaway locomotive. Not being daring enough for such stunts, Gertrude contented herself with taking the boys to the "flicks" whenever she could, especially to see Pearl White and "the cute little girl with the curls"—Mary Pickford. "Little Mary," as she was often called, was the same age as Gertrude, but she continued playing the innocent, lovable child-woman who became America's and the world's sweetheart. For example, in 1918, at the age of twenty-five, she appeared in three films—*The Poor Little Rich Girl, Rebecca of Sunnybrook Farm* and *The Little Princess,* in which she portrayed a youngster with blond curls and a dimpled smile. The stories Gertrude read her children now featured heroines who could all have been played by Mary Pickford.

Ralph was now able to take care of their mother, and so Gertrude, always the romantic, persuaded George to rent a house at 125 Breeze Avenue in Venice, a section of Los Angeles fronting on the Pacific Ocean. Venice had been the dream of Abbot Kinney, a real-estate tycoon with cultural interests. To recreate the glory of its Italian namesake, world-famous architects and engineers set to work in 1900 to build an elaborate system of canals, each four feet deep and forty feet wide. Ocean water was forced in by high tide and retained by locks, the main canal connecting with the ocean at a spot that was appropriately named Playa del Rey. Kinney imported a fleet of graceful gondolas from the original Venice to pick up and discharge passengers from Italianate stucco-built bungalows along the watery streets. He had visualized his Venice as becoming a great art center attracting world-famous opera stars, painters and poets. The enterprise failed to do so, and by the end of World War I, Venice had dissolved into a West Coast Coney Island. Nonetheless, a Venetian ambience was maintained as the gondoliers continued to pole their gondolas through the canals, singing snatches from opera. But soon seaweed drifted into the canals, fungus took root, and an aroma of dying kelp and dead fish filled the air.

About the same time, 1925, as George left the utility company to work as a bookkeeper for the California Bank, the city of Los Angeles incorporated Venice and immediately began to fill in the canals and turn them into paved streets. The Temples moved farther west to Santa Monica, first renting a small house at 334 Twenty-fifth Street. They bought a Spanish-style bungalow at 948 Twenty-fourth Street in 1927. George had been promoted to assistant manager of his bank's branch at Washington Boulevard and Vermont Avenue, and Gertrude had felt they should have an appropriate standard of living to make better contacts. Throughout these years, Gertrude had not lost her fervent interest in the movies, and followed the careers of all the former child stars.

Baby Peggy* had become a star in short comedies at two, and continued her popularity in successful features such as *The Darling of New York* (1923) and *Captain January* (1924). More gamine than "Little Mary," Baby Peggy did charming imitations of Charlie Chaplin and other great comedy stars. She had quickly won the hearts of the movie-going public, and by 1924 was so popular that the Democratic party brought her as a mascot to the Democratic National Convention in Madison Square Garden to vigorously wave the flag as Franklin Delano Roosevelt gave a presidential-nomination speech for New York Governor Alfred E. Smith. With Baby Peggy and Jackie Coogan, who cried real tears with Charlie Chaplin in *The Kid* (1919), leading the way, child stars had burst upon the movie firmament like fireworks on the Fourth of July. Gertrude was not without hope that one of her boys might be the next Jackie Coogan.

Movie magazines proliferated. " 'Your child should be in pictures!' became as commonplace a phrase as 'What an angelic-looking child!' had been a generation earlier," Diana Serra Cary, the mature Baby Peggy, recalled. "In 1921 the Los Angeles *Herald Tribune* headlined a thought-provoking article with: '*Has your baby charm?*' and went on to pierce every ambitious mother to the marrow of her soul. 'Baby Peggy has charm! It has opened the door of the movies to her and enabled the young lady, while still a child, to *earn a salary of a million dollars a year*. Maybe *your* child could do likewise.'

"This was heady stuff, and women from every walk of life were reading such articles every day. As they washed the dishes and shelled peas, they wondered how they could parlay their

---

*"Baby Peggy" was born Peggy Montgomery in 1917. She is known today as author Diana Serra Cary.

own penniless son or daughter into a pint-sized millionaire before another month had passed." And then, with great understanding of women with Gertrude's dreamy nature, Mrs. Cary
adds, "Sometimes they did not even realize how far their plans
had gone in their imagination until someone or some item in the
newspaper triggered the almost ready-made blue print, drawn
up in idle moments during the day's routine. A handful of such
parents made the impressive jump from day-dreaming of stardom for their child to putting it into action, without realizing
what had been accomplished by their own well-defined
schemes."

Gertrude held the dream, but since neither Jack nor Sonny
showed any interest in or talent for becoming performers, she
had no child who could fulfill it for her. Soon, even her story-
times did not command their attention; for by the time they were
both school age, they preferred street games with other boys
their age to stories by their mother's knee, and they had aligned
themselves more closely with George than with Gertrude. By
1927, eight years had passed since Sonny's birth. At thirty-three,
Gertrude already considered herself "middle-aged," and she
decided that before it was too late, she and George should have
a third child—a girl this time. Of course, there was no way to be
certain, but the odds seemed good to Gertrude.*

The new house had absorbed all of George's savings, but he
was convinced that real-estate values would only go up and that
the investment would be sound. Moreover, his wife was happier
than he had ever seen her. To Gertrude, the house was the
beginning of the realization of her vision. Not only did it have
an attached two-car garage (which currently housed only one
car—George's gleaming Graham-Paige sedan) and a large backyard, but on breezy days the wind brought the scent of the
nearby sea. Bougainvillea covered part of the red-tiled roof.
Tropical plants flowered along the front path. The doors, including those of the garage, were of heavily carved wood. A

---

*"My mother was kind of afraid to have a third child," Shirley Temple was later to
recall, "because she wanted a girl but was afraid she would have another boy. So my dad
went to the family doctor, and he said, 'If you have your tonsils out, you will have a girl.'
So they removed my dad's tonsils, and they grew back. He had to have them out a second
time, and nine months after the second operation I was born. There is no medical reason
for the story, but I think it's funny."

massive, tiled fireplace dominated the living room. The Temples had not lived there long when neighbors came to call. Gertrude soon became a member of a local women's bridge club that met once a week.

The film studios had long ago left Santa Monica in favor of the more central regions of greater Los Angeles, where shooting time was not limited by the early-morning and late-afternoon fogs that rolled in from the sea. But the ocean air suited Gertrude, and within a few months of their move she became pregnant. His savings depleted, George borrowed $150 from the bank to cover medical expenses. Gertrude believed strongly in the hypothesis of prenatal influence. Desperately hoping for a girl, she also wanted her daughter to be musically talented and inclined to the arts, especially dancing, a desire of her own which she had suppressed. Therefore, the phonograph spun records endlessly, and Gertrude attended dance recitals and concerts and read and reread her favorite books. At 9:00 P.M. on Monday, April 23, 1928, she and George became the parents of a six-pound eight-ounce baby girl delivered without complications at the Santa Monica Hospital by Dr. Leonard John Madsen. They named the child Shirley.*

Shirley spent the first year of her life in a crib placed in a corner of the living room a short distance from the record player. To lull the baby to sleep, Gertrude played the records she enjoyed most, the popular music of the period. At eight months, Shirley was standing in her crib swaying to the rhythm of the songs. In an early article, Gertrude exclaimed, "She looked like a little dancer, even as a baby . . . she began to walk when she was one year old, as most children do. It was then that the most extraordinary thing appeared in her. She walked on her toes. From the time she took her first step, she ran on her toes, as if she were dancing."

Gertrude believed with enormous pride that her daughter was exceptional and that somehow she was fated for a grand and glorious future. The boys were growing fast (Sonny was nine and Jack thirteen when their sister was born), and didn't require much of her attention, or at least Gertrude convinced herself

---

*Although Temple was later to use the name Shirley Jane Temple, her birth certificate shows no middle name.

this was the case. Life in the Temple house on Twenty-fourth Street was centered upon the comely golden-haired, dimpled child who crooned "Life Is Just a Bowl of Cherries" along with Rudy Vallee and whose chubby but shapely legs seemed constantly in rhythmic motion. When not playing music, Gertrude read her storybooks, enacting the characters (boys' voices deep, girls' pitched higher) as she had once done for Ralph and more recently her two sons. To her delight, Shirley began to mimic her.

It started as a child's game, but soon Gertrude as well as Shirley became wholly caught up in this divertissement.

2 THE TEMPLES were staunch Republicans. Through his connections with the bank, George was allied to the rich, inflexible Old Guard members of the party. When Herbert Hoover won the Republican nomination for president in 1928, they were not pleased, and neither was George. Hoover had served under President Wilson—a Democrat. He had favored membership in the League of Nations. The Old Guard called him "Sir Herbert" because they believed he was pro-British. Nonetheless, his reputation as a great humanitarian while secretary of commerce under Calvin Coolidge had made him especially popular with women voters. He had played a central role in helping the jobless, even during the heady years of Coolidge prosperity. He had been "remarkably sensitive to the plight of Indians, blacks, women, and children," and he had handled relief operations during the disastrous Mississippi flood of 1927 with tremendous zest and with quick aid to the million people made homeless by it.

Hoover had not needed the Temples' votes (although he received them) to defeat New York Governor Alfred E. Smith's second try for the presidency. In addition to the bigoted responses to the governor's Roman Catholicism, there was his "urban provinciality." Al Smith had a New York accent, and "thanks to radio, listeners far beyond New York were able to hear him for the first (foist) time, as the governor spoke to them personally (poisonally) on such matters as work (woik) and research (resoich). And there was snobbishly cruel prejudice in those upper-class drawing rooms where all it took to provoke laughter was for someone to say, 'Can you imagine Mrs. Smith in the White House?' "

Radio had a great influence on Gertrude's life. She listened to its dramas (immediately called *soap operas* because of their commercial sponsors), like *My Gal Sunday,* the lead-in for which was, "Can a coal miner's daughter find happiness married to an English lord?" And *Myrt and Marge,* about a close relationship between a mother and her daughter. George was doing well at the bank, and the Temples were considering the purchase of a second car. Gertrude avidly read a spectrum of popular magazines, from *Good Housekeeping* to *Photoplay* to *Vanity Fair.* A good seamstress, she copied the clothes she saw on modish women and their children for Shirley and herself. And when Shirley's blond, gently curling hair grew to abundance, Gertrude studied photographs of the young Mary Pickford and recreated Pickford's hairstyle on her daughter. A morning ritual entailed dampening Shirley's thick hair with watered-down waving solution, winding exactly fifty-six separate ringlets around her forefinger, securing each with a bobby pin until it was dry, carefully removing the pins and finally brushing the curls loosely in place again over her finger. Gertrude had saved several dolls from her childhood and had kept them propped up on her bed during the seventeen years she had been married to George. These she now gave to Shirley,* no longer having need herself for an inanimate doll. She called Shirley "Presh" for *precious,* and she doted on every clever thing the child did.

Being a girl and so much younger than her brothers, Shirley was coddled by all members of the family. "When Mom and Daddy went out evenings, they'd hire a baby sitter to stay with me," she was to recall. "Jack [her older brother] always got in a tizzy for fear she'd neglect me, so finally the family solved the problem by leaving Jack in charge. If I cried, he'd put on Mom's bathrobe and go in to pick me up, to deceive my youthful innocence into thinking it was Mom in person."

Gertrude concentrated on Shirley. With the boys in school all day, her daughter quickly became the focus of her life, and as Gertrude listened to the music from the radio she would sing

---

*Gertrude's dolls became the first in Shirley Temple's famous doll collection and remained with it when the collection was placed on display in Los Angeles at the California Museum of Science and Industry in Exposition Park in 1960. The collection was moved to the Stanford Children's Convalescent Hospital in Palo Alto in 1979.

and dance with Shirley, who pranced around the room with great agility. When Shirley reached the age of three, Gertrude decided that she should have dance instruction, claiming she planned to give Shirley the fun she herself had missed.

During the twenties, the high-pressure efforts of promoters who were devoted to making prosperity and California synonymous in the public mind forced the state's economy to giddy heights. By 1930, the population of California had increased 65 percent over the previous ten years, outstripping any other state in the Union during the same period. Los Angeles, surrounded by fast-expanding suburbs, became a manufacturing, oil-refining, fruit-shipping and movie-making center. But with the Crash late in 1929, the bubble burst. Jobless newcomers thronged in by the hundreds of thousands, creating an immense burden on California's economy.

Although George was compelled to take a cut in salary, the bank he worked for remained sound. Fortunately for the Temple family, their house and car were paid for. Purchase of a second car was forgotten, and they pulled their belts a bit tighter. George's innate conservatism, his refusal to be swept into any high-risk investment, had kept them solvent, whereas many of their neighbors and friends were not so fortunate and had their investments wiped out. Gertrude had little spare time for the local afternoon bridge games. As neighbors were forced to sell their homes, she became more and more aloof, private, devoting her days to Shirley's care and early education, which included teaching the child the words of songs she played on the phonograph. To her amazement, Shirley had almost perfect pitch, extraordinary in a child of three, an ability to bring expression to her words, to move to the music gracefully and, when shown by Gertrude, to repeat a simple dance step.

The movie *Skippy*, made in 1930, propelled the eight-year-old Jackie Cooper to stardom. Magazines were filled with stories about "America's Boy—blonde, hazel-eyed, clear-skinned, brave, fearless, loved by mother and father—." Actually, America's Boy was the illegitimate son of a Jewish father and an Italian mother, but Gertrude would not have found that information in the magazines she read. They did, however, print stories of how the child was brought by his mother's whim to an audition at Paramount, where out of three hundred boys he was chosen for the role. Articles about other new child stars were frequent—

beautiful "Little Mitzie" Green, who had been cast as Becky Thatcher in *Tom Sawyer* and with Cooper in *Skippy;* Mickey McGuire (soon to be Rooney), the young star of the series that carried his name; and Spanky MacFarland, signed at age three to star in the *Our Gang* comedy series.

Hollywood's "baby boom" came into full swing with the Depression, where every asset a family had was used to put food on the table. Promoters saw gold in this, and "beautiful baby" contests abounded. All parents hoped a published photograph of their darling would catch the eye of a Hollywood casting director. Dancing schools provided another opportunity for a child to be seen while being taught how to take direction. Many mothers enrolled their children in these schools across the country, not to attain a bit of grace but to qualify eventually in the school's ultimate bait—a local performance in an auditorium or theater that might be covered by the press (especially likely in small towns). Class lessons in most such schools cost a parent fifty cents an hour (the median hourly wage in 1930–33). Parents also purchased tap shoes and costumes for their children from the school.

Santa Monica had several of these children's dancing schools, and one of them was owned by a depositor at George's bank. "She told him how healthy it was for a child to dance," Shirley recalled her father telling her. "I was allowed to be a baby for about two years. So I had a couple of years as a lazy baby. I thought every child worked, because I was born into it." After only a few of these local lessons, Gertrude felt Shirley deserved better instruction. The Los Angeles-Hollywood area boasted two of the most professional dancing schools in the country: the Ernest Belcher School of the Dance on Western Avenue and Ethel Meglin Studios, which occupied a building on the Mack Sennett studio lot (leased at this time to a company called Educational Films). In addition to his nationally syndicated column on dance techniques, Ernest Belcher trained fifteen hundred to two thousand pupils a year in a studio that boasted thirty thousand square feet of floor space and a teaching staff (trained by him) of twenty-five. The studio had been financed by Cecil B. DeMille, who relied on the impresario to teach his hundreds of extras how to get through a dancing sequence.

When Ethel Meglin opened her establishment in the summer

of 1930, she had only thirty dance students, all children of a range of ages. With a monthly rental of twenty-seven dollars to meet, drastic measures were necessary. Annually, during Christmas week, Franchon and Marco, producers of the Los Angeles Loew's State Theater's lavish stage productions, presented a huge kiddie revue of one hundred youngsters, "the O'Neill Children from San Francisco." Meglin, who was perhaps even a better promoter than Belcher, approached Franchon and Marco and got them to agree to hire the Famous Meglin Kiddies, an act with *more* than one hundred kids—for which she would charge 20 percent less than the O'Neill Children (after all, being local, she did not have to pay housing and travel costs). When they parted, one condition had been set forth: Mrs. Meglin's kiddie act would have to audition in six weeks. If the producers liked what they saw, the act was in.

Ethel gathered together her present students and offered free lessons to their sisters and playmates in exchange for helping her pad out the act. "The place was bedlam for a solid week," Mrs. Cary reports, "children running in and out at all hours, mothers waiting in cars up and down the street, and rehearsal rooms so few and small, Ethel had to take students in shifts." By audition time, the Famous Meglin Kiddies numbered one hundred and one. Only eight of her best students did solo work, two of them boys, but Mrs. Meglin had taught her small female charges enough basics to form lines, work in unison and, with nymphet legs bared, execute a high and somewhat provocative kick. The group was booked and ran for two weeks over Christmas, 1930, to much publicity and full houses.

Ethel Meglin Studios was besieged with new applicants, almost all with mothers anxious for their children to appear in the next year's Christmas kiddie revue or to be seen by one of the several movie talent scouts who now appeared regularly at Mrs. Meglin's whenever a child was needed for a film.

Several articles about Mrs. Meglin and her school's great popularity with casting directors appeared in the Los Angeles newspapers during the spring of 1931. Gertrude made inquiries and found that lessons were an expensive one dollar for a forty-five-minute class. The dance studio was also twenty-two miles from the Temples' home in Santa Monica. When Gertrude first consulted George about enrolling Shirley, he made it very clear that he thought the price extravagant and that he did not want

Shirley to be exposed to the motion-picture environment. Gertrude persisted. A short time later, she and her three-year-old daughter were traveling—not once but twice—weekly to the school in the Temples' Graham-Paige, after Shirley proved at her audition to have an uncanny and extraordinary talent for learning a dance step by looking away, or closing her eyes, listening to the sound and rhythm of the taps of her teacher's feet and then repeating them with her own.

Despite what has always been written about the Temples' disinterest in their daughter having an early film career, Gertrude, at least, never considered another alternative. Had she only wished to develop Shirley's dancing skills to help her daughter attain more grace and some playmates, she would have selected a neighborhood school. But she was determined to enroll Shirley, who was only a tot at this time, at Mrs. Meglin's highly competitive studio. Shirley would also be one of the youngest in her class, for Mrs. Meglin did not like to take students under the age of five. Without question, Gertrude was—through Shirley—acting out her own fantasies; and the little girl—who had danced to please her mother from the time she was aware of the approval it gained—held on to that love and approval the only way she knew how, by continuing to dance while her mother watched.

Judy Garland was later to recall her own experience at Meglin Dance Studio in 1931, when she was nine years old and still Frances Gumm, one of the three Gumm sisters. Low on funds, her mother, Ethel, played piano for the classes in exchange for lessons for her three daughters. Each one was lectured solemnly beforehand that she was to listen closely to what her fellow classmates had to say (in the event that one would leak some information about an audition) but that she herself must remain aloof, lips sealed about any similar information they might have.*

---

*The author of this book was raised in Los Angeles and recalls attending Meglin Dance Studios at age six in 1933 and being taught a rather titillating version of "Oh, You Nasty Man" to sing and dance to. She can also remember another child her age who collapsed in dance class in pain and with a high fever and who died a few days later of a ruptured appendix. A talent scout was expected the day of the class, and the story that circulated was that the child's mother insisted she attend although obviously not well. Whether true or not, the story points out the atmosphere at the school during the early thirties.

Later, in publicity interviews, Gertrude always claimed that Shirley was accidentally "discovered" in dancing class (just an innocent recreation for Shirley) and that she had never seriously considered a career for her daughter. But from the beginning, she had made the rounds with Shirley to various casting directors. The big kiddie series at the time was the *Our Gang* comedy series. By 1931, many members of the cast had grown into adolescence, and a call went out for new young faces. Hal Roach, the producer of the *Our Gang* comedies, recalled; "About Shirley Temple, her mother brought her in five or six times . . . and nobody'd let her get beyond the outer office. But bear in mind there would usually be dozens of kids out there every single day. You couldn't see them all, and the casting director apparently didn't think Shirley Temple had anything to offer the gang so she didn't get chosen."

Educational Films was established by Earl Woolridge Hammons in New York in 1919. They soon were "a virtual factory for comedy shorts" and did well with such stars as Buster Keaton and Harry Langdon. The combination of talkies and the Crash had nearly bankrupted them, forcing them to close their eastern studios and rent space at Sennett's on the Coast. Jack Hays, a local entrepreneur, was put in charge of production, and Charles Lamont, a director who had made some shorts for Mack Sennett, was hired as director. The idea of putting sound to some of their short silent comedies was abandoned in favor of making a kid's series that might compete with *Our Gang,* but with a difference. The comedies, to be called *Baby Burlesks,* would have small children doing takeoffs of motion pictures by mimicking the adult stars. The original plan was to dub in adult voices, which would have given the shorts a satirical edge.

Still operating from offices in New York, Hammons telegraphed Lamont that he was on his way west on the Twentieth Century and wanted at least twenty-five kids, preferably age five or younger, to begin shooting. Lamont called the Meglin school, which was on the same lot, to say he was coming over in a few minutes. Taking advantage of the short time before his arrival, the mothers swarmed in to primp their daughters' hair and change them into more eye-catching costumes.

The previous week, another scout had come. A notice had been posted on the bulletin board, but Gertrude hadn't seen it.

"There was a lot of excitement [on] that day and the whole class was dressed up in their best clothes," Shirley remembered. "I arrived in an old dancing dress. When Mom discovered they expected a movie scout . . . we left [Gertrude feeling Shirley was not dressed correctly]. . . . She had the car started, ready to go home, when my teacher came out and asked her if she would let the movie scout see me." Gertrude had to stay outside the classroom with the other mothers "while 30 or 40 of us paraded up and down before the movie scout." Shirley had not been selected, a fact Gertrude blamed on her careless attire. Since then, Shirley had attended classes dressed in her best dancing outfit. Still feeling the pain and guilt of the last rejection, caused because she had not looked right, Shirley could think of nothing else to do but hide when Charles Lamont, tall and tanned and wearing *puttees* in the DeMille manner, swaggered in with two assistants. She and another little girl slipped behind the piano.

Most of the children in the class were too old (the script called for these children to walk around in diapers). Lamont was ready to leave when he saw Shirley's and her friend's tiny feet beneath the piano and asked them to come out. Both children were then asked to audition the next day.

George was strenuously opposed to the whole thing. Shirley was just a few months past her third birthday, and he felt she would not be in a position to know if this was what she wanted or not—just that she was doing what pleased her mother. Finally relenting, with Gertrude's insistence and without her parents investigating the content of these one-reelers, which were "exploitative, racist and not necessarily intended for children," Shirley went for an interview.

"And then the fun started," Shirley says. "You never saw so many children in your life . . . children yelling and children having their noses blown, and children getting into fights with one another." She adds that "Mom and I sort of stayed on the sidelines." But Earl Hammons noted, "I was walking across the grounds of the studio talking to Charlie [Lamont]. A lot of kids were waiting. One little girl caught my coat and pulled it a little bit and I looked down and saw the most beautiful little thing, and I picked her up in my arms and I said, 'What's your name?'

"She said, 'Shirley.'

"I said, 'What are you doing here?'

" 'I'm going to work for you,' she answered.

"So I told Charlie, 'You want to watch her. She knows what she wants.' "

Lamont asked all the mothers to walk away and leave the children alone with them for ten minutes.

"Mom gave my curls a few twists with her fingers," Shirley recalled. "She whispered to me, 'If he asks you to dance, or asks you to sing, just do the way you always do, Presh.' "

With Jack Hays, Lamont talked briefly to each child. Twenty-five were selected and the rest told to leave. The mothers of those who remained were called back. "Mr. Hays wanted us all [the children] to get undressed," Shirley remembered. "In the picture they were going to make [we] had to wear . . . diapers, with great big safety pins in front. So all the mothers undressed their children, and Mom undressed me, and we all ran around in our panties. . . . I had to stand in front of the camera in [them], and smile, and wink my eye, and shake my shoulder two or three times."

But she did not get the lead role of Charmaine in the movie titled *War Babies*, a takeoff on the World War I film *What Price Glory?*, which had starred Dolores Del Rio. Audrey Rae Leonard, a pretty English child, was chosen. Shirley was to play a minor role. When Lamont and Jack Hays, the man who was the active producer on the series, saw the rushes, they decided to scrap poor Audrey, who was too stiff on camera, and called the Temples to tell them they had decided to cast Shirley as the vest-pocket Dolores Del Rio. (Shirley adds, "As soon as I made the screen test [Dad] wanted me to get a part more than Mom did. He was so happy when Mr. Lamont finally called up and said that he was giving me the part of Charmaine.")

Lamont and Hays slept well, feeling confident little Shirley had the nymphet appeal they needed. That night, Shirley suffered an ear infection. She appeared on the set the next morning irritable and unresponsive. By the end of the day, she was sent home and told not to bother to come back. Audrey was rehired. On the following morning, Gertrude and Dr. Madsen accompanied Shirley to the set to explain that Shirley had suffered an abscessed ear, which had been lanced the previous evening, and that she now would be fine. Audrey was kept on the sidelines as Shirley was dressed in an off-the-shoulder Mexican blouse, a diaper pinned below it. A giant rose was attached to her hair, and a frilly pink satin garter rolled up just below her right knee.

Hammons had now decided the Baby Burlesk movies should not be dubbed. That morning, on the way to the studio, Gertrude had helped Shirley to memorize her two lines of dialogue spoken in a coy, teasing attempt at French—*"Mais oui, mon cher"* and *"Mais oui, mon Capitaine"*—as she vamped two diaper-clad, bare-chested "soldier boys" with a toss of her rounded and dimpled bare shoulder and planted a kiss on the cheek of each.

George may have originally objected to a movie environment for his daughter but he was now as enthusiastic as Gertrude about Shirley's career, and he personally signed as guardian the contract for Shirley to work for Educational Films, at ten dollars a day for each day of production (the shorts had four-day shooting schedules).* Because this contract predated the restrictive child-labor laws later invoked in children's film contracts, no specification was made for the hours a child could work in a day. Nor was time set apart for lessons if the child was of school age. Shirley made four of these ten- or eleven-minute shorts for Educational in 1932, all opposite Georgie Smith, a four-year-old blond "muscle man." *The Runt Page* (a spoof on the popular Ben Hecht–Charles MacArthur newspaper story *The Front Page*) featured her as "Lulu Parsnips" (movie columnist Louella Parsons); *Pie Covered Wagon* (a takeoff on *Covered Wagon* in which she imitated silent screen star Lois Wilson, tied to a stake as diapered Indians leered and threw dirt at her); and *Glad Rags to Riches,* where she was presented as "La Belle Diaperina," a Gay Nineties chanteuse at the Lullaby Lobster Palace. Dressed from the waist up in a turn-of-the-century show-girl costume, her diaper made of glittering metallic cloth (designed by Gertrude), she sang "She's Only a Bird in a Gilded Cage" inside a big gold birdcage, followed (once "freed" from her imprisonment) by a short tap dance executed with a chorus of four diapered lads, chests bared except for stiff collars and bow ties about their necks, and awkwardly maneuvering top hats and canes.

"All of us wore very elaborate costumes, authentic grown-up clothes from the waist up and diapers pinned with enormous

---

*Her first payroll invoice, dated January 9, 1932, and signed by Jack Hays, notes this amount included overtime.

safety pins," Temple remembered. "Mom worked harder than I did because she had to make all my costumes and press them at night. She created a special panty for me with a flap in front that resembled a diaper [but wasn't as bulky] . . . She spent her days on the set with me and considering the four day shooting schedule, they must have been nightmares." And then, as an added thought: "A movie lot is a fascinating place even for grownups . . . completely Alice-in-Wonderland. Machines and gadgets all over, trees and grass apparently growing right inside a building . . . Mom had never been on a studio lot before, so she was as agog about it as I was."

A daily routine was now formed. Gertrude would drive George to the bank, and then she and Shirley would continue on to the studio, where she would remain by her daughter's side as much as possible. They brought their own lunch—usually a Thermos of hot soup and some small sandwiches. On the drive home, Gertrude would explain to Shirley what she was expected to do the next day. After dinner, George gave her a bath, and then Gertrude set her hair in rag curlers. When Shirley was in bed, Gertrude would read any lines she had to say the next day. Shirley would repeat them "word for word five or six times. She might say, 'You're supposed to feel very happy when you say this line, Presh' . . . or 'You're supposed to be eating a thick sandwich while you're saying these lines,' " and Shirley would practice this bit of action. When the light went out, Shirley was expected to repeat the lines several times as a soporific, so that by morning they would be memorized.*

Gertrude's life was now dominated by her pursuit of Shirley's career, and she was determined that her daughter would make the leap from "cheap-jack comedy shorts" to the eminently more respectable feature film. As in dancing school, she remained distant from the other mothers and kept Shirley apart from their children whenever possible. Costume adjustments were always to be made. She never left the interpretation of Shirley's role to the director (Charles Lamont, in most instances). During a production, she departed with Shirley for the studio by 7:00 A.M., the child's hair set and brushed into curls.

---

*This same routine was religiously followed as Temple's career progressed and the scenes and dialogue became much more complicated.

Pandemonium might have existed among the other children in the cast, but Shirley remained close to Gertrude's side, rehearsing the scene she was about to play. The child's timing was always correct. Her mother taught her to "sparkle," as she called it, by wetting her lips, focusing her eyes so that they gleamed with a little pre-tearing moisture, and then to smile or sulk or laugh as the scene required. Standing behind Lamont as he got set to instruct the cinematographer to start shooting, Gertrude would issue a final instruction: "Sparkle, Shirley, sparkle," and Shirley would. (The pet name "Presh" was used by her mother only in their private moments, and "Shirl" employed in a disciplinary tone; Gertrude called her daughter "Shirley" in most public situations.)

Jack Hays was a shrewd promoter. A good chunk of the financial backing for the Baby Burlesk shorts was secured by using products that could be easily identified by their packaging (Carnation milk, Kellogg's Corn Flakes). For her ten dollars a day, Shirley and her tiny co-performers were also expected to pose for advertisements for these products between film scenes. Gertrude offered no objections. She had already learned that *exposure* was an important part of a film career, both for Shirley to be seen and for the child to begin to feel natural before the cameras.

Shirley's early footage reveals a lissome child with camera appeal but no indication of any exceptional talent other than charm. The song that she sang and the dance steps she executed for *War Babies* and *Glad Rags to Riches* (which she made at the end of 1932 when four and a half) show precociousness rather than inspiration. The simple steps are mastered and the song rendered on key, but several other children in the shorts exhibit far greater musical talent and dancing ability. Her acting was more mimicry than performance, especially when measured against a child like Margaret O'Brien, who at the same age gave such a stunning performance in *A Journey for Margaret,* or Jackie "Butch" Jenkins, who was five when he brought tears to moviegoers' eyes as Ulysses, the dreamy, Depression-bound little boy who symbolically waved to passing trains in William Saroyan's *The Human Comedy.* But Shirley did possess a tremendous camera appeal that brought the viewer's eyes to her in almost every scene in which she appeared.

The Baby Burlesk films did not make an overnight star of Gertrude's little girl. No outside producer fought to get her away from Educational, perhaps because the Baby Burlesks did not have the popularity of the *Our Gang* series. The shorts were played in neighborhood theaters at matinees or to accompany a double feature, and audiences were lured in by long programs and giveaways of kitchen dishes. Without Gertrude's enthusiasm and perseverance, Shirley Temple might have ended her career at five—the cutoff age at Educational—as did her co-star Georgie Smith. But on film, Shirley *did* sparkle, and this, in the beginning, was her greatest attribute. Something about the glint in her eye, the golden ringlets that bobbed as she moved and the irrepressible dimples brought a smile to her beholders, most of whom were going through grim times when a child's smile was far more moving than its tears.

"[My father] said there was no use bothering about the movies any longer," Shirley recalled. "He said that I had about three hundred dollars in the bank—that was all the money I had made working for a whole year. . . . Mom though . . . kept saying she wished I could get a contract . . . she didn't care about the money—just so long as I had a chance to get a good part."

Gertrude knew Shirley had a better opportunity of being "discovered" in a feature picture, and she jumped at the chance offered her for Shirley to appear in *The Red-Haired Alibi,* for Tower Films, a subsidiary of Hammons's company.

The part was little more than a bit role. When the picture was reviewed in *Variety,* Shirley's name was not even listed in the credits. It starred Merna Kennedy (who later became Mrs. Busby Berkeley) as a redhead accused of murder, Theodore von Eltz as the gangster she is involved with at the time of the murder and Grant Withers as the man she finally marries.* To make Kennedy's and Withers's roles more sympathetic, they were given a little girl (Shirley) who appears in two scenes, once in close-up, eyes saucer-wide and appealing as she clings to and looks up to her mother—the message being, "If this innocent

---

*Theodore von Eltz was to gain recognition as a shady pornographer-blackmailer in *The Big Sleep* (1946) and as the star of the 1950's television serial *One Man's Family.* He also appeared in three more films with Temple: *Change of Heart* and *Bright Eyes* (1934) and *Since You Went Away* (1946). Grant Withers appeared again with Temple in *Fort Apache* (1948).

child can love her mother this much, the woman must be innately good." *Red-Haired Alibi* suffered from a script that was "sufficiently bad to relegate the feature to the country's least important locations." Gertrude and Shirley were back to work at Educational.

Four more Baby Burlesks were made starring Shirley. George and the boys became self-sufficient as Gertrude devoted herself to Shirley's career. First there was *Kid's Last Fight,* a Jack Dempsey spoof, with Georgie Smith as the fighter and Shirley as his girl friend who is kidnapped by gangsters to force Georgie to throw the championship match. Shirley next made *Polly-Tix in Washington,* dressed in a black lace bra and undies designed and made by Gertrude, and playing "a wealthy gold-digger intending to elect a cowboy politician [Georgie Smith] to office . . . she vamps her way into the life of a mighty important man in Washington. Will she lead him astray, or will he have some effect on her and make her mend her ways?" Jack Hays's intentions were obvious. The Baby Burlesks were meant to titillate male matinee audiences. *Kid 'n' Hollywood* followed, with Georgie as "Frightwig Von Stumblebum" (a takeoff of Eric von Stroheim) and Shirley as "the incomparable Morelegs Sweet Trick" (a blatant parody of Marlene Dietrich), "wearing lots of blue feathers and sequins," which she later claimed she considered "really dreamy . . . The most sirenish outfit" she was ever to wear.

In *Kid 'n' Africa,* Shirley played Madame Cradlebait, a missionary caught by the cannibals she has been sent to civilize. While she is being cooked in a big pot over a fire, the natives drink the water in which she sits. Rescued by Diaperzan (a mini-Tarzan) on an elephant, she insists he marry her and then domesticates him into becoming her slavey and the cannibals into hucksters. *Kid 'n' Africa* was the most tasteless of the eight Baby Burlesks that Shirley made, and with its release, the series was discontinued.

During production of the Baby Burlesks, the children were constantly faced with dangerous situations. Shirley recalled that while making this final film, "I was Jane to a little boy who was Tarzan and we had to run through a jungle. I was being chased by little black boys who were playing the African natives. . . . [The director] wanted all the children to fall at one time. [I] got through on the path and then they put a wire up and tripped all the little black boys at once and, of course, they all fell in a heap and some of their legs were cut." For a scene in *Polly-Tix in Washington,* Shirley was to take a wild ride in an ostrich-drawn carriage. To get the proper effect, Hays and Lamont had the animal blindfolded before the camera began to roll. The moment "Action!" was called, the blindfold was ripped away. The ostrich, terrified by the bright lights, bolted forward, surprising Shirley (exactly the effect they had wanted), who had not been warned and who would have been thrown to the ground from the fast-moving vehicle if not for the quick thinking of a nearby assistant director, who caught her in midair. Gertrude had either not been consulted or had not thought Shirley was in danger.

George did not often accompany Gertrude and Shirley to the studio, and it is doubtful if his wife informed him of the risks to their daughter. Jack Hays interpreted the eight-hour daily federal child-labor law to mean eight hours' work *before* the cameras. Children could therefore be on the set, ready and waiting for their scenes, from eight in the morning until six at night. Movie parents tended to think their children were special and could handle anything. Gertrude was no exception. But a film clip from *Kid's Last Fight* of a "speakeasy" scene in which a "free-for-all" ensues as the place is being raided by the "cops" reveals an utterly disoriented, bewildered and frightened expression on Shirley's baby face.

"Children were treated as children by directors, crew and other actors until the cameras rolled," Diana Serra Cary says. "Then there were no holds barred. . . . One take, no wasting time or film, no excuses. [You] were a 'responsible' child. When I turned four and made *Captain January** . . . I ceased being a child and became a grown-up."

With brothers considerably older than herself (Jack graduated from high school in 1933) and her days taken up with the pursuit of her career—filming, auditioning and dance lessons— Shirley had little contact with children her own age other than movie kids, who were pitted against each other professionally and whose parents harbored attitudes of mutual mistrust.

When Shirley's first Baby Burlesk, *War Babies,* was exhibited

---

*The 1924 silent version (made the previous year) of the movie Temple remade as a talkie in 1936.

at their local theater, the Temples invited all their friends. Gertrude was to recall: "The picture lasted ten minutes. Shirley merely flitted across the screen a few times and said only two lines. But my head swam and the goose flesh popped out on my arms. I think I cried a little. George squeezed my hand. Oh, well, we were proud. It was our little girl doing something wonderful, like saying her first words, and we were happy." Shirley, who had accompanied her parents and their friends, added, "She kept whispering to me, 'Do you see yourself, Presh? That's *you!*' "

Gertrude continued to believe, correctly, that Shirley needed to be seen in a full-length picture to get her "big chance." Though Shirley was under contract to Hays, Gertrude made contacts in studio casting departments and began to make the rounds and "calls" (open auditions) with her on the child's free days, but these independent attempts were not successful. Shirley later remembered one of these "calls" as having "about three hundred other little girls there with their mothers, and many of them with their agents—so we couldn't get very near Mr. White [George White, the producer-director]. Mom was quite disappointed. But a man finally came over to us [Leo Houck, the assistant director] . . . he recognized me from seeing me in the *Baby Burlesks.* . . . He told Mom he didn't think there was much use in expecting me to get a part in Mr. White's *Scandals.* The 'call' was only to see what little girls they could get *if* they really made up their minds they wanted any."*

Early in 1933, Shirley played a bit role in the Universal feature *Out All Night,* starring Slim Summerville, ZaSu Pitts and Laura Hope Crews. The story, an amusing comedy, had Pitts, as a nurse in the baby-checking department of a large retail store, in love with Summerville, another store employee. The couple accidentally get locked in the store overnight and have to marry. The rest of the film has to do with Pitts's problems with her husband's attachment to his mother (Crews). Shirley appears with several other children in two baby-checking scenes. She played a loving but mischievous child whose antics harass the

---

*George White made three *Scandals* films in 1934, 1935 and 1945. Temple is referring to the 1934 *George White's Scandals* (filmed in 1933) which starred Alice Faye in her film debut singing "Oh, You Nasty Man," a lavish production number that did include some small girls.

fluttery Miss Pitts. Listed in the credits under *children* along with several others, she was not singled out in any of the reviews. *Out All Night* was a turning point in her career, however.

Although competitiveness was partially responsible for Gertrude's aloofness from other movie mothers, a certain amount of snobbishness was also involved. Some of the children came from vaudevillian backgrounds, and Gertrude believed she had little in common with their mothers, who were relying on their children as wage earners to support whole families. Gertrude *always* refused to consider that she and George were exploiting Shirley. After all, George held a respectable position, and they owned a house and a car. To Gertrude, this meant she was a breed apart from the other mothers—and Shirley from their children. She also did not mingle with the adult cast. However, during Shirley's work on *Out All Night,* Gertrude made friends with ZaSu Pitts, and this friendship would eventually have an influence on the lives of both Gertrude and Shirley.

Raised in California, Miss Pitts had been on the scene since the early days of films. She began her career in two Mary Pickford films, *The Little Princess* and *Rebecca of Sunnybrook Farm,* and gained prominence as the dramatic lead in Erich von Stroheim's great silent movie *Greed.* With the advent of sound, her humorous, trembling voice caused her to appear almost exclusively in comedy. She worked constantly and became well known for her portrayals of scatterbrained, zany women. But she was anything but light-headed. An excellent businesswoman and an ardent Republican, she was financially secure despite the shakiness of the times. Gertrude admired her sense of fashion (following the star's lead, she bought an elegant pair of alligator shoes with matching pocketbook, one of her few early extravagances) and her confident attitude, and although Shirley worked only five days on *Out All Night,* by the end of that time the two women had become friends. Miss Pitts gave Gertrude wise advice—to begin being selective about Shirley's roles. What a producer or casting director saw on-screen, she told her, was how a performer was perceived. She warned against Jack Hays's questionable taste, and suggested Gertrude have more to say about the stories Shirley did.

Still under contract to Hays, Shirley made two more films for Educational in 1933, *Merrily Yours* and *Dora's Dunkin' Doughnuts,* both shorts but with longer (twenty-two-minute) formats. Her role in the ZaSu Pitts film had given Hays (as Pitts had predicted) a new image of Shirley as a mischievous little girl with an angelic face. Now five, she was able to handle dialogue and developed scenes. Both these shorts were simple comedies slanted toward family entertainment. *Merrily Yours* was the first of four stories (part of a series called Frolics of Youth) that Shirley would do about the Rogers family, teenage Sonny (Junior Coughlin), Mary Lou (Shirley) and their parents (Harry Myers and Helene Chadwick*). The Rogers family series had all the earmarks of latter-day television situation comedies, and Shirley was winning as, with innocent guilelessness, she poured water over the kid (Kenneth Howell) who bullies her older brother. In *Dora's Dunkin' Doughnuts* (which also featured the Meglin Kiddies Band), she effectively played second banana to bumbling comedian Andy Clyde's absent-minded teacher, sabotaging his radio appearance to advertise the doughnuts made by his sweetheart, Dora (Florence Gill).

Gertrude saw no future in the short comedies Hays was making. Hays, however, still had a contract for Shirley's services. Her salary with Educational was now fifteen dollars a day, but she had been paid fifty dollars a day for *Out All Night,* the difference going directly to Educational. Hays saw Shirley's potential, and hearing of a feature western at Paramount that had some kids' roles in it, went to see the director, Henry Hathaway, whom he had known for years.

The film, a Zane Grey story, *To the Last Man,* was to star tall, rugged Randolph Scott and vivacious, blond Esther Ralston as star-crossed lovers in a war between two western families. A small girl was needed to play Ralston's little sister. "[Hays] came to me," Hathaway recalled, "and said, 'Henry, I have this kid under contract and her mother won't let me off the hook [to find parts for her, but] she's getting too big to play these kids in diapers.' " He showed Hathaway some photographs of Shirley and asked him to audition her. She bore a resemblance to Ralston, and Hathaway readily agreed. After seeing her, he gave her the part. For the first and only time, she was listed in the credits

---

*Chadwick had been a leading lady in silent films, but had not weathered the transition to sound.

as Shirley Jane Temple, Gertrude's choice, perhaps to distance her from the Baby Burlesks.

Cast as her brother was another child actor, Delmar Watson, one of nine Watson children who all appeared in films. "The family lived near Mack Sennett's studio, so when they needed a child they'd say, 'What size kid do you want, boy or girl? Go down to the Watsons,'" fellow child-actor Dickie Moore remembers. The Watsons were managed by their father, Coy Watson, who had been a propman, assistant director, a special-effects artist and a cowboy (and often an Indian) in early western films. "Many of us [child actors] felt Coy would go to any length to advance his kids' careers," Moore adds. "You had to watch your ribs when you were in a scene with them," Moore says Jackie Coogan told him, "[or] they'd poke you out of the way with an elbow." Coy Watson had a rough manner. "He wore plaid shirts with striped ties, blue socks with green pants . . ." but he knew movies inside and out, and especially what had to be done to protect and promote the financial resources of the children in his charge.

Gertrude was quick to see that she could learn a lot from Coy Watson and, despite his reputation, became friendly with him. Watson advised her to take a year off Shirley's age* at all job interviews to prolong her juvenile status. He did not believe in signing a child to a studio contract, since the studio usually profited more from this than the child. "I was seven and Shirley four or five [actually she was five] when we made *To the Last Man*," Delmar Watson recalls. "She was fun and had true charisma—and she went after whatever she wanted. Once she pushed me off my father's lap and sat there herself. Whenever she could she would try to run off and hide from Gertrude. It was supposed to be a game. I remember Gertrude then as being matronly. She wore hats and had no sense of humor. She was very protective of Shirley, called her *Shirl* in a tone that meant *behave,* and usually Shirley did."

Henry Hathaway had memories of a scene that "called for

---

*Until 1936, when an enterprising reporter sought out her birth certificate, Temple was believed to have been born in 1929. The studio still gave out the later birth date so that the general public, and even Shirley herself thought she was younger. Not until Shirley's twenty-first birthday, on April 23, 1949, did she publicly admit she was one year older than the original printed record.

Shirley to be playing by herself at a little table in a barn, having a tea party. Close by, we had a mule. As Shirley, following the script, poured tea for herself and a pretended guest, the mule wandered over, attracted by the sugar the propman had placed on the table, and began to lick at it.

"Now this wasn't in the script. Shirley was irritated and tried to shoo him away. I ordered the camera to keep going, because this began to look good. The mule refused to move and kept on eating the sugar. At this point, Shirley got up from the table and, with her two small hands, tried to push him out of the way.

"This got the mule irritated. He turned around, and with his two back legs he hauled off at her with a kick. She ducked back and he missed, but instead of stopping or running away, and before we could rush in and grab her away, she strode over and kicked the mule back. She gave one hell of a boot in the ass. This surprised the mule, who ran away . . . She had a magic you couldn't define . . . an unpredictability . . . inventive, rare for a youngster that age."

The film was previewed at the Hollywood Paramount Theater on Thursday, September 7, 1933. "Pair of kids, Delmar Watson and Shirley Jane Temple, are swell troupers," *Variety* reported the next day. "Boy's saving some pups in the height of battle is an effective piece of hokum."

Shirley was not yet on her way to stardom. But Gertrude had learned a lesson from Coy Watson: Make sure no other kid in a film is able to steal a scene from your own. In her next picture, *As the Earth Turns,** a Warner Brothers potboiler about two warring families, that axiom was put to immediate use, because the cast included fifteen youngsters along with the stars of the film, Donald Woods, Sarah Padden and Russell Hardie. One of the children, Cora Sue Collins, was to become a child star within a year, and had the main child's role in the movie. Shirley was cast as Betty Shaw, the youngest of the Shaw family's ten children. Gertrude signed the contract, which paid two hundred dollars for two weeks' work.

As Christmas, 1933, approached, Shirley was steadily em-

---

*Previously unknown as a film in which Temple appeared, *As the Earth Turns* was made at Warner Brothers in November 1933. Temple's contract is dated October 31, 1933, and holds Mrs. Temple responsible for her daughter's attire in the movie. The contract is in the Warner Brothers Film Archives at the University of Southern California.

ployed, first with *Pardon My Pups* (released in 1934), and then *Managed Money,* and *What to Do?,* all part of the series on the Rogers family. Educational had gone bankrupt. With the bill collectors at his heels, Jack Hays had vanished. Charles Lamont had been signed as a director by Universal, but Shirley and Gertrude were on their own, making the rounds.*

The House of Connelly by Paul Green had been a successful Broadway play. Fox Pictures bought it as a vehicle for Lionel Barrymore (as Bob Connelly, titular head of the Southern Connelly family) and Janet Gaynor (as the Yankee farm girl he does not want his son, Robert Young, to marry). Set in post-Civil War times, the story, retitled *Carolina,* was a romanticized vision of a fading South and a family's restoration to its once proud and supercilious state. Shirley was hired by director Henry King for some tag scenes at the end of the film, which showed Gaynor and Young happily married and the parents of a crinolined, curly-topped daughter.†

"Shirley was too young to read," Robert Young recalls. "In order for her to learn her lines, her mother would read the script to her . . . so eventually in this process . . . she literally learned all of the lines, which wasn't particularly unusual or outstanding, but everyone thought it was somewhat miraculous. Her mother coached her on which way to look when a person spoke, and so forth. You might say the direction was done by her mother and not by the film's director.

"In this one scene she was in with Lionel Barrymore, she was told to stand by the rocker he sat in. He suffered with severe arthritis, so painful he couldn't walk except with a cane and with difficulty. Anyway, I was standing behind Shirley and there was a nice little casual scene—not terribly important—and Lionel (who was on drugs, pain killers and things—'cause he was in a great deal of intense pain) got stuck, couldn't remember his lines.

"Shirley, in that sweet, wonderful, innocent naïveté of a

---

*Two years later, in 1935, Hays reappeared and, claiming that he still had Temple under contract, attempted to sue for a percentage of her earnings, but Educational Films' bankruptcy had invalidated the contract, and the case was dismissed.

†All prints of this film have been lost. Robert Young has reconstructed the plot printed here as he recalled it. He also places the Barrymore-Temple confrontation as occurring during the making of *Carolina,* and not in a later film, as has been previously reported.

child, told Mr. Barrymore what his line was—'Mr. Barrymore, you're supposed to say so-and-so here'—having no idea of what impact that would have on him. Well, he let out a roar like a singed cat, and people came running. I grabbed her by the arm, because I thought surely if he ever got his hands on her, he'd crush her head or choke her to death. I don't think he would have. But . . . this was a dramatic moment. There was a great deal of scurrying around on the set. Finally, the director [King] came, and they talked for quite a little time and eventually Barrymore calmed down and the scene went on from there. I'll never forget that moment. . . . It was never photographed, but it was a memorable moment in the shooting of that film."

With stars of the caliber of Barrymore and Gaynor, and with Henry King's recent great success with *State Fair,* Shirley's small role in *Carolina* seemed to be that big break for which Gertrude had been praying. But Gertrude's hopes were smashed when *Carolina* opened at the Music Hall in New York on February 20, 1934. Not only had Shirley's name been omitted from the credits, her scene with Barrymore had been severely cut, along with some nice footage with Gaynor and Young. She appeared in two short scenes, but the child who knew everyone's dialogue never uttered a word on screen.

3

THE BETTER PART of two years had passed since Shirley had made her first short film. She could now be called "a screen veteran," and had appeared in four feature films. But, unlike Dickie Moore, who had played the title role in *Oliver Twist* (1933), and Jackie Cooper, who starred with Wallace Beery in *The Bowery* (1933) and as *Peck's Bad Boy* (1934), Shirley was a bit player. Gertrude was beginning to despair. Her fortieth birthday had just passed and Shirley was approaching her sixth, and would soon have to be enrolled in the first grade.

The country boasted a new president, a Democrat, Franklin Delano Roosevelt, and a new Cabinet. For the unemployed, whose condition was desperate, there was federal relief. The New Deal had gone to the rescue of the farm population. Prohibition, after a reign of nearly fourteen years, had finally been repealed. Because the five-day week had been begun to appease workers whose pay had been drastically reduced, millions of people, rich and poor, found themselves with Saturdays free. The capital investors in the movies preferred to steer clear of awkward issues, not to run the risk of offending audiences abroad or at home. In the first three years of the decade, Paramount had been on the verge of bankruptcy, Radio-Keith-Orpheum (RKO) was in receivership, and with the exception of Warner Brothers and Metro-Goldwyn-Mayer, all the other film companies were struggling to remain solvent. Now, movies became the great escape. And they prospered.

More pictures, some of them excellent, were produced in 1934 than in 1932 and 1933 combined; comedies like *It Hap-*

47

pened One Night and *Twentieth Century*, historical dramas like *Cleopatra* and *Catherine the Great*, adventure stories like *Treasure Island* with Jackie Cooper and Wallace Beery and *Viva Villa!* with Beery as Pancho Villa, and musicals, musicals, musicals—Astaire and Rogers in *The Gay Divorcee*, Maurice Chevalier and Jeanette MacDonald in *The Merry Widow*, Al Jolson in *Wonder Bar*, Ruby Keeler and Dick Powell in *Dames*, Eddie Cantor in *Kid Millions*, Bing Crosby in *Here's My Heart*, Rudy Vallee and Alice Faye in *George White's Scandals* (the film to which Shirley had gone on "call" while it was in preproduction). Gertrude stepped up Shirley's dance lessons and taught her all the popular songs of the day.

Studios often did two-reel featurettes (running time: about twenty minutes) that served as screen tests for a newcomer with promise. Shirley's musical ability had not been proved. What singing she had done in the Baby Burlesks had been parodies of adult stars. With Henry Hathaway's help, she was placed in a Paramount two-reeler titled *New Deal Rhythm* with Charles "Buddy" Rogers and Marjorie Main. Rogers was under contract to Paramount as a light, romantic lead. Between movies, he sang with and led his own band on tour. *New Deal Rhythm* was filmed with a threefold purpose—to see if Rogers was suitable for musical leads, if Marjorie Main (who had been playing dramatic character parts) had comedy appeal, and to test Shirley's ability. The darkly handsome, dreamy-eyed Rogers was known to be having an affair with the decade-older Mary Pickford, still married at the time to Douglas Fairbanks. (Asked by a columnist if he ever intended to marry, Rogers had replied, "No, the woman I love is already married.") Shirley came alive in this short film. She radiated charm, sang one song alone and one in a duet with Rogers, followed by one of Ethel Meglin's tap routines. Paramount was impressed. They had a Damon Runyon story, *Little Miss Marker*, in development that had a girl her age as a main character. But studios were wary of signing a child for a film not scheduled for immediate production. A great many changes could take place in a moppet's appearance over a few months— size, missing teeth, weight loss or gain. With their finances still shaky, Paramount did not want to encumber itself with a salary for a performer who might be idle for many months. Once again, Gertrude was left to make the rounds of the studios.

Her spirits were lifted when a call came for an audition at Warner Brothers Studios in Burbank for a role in a Kay Francis film, *Mandalay*. After they had made the hour drive over the mountains in teeming rain from Santa Monica to the valley, she and Shirley found the huge, barnlike audition room crowded with other little girls, many of them Meglin tots. Shirley won the role, but it turned out to be little more than a walk-on (she played the child of a couple* who ran a boarding house), and was not included in the cast credits.†

George had begun to lose heart in Gertrude's enterprise. He did not doubt Shirley's intelligence or her ability to "sparkle" on screen, but he saw the situation more realistically than his wife. The auditions and the work experience were not child's play. Shirley's Alice-in-Wonderland view of film-making could quickly become a child's nightmare if a lack of success made her feel responsible for her mother's disappointment. Then there was his own guilt. The money Shirley had earned in the two and a half years she had been acting had not been a large enough sum to cover much more than the cost of the costumes Gertrude made for her, her lessons, and the running of the car. The eight Baby Burlesks had paid an accumulative $320 over two years; the four Frolics of Youth (the Rogers-family films) $240; the four appearances in feature pictures a scant $500 and the featurette at Paramount $75: a total of $1,135. He asked Gertrude to give up, enroll their daughter in the first grade (she would be six on April 23); and if Shirley eventually decided to become an actress, then they could reconsider.

On the night of January 29, a Monday, Shirley's last Frolics of Youth, *What to Do?*, was being shown at the Fox Ritz Theater along with the Warner Baxter–Dick Powell–Ruby Keeler musical *42nd Street*. Short subjects and newsreels were always first on the bill (to allow patrons time to buy popcorn, find their seats and go with the kiddies to the bathroom). The Temples took Shirley to see herself on-screen. They left directly after the short. Because it was raining, Gertrude and Shirley waited under the marquee while George went to fetch the car.

At precisely this time, songwriter Jay Gorney entered the

---

*Ruth Donnelly and Lucien Littlefield
†When rereleased many years later, Temple's name was inserted in the credits.

theater with his wife. Gorney had wanted to see *42nd Street* (released several months earlier), since he had just been signed by the Fox Film Company to write the music for Baxter's next musical, then titled *Fox Movietone Revue*. As he and Mrs. Gorney stepped up to the box office, he noticed Shirley looking at the display photographs of Ruby Keeler dancing in *42nd Street*. As she studied them, Shirley hummed out loud and did a few tap steps.

Gorney recalled:

I stopped and said to my wife, "Have you ever seen a cuter child?"

"She's adorable," she said.

I looked around to see who was accompanying her, but saw nobody. Well, I don't usually talk to strange little girls, but this one was just charming, so I went up to her.

"Hello," I said. "What's your name?"

"Shirley."

"What's your last name?'

"Temple."

"Where did you learn to dance?"

"I go to school."

"Are you here alone?" I asked.

"My mommy's over there." I saw a tall attractive woman a few feet away. I went over to her and said I had been talking to that little girl (pointing to Shirley) and she said you are her mommy. "I am," she said.

"Has she ever been in the theater or done anything in pictures?" I asked.

The woman explained that her daughter had been in a number of shorts but nothing more.*

"Would she like to be in a major film?" I asked.

"I think so. Certainly, certainly."

"Cer'nly would," Shirley chimed in.

The mother was a charming woman and she did seem very eager. So I asked her to bring Shirley to my office at the studio the following day. She asked what time, I told her two o'clock. She said she would have her there.

---

*This, of course, was not the truth. Temple had appeared in four feature films by this time, albeit in small roles.

"You promise?"

"I promise."

I went back to Shirley, who was still looking at the pictures.

"Your mommy said she will come to my office at the studio and you will come with her," I said.

She gave me a big smile.

Shirley's version of the meeting at the theater eliminated the element of chance. She claimed Gorney came to see the short, not the main picture, and that he had been brought by Leo Houck, the assistant director from the *Scandals* audition, with the idea that she should be considered for a part in *Fox Movietone Revue*. "[Mr. Gorney] asked Mom if I could sing, and she said she guessed so." Gertrude appeared at the gates of Fox Movietone Studio lot in Hollywood, but the guard told her no one by the name of Jay Gorney worked there. This supposedly went on daily for three days. Finally, Gertrude located Gorney's home telephone number and called him that same night. It turned out Gorney had been so newly signed by Fox that the news had not yet reached the front gate.

"If it wasn't for [Mrs. Temple's] astuteness and drive, that little thing might have been lost to the world," Gorney mused. Gertrude appeared at the studio the next day. "I had a little cottage on the lot, with a big grand piano . . . The doorbell rang . . . There stood mother and daughter. 'We haven't got much time,' I told them. 'I want Shirley to learn this song quickly.'

"I went to the piano and hoisted Shirley on top and ran through the words just twice [Shirley recalled the song being 'St. Louis Blues']. Well, she amazed me. She sang it through perfectly . . . I asked her, 'Can you dance to that rhythm?' She said she could, so I told her to stand on the piano and I played a little introduction, ta-da, ta dum-dum-dum, and she went into a tap routine for two choruses." Shirley remembered doing a buck-and-wing and that Lew Brown, who collaborated with Gorney on songs and had written the screenplay and would co-produce the movie, was also present. They asked her to sing again and she sang a new Rudy Vallee song that Gertrude had rehearsed with her.

Brown was enthusiastic, and Gorney was ecstatic. They had

auditioned close to 150 little girls for the picture, and none of them had been right. Shirley was exactly what was needed. The absurd story of *Fox Movietone Revue* had the president appointing a secretary of amusement (Baxter) to cheer people up during the still-current Depression. Baxter books touring companies of performers (to be paid by the government) to entertain the population. Somehow gangsters put a snag in the plan, but in the end they are found out, and happiness prevails throughout the land. The song Shirley was to sing, if she got the role, was the big number at the end of the movie. Since Lew Brown had given Jackie Cooper his first featured part in another Fox Movietone Follies (1929), Gertrude was convinced Shirley's break had finally arrived.

Gorney had written the music (E. Y. "Yip" Harburg the lyrics) for one of the most popular songs of the Depression, "Brother, Can You Spare a Dime?," and the studio had great hopes that "Baby, Take a Bow" would be equally successful. What the song required was a natural child who could light up the screen with cheer and hope. Gorney went right to the telephone and called Fox's production head, Winfield Sheehan, and asked him to come over to his bungalow to hear Shirley. Sheehan, a man who considered himself God to his employees, refused; but because Gorney was so insistent, Sheehan finally agreed to be there in fifteen minutes.

"As we were going through the number again," Gorney remembered, "the door to my cottage opened and Mr. Sheehan came in. Shirley, still on top of the piano [went through the song and her improvised dance] for him."

Sheehan was won over and Shirley was signed for the film (now called *Fox Movietone Follies of 1934*), to be paid twenty-five dollars a day for a minimum of five days work. Gertrude, wanting to make sure that Shirley felt comfortable, insisted she wear one of her own dresses and brought several in for the approval of the costume department.* Her name appears for the first time on the daily cast call sheets for the picture on February 9, 1934, under *Specialty Numbers*.

---

*The one chosen, copied and adapted, a red-dotted white organza with puffed sleeves and a short full skirt over many ruffled petticoats (flattering to Temple's chubby legs) became a Temple trademark. Instead of the *de rigueur* black patent-leather Mary Jane tap shoes worn by most "Meglin Kiddies" at that time, Shirley wore white shoes.

That day, she claimed, "was the start of my great romance with Jimmy [James] Dunn," who was one of the supporting players in the picture and was to work with Shirley in the "Baby, Take a Bow" number. "I came in at the close of it," she remembered, "making my appearance by crawling out from between Jimmy's legs and joined him in the finale. The studio decided that it would be easier for me to teach Jimmy the dance routine I knew already than for me to learn something different, so my first job at Fox was giving Jimmy Dunn dancing lessons." For the next five working days, she and Dunn rehearsed their routine between the few nonmusical scenes she had to do. When Sheehan saw the daily rushes, he became as enthusiastic about Shirley as Gorney had been, and additions were made to her role and a scene (considered an outtake, to be disposed of) where she fed Dunn his lines (a repeat of the disastrous incident in *Carolina* with Barrymore, except that Dunn was amused) was kept in the film.

Because of the problems of sound recording, musical numbers have always been filmed with the performers going through the motions of singing a song before the camera. The orchestra and voice have been prerecorded in a soundproof studio. Sound and action are then put together in a mixing room.

Shirley rehearsed all morning on the day they were to record the music track and then film the production number. Around 1:00 P.M., she and Gertrude went to their small portable dressing room to wait to be called to do the recording. After an hour, the child fell asleep, exhausted. "I hadn't been asleep fifteen minutes," Shirley remembered, "when they called for me, so up I got, all sleepy-eyed, and we went over to the recording room. [It] was enormous, and the orchestra was enormous, and there were 50 chorus girls in slinky black costumes sitting [on the floor against] . . . the walls. This was the first time I had ever seen an orchestra.

"They stood me on a table in front of the microphone I was to sing into. We rehearsed once and then made two recordings and in half an hour it was over. . . . Mom and I thought it was all quite ordinary, but apparently everyone, including the director [Hamilton MacFadden], was impressed because I had made two okay recordings after a single rehearsal."

That evening, after Winfield Sheehan viewed the rushes of

the scene, he called Gertrude and asked if she and George could come in to see him the next morning to discuss a long-term contract for Shirley.

Gertrude remembered Coy Watson's warnings about signing such a contract with a studio, and George feared that Shirley might lose control over her own wishes. Sheehan offered $150 a week starting salary for a seven-year contract, with incremental raises commensurate with her progress. "I almost fainted from the shock," Gertrude was quoted as saying a short time later. "I sensed rather than saw, that all this would mean a great change for Shirley. I couldn't give an answer right then, because I wanted to talk it all over with Mr. Temple." Sheehan gave them some additional time to think about it. Gertrude convinced George of "the vista of enormous opportunity that was opened to Shirley—the priceless training it would give her, the certainty of a solid financial background when she grew up." Two days later, they came with Shirley to Sheehan's office and signed a contract. "We took a taxi all the way [there and] home." Though the trip was expensive, Gertrude said they could afford to "celebrate." "Fox wasn't quite sure how to handle me after *Stand Up and Cheer* [the final title of *Fox Movietone Follies*]," Shirley later explained. ". . . [I]t wasn't easy to find good parts for anyone my age and size. Mr. Sheehan took a personal interest in me and protected me with special orders in the studio. He wouldn't let me eat in the Fox commissary for fear the other actors would spoil me." (Actually, she was a bit chubby, and Sheehan and Gertrude were monitoring her meals and did not want her tempted by seeing others served ice cream or french-fried potatoes.)

Winfield Sheehan was always to be remembered by Shirley as her great protector, the man who made her a star and who kept her safe from danger (kidnapping, overzealous fans) and any undue bad influences. Sheehan was perfectly cast in this real-life role. Once a police reporter on the *New York World,* he had in 1910 become secretary to the New York fire commissioner and shortly after secretary to the police commissioner, and involved but never indicted in several police-graft cases (one that ended in an unsolved murder). He entered the film industry as strong-arm protection for William Fox, who was fearful of gangster retaliation because of his fight against the

Motion Picture Patent Company.* In 1914, Fox rewarded Sheehan with a hundred-dollar-a-week job as his personal secretary. Within two years, Sheehan was made Fox Company's vice-president and general manager at twenty thousand dollars a year. In 1927, his salary soared astronomically when he became head of production and established distribution centers in London, Dublin, Paris, Berlin, Rome and Australia.

William Fox, Sheehan's mentor and boss, in 1929 acquired the Gaumont chain of theaters in Britain and attempted to take over Loew's, Inc. (the parent company of Metro-Goldwyn-Mayer). The bid failed because of the Wall Street crash and the intervention of the Justice Department, which ordered Fox Film Corporation to divest itself of 660,900 newly acquired shares of Loew's, Inc. In an emotional state, his personal finances near bankruptcy, the film tycoon was to find his problems were not yet over. At this point, he suffered temporary but severely disabling injuries in a car crash. The bankers who held notes on Fox (he had quite recently controlled a three-hundred-million-dollar film empire) deposed and replaced him with Winfield Sheehan ("the same man," Fox told author Upton Sinclair, "whom I had picked up in 1912 . . . and had rescued from the murder charge they were making against him as Secretary to the Police Commissioner.")

Sheehan's salary leaped from $130,000 a year to $250,000 (within a year this figure would double). Having divorced the Ziegfeld beauty Kay Laurel, he married Metropolitan Opera soprano Maria Jeritza. They lived on a scale considered lavish even for Hollywood, with thirty-three servants employed to care for a forty-room Mediterranean-style palace in Beverly Hills, with its ceilings, doors, grillwork, furniture and art treasures imported from castles in Spain, Italy and France. He kept a five-room suite at the Savoy Plaza in New York, the Savoy in London, and the Ritz in Paris (all paid for by his company).†

---

*Gangsters had taken over the Motion Picture Patents Company, which claimed control of (and was collecting fees for the use of) the patents of all the cameras and projectors designed by Edison, Kalim, Selig, Lubin Biograph Pathé, Essanay and the Vitagraph Company of America. Fox won a stunning victory over the Motion Picture Patents Company in 1912, after four years of constant court litigation, during which time his life had been threatened.

†The great Savoy Plaza Hotel in New York was later torn down and replaced by the General Motors Building.

Glendon Allvine, who was director of advertising and publicity for Fox from 1927 to 1932, claimed Sheehan was "loved, feared and hated, he was Dr. Jekyll and Mr. Hyde," in all those cities.

"He was a complex character: affable, sentimental, suspicious, cynical, ruthless, and a squat dynamo of energy. His baby-blue eyes popped out from a florid face that was seldom relaxed . . . Sheehan loved to play God . . . Discovering new talent was one of his favorite preoccupations, for the Fox studios had few big stars under contract, and were not in the same name league with Metro-Goldwyn-Mayer ('more stars than there are in heaven,' was their publicity slogan)."

Sheehan had paired Janet Gaynor with Charles Farrell in the days of the silents, and both were under contract to Fox, as was the ever-popular Will Rogers. But this still left Fox in a position of having to borrow stars from other studios at high loan-out fees. To circumvent this problem, Sheehan set out on a path of "manufacturing new young stars to his own specification." All-vine recalled that about 1929 Sheehan had "dreamed up the name Dixie Lee and asked me how I liked it. I said it was short, sweet, memorable and would look good in electric lights. . . . He said that he wanted a red-headed blues singer to flush out his Dixie Lee, and told me to run a display ad on the theater page of the [New York] *Daily News* asking blues singers with red hair to audition . . . Some sixty girls showed up—a few with the red hair dye still wet—and sang their blues. . . . One little girl seemed to have a youthful flair and said she had been in the chorus of *Good News* . . . I asked her if she would mind changing her name [Wilma Wyatt] . . . to Dixie Lee. For a hundred dollars a week she said that would be O.K."

Dixie Lee made several films, then fell in love with and married Bing Crosby, and retired from the screen, but Sheehan had not given up trying to bolster Fox's star roster. About the same time as Shirley's association with Fox, the company had signed Alice Faye, James Dunn, Loretta Young and Warner Baxter. But none of these performers had the box-office power of Greta Garbo, Katharine Hepburn, Jean Harlow, Clark Gable, Joan Crawford, Jeanette MacDonald and Norma Shearer—all at Metro-Goldwyn-Mayer. Or Bette Davis, James Cagney, Paul Muni, Edward G. Robinson and Barbara Stanwyck, who were at Warner Brothers.

Fox was, in fact, reliant financially on one man, Will Rogers, who had won the love of moviegoers around the world in such films as *A Connecticut Yankee* (1931), *State Fair* (1933) and *David Harum* (1934). Sheehan was not yet sure what to do with Shirley, but he had an instinct that she could follow in Jackie Coogan's and Jackie Cooper's footsteps as a major child star if the right format could be found and if the public became familiar with her face and personality.

Within six weeks of Shirley's appearance in *Stand Up and Cheer,* Sheehan had cast her in two Fox films already in production, *Now I'll Tell,* a melodrama about a gambler (Spencer Tracy) who becomes associated with gangsters, and *Change of Heart,* which once again paired Janet Gaynor and Charles Farrell (along with Ginger Rogers and James Dunn). Shirley's appearances in both these films are brief, and the parts seem to have been written into a final script. She doesn't sing in either picture. Published credits of the movies in most film books list Shirley as playing Tracy's daughter in *Now I'll Tell.* She does not. Her role is that of Mary Doran, daughter of Tracy's lawyer, character-actor Henry O'Neill. In *Change of Heart,* she appears as James Dunn's neighbor's kid and has a scene playing with a paper airplane that is used as a dissolve to get Dunn on the real thing. However small the roles, Sheehan made sure that the camera caught Shirley in a charming, full-frame close-up. ("Shirley Temple sparkles in a brief bit," *Variety* reported in their review of *Now I'll Tell.* None of the trade papers were to mention her in their future reviews of *Change of Heart.*)

Gertrude had hoped for more immediate rewards. Her fear was that Coy Watson had been right and that Shirley would be relegated to bit roles for the next seven years. On one of her daughter's free days, Gertrude decided to do something about it. "Mom remembered a man who had been especially nice to us [Henry Hathaway] when I'd taken a part in a Western picture [at Paramount]. She asked me if I'd like to drop in and say hello. . . . So in we went [to Hathaway's office at the studio] and while we were there somebody suggested that we see . . . the director Al Hall." Gertrude had read items that Paramount had decided to go ahead with the Damon Runyon story *Little Miss Marker,* to be directed by Hall. Though Shirley was under contract to Fox, a loan-out was always possible, so "on the theory that we had nothing to lose but five minutes," Shirley went to Hall's office, virtually down the corridor from Hathaway, while Gertrude waited outside. Hall took very little persuading that Shirley was right for little "Marky" in his film. He gave her what Shirley called "a three-word test—*aw nuts!* and *Scram!*"

Negotiations between Paramount and Fox over loaning Shirley out for the film began. Despite the uncertainty, Shirley and Gertrude trekked over to Paramount several times to have her costumes fitted. With Gertrude coaching her, she learned the entire part. Still, Fox had not agreed to terms. Finally, a weekly fee of $1,000 payable to Fox was established (Shirley received $150 weekly, as her contract stipulated). But Sheehan wanted her to do *Change of Heart* first. There were innumerable delays in the shooting of Shirley's few scenes in this film, and Gertrude was terrified they would lose *Little Miss Marker.* Finally, "at long last," Fox put Shirley on call for her last scene, the indoor paper-airplane shot to be done that next Monday—if it rained. "Mom prayed for rain all day Sunday," she recalled. Monday it did indeed rain, and Shirley began work on *Little Miss Marker.*

Stand Up and Cheer was premiered the week of April 19, while the Paramount film was just finishing production. "If nothing else," *Variety* led off in its review, " 'Stand up and Cheer' should be very worthwhile for Fox because of that sure-fire, potential kidlet star in four year old Shirley Temple [the age Fox had given Shirley in all publicity releases]. She's a cinch female Jackie Cooper and Jackie Coogan in one, excepting in a more jovial being. She's the unofficial star of this Fox musical."

The other newspapers joined in with their enthusiasm for Shirley:

> *New York Daily News:* "Although *Stand Up and Cheer* was designed to wipe away our fears and blues over these hard times by insisting the Depression is over, I'm afraid it is going to have just the opposite effect. Little Shirley Temple earned the only burst of spontaneous applause."

> New York *Journal:* "Despite the fact that the cast contains plenty of high-powered names, an individual triumph is scored by four-year-old Shirley Temple."

Los Angeles Times: "You must see Shirley Temple. The most adorable four-year-old on the screen today, she does a dance number and song with James Dunn that is amazing."

No one can question Shirley's unique and precocious talent. But she did have an edge. Considerably short for a six-year-old, she had no problem being presented as two years younger. Her "amazing coordination" was partially illusion—as audiences looked at her as just two years past toddler age. Fox, however, did not know that Shirley was six. Her birth-date had been given to the studio by Gertrude as April 23, 1929, and Gertrude had taught Shirley to memorize that date. The child believed she was five years old. A few years later, when the press published articles suggesting her real age, she was kept from seeing them. A girlhood friend, Nancy Majors Voorheis, recalls Shirley's shock at finding out in 1941 that she was about to celebrate her thirteenth, not her twelfth, birthday, that she was a teenager.

THE EXPLOITS of gang leader John Dillinger dominated the headlines the spring of 1934: DILLINGER FORCES DOCTOR TO TREAT HIM, DILLINGER HALTS FOUR COPS. Author and editor Edmund Wilson wrote in his diary for April 17–May 2, 1934: "Dillinger is Surrounding the United States." Dillinger's name (or any violent crime, for that matter) sold newspapers. Hollywood took note. Warner Brothers were grinding out gangster films at an accelerated pace. Metro (*The Thin Man*) and Fox (*Charlie Chan*) had found the detective genre brought good box-office returns. One of the biggest money-makers in 1933 had been a Columbia film, the sentimental comedy *Lady for a Day,* which had gangsters help an old apple seller to pose as a rich woman when her daughter visits. The story had been written by Damon Runyon. Paramount, which was fighting to get back on its feet after being declared bankrupt the previous year, hoped the new Runyon story, *Little Miss Marker,* would pay off as handsomely for them. The same soft-hearted gangsters were in evidence, this time a child rather than an old woman melting their otherwise hard hearts.

The story revolved around little "Marky" (Shirley), who is left by her father (Edward Earle) with a bookmaker (Adolphe Menjou) as the marker (security) on a racetrack ticket. When the horse, Dream Prince, loses the race, the father commits suicide and Marky is taken in by the bookmaker, Sorrowful Jones. The little girl had named Sorrowful and his gang after the members of King Arthur's Court, Tennyson's tale being her favorite bedtime story. Without a copy of the *Legends* at hand, Sorrowful improvises by reading to her from track magazines. When the child begins to speak in racetrack slang, Bangles (Dorothy Dell) the girl friend of hardened underworld boss, Big Steve (Charles Bickford), persuades Sorrowful to stage a medieval pageant to restore Marky's belief in fairy tales. With Big Steve away, his gang take over a nightclub and dress up as Knights of the Round Table. Marky is riding Dream Prince around the dance floor when Big Steve walks in. Dream Prince, who fears the gangster, rears, and Marky is thrown. Unconscious and suffering internal bleeding, the child is rushed to the hospital and saved by a transfusion from Big Steve, the only person to have her unusual blood type. Sorrowful and Bangles find love and a ready-made family, and Big Steve softens.*

For the scene where she was thrown from the horse, Shirley (who had never before ridden one) was wired to an overhead crane, not visible in the final print. When the horse bolted, she flew off and was carefully lowered by the crane, which controlled the wires to the ground. Only one rehearsal and one take were required.

"Shirley Temple, the greatest child actress, or actor, for that matter, yet to be seen on the screen, takes this picture, wraps it up and walks away with acting honors . . . she seems to have the ability of a grownup combined with a delightful, childish charm," Louella Parsons enthused.

"What took Mom off her feet," Shirley later commented, "was the . . . *Variety* headline, saying 'Temple Holds 'Em Three Weeks' [at the Paramount Theater in New York]." Gertrude's Shirley was now a star—but she was only being paid $150 a week at Fox. Paramount offered to buy out the contract and pay Shirley $1,000 a week. Gertrude went to see Mr. Sheehan, who agreed to tear up the original contract. New terms were made. Shirley's salary would begin at $1,250 a week and rise in yearly increments of $1,000 a week for seven years. Shirley would make only three films a year. Gertrude, as her "coach," would receive

---

Little Miss Marker was remade three times: *Sorrowful Jones* (1949) with Mary Jane Saunders in Temple's role and Bob Hope as the bookmaker; *Forty Pounds of Trouble* (1963) with Claire Wilcox and Tony Curtis; *Little Miss Marker* (1980) with Sara Stimson and Walter Matthau. Each of the remakes was compared unfavorably with the original, and none of the children playing Marky found it a stepping stone to stardom.

$150 weekly, a figure that would rise by $100 increments yearly during the time Shirley was under contract to Fox.

Sheehan claimed Gertrude was an astute business woman (within a year, she renegotiated the contract with the legal assistance of attorney Loyd Wright and got four thousand dollars a week for Shirley, five hundred dollars for herself and a twenty-thousand-dollar bonus per film with the same yearly raises as had been designated in the previous contract).* However, Sheehan could afford to be generous. Shirley's fan mail was tremendous. Fox had spent almost nothing to develop her, but already they were being offered handsome contracts for the use of Shirley's name in the manufacture of children's dresses, toys, books and a list of other, less child-related items. (Gertrude was shortly to win back this franchise as well.)

Shirley made three films (for Fox) from July to December 1934: *Baby, Take a Bow, Now and Forever* and *Bright Eyes.* This brought the total to three shorts and nine features filmed in one year. No fewer than fourteen magazine covers carried her photograph. Dozens of articles about her with pictures appeared in all the film-oriented or women's magazines. Her exposure was extraordinary. Many of these stories carried the name and branch of George's bank. He was sought out by depositors (Shirley claimed children's accounts in this branch went up 500 percent when it was announced that her father was handling her financial affairs). George was given a raise and a bonus.

The house in Santa Monica was too cramped for the Temples' new life. They moved to a larger, but fundamentally middle-class, house, a few blocks away. Gertrude hired a housekeeper (Katie), and the studio supplied a car (a black limousine) and a chauffeur.

"I first met Shirley on Christmas day, 1934, when I was seven," Nancy Majors Voorheis recalls. "We [the Majors family] lived on Twenty-First Street in Santa Monica, and Shirley had just moved into a rambling California ranch-style home on [259] Nineteenth Street. Because it was Christmas, my little sister, Marion, and I had three [small] cousins visiting from Berkeley. We'd all seen Shirley's latest great hit, *Bright Eyes,* and we were

---

*Even this contract would be renegotiated for much higher terms by Joseph Schenck, chairman of the board when Twentieth Century and Fox merged.

all in love with Shirley. . . . Our most exciting Christmas present
was our Shirley Temple dolls, which we carried everywhere.*
Without any adult and dressed in some long costumes made by
an aunt, we walked the two blocks to Shirley's house determined
to play with our new idol [a neighbor had told the Majorses
which house was now occupied by the Temples].

"There seemed to be lots of activity around the house—cars
coming and going, people going in, then out—but a conspicu-
ous lack of children. There was an air of excitement as we little
girls stood on the sidewalk in costume, each holding her Shirley
Temple doll. . . . We were terribly excited, scared but determined to meet Shirley. We three older girls prevailed on the
youngest to do our 'dirty work.' We knew she was by far the
cutest, with her enormous brown eyes and little lisp.

"We pushed her to the door, stood over her until she'd
knocked, then withdrew. We could hear her lisp, 'Could Shirley
come out and play with us?' "

George answered Marion's knock and invited the unusually
dressed group in, where they stayed and played with Shirley for
two and a half hours.

The Majors sisters were the daughters of Helen (née
McCreary) and Cort Majors, a leader in the paper industry. For
Gertrude, their appearance on the Temple doorstep was most
opportune. She had been determined that Shirley's life would
be as "normal" as she could make it, given the extraordinary
circumstances. The Majorses were a good solid family, and the
sisters provided two playmates not in movies, which meant the
competitive edge was avoided. Helen and Gertrude also became
friends, and would talk on the telephone "for an hour at a time,"
Nancy relates. The Majors sisters were now invited (and expected) to play with Shirley on Sundays, her only free day.
Except for Mary Lou Islieb, Shirley's stand-in at the studio,
she was not exposed to many other children for fear that she
would contract a contagious childhood illness, and to prevent
her from becoming dissatisfied with the abnormal pressures of
performing.

Nancy Majors Voorheis's earliest recollections of Gertrude

---

*The first Shirley Temple dolls, books, clothes, etc., were sold in stores the fall of
1934.

are of "a very handsome woman—tall, fine bones, patrician features . . . forever straightening up either Shirley or the house: ashtrays, pillows or a misdirected curl on Shirley . . . nothing escaped her need to make it perfect. George was jolly . . . always joking with us. He was as outgoing and nonserious as Gertrude was withdrawn and *so* serious. Shirley looked and was more like her Dad, with his warm brown eyes, long eyelashes, olive skin and twinkle. She had a mischievous nature, a sense of humor, but she did not seem to mind Gertrude's fussing over her, and Gertrude's stern 'Be good, Shirley' always brought her straight up to attention."

David Butler, who directed Shirley in *Bright Eyes* (and three other films), said, "Gertrude had a firm hold on her all the time." Columnist Sidney Skolsky observed that Gertrude "monitored Shirley's entire existence." And Allan Dwan, who also directed her in three films, commented that "Shirley was the product of her mother. Shirley was the instrument on which her mother played. I don't know why the mother was like that— but I'd seen it before with Mary Pickford and her domineering mother."

"I wouldn't stand for any funny business [from Shirley]," Gertrude once declared. "I never coddled or babied her . . . [or] allowed her to be rocked or petted too much. . . . If she ever offered to rebel against my wishes I would use force to see that she did what she was told. I have spanked her soundly upon three or four occasions when she was slow about minding me, but I do not find it necessary to use force often . . . I believe children should really be seen more than heard."

Allan Dwan was to observe, "The mother was very alert and would listen to all the instructions that were given. Absentmindedly I would tell Shirley something I wanted her to do and she would say, 'Yes Sir,' and hurry away.* If she didn't go over to her mother, who would repeat to her what was to be done and take her off to a corner and rehearse her a little bit, she wouldn't do it right. She would do it her own way or whatever she made up, and so we were constantly having the mother come up and convey to her what we wanted. You knew better than to go up to Shirley and [give instructions]. You talked to the mother

---

*This would have been *Heidi*. Temple was nine when this picture was made.

. . . the mother had her strictly controlled at home, and so she could control her in the studio."

Baby, Take a Bow, which followed *Little Miss Marker,* also had Shirley reforming a gangster (James Dunn, her father in this one). The title came from the song Shirley had sung in *Stand Up and Cheer.* She worked well with Dunn, who would be teamed with her in several films, Shirley always receiving the top credit. A pleasant, sentimental film, *Baby, Take a Bow* had very little other than Shirley to recommend it at the box office. Yet her appeal was so great that the picture did as well as the Will Rogers classic *David Harum,* released about the same time.

Paramount claimed her services (they had a second-film option clause in the *Little Miss Marker* contract) for a Gary Cooper–Carole Lombard* film, *Now and Forever.* Once again, she reforms a criminal father (Cooper). She received third credit, but in print of equal size to her co-stars' names. The script managed to find a place for her to sing "The World Owes Me a Living." Louella Parsons marveled "at the ease with which she reels off her lines, saying big words and expressions. There is nothing parrot-like about Shirley. She knows what she is talking about." Despite the weak script, Shirley Temple fever had spread. While Paramount reaped a large profit, Fox reaped the benefit, and Shirley's fan mail, which numbered four to five hundred letters a day, had to be delivered to the studio in huge mail sacks.

A secretary, Dorothy Drum, was hired just to answer the letters for Shirley, who was now an international sensation. Paramount, Warners and Metro offered to buy her contract from her home studio, Fox, which was suffering substantial losses. Stockholders demanded action—better pictures or a sellout to Joseph M. Schenck and Darryl F. Zanuck, who were "hungrily eyeing" the studio. Sheehan took a train to New York to appear before his gloomy board of directors.

"Gentlemen," he said, opening his briefcase and extracting some papers, "here is ten million dollars. Here are the offers and the figures to prove we have such an asset in this five-year-old child."

Sheehan returned to California with a new and better con-

---

*Dorothy Dell, who had played with Temple in *Little Miss Marker,* was first cast in this role, but was killed in a car crash after only three days of shooting.

tract for himself and money to complete work (begun years before) on an eighteen-million-dollar studio located on Pico Boulevard in the Beverly Hills Westwood area with 250 acres of land far from any high-rise office or housing development (originally, this acreage had been used as a "location" for cowboy-star Tom Mix's westerns). The site provided the ideal locale for the "permanent" outdoor sets of the movie company and the construction of much-needed film stages and offices. The top-budget pictures were made at this studio, the B films, or companion features, on the old Fox Movietone Western Avenue studio. English musical-comedy star George Grossman claimed the new studio looked "rather like an Earl's Court Exhibition" and beautifully described the old studios on Western Avenue where he was employed:

> On the one side of the Avenue there are four huge stages which look like Zeppelin hangars or a series of Paddington Stations . . . At the other side of the Avenue are the executive buildings, the bungalow offices, the projection rooms, which are like miniature theatres, the make-up department, which resembles the laboratory of a modern hospital, the rehearsal rooms and Writers' Row. This last consists of a beautiful garden kept in perfect order by a Japanese gardener and surrounded by the bungalows of the scenario writers . . . The garden is crossed by four little streets or paths, each with a sign-post painted . . . "Broadway" . . . "Piccadilly" . . . "Rue de la Poix" . . . and . . . "Unter den Linden."

Stand Up and Cheer and *Baby, Take a Bow* had been filmed on this lot. As if to recognize Shirley's star status, *Bright Eyes,* her next film, was not only written and developed especially for her, it was shot at the new studio. (While with Fox, she would never again film on Western Avenue.) She was given the English actress Lilian Harvey's dressing-room bungalow, *La Maison de Rêves* (Dream House), which had its own garden and a fence around it. Harvey had failed in her bid for Hollywood stardom and, after three badly received films, had returned to Europe. Shirley ate and napped in the bungalow. She rehearsed her dance numbers on an empty sound stage. "Mom always went with us [the dance director and co-performers]. She just sat on the side and watched. When I looked over at her, she smiled. If I did a wrong step, she shook her head a little."

Winfield Sheehan was "very anxious that I shouldn't become spoiled," Shirley recalled, "because if I started admiring myself, it would be sure to come out on the screen. 'It would show in the eyes,' said Mr. Sheehan. No one was allowed to ask me to dance or recite, and no one was supposed to congratulate me on my work except the director."

When Gertrude read the script of *Bright Eyes* for the first time, she was alarmed. The story included another little girl, Mary Smythe, the rich, mean, snobbish opposite to Shirley's winsome, lovable character. Recalling Delmar Watson's reviews in *To the Last Man,* she went to see Sheehan to convince him that the second child's role should be considerably cut. Sheehan held fast, believing that the contrast of the two children would add sympathy for Shirley's character.

David Butler called in thirty girls to audition for the role of the obnoxious Mary Smythe. After interviewing eight-year-old Jane Withers, he sent the rest home. While Withers was not pretty, she had a memorable speaking voice, mischievous charm and boundless energy. She had made only one feature film, but had performed in vaudeville and on the radio from the age of four, and was extremely professional. Gertrude hovered closer than ever over Shirley. Withers remembered that

> I couldn't even talk to her. . . . Later, our director, David Butler, said he always felt his hands were tied and he had a gag in his mouth through that whole movie. He told me, "You stole the picture. When we were working with you, we knew it would happen and we knew it was going to be absolute misery for all of us."
>
> I was not permitted to talk to Shirley at all. I even was told to go and wash my hands before I went into a scene with her. That upset Mother a lot. She wanted to go and talk with Mrs. Temple.
>
> She told the studio people, "Jane is a very clean child. And don't worry. I'll make very sure that her hands are washed before she goes into a scene with Shirley." And she did. But they wouldn't let Mother talk directly to Mrs. Temple.

The camera operator on this (and many Temple films), Joseph LaShelle, recalled that Gertrude "was on the set all of the time, leaving only at short intervals—five minutes or so—when necessary. During those short moments, Shirley could be a little devil. I remember her jumping on the camera seat and saying, 'I'm going to shoot this scene myself.' I told her to come down from that camera and she did.

"In one scene Shirley was told to slap Jane [Withers]. Shirley said, 'I can't!' David Butler told her she had to—Shirley again said, 'I can't!' Finally, Butler said, 'Shirley, you've got to, now do it!' Then Shirley, wincing, slapped her so hard poor Jane burst into tears and so did Shirley."

"I wanted desperately to know her," Withers says. "I didn't know if she was afraid because of what her mother said or what. . . . Naturally, Shirley was the star of the picture, but we were the only two children in the film. When the shooting ended, they had a little party. I wasn't even invited to it. But when . . . Lois Wilson* finished her part in the film, she brought this beautiful doll to Shirley. . . . I'm sure she didn't realize what it would do to another child but we were both there, you know."

The film came out Christmas week and was Shirley's best and most successful to date. Sheehan had calculated right. The two children played well off each other. Fox now had a second child star. Withers says:

> . . . after *Bright Eyes* was released and we were getting telegrams and wonderful letters congratulating me . . . We saw Shirley and Mrs. Temple on the lot and Mother said, "Oh, we must go thank her and tell her how much this means to us."
>
> She saw us coming and she crossed the street and started down the other way with Shirley. Shirley kept looking back and smiling and waving. I was saying "Hi" to her, and Mother was bound and determined to say thank you. So she crossed over and we ran and got in front of her, so she had to stop. I remember this as though it were yesterday.
>
> My mother said, "Hello, Mrs. Temple." She replied,

---

*Lois Wilson played Temple's mother in *Bright Eyes*. Wilson was the same actress whom Temple had satirized in one of her Baby Burlesks—*Pie Covered Wagon*.

"Hello," and was very curt. Mother said, "I have been
trying to talk to you all through the film . . . I just wanted
to thank you for the great opportunity that Shirley's picture afforded Jane . . ."

. . . Mrs. Temple said, "Come, Shirley, we must be
going." then she grabbed Shirley. Shirley looked a little
bewildered and she started to say something. Her
mother literally jerked her away. I never saw her again
[when they were children].

This was, in fact, to be one of the last times Withers was on
the Pico Boulevard lot.* From that point, all of her films (also
very successful) were shot at Western Avenue.

Bright Eyes had Shirley as an orphan whom James Dunn battles to adopt. Dunn this time was a flier, and in one dramatic
scene he is forced to parachute out of his plane (the "ship" of
"On the Good Ship *Lollipop*," the song that Shirley sang in the
film) with Shirley grasped tightly in his arms.

The child's life could not be measured by any normal com-
parison. ("Well, I started in Baby Burlesk films at about three,"
Shirley once commented, "and worked for the rest of my childhood. The studio didn't control my life, but I went to work *every
day*. . . . I thought every child worked, because I was born into
it.") Shirley could no longer go anywhere without a bodyguard,
and even then there was danger of her clothes being torn from
her by fans in search of a memento.

"I don't have many memories of other children or their
parents," Shirley claims, "because I didn't socialize with my
peer group at the studio. . . . I had a lot of concentration to do.
I just didn't have that experience. . . . I was going back to the
studio, back to the set, back and forth to lunch, to home." And
she thoughtfully adds, "[Acting] was something I did during the
day, along with school. Then I came home at a certain time and
went to bed. I liked the work, especially the dancing, and I knew
I was good at it."

All other child stars had agents and studio personnel direct-

---

*In 1944 (age seventeen), Temple wrote. "Some writer started a story about a
deadly feud between Jane Withers and me. . . . Jane and I, as a matter of fact, got along
fine."

ing their lives. After *Stand Up and Cheer,* Gertrude claimed "practically every agent in town had been after us, and we didn't know which way to turn." One day, Arthur Bernstein, Jackie Coogan's manager and stepfather (who was to use up all the former child star's huge earnings), came to see the Temples, "and walked up and down waving a check for a million dollars in my face. He told me he had just gotten that much for Jackie and we ought to let him handle Shirley, because we didn't know anything about the picture business. . . . Bernstein declared he could handle the Fox contract for us. . . ."

When Bernstein would not give up, George, a great admirer of the medical profession, called their family doctor, who came right over and advised them to sign no paper with Bernstein or anyone else. The Temples did not employ an agent or a manager (although attorney Loyd Wright was placed on retainer). George now began carefully to invest his daughter's money for her future; Gertrude dealt with the studio, and Wright handled the final contractual arrangements.

By now, the entire Temple family, even Sonny and Jack, had been "drawn into the vortex of Shirley's fame." Despite George and Gertrude's disclaimers, La Temple, as her brothers teasingly called Shirley, was the breadwinner in the family. Shirley was responsible for her mother's salary and her father's raise at the bank. Her money, after all, supplied the many comforts they had never known and the celebrity that they could never have imagined.

<table>
<tr><td>

5

</td><td>

HOLLYWOOD'S BOLDEST and most enterpris-
ing producer in 1934 was Darryl Zanuck. He
began his career in 1923 as a scriptwriter for
Fox Films. Two years later, he had moved to
Warner Brothers, where he created the
highly successful Rin-Tin-Tin series. Zanuck
swiftly rose to head his own production com-

</td></tr>
</table>

pany while supervising the studio's production schedule. Under
his aegis, Warner Brothers emerged with one of the most effi-
cient and profitable film-making formulas—fast-paced, action-
packed, good scripts, top names, low budgets. Recognizing his
contribution to Warner Brothers' success, Zanuck battled Harry
Warner for higher stakes. The dispute reached an impasse, and
in 1933 Zanuck accepted an offer from Joseph Schenck of
United Artists to form a new company, Twentieth Century Pictures, which would distribute his films through United Artists.*

He realized that without major stars Twentieth Century Pictures would never be able to compete with either Warners or
MGM. What he had going for him was one of the best story
minds in Hollywood and the shrewdness to know that a great
role would attract a major star.

His top writer, Nunnally Johnson, said later, "Darryl always
thought of himself as a writer although he wasn't. He could

---

*Some of the classic films Zanuck produced and in some cases also adapted for
Warner Brothers were: *Disraeli* (1929, producer); *Little Caesar* (1930, screenplay, pro-
ducer) *The Public Enemy* (1931, producer); *The Mouthpiece* (1932, screenplay, producer);
I Am a Fugitive from a Chain Gang (1932, screenplay, producer); *42nd Street* (1933, pro-
ducer). Zanuck had also written dialogue for the first successful talking film, *The Jazz
Singer* (1927).

hardly spell *cat*. He was an ideas-man pure and simple. We would go to the Brown Derby at two in the morning and look through the early editions of the papers, and he would tear out a story and say, 'How about that?' and it would be a story of the suicide of Kreuger, the Swedish match king, and he would say, 'How about that?' . . . and by the next morning he would have an outline ready to be turned into a script and handed to a director.''

Twentieth Century, with stories that were first class, attracted such stars as Wallace Beery and Jackie Cooper (*The Bowery*, 1933), George Arliss (*The House of Rothschild*, 1934), Ronald Colman (*Bulldog Drummond Strikes Back*, 1934), Colman and Loretta Young (*Clive of India*, 1935), Charles Laughton and Fredric March (*Les Misérables*, 1935), and Clark Gable (*Call of the Wild*, 1935). In the short space of two years, Zanuck's company had become extremely successful. What was needed now were greater studio facilities and a distribution system more far-reaching and less money-grabbing than United Artists. Schenck joined forces with Zanuck, and a merger with Fox Films, which remained in dire financial trouble because of mishandling, bad movies and double dealing (Sheehan against Fox), got under way. When the deal was finally negotiated and Twentieth Century-Fox established, Sheehan, realizing his days were numbered, agreed to retire, having been paid a million and a half dollars for his share of the takeover. "They didn't buy the Fox studio," Sheehan said. "They bought Shirley Temple."

The story is told that "the first time Zanuck and Schenck drove through the Pico Boulevard Fox studio, it was a secret and unofficial visit. Schenck looked over the ninety-six-acre lot, with its five miles of streets, its twelve stages, its complex of one-story administration buildings and said scornfully, 'It looks like a bunch of stables, and we've got a lot of shit to sweep out of them.' " But Zanuck, measuring this studio against Warner Brothers, found this one "bigger, richer, better equipped territory than Warners ever had been." And he was now, at the age of thirty-three, its boss.

Hollywood, he felt, was waiting for him to fail, and all he had to rely upon at Twentieth Century-Fox were the two proven money-makers, Will Rogers and Shirley Temple. Within six weeks of Zanuck's takeover, Will Rogers was tragically killed in an air crash in Alaska. Shirley became the focus of Zanuck's production schedule.

Quite simply, after four films, *Little Miss Marker, Stand Up and Cheer, Baby, Take a Bow* and *Bright Eyes,* the public had fallen in love with Shirley. Her success had been the combination of her own charm, Gertrude's ambition, the world's condition, good exposure and film stories that had *accidentally* placed the child in a position of being "Little Miss Fix-It" in the lives of adults. This was mid-Depression, and schemes proliferated for the care of the needy and the regeneration of the fallen. But they all required endless paperwork and demeaning, hours-long queues, at the end of which an exhausted, nettled social worker dealt with each person as a faceless number. Shirley offered a natural solution: to open one's heart. In all of the feature films she had made since *Stand Up and Cheer,* she turned "like a lodestone toward the flintiest characters in her films [the grouchy Warner Baxter in *Stand Up and Cheer*], the wizened wealthy [the Smythe family in *Bright Eyes*], the defensive unloved [Dorothy Dell as the moll in *Little Miss Marker*], the bratty [Jane Withers in *Bright Eyes*], and tough criminals [again, *Stand Up and Cheer;* also, *Little Miss Marker, Now and Forever* and *Baby, Take a Bow*]." Zanuck's first move at Twentieth Century-Fox was to call a story conference with his best writing talent. Top priority, he told them, would be given to develop projects for Shirley that followed this formula. He added one more—Shirley melting "figures of cold authority like Army officers."

The Twentieth Century-Fox archives* list nineteen writers who were assigned to develop eleven original stories called simply "Shirley Temple Story Development." Adaptations of some classics were also delegated. Vera Caspary was the first writer to be given *Daddy Long Legs* (to become *Curly Top* in the hands of two other writers). By March 1935, Zanuck had writers exhuming Baby Peggy's big hit, *Captain January.* The work on Shirley Temple projects was a veritable factory.

The scripts finally selected for Shirley's pictures all had one driving and cohesive theme. As one filmographer wrote, "She assaults, penetrates and opens [the flinty characters] making it possible for them to *give* of themselves. All of this returns upon

---

*At University of California, Los Angeles

her at times forcing her into situations where she must decide who needs her most. It is her agon, her calvary, and it brings her to her most despairing moments . . . Shirley's capacity for love . . . was indiscriminate, extending to pinched misers or to common hobos, it was a social, even a political, force on a par with the idea of democracy or the Constitution." President Roosevelt had even made the statement, "It is a splendid thing that for just fifteen cents an American can go to a movie and look at the smiling face of a baby and forget his troubles."

Shirley was unaware that she was the central force in so many machinations of power, money and Depression-bred neuroses. The only other children whose lives were as pivotal to either big business or political stratagem were both of royal birth and close ascension to the crown. But in the mid-thirties, even England's little princesses, Elizabeth and Margaret Rose, were able to lead more normal existences than Shirley. The word *normal*, of course, has to be placed in proper context. The princesses had been born into their royal life, which involved from their earliest memory a public and private persona. They may not have understood *why* throngs of people cheered as they rode past in an open coach, but they were not surprised by it. Until Edward VIII's abdication in 1938, when Elizabeth was closer to the teenage years than childhood, they had far less responsibility and far more personal freedom as small children than Shirley had been given.

A cover article for *Time* in 1935 stated that "[Shirley's] work entails no effort. She plays at acting as other small girls play at dolls. Her training began so long ago that she now absorbs instruction almost subconsciously. While her director explains how he wants a scene played, Shirley looks at her feet, apparently thinking of more important matters. . . . When the take starts, she not only knows her own function but frequently that of the other actors. . . . She is not sensitive when criticized . . . In one morning . . . tap dancer Bill Robinson [during *The Little Colonel*] . . . taught her a soft shoe number, a waltz clog and three tap routines. She learned them without looking at him, by listening to his feet."

Gertrude was quoted as saying, "Motion picture acting is simply part of her play life. It is untinged with worry about tomorrow or fear of failure. A few times when we have left the studio together, she has looked up at me and said, 'Mommy, did

I do all right?' . . . I have replied, non-committally, 'All right.' That was the end of it. . . . Her playing [acting] is really play. She learns her lines rapidly, just as any child learns nursery rhymes or stories. . . . We usually go over the script the first time with enthusiasm. Sometimes when it is issued, Shirley cannot wait until we get home to hear her lines read. 'Turn on the dashboard light,' she said one night, 'and read my lines while you drive.' "*

During any drive, Shirley's new bodyguard, Grif (who frequently drove the car), would accompany mother and daughter. Grif's real name was John (Johnny) Griffith, and he had been a childhood friend of Zanuck's. Shirley was seldom alone. From the time she began *The Little Colonel* in February 1935 (still under Sheehan's aegis), until many years later, unless traveling, she would spend every day but Sunday at the studio, arriving "on the dot of nine," whether she was filming or not. One of Sheehan's last gestures before he resigned was to have a bungalow built for Shirley on the lot, supposedly to provide her a normal environment. Painted white and trimmed in a blue scalloped and polka-dotted design, the four-room bungalow (living room, bedroom, kitchen and schoolroom/office) had on its grounds a garden, a picket fence, a tree with a swing and a rabbit pen. Furniture in Shirley's bedroom (including a white "baby grand" piano) was scaled to her size. The ceiling was sky blue with silver stars. On one wall in the living room was painted a mural of Shirley in fairy-tale princess costume, a gold shiny star atop her curly head. The furnishings in the room were cherry red and white. A studio set designer had conceived it "as outside Hansel and Gretel's cottage—inside pure Sleeping Beauty."

Shirley's days were spent going between the bungalow, the set and the recording room. Her stand-in, Mary Lou Islieb,† was not able to join her for lessons in the bungalow "because our schedules were exactly opposite."‡ During Shirley's early films, her teacher had been Lillian Barkley, a tall, handsome, strong-

---

*This suggests that Shirley was returning from the studio after dark.
†Islieb was Temple's stand-in from the time of *Bright Eyes*, and was to work with her for fifteen years. Marilyn Granas, the child who had appeared with her in the Baby Burlesks films, had been an earlier stand-in.
‡Islieb stood in front of the cameras when lights were being set up for Shirley or when the cast was rehearsing. Shirley seldom did more than one rehearsal, except for musical numbers.

minded woman. Shirley's contemporary, child star Edith Fellows, recalled that for the five years she had been under Mrs. Barkley's tutorage, "Lillian was not just my teacher. She was my psychiatrist, my friend, mother, sister—she was everything. She kept me from blowing to pieces. I didn't learn my three R's, but I survived. She knew that it was more important that I have someone to talk to than learn my lessons." But with Gertrude ever present, Shirley could not share that same kind of familiarity with a teacher. Toward the end of 1935, Barkley was replaced as Shirley's private tutor by Frances Klampt, a younger and less authoritative woman. Shirley was fond of "Klammie," who knew how to make games out of lessons, but Gertrude remained her real confidante.

Although her contract called for three pictures a year, Zanuck prevailed upon Gertrude in 1935 to add a fourth film. (She would make four movies in 1936 and 1937, as well.) To sweeten the request, he agreed to double Gertrude's salary to one thousand dollars a week and to increase Shirley's bonus arrangement.

Shooting schedules for Shirley's films were six to seven weeks. The law now required she "attend school" three hours a day. She seemed more alert in the morning, and so, when possible, her most difficult scenes were filmed then. She would break for lunch in her bungalow with Gertrude and Klammie (a half hour), take a nap (a half hour—she hated this), then put in an hour or two of studies before she went back to the set, returning to the bungalow in the late afternoon to complete her schoolwork. Between films, she was still expected to be at the studio for six seven-hour days a week for interviews, costume fittings for upcoming pictures and photographic sessions.*

George Hurrell, one of Hollywood's most distinguished photographers, did a series of portraits of Shirley in his studio in 1935. Their first session was lengthy and Shirley never complained, but he could see how exhausted she had become. "I remember once she fell asleep when I was changing a background." Hurrell was moved by this and "photographed her that way. She must have been tired all the time because of her

---

*Mrs. Temple later stated Shirley was photographed on the average of fifty times a day, six days a week, during the years of her contract with Fox.

hectic schedule." At the next sitting, when Gertrude sharply disciplined her for squirming when Hurrell was photographing her, and he tried to intervene, he was warned sharply by Gertrude, "You tend to your photography, Mr. Hurrell, and I'll tend to my daughter."

Looking back, Shirley claimed, "To me [making movies was] always a great big gorgeous game of let's-pretend. Children spend most of their time pretending to be somebody else anyhow. . . . I had a studio full of people to play with me and all the costumes and scenery I needed."

Her studio "friends," with the exception of Mary Lou, were all adults who depended upon her or her services for their livelihood. There was Klammie, a tall woman in her thirties, protective, intelligent, and mildly martinet; Grif, the guard (so tall that Shirley couldn't talk to him when he stood up), who "carried a marvelous pair of handcuffs in his pocket" that she could "beg" away and "handcuff people to chairs"; and there were her directors, who would from time to time enter into the spirit of childhood games with her. Most of her co-performers claim she was "whisked away" by Gertrude after a scene was completed and marched directly back to her bungalow. She listed as great studio games "looking through the camera, and listening to sound through the ear phones, lots of fun." Joseph LaShelle, the assistant cameraman who had to measure the distance from the camera to the actors, would let her guess the yardage. "Sometimes he pretended I was wrong . . . and then I'd get even by snarling it up." Klammie invented a game in which she was Shirley's age and co-pupil, "a droop of a girl named Mergetroid who was barely able to read and write." Klammie would give a wrong answer as Mergetroid, and Shirley would correct her. Doc Bishop, the studio's top publicity man, taught her to ride a bicycle, and then, fearing she might fall off, ran beside her for ten minutes to an hour (suffering huge blisters from the effort). Hulda Anderson ("Ande"), the wardrobe mistress, cut doll clothes for her in her free time. One boon was that almost all of the staff working on the Temple films remained for years, so that there was a continuity.

Saturday was her "big day." Lessons were abandoned, so she had an extra three hours. During that time, Klammie read her stories, or Shirley engaged the crew in games.

Gertrude and George had made arrangements to take Shirley from time to time to a house they rented in Palm Springs "to have a complete rest from all studio photographers and publicity men." When Doc Bishop discovered this, he decided that doing a photo layout at Palm Springs would be a good way to show how America's princess relaxed. "After the studio sent down their publicity man, I had to stop playing hide-and-seek and riding my pony and going swimming so that they could take pictures of myself playing hide-and-seek and riding my pony and going swimming."

Sonny was sent to military school in Arizona in the fall of 1935 and came home only for the holidays, and Jack was attending Stanford University. Gertrude remained Shirley's constant companion. David Butler has said that the two no longer had to exchange words to communicate. All it took was a look from Gertrude, a nod of the head, and the child would react appropriately.

On February 27, 1935, Shirley was presented with a miniature Oscar "in grateful recognition of her outstanding contribution to screen entertainment during the year, 1934." For the first, and only, time, the Academy of Motion Picture Arts and Sciences had thrown the voting open to write-in ballots, and Shirley had received an overwhelming number of these votes for her performances in *Little Miss Marker* and *Bright Eyes*. Child actors had not previously been recognized by the Academy at awards time. They therefore decided to give her a special award. She attended the evening ceremonies with her parents, and fell asleep before her turn came. Gertrude woke her up, and she instantly bounced down the aisle and up onto the stage, and later joined hands with Clark Gable and Claudette Colbert, who had won the Best Actor and Best Actress awards for *It Happened One Night*.

By now, Shirley was virtually unable to appear in public. Hordes of people would wait at the gates of the studio for a glimpse of her getting into or out of her car. The same was true at the gates of her home. There was no opportunity to go down to the beach and play in the sand occasionally as she had done in Santa Monica. Enterprises such as setting up a lemonade stand in a back alley were ended. Such open exposure was believed to be far too dangerous. There was talk of kidnapping threats, but no concrete evidence was ever revealed. Nonetheless, these were hard times, and Shirley was a natural target for ransom, and she recalls numerous times when she was ordered by Gertrude or the chauffeur to ride crouched on the floor of the car as there had been threats to her life.

The famous came to the set to meet her—the great writer Thomas Mann had his picture taken with her, as did the First Lady, Eleanor Roosevelt. Other stars valued publicity shots with her to plug their own new films or to boost their popularity. Later in 1935, she traveled to Washington at FDR's invitation. The Temples were Republicans and not Roosevelt supporters, but the honor of being asked to the White House was not to be dismissed. For Roosevelt, with the Depression still grinding on and an election coming up the following year, Little Miss Bright Eyes was a definite crowd-pleaser to have on his side.

"I liked the President a lot," Shirley later commented. "I had lost a tooth just before I met him. Franklin said, 'I'm concerned! Shirley Temple is supposed to smile a lot.' Well, I wouldn't smile, because I was trying to cover up my lost tooth, because I was embarrassed by it." The Roosevelts invited Shirley and her parents to Hyde Park. The Temples went grudgingly, but once there, were charmed by Franklin and greatly impressed by Eleanor.

"Mrs. Roosevelt was bending over an outdoor grill cooking some hamburgers for us," Shirley remembered. "I was in my little dress with the puffed sleeves and white shoes and had this very feminine lace purse—which contained the slingshot I always carried with me. When I saw Mrs. Roosevelt bending over, I couldn't resist. I hit her with a pebble from my slingshot. She jumped quite smartly and the Secret Service men assigned to her were extremely upset for a while. But no one saw me do it except my mother, and she didn't blow the whistle on me until we got back to the hotel. Then she let me have it in the same area I'd attacked the First Lady."

Shirley's films in 1935 all proved to be crowd-pleasers. *The Little Colonel,* a story of the Old South, had her up against crusty old Lionel Barrymore (again as the grandfather who had disowned one of her parents), this time with better results. As her sidekick, she had the legendary "Bojangles," Bill Robinson, and the two of them were sheer magic together. This is the film in

which they executed their famous staircase dance.* After the
first rehearsal, Robinson sat down and "kissed each of her dancing feet. . . . Uncle Bill doesn't tell her feet where to go, her heart
tells her," he is claimed to have said.

Unfortunately, the film has a long story to tell that is both
sentimental and predictable, and the best scenes with Robinson
are toward the end. Until that time, Shirley pouts a lot as she
attempts to show she is of the same crusty fiber as Barrymore.
Of course, she patches things up between her mother (Evelyn
Venable) and her grandfather, and in so doing saves her father
(John Lodge) from bankruptcy and an attempt on his life. The
finale takes the form of a "pink party" given by the grandfather,
and is photographed in Technicolor, one of the few times Shirley's films used color. This film had been begun while Sheehan
was still at the studio, as was *Our Little Girl*, released only two
months later (May 17, 1935), in which the story and Shirley's
character are both undeveloped. In it, Shirley runs away to the
circus when her parents fight. Joel McCrea portrays the father
in this least interesting of Temple vehicles that year, but the
scenes with Shirley and Poodles Hanneford the clown are extremely winning. Shirley's name alone made this picture pay off
at the box office.

To understand just how constantly Shirley was working and
how fast the studio was turning out her films, one only need
note that her next feature, *Curly Top*, was released on August 7,
less than three months later. This was the first of four Temple
remakes of Mary Pickford silent films, and one of her most
winning movies. In this, she and her older sister (Rochelle Hudson) are orphaned (a frequent Temple story device) and rescued
from an asylum by a rich bachelor (John Boles), who eventually
marries the sister. The score is lively and the musical numbers
well choreographed. Shirley sang "Animal Crackers (in My
Soup)" with a chorus of sixty orphans, as she danced up and
down the aisles of the orphanage dining room, on and off chairs,
with incredible expertise. She performed a hula and tapped to
John Boles's accompaniment of "Curly Top" on the lid of a

---

*Robinson claimed he originated the dance after he awoke from a dream in which
"I was being made a lord by the King of England and he was standing at the head of
a flight of stairs. Rather than walk, I danced up to get it." He also claimed he soaked
his feet in hot water and two quarts of strong liquor nightly, "until they are drunk."

white baby-grand piano. In "When I Grow Up," she performs an entire tabloid with several changes of costume from small child, to teenager, bride and old woman. Her diction is perfect, her phrasing excellent, and her voice changes (especially as the elderly lady) in fairly astounding fashion. *Curly Top* is the quintessential Temple film. She is bright, always surprising you with her tricks. She makes you laugh and shed a tear even though you know perfectly well all will end happily. The arch and delightful Arthur Treacher was Boles's butler and Shirley's cohort. Although he had left the studio long before its release, *Curly Top* was the last Temple movie to have been supervised by Winfield Sheehan, and it was a gratifying end to their relationship.

Released during Christmas week, 1935, *The Littlest Rebel* was a Civil War story, produced personally by Zanuck and directed by Shirley's old friend David Butler. She was again teamed with Bill Robinson. The film was based on a successful play by Edward Peple. Her father (Boles again) goes to the front to fight, and Shirley is left in the care of her ailing mother and the family's black servants: Robinson, Willie Best, and Bessie Lyle as Mammy. In *The Little Colonel,* Robinson had proved himself "a well-behaved, mannerly negro attendant," as he glided up the stairs with Shirley saying, "Now, Honey, all you gotta do is listen with your feet." His "good old Bill" stood patiently by as the old Southern Colonel Lionel Barrymore "cursed and cussed and fussed at him." He was presented as the definitive Uncle Tom who "knew de ole massa didn't mean no harm." His character in *The Littlest Rebel* was at least a trace more dignified.

Bill Robinson was called the "Brown conqueror of a white world," but this was not exactly true. Without question, "Bojangles" had received more recognition from white organizations and societies than any other black man in the United States at that time, and he was "tremendously proud of this triumph over race prejudice." But he remained cast in the stereotypical roles of the Jim Crow Negro. When appearing in theaters across the country, he had to enter through rear doors, could not eat in the same restaurants as other members of the cast (although he was the star), or use the same toilets. He liked to tell the story of how on one tour the predominantly white company, when told that "Bojangles" had to ride the service elevator, got in and rode it with him, a sad comment on his "triumph over racial prejudice."

He had been raised in Richmond, Virginia, by his grand-mother, an emancipated slave. At the age of six, he was already earning nickels and dimes in Richmond beer gardens. By 1906, when he was twenty-eight, he was a star earning thirty-five-hundred dollars a week in theaters and nightclubs. Zanuck had signed him to a five-year contract that paid him sixty-five hundred dollars a week when he worked in a film and gave him the right to also appear in theater and nightclubs, an unusual studio concession. Critics showered him with praise. He was the great-est dancer in America and a tremendous box-office attraction. Still, he met with much prejudice on the Fox lot (as did black performers at most studios).

In *The Littlest Rebel*, Robinson remains the good-natured ser-vant, but with a difference. In *Gone With the Wind*, Scarlett must protect and care for the black servants in her household when the Yankees invade her plantation, but in *The Littlest Rebel* Shir-ley turns to Uncle Billy (Robinson) for safety, and he provides just that. When her mother dies and her father is captured by Union troops and hauled off to a Northern prison camp, he becomes her guardian-companion. They trudge off to Washing-ton to see President Lincoln, street-dancing on the way to raise funds while sleepy-eyed Willie Best passes the hat.

Throughout most of her films, Shirley was surrounded by black servants who were willing to lend a helping hand. As they shared good times together, often through tears or in the face of adversity, Depression audiences came away feeling that if everyone could be kinder to one another, they might survive the bad times.

"During this period of bread lines, of labor problems, of fireside radio chats from President Roosevelt, and of W.P.A. Programs, of intellectual Leftist activities, blacks in films were used to reaffirm for a socially chaotic age a belief in life and the American way of living itself," says black historian Donald Bogle. An "inside" industry joke was that a Temple picture was incomplete without at least one "darky."* It was with the

---

*The major black performers in Temple's films were Stepin Fetchit, *Stand Up and Cheer*; Bill Robinson, Hattie McDaniel and several children, *The Little Colonel*; Willie Best, *Little Miss Marker*; Hattie McDaniel, Robinson, Best and Bessie Lyle, *The Littlest Rebel*; Fetchit, *Dimples*; Robinson, *Rebecca of Sunnybrook Farm*; Robinson, *Just Around the Corner*; McDaniel, *Since You Went Away*; and Lillian Randolph, *The Bachelor and the Bobby Soxer*.

"black low-lifers—the livery keepers, the faithful old butlers, the big bossy maids, the doormen, the cooks . . . and the pickaninnies . . ." that Shirley's character could relax and be herself, to kick up her heels and have some good clean fun (although *The Little Colonel* had her making mud pies with her small black friends). While the world looks bleakest for her, Shirley and Robinson have a rollicking time doing a sidewalk dance to "Pollywolly Doodle" in *The Littlest Rebel.*

Both Boles and Robinson nearly drowned while shooting a Civil War escape scene for this film. A deep fifteen-foot rushing stream, part of the old Tom Mix ranch, existed on the back lot. The two men were to cross the stream on an enormous log, to which the bare branches were still attached for purposes of camouflage. But their combined weight caused the log to overturn, and Robinson's hand somehow was caught in a branch. He shouted for help as he went down. Still clinging to the whirling limb that was being carried quickly downstream, he was jerked up and his head struck the log with such force that he was knocked unconscious. Boles managed to swim to the bank, but Robinson's hold was broken and he went to the bottom. A special-effects man at the scene ran along the bank, jumped in and finally pulled a terrified Robinson to safety. Badly bruised, Robinson nonetheless returned the next day for a scene with Shirley.

Halfway through the year, Shirley topped the box-office charts as the most popular star in the world. Her films grossed unheard-of sums in India and Japan, as well as in North America. And her pictures had solved Zanuck's and Twentieth Century-Fox's financial problems and made the studio competitive with Metro and Warner Brothers. Gertrude had fulfilled part of her dream. Shirley was as big a star as Mary Pickford had been. Now her position had to be maintained.

Zanuck's influence on Shirley's films can be seen in the margin notes he made on the script of *The Littlest Rebel.* "Perfect Temple formula," he inked on the first draft—"real sincere drama or comedy, then put her in it and tell it from her point of view." He suggests that the film "[o]pen on an old Southern plantation—birthday party for Virgie (Shirley Temple)—6 years old—all children from neighboring plantations—twenty kids—old costumes—cut cake—music—dancing—chance for comedy as kids waltz and change partners—Sally and Negro kids love Virgie—they bring presents—ten kids—she thanks them—then go into dance—at height of comedy—rider arrives—news of war—party broken up at once—parents hurry kids home—kids bewildered—what is war—all festivities close—everybody leaves—adults nervous—women start to cry—men worried— Virgie left alone with huge empty ball room—partly forgotten— she feels like crying—scene with Bill (Robinson)—'What is War?'—Fade."*

The script was not written by Zanuck, but the writers merely fleshed out what he outlined above. Zanuck also altered history a bit by having Virgie present ("Leave her here. She may be an inspiration.") when Lincoln thoughtfully begins to write "Four score and seven years ago . . ."

Within a year, the house in Santa Monica that had seemed so grand to Gertrude proved too small to accommodate the gifts of dolls and toys being sent to Shirley. Besides, its design would never allow Shirley protection and privacy, as fans peered into windows and knocked at the front door. Gertrude found her family a suitable home at 227 North Rockingham Avenue in Brentwood Heights, next door to her old acquaintance ZaSu Pitts. A massive stone wall was erected around the property, with an iron electronic gate that could be operated from the house. No matter what the time of day, fans stood pressed against the bars of the wrought iron waiting for a glimpse of America's first little princess.

The house was of a French-Normandy design, its front hidden from the road and its rear looking down across a slope of hills to the Will Rogers Memorial Polo Grounds. There was a shallow swimming pool on the property (so Shirley would be safe). Next to the pool was a glass-brick playhouse, the gift of "a modernist construction company." The estate also contained a badminton court and a stable where Shirley's new ponies, Spunky and Little Carnation, and a horse for Sonny were

---

*There is a strong possibility that Margaret Mitchell, when writing *Gone With the Wind*, could have been influenced by the opening of *The Littlest Rebel*—the party, the advent of the Civil War intruding upon it and the young Southern child's dilemma about and boredom with *war*. Although the main body of *Gone With the Wind* was complete by early 1935, the opening had not been written and was not done until late that year. Mitchell was a moviegoer, and Temple films among her favorites.

kept.* Corky, a Scotty dog, Rowdy, a Cocker Spaniel and Ching-Ching, a Pekinese (Shirley's favorite), completed the menagerie.

Shirley's bedroom on the second floor had a wall of windows that looked out to the ocean. Adjoining the bedroom was a mirrored dressing room and a lighted makeup table, which, though inappropriate for a child of eight, was where Gertrude set and combed her hair. The interior of the playhouse looked "like a department store display window the week before Christmas." By now, Shirley had one of the largest doll collections in the world, with Gertrude's dolls as a part of it.

About this time, the Majors family and the Temples were reunited as close friends (the difficult schedule of Shirley's first two years at Fox had disallowed social relationships). Nancy was appearing (with a monkey named Chico) in an amateur charity production of *The Little Princess* at the Santa Monica Children's Little Theater, and her mother asked the Temples to attend. "They arrived—Shirley, Gertrude, George and Shirley's bodyguard [Grif]—in the family's mile-long black limousine. The limousine must have been half the size of our tiny [theater]. They all wanted to meet me (or probably Chico!) when it was over. I believe Shirley was intrigued with two things: first, that I got to handle a *real* monkey . . . Shirley was always drawn to adventure and she was definitely attracted to my little Chico [who] had been loaned to us by the world-famous explorers Osa Johnson and her husband. The other thing that interested Shirley was our lines. In the movies, Shirley never had to memorize more than a handful for one 'take.' In the play, we had to remember line after line after line. . . .

"From that point on, we were invited to the Temples' home every single Sunday. This was their one 'social' time, and I know it was a sacred time for them. There were *never* any celebrities—it was always a family affair . . . and we [the Majorses] became family . . . George Temple and Daddy became fast friends, while mother and Gertrude became intimate . . . [Sundays were] very, very private and low key. . . . Katie always left a gorgeous chocolate cake made the day before.

---

*Spunky, who was bred on one of Great Britain's finest horse and pony farms, owned by Lady Hector MacNeal, was a gift from Zanuck and had been brought from England by boat and presented to Shirley by the breeder's daughter, Carolyn Wainwright.

"This went on for about five years until I began to resist. I wanted to do 'other things.' [Nancy Majors would have been fourteen by then.]

"One vivid memory was that Shirley always had her hair in pin curls. Her mother always washed her hair on Sunday morning and kept it in pin curls all day to dry to be ready for an early set call on Monday morning. Because we were all so close, this didn't seem like a big deal to us. We entertained ourselves [with Shirley's many toys] . . . the Temple grounds [in Brentwood Heights] really did resemble a miniature Disneyland. It was all there—anything you could dream was there—the junior-grade roller coaster, the real merry-go-round, the real live ponies, the large glass brick playhouse and, of course, the swimming pool. Shirley never ever swam [because of her hair set] . . . and so we weren't allowed to either.

"Shirley was . . . exactly like her wisecracking dad and so unlike her ever-so-serious mom [who] was . . . a bit forbidding. . . . I guess that she probably scared me a little. . . . [From about this time] she always wore her huge rings—one a fine ruby, a very large diamond and a star sapphire. She had told us these were *good* investments, so even at our family gatherings she always wore them.

"Jack [Shirley's brother] . . . was very, very nice—fatherly and kind to his little sister and her friends—like his dad, he was fun, too, and so we loved to be around Jack. Sonny was *very* serious—so much so that I felt I could never talk to him. He never tried to be friendly with us. I suspect he was just terribly shy."

The Sunday sessions with the Majors family, although spent in a controlled environment, proved a great release for Shirley, although the Majorses going to her house—never she to theirs—was an understood axiom of the friendship. She did not attend other children's gatherings or parties, although Jane Withers (who was the most personally popular child performer among their peers) claimed Shirley was often invited by the children who played in films with her.

Zanuck had begun his reign at Twentieth Century-Fox skeptical about the genuineness of his prized "kidlet" star, but he soon was won over by her. "What a shame it is that she has to grow up," he would say. On her part, Shirley soon transferred her affection for Winfield Sheehan to Zanuck, who she claimed later had been like "a second father" to her. George Temple also looked up to Zanuck, who gave him advice—business and personal—from time to time. Zanuck often told the story of how George came to see him at the studio one day. "He hemmed and hawed . . . 'I've had some letters . . . from women.' Long pause. 'They make propositions. They want me to father a child for them.' "

"Can you guarantee you'll give them a girl?" Zanuck asked. "Or even another Shirley?"

"Nope," said Mr. Temple.

"Then don't be unfaithful to your wife," Zanuck advised.

One of the rare excursions the Temples took with Shirley was to the Zanuck ranch in Encino. Unlike his own children, who were awed by him, Shirley called him "Uncle Pipsqueak" (because he often referred to her as Pipsqueak) and would joke with him. But in 1935–36, Shirley alone stood between the studio and bankruptcy: In each year, her films brought in over six million dollars in profit.

"[My father] was a very scary person to me," Richard Zanuck later admitted. "I wasn't a shy little kid hovering in a corner or anything, but I did find his presence overwhelming. I was always aware of my father's need to compete [with] and dominate everyone with whom he came in contact [directors, stars, writers who came to the house]. Sometimes he didn't even look at them when he was talking to them, but just rasped out words at them while he busied himself with something else. And they took it. They were big stars, big names, and they let him push them around. And I sensed that everyone feared him, was afraid to stand up to him, and capitulated to his domination."

"You know that Darryl was mad about women," Milton Sperling, a screenwriter and producer at Fox (previously Zanuck's secretary) said. "Everybody talked about it in Hollywood, and the rumor was that his prowess as a cocksman was just unbelievable. . . . I knew that every day at four o'clock in the afternoon some girl on the lot would visit Zanuck in his office. The doors would be locked after she went in, no calls taken, and for the next half-hour . . . headquarters shut down. Around the office work came to a halt for the sex siesta. It was an understood thing. While the girl was with Zanuck, everything stopped and anyone [in the offices, not on the sets] who had the same proclivities and had a girl to do it with, would go off somewhere and do what he was doing. . . . Any pretty and willing extra was picked . . . and after her erotic chore was completed, she departed by a side door, with or without a little present or promise from her temporary lover. Only then would Zanuck's door be unlocked again. The telephones would begin to ring, work would be resumed, and conferences would be called." Gertrude kept Shirley isolated from studio gossip in a successful effort to retain her daughter's naïveté.

But Jane Withers was not as protected as Shirley and confesses that "Darryl Zanuck was the only man I've ever met in my entire life that I didn't like. I didn't respect him, his attitude, or the way he treated people. I felt strange around him, like I wanted to take a bath. Luckily, I didn't usually have to worry about him, because I was in 'B' pictures.

"I had to go to conventions for exhibitors because they demanded to see me [Withers's films were very popular in 1935–38]. It would make Zanuck so mad, and it used to tickle me to death. Those guys would say to me, 'Hey, kid, we can always count on your movies to save us from those tacky things he [Zanuck] puts out.'

"When they introduced Shirley Temple, of course, she'd get thunderous applause. But when they mentioned my name, those exhibitors would get up and scream. And Zanuck would be furious. He would get red in the face, he'd be so angry. Instead of being thrilled and proud that mine was another film from his studio, it just killed him when they carried on so."

Zanuck was "a health fanatic, worried about his lung power, his weight, his muscles." One of his biographers, Leonard Mosley, wrote that "after a session on the trapeze or a half-hour boxing with his trainer, Fidel La Barba, he would spend some time in front of the full-length mirror in the [studio] gym, scrutinizing his body." He devoted a good part of the night at the studio to seeing rushes and movies, arriving home in the early hours of the morning, slept until nine, breakfasted on yogurt and fruit while a teacher gave him French and Spanish lessons. "Then he was off in his Zanuck Green Cadillac to the studio, driving at breakneck speed over the hills to Westwood [the location of Twentieth Century-Fox], where he arrived promptly at 11 A.M. Everybody else had to be in the studio by eight o'clock [including Shirley] and work was already in progress, but somehow the atmosphere of the place subtly changed as the Cadillac swerved through the gate . . ."

The first items on Zanuck's agenda were his story conferences, and Shirley's scripts had top priority. In July 1935, while Shirley was filming *The Littlest Rebel* (and *Our Little Girl* and *Curly Top* and *The Little Colonel* were still in general release), screenwriters Sam Hellman and Gladys Lehman were working on the script for *Captain January*, the same film Baby Peggy had made in 1924. Shirley was to play "Star, a waif cast ashore by the sea." Captain January, who rescues Star when her parents' boat capsizes and they are killed, is a gruff old sea captain in charge of a lighthouse at Cape Tempest, Maine. The salty Captain January then proceeds to raise the spunky child. The earliest script, dated July 30, 1935, concludes with "the arrival of relatives who will take Star away from the captain. January, aware that his days are numbered, pleads with them to let Star remain with him a while longer. On their final evening together, [he] allows her to light the lamp in the lighthouse [something she had wanted always to do]. She is unaware that . . . the Captain has suffered a massive heart attack and is unable to carry out his duties. January sees the lamp lit and dies." Star, nescient of this tragedy, goes off singing with the lighthouse inspector to join her relatives. Zanuck found this script, because of the death of January, unacceptable, and made extensive suggestions—"a chase scene in which January and Star manage to hide for a time from the authorities. The relatives appear, but turn out to be . . . wealthy . . . wonderful people." The relatives end up giving Star a yacht and hire Captain January to be at the helm.

The second script, dated August 5, 1935, followed Zanuck's notations but added a parrot who could say "Why, shiver my timbers!" The parrot was excised by Zanuck. *Captain January* went into production in late October and was ready for postproduction work in time for Shirley to have two weeks off at Christmas time. Guy Kibbee was cast as January. Tall, lanky Buddy Ebsen, who carried the slender love interest lead opposite June Lang, was Shirley's new dancing partner, and they did a stunning turn to "At the Codfish Ball."

June Lang (her schoolteacher in the film) was one of the few contract players on the lot. (The other major studios kept several dozen performers under contract, but Twentieth Century-Fox was still borrowing players when they needed them.) She felt that Shirley "was not a normal child, due to her outstanding talent at such an early age. She had a mature personality and yet a darling baby face and voice. She was never late on the set, never fluffed her lines . . . Shirley was never allowed to associate with anyone. After every scene, if the director [David Butler] didn't want to talk to her or redo the scene, Shirley would always go to her mother, who sat in a director's chair with her name on it just to the side of the camera. If not needed, they would go to Shirley's dressing-room suite. There was never a time actors could talk to Shirley between takes.

"[I remember hearing] that one day Slim Summerville [an actor in the film] said to Mrs. Temple, 'So you're the goose that laid the golden egg,' after she asked him for her director's chair, [which] he happened to be sitting in when she came on the set."

While Shirley was shooting *Captain January,* its original star, Baby Peggy (Diana Serra Cary),* had a "small bit-part" in the film *Girls' Dormitory,* a Twentieth Century-Fox movie. She recalls that "someone responsible for publicity on that opus got the bright idea he could make a little hay with me by photographing Shirley and me together. I agreed because I was sixteen and very determined to make a comeback in films so that I could set my parents up in satisfactory lives of their own [they had, through bad investments, used up her vast early earnings]. I had it in my head that if I could have even ten years of success . . . I could earn enough to enable me to walk away, as I longed to do, and start living my own life.

"Shirley was entirely alone . . . There was a daybed [in Shirley's dressing room] with a white phone beside it, and she stood up there in her famous high-topped white shoes. Pretending she was her mother (which I am sure fooled no one!) she ordered ice cream sent in from the Chez Paris [the commissary]. . . . I think I mentioned to her having made *Captain January* in an earlier version. I was just a little ill at ease, feeling a bit out of it. I was also disappointed when someone from the portrait

---

*Baby Peggy's family name was Montgomery. Baby Peggy, Peggy Montgomery and Diana Serra Cary are all the same person. *Girls' Dormitory* starred Herbert Marshall and Simone Simon and featured Tyrone Power.

gallery came in and said they couldn't do the pictures that day. I felt it was a lost opportunity for me. I recall thinking how in control Shirley seemed to be, how much 'bossier' than I had ever dared to be at her age [eight]. I remember thinking what a precocious child she was (not surprisingly). She was very mature in expressing her sympathy that we couldn't do the pictures, and treated me with great courtesy and in a very ladylike manner.''

Captain January proved to be another Temple hit, but with its release began an ill-fated relationship between Shirley, the studio and the English author and critic Graham Greene. He saw in Shirley something of the nymphlike coquette that she had portrayed in the old Baby Burlesk shorts. In his review of *Captain January* in *The Spectator,* he wrote, "Shirley Temple acts and dances with immense vigour and assurance, but some of her popularity seems to rest on a coquetry . . . and on an oddly precocious body as voluptuous in grey flannel trousers as [Marlene] Dietrich's.'' He also called the film "sentimental, a little depraved, with an appeal interestingly decadent.''

Not long after, he visited Hollywood and met Shirley on the set where she was filming. He carried away the same mature image of her. These impressions would soon create an international stir. But whatever maturity Graham Greene might have attributed to Shirley, it applied only to her role as a performer. In her private life, she was, in fact, kept very young and naïve.

George's salary at the bank in 1936 was ninety dollars per week, considered substantial for those times.* The house in Brentwood Heights had been bought with Shirley's money and the proceeds of their former home. The studio also provided several "perks," including Grif, the car and Shirley's private schooling. Their housekeeper, Katie, ran the house single-handedly. Nonetheless, there was a laundress, two Japanese gardeners, a pool man and a cleaner who came in twice a week to do the heavy chores.

For a comparative view of how *very* much Shirley was earning, consider that Darryl Zanuck's salary at Twentieth Century-Fox in 1937 was $265,000 yearly, and the chairman of the board, Joseph M. Schenck's, $106,000. Shirley earned in the same year $307,014 in salary alone. This did not include the monies she

---

*Tellers in the same bank drew a weekly salary of approximately forty dollars.

received for the licensing of her name to products.* Metro-Goldwyn-Mayer's three top stars, Clark Gable, Greta Garbo and Spencer Tracy, drew yearly paychecks of $272,000, $270,000 and $212,000, respectively. Over at Warner Brothers, James Cagney took home $243,000 and Errol Flynn $181,333. And at RKO, Fred Astaire made $266,837 and Ginger Rogers $208,767. These stars had very little additional revenue from the commercial use of their names. A study called the Motion Picture Research Project, begun in January 1939 and financed by the Rockefeller Foundation, found that only nine Hollywood actors earned three hundred thousand annually, and that Shirley Temple "earned fifteen times as much [$4.5 million] from her sponsorship of by-products as from her acting."†

Clearly, with the huge sums Shirley was earning, the money could not be allowed to slip away through mishandling and high taxes. Shirley was in the 70 percent tax bracket, but another 10 to 20 percent could be saved from taxes with good management and investment. Gertrude remained strong in her feelings that outsiders (agent or manager) should not be brought in. To begin with, she believed that they would take a percentage of Shirley's earnings equal to or more than what they might save her. Moreover, she did not trust these people. This left only one alternative. George resigned from the bank to set Shirley up as a corporation, and then he was "hired" by the company to handle all financial investments at approximately the same salary that the studio was paying Gertrude. The amounts the Temples now made meant that they could personally pay for all the family housing expenses. George then began investing Shirley's own money in United States government bonds, annuities in old-line insurance companies and guaranteed trust funds with several strong banks as trustees.‡

---

*The figures quoted come from information released in the year 1938 (for the previous year) by the Treasury Department and the Securities and Exchange Commission. All salaries at Twentieth Century-Fox had to be reported because they were a publicly held stock company. Zanuck's salary does not take into consideration his share of the profits of the studio.

†In 1935, 1936 and 1937, the Motion Picture Research Project reported that Temple films "earned over $20,000,000 in profits for Twentieth Century-Fox." That is an accumulative figure for eleven films. *Bright Eyes*, made in 1934, was released Christmas week: Its profits were therefore reflected in 1935.

‡George's position as Shirley's financial adviser attracted other people who wanted to invest conservatively, and soon he had a thriving career as a business counselor.

The arrangement was conservative and the yields comparatively low, but George felt that safety should be their first consideration. The annuities were so arranged that the first returns from the insurance companies would not come to Shirley until she was twenty-one. For each of the five years thereafter, a considerable amount would be paid her.

Shirley Temple, the business, was now protected and secure, but what of Shirley Temple, the child?

For what was actually her eighth birthday, though she celebrated it as her seventh (April 23, 1936), Zanuck instituted what would become for the next four years an annual birthday party, inviting as many as a hundred children—other performers on the lot and children of actors, directors and other personnel—"who came all dressed up, dived into the mountains of cake and ice cream . . . watched the entertainer," and posed for cameramen. "They were children of people at the studio, newspaper reporters and editors," she later said. "It was fun but impersonal."

Delmar Watson adds, "I felt so darned sorry for her. She seemed so lonely. . . . There she was, a big star, and no chance of having any fun. I always felt she was almost like the character she . . . played in . . . *Poor Little Rich Girl* . . ."

"I do not let Shirley get the idea that she is too important in our scheme of existence," Gertrude stated. "At home she feels everything revolves around her father." Then she added, "The mother of a famous star has a difficult road to travel. No mother can know how difficult until she has a small celebrity in her own home."

While Gertrude was being interviewed on the set of *Poor Little Rich Girl,* Shirley strolled over. "Why don't you talk to me?" she asked the reporter. "I'm the star."

6

FROM A BUSINESS VIEWPOINT, the studio found many advantages in the star system. A person could be marketed and sold as a standardized product that a movie audience, banks and exhibitors could understand and regard as security for large profits. Studios stood to have a better chance with a film if they could promise the exhibitors a Jimmy Stewart, Gary Cooper or Clark Gable movie. One contemporary film historian claims this was the case because the star system gave "a psychological security to men who know little about the art of storytelling. It is therefore, logical, from the point of view of studio executives, to build up and exaggerate the star system."

The stars who enjoyed the longest tenure at the time were usually those who could appeal to both sexes. Male stars with a strong masculine personality were able to do this more successfully than females. The popularity of certain child actors, like Baby Peggy, Jackie Coogan and Jackie Cooper, may well have been due to a great extent to the fact that their fans included both sexes and all ages. For this reason, Shirley's scripts were never geared toward the kiddie audience. A love story was always a part of the script, and to mitigate the possibility of women audiences only, Shirley's cuteness was paired against the strongly masculine or brusque personalities of actors like Warner Baxter, Lionel Barrymore, Arthur Treacher and, later, Frank Morgan and Victor McLaglen. The same approach had worked in teaming both Jackie Coogan (*The Kid*) and Jackie Cooper (*The Bowery*) with Wallace Beery.

Darryl Zanuck was working hard to hedge his bets, being well aware that Shirley could at any minute turn from the dimpled darling that the audiences adored to an awkward preadolescent. In little girls particularly, the years eight to eleven could be difficult, and eleven to fourteen disastrous. The studio's many resources could not reverse the aging process, and the studio was busily developing other potential contract stars—Tyrone Power, Loretta Young, Alice Faye, Don Ameche and Robert Young. And Zanuck had just signed the Norwegian ice-skating champion, Sonja Henie, and was bringing her to Hollywood.

Shirley was oblivious to the fact that despite her tremendous popularity, Nature could play tricks on her and end her career without any real warning. When you are eight years old, it seems life will keep on going exactly as it has been. This child's innocence kept her safe from the fear of losing what she had, whereas Alice Faye knew she could be affected by the studio's signing Betty Grable.

Natalie Wood, one of the very few child stars who held her position as an adult, once said, "We [child stars] had an inordinate sense of being responsible and guilty. Guilt, that was the universal feeling [among her peers]."

Jane Powell adds, "We all knew we had a duty to perform and we were trained to follow orders."

Dickie Moore says that he was aware of the fact that his star days could be numbered. "When I came down with scarlet fever, I overheard Mother tell Dad that Freddie Bartholomew, a stranger from England, had won the role of *David Copperfield* (1935). He was now the hot new boy in town under contract to M.G.M., and I was by then [at ten] reduced to going out on interviews for parts. . . . I also felt keenly competitive with Bobs Watson [Delmar's brother, who had starred with Tracy and Rooney in *Boys Town*] and Darryl Hickman [*The Grapes of Wrath*], neither of whom I really knew."

The catalyst for Moore's film decline at age ten had been scarlet fever. Mathew Beard (Stymie in the *Our Gang* comedies), at ten "outgrew the other kids and that didn't work." Edith Fellows, who played "rotten but nice roles," had been receiving twelve hundred dollars a week when Jane Withers, who had a similar feisty quality but was three years younger, entered the scene, and Fellows was let go from her studio.

But if Shirley was not aware of the treacherous factors of

her "play world," Gertrude was; and she knew as long as her daughter was the studio's number-one box-office attraction, she did not have to worry about competition. She therefore put up no objection to the hours Shirley had to work.* Posing for still pictures was one of the tasks that Shirley disliked most. At that time, a picture took a full second to catch, and the subject had to sit absolutely still or ruin the shot. "A whole second," Shirley remembered, "that's longer than you would imagine. . . . I used to pose for about 30 stills every day [between takes of her scenes], and it was difficult to hold my pose, then hold it again for more shots. And then take another pose and do it all over again."† In addition, there were the fashion shots of the dresses that carried the Shirley Temple label and that were a great source of income. "Each dress would be photographed four times and since there were some 25 dresses [each three-month season], that made one hundred shots, sometimes more, in an afternoon. Mom wouldn't let a dress be advertised with the Shirley Temple name unless I'd tried it on and we all liked it.

"Seasonal stills always had to be done ahead of time. About August I'd be posing, in all that California sunshine, for Christmas pictures." Then there were the fittings for her costumes to be worn in each film. After making a movie, Gertrude took the costumes home, and one entire wardrobe in Shirley's dressing room was filled with them. Shirley also had to pose on the set with her distinguished visitors; Eleanor Roosevelt came twice, Henry Morgenthau, Harry Lauder, John McCormick, Rosa Ponselle, Edwina Mountbatten, Ilya Tolstoy.

Gertrude loved to travel, but trips with Shirley seldom worked out well anymore. They had made a pleasant family excursion to Erie, Pennsylvania, to visit George's family just before *Little Miss Marker* had been released, and a few months later they had a mostly untroubled vacation to Hawaii. Now,

---

*Mondays through Fridays, school-age child actors worked five hours and had classes for three hours. But on Saturdays and all school holidays, they could be expected, if necessary, to work a full eight hours. Studios, therefore, whenever possible, scheduled pictures featuring child stars for summer production. Shirley almost always worked on Saturday, and from 1933 straight through to 1939 made one film, and sometimes two films, during the summer months.

†Most of Temple's stills at Twentieth Century-Fox were photographed by Anthony Ugrin.

Shirley's great celebrity made travel difficult. Crowds followed wherever she went, and Grif and the Twentieth Century publicity man, Doc Bishop, always accompanied her. In whatever city she visited, she was expected to pose with local dignitaries and to say a few "cute" words. In Seattle in the summer of 1936, while she was en route to Canada for a premiere of one of her films, three thousand fans blocked her way as she went to leave the hotel. "The hotel people formed a kind of flying wedge around us, and Daddy put me on his shoulders and we went through the lobby," she recalled.

In Victoria, they had an even worse time with the crowds. In order to get out of the hotel, "the police took a rope and made a circle around us, and then they actually started to kick and club people out of the way."

The normal loss of a baby tooth was a trauma in Shirley's life. A dentist made porcelain copies of all her teeth, and if one fell out during filming, it could be quickly replaced with a replica in a plate that Shirley had to wear in her mouth. Zanuck once hurriedly left an important financial board meeting and ran to Shirley's set when he heard she had lost a tooth. Unless it was immediately replaced, a day's shooting could be wasted. When her own tooth would grow halfway in, the plate would be removed and a cap sealed into place with dental powder. Gertrude always carried "two or three spare teeth and some dental powder for emergencies." And if Shirley was wearing a false tooth or cap, it had to be removed when she ate, kept in a glass of water and then replaced again when she went before the cameras.

She followed *Captain January* with *Poor Little Rich Girl,* which took five authors to script and co-starred Alice Faye, Gloria Stuart and Jack Haley. "We all loved our director, Irving Cummings," Faye says. "He was a real gentleman and very good with Shirley and her mother. We were all aware that to be an adult in a Shirley Temple film was a pretty thankless job. You had to work to hold your own." Though the film had been made as a silent by Mary Pickford, little of the former movie remained. Shirley was the neglected poor-little-rich-girl daughter of a soap tycoon (Michael Whalen). When her nurse is hit by a car as she and the child are on the way to her private school, Shirley wanders off and follows an organ grinder (Henry Armetta) home. In the same apartment building lives the vaudeville team of Dolan (Alice Faye) and Dolan (Jack Haley). Shirley joins the act. This leads to a radio contract advertising the soap of her father's chief competitor. The end finds the two merging into one happy company, and Shirley's dad with a new mom (Gloria Stuart) for her. A long dance routine that Alice Faye, Shirley and Haley execute in the film was "nothing less than marvelous." Shirley also sang the Harry Revel and Mack Gordon song "Oh My Goodness," which was thereafter always identified with her.

The acerbic critic Frank Nugent (who had a running battle of quips with Zanuck) wrote in *The New York Times* when *Dimples*, her next film, opened, "The Shirley Temple-for-President Club reconvened yesterday at the Roxy and displayed flattering attention to their candidate's latest assault upon the nation's maternal instinct. . . . Why they bother with titles, or with plots either for that matter, is beyond us. The sensible thing would be to announce Shirley Temple in 'Shirley Temple' and let it go at that. Or to follow the example of the authors of children's books and call them 'Shirley Temple in Dixie,' 'Shirley Temple at Cape Cod,' or [as he suggested for *Dimples*] 'Shirley in Little Old New York.' "

Dimples is an orphan, the granddaughter of a slightly addled and often gruff actor (Frank Morgan) in the 1850's. Stuck with the child, Morgan casts her in his company's first production of *Uncle Tom's Cabin* to play Little Eva and she becomes a big success, wins over her grumpy gramps and plays her usual Miss-Fix-It between two young members of the company (Robert Kent and Astrid Allwyn). A portent of what might be heading Shirley's way can be found in Louella Parsons's negative review of the film. "The Golden Temple baby is growing up—both taller and broader—but her million-dollar personality remains the same fortunately and she needs it for *Dimples*."

Christmas week, *Stowaway* was released, and to Zanuck's and Gertrude's relief, it regained whatever ground *Dimples* had lost. "No exhib[itor's] worrying necessary for this one," *Variety* reported. "It's a nifty Shirley Temple comedy with musical trimmings." As the orphaned child of missionaries in China, Shirley spoke forty words in Chinese, imitated Eddie Cantor and Al Jolson (the latter singing "Mammy") and, with a full-size male doll painted to look like Fred Astaire strapped to her toes as she danced, pretended she was Ginger Rogers. Somehow *Stowaway* charmed critics despite an incredible script. Shirley's parents are murdered by Chinese bandits and she escapes with her dog (her own Ching-Ching) grasped in her arms to the dockland area of Shanghai. Here, she picks up with a youthful American millionaire (Robert Young) and follows him to find herself on board a round-the-world ship as a stowaway and then proceeds to act as cupid between Young and Alice Faye (also on board). Shirley played very well with Faye, and the director William Seiter seemed to hit the right chord with Shirley. "Whether or not due to Seiter's efforts," *Variety* commented, "[Shirley] does not appear to have outgrown . . . the 'Little Miss Marker' stage in this one as she had in her last pictures."

Her ninth birthday was approaching, and she was losing the pouting, baby look. She had been tested and found to have an IQ of 155, which is in the genius classification. Her lessons with Klammie were not sufficiently challenging, and Gertrude knew it. Publicity releases bragged that in school Shirley was "a year-and-a-half ahead of the average child of her age." However, the studio, the public and Shirley herself believed she was eight, not nine. Once again, she had topped the box-office charts. Zanuck had the studio on a profit-making climb, and he was not ready to let go of their little gold mine. His hope was that Shirley would develop into a popular preadolescent in classics the way Freddie Bartholomew had done at Metro-Goldwyn-Mayer, and he assigned his writing staff numerous old favorites to adapt for her.

Gertrude, who had been disconcerted when Zanuck produced *The Country Doctor,* starring Jean Hersholt and the five adorable and world-loved Dionne Quintuplets, was doubly concerned when he scheduled a sequel for the following year. Her life remained wound around her daughter. Evenings they still studied the scenes to be shot the next day. They drove together to the studio, and she continued to work with Shirley on the interpretation of her parts and remained with her in the bungalow between scenes. They ate lunch together every day, and when Shirley was called to perform in front of the cameras, Gertrude would give her last command by the director's side, "Sparkle, Shirley, sparkle!" Then she would sit down in the chair marked "Mrs. Temple" by one side of the camera and watch intently as her daughter went through her paces. Shirley was her world and she was Shirley's. But somehow, a certain amount of spontaneity had been lost. The *play* had become, quite frankly, hard work, and she was fearful the same might be the case for Shirley.

Although it would be two years before it ever reached the screen, what the film people were talking about in 1937 was *Gone With the Wind*. Since the publication of Margaret Mitchell's best-selling book in June 1936,* Rhett-and-Scarlett fever had swept the country. Shirley has said that David O. Selznick, the man who had bought the film rights, had considered her for the film. In the final script for the movie, Bonnie Blue (Scarlett and Rhett's daughter) emerged as the only fair-sized child's role, and Shirley, even in 1936, was too old to play the character. However, in Margaret Mitchell's book, Scarlett had two children, Wade Hamilton and Ella, by a previous marriage. Selznick had originally planned to develop Ella but abandoned both the two earlier children almost from the start of work on the script. Selznick might have had the role of Ella in mind for Shirley. The only other possibility, Scarlett's younger sister, Careen, was too mature in the Reconstruction scenes for Selznick to have considered Shirley.

Shirley remembers yearning for the glamorous dresses earmarked for Alice Faye and Loretta Young she saw hanging in the wardrobe department, aware that her fitting form was flat at the chest and theirs were not. Her babyishness was fast diappearing. But her popularity and box-office appeal were as strong as ever. In 1937, once again she reigned supreme. Gertrude had Zanuck to thank, because of his commercial choice of story material. Only two Shirley Temple films were released that year, both classic children's stories: Rudyard Kipling's *Wee Willie Winkie*, and Johanna Spyri's *Heidi*. Zanuck believed "whole-heartedly in the theory that stars didn't make pictures, but pictures made stars." Shirley was no exception.

The basic ingredients of her film formula were changed by

---

*A small first edition of *Gone With the Wind* dated May 1936 was distributed to publicity sources, newspapers and store book buyers, but the books marked June 1936 were the first to go on sale.

Zanuck. Her naturalness and naïveté were encouraged , but with preadolescence approaching, the baby innocence was no longer acceptable. When the Temples traveled to Bermuda on the *Queen of Bermuda* for a holiday late in 1937, the great English star Gertrude Lawrence was also on board. Shirley tells the story that Miss Lawrence came in to dinner one evening wearing a dress with long, full sleeves, the vogue at the time, and kept pushing them up while dining. Shirley, wide-eyed, "in all the innocence of my nine years . . . announced to the table at large [they were both seated at the captain's table], 'My, that dress doesn't fit you very well, does it.' " There was deadly silence. Eventually Miss Lawrence laughed at the incident, but she also commented to a friend, "That Temple child should be taught some manners." What might seem guileless in a six-year-old child appeared rude at nine.

Zanuck's idea was to bring out Shirley's tomboy quality and to present her in a film with larger production values and more background activity, much as Metro had done with Mickey Rooney and Freddie Bartholomew in movies like *Captains Courageous, Ah, Wilderness* and *The Devil Is a Sissy.* He increased the budgets on her films and turned to top directors. For *Wee Willie Winkie,* the feminization of the old Rudyard Kipling hero, he chose John Ford, who had won the Academy Award two years before with *The Informer.* Ford, on contract to Zanuck, accepted the assignment good-naturedly. As he remembered, "One day Darryl said, 'I'm going to give you something to scream about. I'm going to put you together with Shirley Temple.' He thought that combination would make me . . . howl. I said, 'Great' . . . I remembered the story from Kipling, and it was just great . . ."

Ford and Zanuck had at best "a quarrelsome relationship." Ford thought Zanuck ran the studio like a "Versailles Court," and refused to become one of "Zanuck's flunkies." According to him, Zanuck "lacked artistic integrity . . . he was more interested in making safe commercial pictures." Yet each man had a grudging respect for the other. Ford admired Zanuck's promotional instincts, and Zanuck believed Ford was a consummate director—and after all, Shirley was Twentieth Century-Fox's most valuable asset. Ford put together a supporting cast of actors he knew well: Victor McLaglen (who had won the Best Actor award for *The Informer*), C. Aubrey Smith and Cesar

Romero. McLaglen's Scottish character was killed halfway through the film. "I'd like to keep him," Zanuck told Ford after seeing the rushes. Ford said the story could not work otherwise. "Well, we have all those bag pipes. Can you give him an impressive military funeral?"

Shot in sepia to enhance the exotic Indian background, the Kipling story with its new sex-change was an adventure yarn about a young American widow (June Lang) and her daughter (Shirley) who journey to India in the latter part of the nineteenth century to join the child's maternal grandfather (C. Aubrey Smith), a colonel of a Highland regiment stationed on the frontier. The menace of native insurrection and massacre provided the melodramatic suspense. "When open warfare is threatened between the territorials and the natives, the little girl on a peace-pleading mission is delivered into enemy hands. She is the means of reconciling the two factions."

The story was simple, but Ford gave the production realistic backgrounds, and his handling of the principals, the crowds and the cavalry was excellent. The *New Yorker* critic, who was not generally a Shirley Temple aficionado, wrote, "Under John Ford's expert hand, Shirley has become something more than just a pretty puppet. The child is growing up, seems to understand the emotions she is portraying and there is a definite expansion of personality. She is developing the same appeal, puffed sleeves, the ability to smile-through-tears, that made Mary Pickford 'America's Sweetheart.' Zanuck is very wise in planning to star Shirley in Mary's early vehicles."

At this time, Graham Greene was to discover the dangers of film reviewing. As in his earlier critique of *Captain January* and his personal meeting a few months later with Shirley when she was filming *Wee Willie Winkie*, he found Shirley's appeal far more sensual than her years would warrant. (He had seen her for the first time in *The Littlest Rebel* and kindly written, "I had not expected the tremendous energy which her rivals certainly lack.") Greene's review for *Wee Willie Winkie*, which appeared in a new magazine called *Night and Day* (October 20, 1937), never reached the States and was pulled from the newsstands shortly after publication in England. According to the stories in the American press, Greene wrote that Shirley was a midget with a seven-year-old child of her own. (Shirley herself believed this is what Greene had written.) No such statement appears in the banned article, but Greene does again accuse Shirley of being too nubile for a nine-year-old girl. He claims, "I had accused [in the magazine] 20th Century-Fox of 'procuring' Miss Temple 'for immoral purposes.' " As soon as the review appeared (and was immediately withdrawn) a libel action was brought against Greene and his publishers by solicitor Roy Simmonds on Shirley's behalf, and by Twentieth Century-Fox Film Corporation (New York and Great Britain branches).*

Zanuck's new formula of starring Shirley in a popular classic was next applied to Johanna Spyri's *Heidi*, which was perfectly suited to Shirley's slightly more mature personality. The book had been purchased in 1923 from the author by Sol Lesser and the Baby Peggy Corporation for Baby Peggy, but had not been made.† Zanuck bought the rights from Lesser and put writers Walter Ferris and Julien Josephson on the screenplay. This time, the story remained fairly loyal (at least in essence) to the original sentimental tale of an orphaned child brought up by her elderly, hermitlike grandfather (Jean Hersholt) in a Tyrolean Alpine hut. Heidi is ideally happy with her mountain life and friends, including Peter the goat boy (Delmar Watson). Then an aunt (Mady Christians) virtually sells her to be a companion to a wealthy crippled girl (Marcia Mae Jones) in the city of Frankfurt. The child is torn between her desire to stay with the girl, her wish to return to her grandfather and her suffering under the harsh

---

*The case appeared before the King's Bench on March 22, 1938, and May 23, 1938. Greene, who was in Mexico on assignment, did not appear *(in absentia)*. *Night and Day*, referred to as the "beastly publication" in court, also had on its staff Elizabeth Bowen as film critic and Evelyn Waugh as chief book reviewer. The magazine was intended as a British counterpart of *The New Yorker*, and Greene's reviews were often acerbic or tongue-in-cheek. The case was won by Temple and the two branches of Twentieth Century-Fox. Temple received £2,000 plus costs, Twentieth Century-Fox Film Corporation New York £1,000 and the British film company £500. The settlement remained in trust for Shirley in England. The trial transcript and Greene's article are in the appendices of this book.

†Lesser (1890–1981) had begun his career as a film exhibitor. In 1919, he established himself as an independent producer in Hollywood. He joined forces with child star Jackie Coogan's father, Jack Coogan, and presented the boy actor in several silent films. Diana Serra Cary says, "Lesser was one of the first men in the industry to recognize that even though a child star's career was necessarily brief, a great deal more money could be extracted from those few years than might be surmised." Baby Peggy was at the top in 1923 and earned $1.5 million in salaries and product endorsements. As an independent producer, Lesser made a fortune during the 1930's with the Tarzan films.

treatment of the housekeeper (Mary Nash). In the end, she returns to her grandfather and the mountains she loves.

Allan Dwan, the director of *Heidi*, recalled, "Shirley hit her peak and was sliding [in 1937]. Zanuck would like to have made a trade [a loan-out in exchange for another studio's star], but nobody was interested, and I liked to avoid children, especially those who were [aging fast]. In a kind of left-handed way he gave me *Heidi* and said, 'See what you can do with it.' *Heidi*'s a very down story, stiff and heavy, but Zanuck loosened the purse strings a little. We got to use Lake Arrowhead locations for the Alps and a lot of tricks. Shirley helped invent the dream sequence where she's in Holland because she [instinctively] knew it was a good spot for a musical number."*

Gertrude, who now had a great deal to say about her daughter's scripts, was the one who first came to Zanuck and asked that a musical number be inserted to liven the movie. But *Heidi* screenwriters have, along with Dwan, credited Shirley with the idea of the wooden shoes and the placement of the number. Her theatrical acumen seemed to be developing along with her little girl's body. She was four feet tall, short for nine. Her golden hair had turned to dark ash blond and the ringlets brushed back into soft curls.

Delmar Watson had been called by Dwan with about twenty other young boys to audition for the role of Peter the goat boy. Watson remembers that as they all lined up ready to go through the first weeding-out process (judging size, appearance and voice quality), Shirley and Gertrude entered.

"Which one of these boys would you like to play Peter with you?" Dwan asked Shirley, who motioned to Watson.

Watson recalled that "Mrs. Temple had become much more sophisticated in the years since I had worked with Shirley [1933]. Funnily enough, she seemed to have changed more than Shirley, who I found just as good-natured and, considering her position, not in the least affected. [Mrs. Temple] was now not only protective about Shirley, she allowed nothing to pass regarding her without her knowledge. But she was never unpleas-

---

*The dream sequence had Temple as a Dutch girl singing and dancing with a group of other children to the Lew Pollack and Sidney D. Mitchell song "In Our Little Wooden Shoes."

ant. My dad was on the set, as always. But she was not too friendly with him this time. Marcia Mae Jones's mother was also on hand, and I don't think they were that friendly. Mrs. Temple sat right by the camera during every take Shirley was in. She always wore a hat, which—since it was a very hot summer when we filmed *Heidi*—stood out in my mind. And she wore very smart alligator shoes and a pocketbook that matched.

"One of the first scenes I did with Shirley involved Heidi teaching Peter the ABC's up on the mountain. The two of us improvised a lot during it, and when it was finished, Allan Dwan, the cameraman, all the technicians were confident it would be one of the best scenes in the final picture. But then I heard it was being cut. Of course it was hard not to think that Mrs. Temple might be responsible.

"I was never given my lines to study in advance. My dad asked Allan Dwan about this, and he said they wanted Peter to be kind of dumb, but it was the only time I was in a picture of that length where they would not give me my lines until the night before I was supposed to do a scene."

Coy Watson blamed the studio. "They're not being fair to the boy," he complained to his family when he and Delmar returned home in the evenings. "They're changing his dialogue right on the set. It's almost like they're making him stumble over his lines to make Shirley look better."

Marcia Mae Jones, who was cast as Clara Sesemann, the crippled girl in the film, had no such feeling about the studio or about Gertrude. "I do remember that Mrs. Temple always had on a hat, gloves and a purse . . . and that she was always on the stool sitting next to the camera. Mrs. Temple was always lovely to me—she would invite me in the afternoon to come into the dressing room with Shirley, where she would give each of us a piece of Hershey [chocolate] at four o'clock. It was instead of having tea . . . My mother [Freda Jones]* was on the set at the same time as Mrs. Temple, and they seemed to get along fine. But my mother never intruded on anyone—she spoke to Mrs. Temple when Mrs. Temple spoke to her—and I guess they had some conversations together. I couldn't tell you what they were

---

*Freda Jones was to have a small movie career of her own later in life, and appeared in a featured role with Kirk Douglas in *The Moneychangers*.

about—but I know my mother liked Mrs. Temple and never had any complaints."

Like the Watson family, the four Jones children—Marcia Mae and her two brothers and a sister—were all in the movies. But only Marcia Mae had become a child star. Her debut had been made at the age of six months in the Dolores Costello silent film *The Mannequin* (1924). By the age of seven, she was playing strong, dramatic roles in major films such as the potent *Night Nurse* (1931), starring Clark Gable and Barbara Stanwyck, and *These Three* (1936—based on Lillian Hellman's *The Children's Hour*). Then there had been persuasive performances in *The Garden of Allah* (1936) and *The Life of Emile Zola* (1937). Marcia Mae was a sensitive and talented actress, and Gertrude appeared respectful of her abilities. And perhaps because she was thirteen when she made *Heidi,* four years older than Shirley, Gertrude did not consider the role Marcia Mae played in the film competitive.

"The movie was made during the summer," Marcia Mae recalls, "and an enormous tent had been set up on the back lot and inside there was a complete street scene with the Sesemann house and so forth. They used a great big machine to create the snow, and it was very, very hot in there. It wasn't the best conditions at that time [no air conditioning], and the artificial snow sometimes got in your eyes and your mouth—but . . . I loved the clothes . . . I wore a royal-blue princess coat with an ermine collar and shoes to match with ermine on the boots— and, oh, my dear, I cried when I had to leave that [at the studio].

"I had my own dressing room . . . but I used to love to eat in the commissary, because at that time I was madly in love with Tyrone Power, and it's my understanding that they told him, and he would smile and wave at me and my heart would just go pitter-patter . . .

"Allan Dwan—well, he didn't seem to give any direction. I remember my mother talking to me when I had to get up and pretend like I was trying to walk, and I was told just to get up and do it. I was really quite frightened, because not being crippled I didn't know how to do it, so I imagined—on my own— what it would be like—which is the key to acting . . .

"Poor Jean Hersholt was extremely uncomfortable throughout the film. As I said, the tent was stifling, and he had to wear tremendous padding to make him heavier, and a beard and longish hair to make him look older [and more like a hermit]. Unfortunately, he had a lot of [action scenes] and one day he collapsed from heat exhaustion."

The heat was difficult for all the cast and crew, including Shirley, who tripped on an electric wire, sprawled head first and received a cut over her eyebrow. The eye began to discolor quickly. This was a Saturday, and the film was already two days behind schedule. The makeup artist on the film covered the discoloration and the abrasion, and Shirley completed the day's scenes. A few days later, the artificial snow had caused her throat to close up, and the crew was forced to shoot around her for two days. Despite these problems, *Heidi* was one of Shirley's favorite movies. Her old sidekick Arthur Treacher was also in the film.

"He was marvelous to all us children," Marcia Mae says. "We just loved him."

For the Swiss Alpine scenes, shot on the slopes of Arrowhead Peak, the members of the company either lodged in Arrowhead Village's single hotel or had rooms in private chalets. Shirley was given her own trailer home "parked on the side of a hill." Watson claims, "She was there all the time with [Grif] and, of course, her mother. Only a few studio people were allowed up there. . . . She had a stand-in [Mary Lou Islieb] for the sound and lights. Then, when everything was set, she'd . . . come down at the last minute, we'd do our scene together, and when it was finished, she would be escorted back up the hill and disappear into her trailer.

"Once, I was playing horseshoes right after lunch with the lighting guys, and she came out of her trailer. I said, 'Hi,' and she greeted me and asked if she could play. Sure, we told her. She picked up a horseshoe and tossed it. I think she missed. She played with us for exactly two minutes, and then her bodyguard came down and took her away, back up the hill into the trailer. I heard him tell her she wasn't supposed to be there. As she left, I said to her, 'Bye. Maybe you could do it later.' Shirley didn't say anything, but obediently returned to the trailer."

On the other hand, Marcia Mae Jones felt that a camaraderie existed between herself and Shirley. "We talked and we laughed . . . I think most of us children [who worked with her] were a little in awe of her because Shirley was always bubbling . . . I remember that at Lake Arrowhead there was a miniature golf course, and Shirley and I were playing and I think we had about seven or eight bodyguards watching us—and I know that I was uncomfortable and I just wanted them to go away and leave us alone and let us play, but it didn't seem to bother Shirley.

"One funny thing I remember: I was only thirteen when I made *Heidi,* but I had my full height then—I was extremely tall for my age—I was five feet six inches and Shirley was very tiny and very petite [she would have been eighteen inches shorter than Marcia Mae]. She had to help me out of my wheelchair . . . my God, if I had really leaned on Shirley, I would have crushed her to the floor. When I saw the film years later as a mature woman, I just seemed to get bigger and bigger as I rose from the chair, and my husband, who was with me, said, 'My God, it's a giraffe!' "

Allan Dwan has recalled, "In *Heidi,* we had a lot of kids dressed as little Dutch girls doing a folk dance. One of the steps, a fairly intricate one, called for them to place one leg over the other. Many of them became confused and got it all wrong and would even fall down trying to do it. Shirley would bawl them out and say, 'Look, you do it this way.' They would argue back and forth. She was stubborn and would say, 'No, it's *this* way,' and show them again. Well, the dancing master finally got them all together and straightened them out.

"Since she obviously wanted to take charge . . . I had a bunch of little badges made with SHIRLEY TEMPLE POLICE stamped on them. Every kid who came on the set had to wear a badge and join the force and swear allegiance to Shirley, guaranteeing to obey her. Pretty soon, we had almost everyone on the set wearing a badge, with Shirley sporting one labeled CHIEF. . . . She was a little big shot and loved it. If I had to leave the set, I'd tell her, 'Shirley, now you take charge of things,' and she did. She strutted around giving orders, like 'I want you to take that set down and put up a castle.' The grip would pretend to carry out her instructions, satisfying her, going along with the game."

Filming was completed on *Heidi* the first week in July.* Two

---

*Heidi gave Shirley greater dramatic opportunities than she had had in *Wee Willie Winkie,* and for the third straight year, and with only two pictures in release in 1937, she was box-office champion.

days later, the Temples and Shirley boarded the Matson liner *Malele* for Hawaii. Jack Temple was working that summer as a second assistant director at Twentieth, and Sonny seems to have been left at home. The boys were now grown (Jack was twenty-two, Sonny, eighteen), and they appeared to love their little sister. Still, the inequity between their relationship with their parents and Shirley's could not be disguised. Both George and Gertrude doted on Shirley (George still gave Shirley her evening bath, a ritual between them since she had been a baby and a daily occasion that did not cease until her tenth birthday). Their lives and livelihoods revolved around her, and she had been at the center of the entire household during her growing-up years. A school friend of Jack's says, "He didn't like to talk about Shirley. He hated for people to refer to him as 'Shirley Temple's brother.' "

In her family, Marcia Mae Jones was the star, although never to equal Shirley's celebrity. "I don't know if I could have done as well as my mother if the tables had been reversed," she admits, "but she did love me way too much, and it did cause trouble and jealousy with my brothers and my sister. I can understand today how they must have felt. It was always—'Marcia Mae has to go to work, and Marcia Mae's making the money.' . . . My mother was an orphan and . . . my father a telegraph operator and worked on the railroad, and she was just in this flat with [all of us] children. [It was financially difficult] and she didn't know what else to do. In those days, anybody could work in pictures, so she put us all in pictures so that we could have better clothes and have things nicer. . . . I was the only one who was successful, and so all her energy and attention went into me, and the others resented it."

When Shirley came down the gangplank of the ship that had brought them to Honolulu, she was carried on the shoulders of Hawaiian swimming star Duke Kahanamoku. The two of them were surrounded by a dozen policemen who tried to steer them through the eight thousand people who had come to greet Shirley. The progress was slow and the shouting (in Chinese, Japanese, Filipino and English) deafening.

Jackie Cooper recalls, "The first crowd that shoved around me frightened me a little. I didn't know what they wanted. My mother said nobody wanted to hurt me. They just wanted to see me. That was a concept you might expect a child would have difficulty in understanding. But [I had been told] I had a job to do and it was all part of that job. I was different from other kids—not better, just different. And the key to that difference is that I had a job . . . I had to work at the studio; that meant I couldn't go to regular school but had to study with my tutor . . . [Facing crowds] was simply another facet of that same situation."

Gertrude employed similar psychology. She could not satisfactorily explain to Shirley why all the people wanted to see her. She could only tell the child that this was the way things were for her, and that she had to accept them.

The Temples remained in Hawaii for sixteen days. Almost immediately upon their return, Shirley was back at work doing advance recordings of the song numbers for her next film, *Rebecca of Sunnybrook Farm.*

Zanuck's remake of the Kate Douglas Wiggin children's classic bore little resemblance to the original book or to the Mary Pickford silent based on it. But it did reunite Shirley with Bill Robinson, and the two of them updated their stairway routine to Raymond Scott's engaging number "Toy Trumpet" (based on "The Parade of the Wooden Soldiers"), during which she had to handle some tongue-twisting lyrics that demanded expert enunciation.* The film could well have been called *The Big Broadcast.* The story has Randolph Scott as a young radio executive desperately searching for a child performer for his top sponsor. Shirley, an orphan being raised by a crotchety stepfather (William Demarest), auditions and is accidentally turned down. Demarest takes her to Sunnybrook Farm and leaves her there in the care of her equally gruff aunt (Helen Westley) and her pretty and sympathetic cousin (Gloria Stuart). Robinson is a farmhand who befriends Shirley. Scott's country retreat fortuitously neighbors Sunnybrook Farm. He finds Shirley and falls in love with Stuart. They all return to New York, and Shirley becomes a radio star along with Robinson.

"The national No. 1 box office star seldom has shone so

---

*Temple's songs in *Rebecca of Sunnybrook Farm* were "If I Had One Wish to Make," "Crackly Grain Flakes," "Come Get Your Happiness," "Alone with You" and, with Robinson, "Toy Trumpet." She also sang a medley of her earlier hits, including "On the Good Ship *Lollipop.*"

brilliantly in her singing, dancing and repartee. That means she is going right ahead to bigger and better grosses," *Variety* proclaimed. But Zanuck was not taking any chances. The competition that Gertrude had so feared did not come from another child star (not even the five quints), but from the Norwegian ice-skating champion, Sonja Henie, who he said ". . . looks and acts like the girl-next-door's ugly sister . . . But on the rink, she [is] a princess, a flying angel, a quick-silver goddess, and she hit everyone who watched her right in the heart and the stomach." He cast her in a bland story called *One in a Million,* which made a fortune at the box office. Next he cast her in the equally successful *Thin Ice.* When preparing her third film, *Happy Landing,* he exhorted his writers at every script conference, "for Christ's sake keep the dame on ice." Henie's films made so much money in 1938 (her three films doubling the gross of Shirley's two) that "the studio had a surplus at the bank for the first time in twenty years."

Twentieth Century-Fox was riding high, and Henie and Shirley were not its only commodities. Tyrone Power's career had taken off (Zanuck had commented, "It couldn't have happened to a duller guy") with starring roles opposite Henie in *Thin Ice* and Alice Faye in *In Old Chicago* and *Alexander's Ragtime Band.* The following year, Don Ameche's star would rise with the release of *The Story of Alexander Graham Bell.* But if Gertrude sensed that Shirley's days of celebrity might be numbered, her quote to a reporter on the set of *Rebecca of Sunnybrook Farm* did not reveal it. "My secret ambition is to take a leisurely train trip across the continent and let Shirley greet people at railroad stations. Then anyone could see her and it would not be necessary for people to pay admission to see her." And she reminded the press, "There is a Shirley Temple fan club of 625,000 members in upper England and Scotland alone, and 135,000 persons sent gifts or greetings for her eighth birthday."

Shirley was actually approaching her tenth birthday when this was said. Her films continued to be successful, and miraculously there was still no hint of encroaching adolescence. Yet for four years, she had been doing the same things over and over on the screen; the public now was very familiar with what she could do, and they were beginning to expect her films to be a little more real and considerably more artistic. Zanuck was a clever producer, a brilliant showman. But having done well with children's classics for Shirley enhanced with music and dimpled charm, he decided to stick with that formula, a choice that was to set Shirley, the studio and the box office on a three-way collision course.

ON APRIL 11, 1938, at the age of twenty-three, Jackie Coogan filed suit against his mother and stepfather to recover what he could of the estimated four million dollars he had earned in the 1920's as a child star. The case was front-page news and remained so for many weeks in Great Britain, Australia, Canada, France and the United States. Arthur Bernstein, Coogan's stepfather (the same man who had tried to pressure the Temples into letting him represent Shirley), retaliated by announcing, "He'll not get a penny from us, the law is on our side. Lawyers tell his mother and me that every dollar a kid earns before he is twenty-one years old belongs to his parents." Lillian Coogan Bernstein, Coogan's mother, added, "There never has been a cent belonging to Jackie. It's all mine and Arthur's . . . No promises were ever made to give him anything."

Bernstein had been hired by John Henry Coogan, Jackie's father, in 1923 as "efficiency man to keep down expenses of production [on Jackie's films.]" The senior Coogan had been killed in a car crash in 1935, just three months short of his son's twenty-first birthday. His widow had married Bernstein three weeks later, and they had taken over the estate. The Bernsteins had spent a sizable portion of Jackie's money on a palatial ten-acre Van Nuys estate, two Rolls-Royce limousines and another lavish estate in Palm Springs, as well as on assorted real-estate and security holdings, which were purchased in their names. What was left had been dissipated by Bernstein's huge gambling losses at the racetrack. The long, embittered battle for a share of his childhood earnings did not end for Coogan until August

1939, when the court settled the suit giving him one half of what remained of the estate left by his father. The Bernsteins were forced to liquidate their holdings. But by this time Bernstein's real-estate investments had proved to be almost worthless. Coogan received $126,000.*

Other child stars had been the center of court disputes over their earnings: Freddie Bartholomew's case was almost as well known as Coogan's. Young Freddie had been raised from the age of three by his Aunt Cissy, his legal guardian. Between the years 1934 and 1937, Bartholomew was in court at least twice a month as some twenty-seven separate lawsuits were filed by members of his English family, each trying to get a percentage of his earnings. The expense of these hearings stripped the young man of virtually every cent of the one million dollars he had earned as a child star. Edith Fellows was caught in a three-way custody battle among her paternal grandmother (who had raised her), her mother and her maternal grandmother, each fighting for a portion of her one-thousand-dollar weekly salary. The judge ruled in favor of the grandmother with whom she lived, but the legal battle had proved costly for the child, and she was never to regain her early and highest earnings. Although Judy Garland never took her grievances to court, her mother, Ethel, and her stepfather, William Gilmore, lost all her childhood earnings in a series of ill-fated promotions and land schemes.

When Jackie Coogan had been at his height as a child star, his father had given out in interviews, just as Gertrude Temple had, that the child's millions were safely invested, and that the youngster would be well taken care of as an adult. Shirley's future was subject to great speculation by the press during the Coogan court case. "The Temples naturally adore Shirley, and such a thing as ever fighting with her over money seems now as remote and impossible as the end of the world," Louella O.

---

*Much of Coogan's settlement was lost in legal and court costs and to a divorce settlement to Betty Grable, his bride of one year. Grable was only an aspiring starlet at this time. She was to be signed by Zanuck, and became a Twentieth Century-Fox star. Coogan did not work in films for a decade. He then appeared in small roles until the mid-sixties, when he was cast as the bald, grotesque Uncle Fenster in the successful television series *The Addams Family*. Some years after Arthur Bernstein's death, Coogan and his mother reconciled.

Parsons wrote, and then lauded Winfield Sheehan, Joseph M. Schenck and Darryl Zanuck, who, she claimed, "inserted in Shirley's contracts at their insistence, where and how much of her earnings shall be invested in a manner to safeguard them for her maturity."

Because of Jackie Coogan's plight, the future of all child film performers was made secure. Ten days after his case was filed, Superior Judge Emmett H. Wilson, who approved most of the screen contracts between minors and studios, announced inauguration of a court move to require all who employed juveniles to pay at least half of the minor's income into a trust fund. As a result, the State Assembly in Sacramento, California, passed a Child Actors' Bill, commonly known as "The Coogan Act," under section 36 of the California Civil Code. The bill gave the court the authority to demand that the studio or other employer pay one half of the minor's earnings directly into a trust fund established for the minor's benefit and subject to the court's approval. Singing star Deanna Durbin was the first child to become subject to the new bill when she signed a long-term contract with Universal Studios. "The Coogan Act" unfortunately was not retroactive, which meant that existing contracts between child actors and studios were not affected and left the majority of the children, including Shirley, unprotected. Within a year, the act was extended to cover past contracts still in effect. This addendum was called "The Shirley Temple Amendment."

Each child performer who signed a new contract was now obliged to enact a similar ritual. "The documents had all been read and approved by lawyers for both sides, but the legal traditions had to be upheld," Jackie Cooper remembers. "A judge had to give his official approval to the arrangements. One phase of that ceremony was, as I remember it, always the same.

"The judge would peer at me over his glasses and summon me up to sit beside him on the bench with a wag of his finger. My mother would pat me on my shoulder and send me on my way—'Be nice, Jackie'—and I would smile my way up to the bench and shake the judge's hand.

" 'Well, Jackie,' the judge would say, 'tell me. Do you like what you are doing?'

" 'Oh, yes, sir.'

" 'Good, good.'

"And that would be that for another few years. I hadn't lied. I did like what I was doing. By and large."

Despite the commercial success of several of Twentieth Century-Fox's films in 1938, not one was well received critically, nor was any one of the thirty-five movies made by the studio that year likely to be rediscovered one day as a classic. The list included two of Shirley's least interesting efforts: *Little Miss Broadway* and *Just Around the Corner*. Zanuck's biographer Leonard Mosley states, "Looking at some of [Zanuck's 1938 films] nearly fifty years later is a revelation of the kind of trash movie fans so easily swallowed two generations ago, when twice-a-week visits to the movies were a national habit and hunger for entertainment was more easily appeased."

Zanuck is said to have written most of the final screenplay of *Little Miss Broadway,* which had Shirley yet another time as an orphan, adopted this time by George Murphy, the owner of a theatrical hotel. Prune-faced Edna May Oliver was "the mean old pumpkin" who tries but fails to send Shirley back to the orphanage. Shirley not only plays cupid in this one (between Murphy and Phyllis Brooks), but single-handedly saves the hotel from bankruptcy, while giving all the vaudevillians who live there, including the irrepressible Jimmy Durante, a new lease on life.

With *Little Miss Broadway,* Darryl Zanuck's great instinct for casting was more evident than his talent for screenwriting. Whatever its story clichés, Shirley and Durante's song-and-dance duets were surefire entertainment and bound to succeed at the box office. Yet even reuniting Shirley and Bill Robinson and casting the brilliantly comedic Bert Lahr as a foil could not save her next film, *Just Around the Corner* (adapted from Paul Gerard Smith's book *Lucky Penny*). Using the pseudonym Darrell Ware, Zanuck collaborated on this script with "J. P. McEvoy," who turned out to be none other than the director of the film, Irving Cummings.

The plot had Shirley's widowed, Depression-hit father (Charles Farrell), an architect forced by reverses to live with his motherless daughter in a dreary basement flat, confiding to her that "a harassed Uncle Sam is doing all he can to help the country, but he needs the cooperation of every citizen." Above them, in the penthouse, lives a grumpy old financial czar, Samuel G. Henshaw (Claude Gillingwater), whom Shirley overhears being called Uncle Sam by his nephew. She assumes this is the "harassed" gentleman of whom her father spoke. To help "Uncle Sam," Shirley runs a benefit show and collects nickels, which she presents to the old codger. Henshaw is so touched, he begins a massive construction project to employ thousands, with—you guessed it—Shirley's dad as architect.

Frank Nugent, the movie critic on *The New York Times*, continued his acerbic attacks on Shirley's films. "Fee-fi-fo-film, and a couple of ho-hums . . . have you heard that Shirley has ended the depression? . . . Certainly nothing so aggravating as this has come along before," Nugent accused in his review of *Just Around the Corner*, "nothing so arch, so dripping with treacle, so palpably an affront to the good taste or intelligence of the beholder. . . . Shirley is not responsible, of course. No child could conceive so diabolic a form of torture. There must be an adult mind in back of it all—way, way, *way* in back of it all."*

Gertrude requested a meeting with Zanuck shortly after the release of *Just Around the Corner*, the first Shirley Temple film to founder at the box office. Shirley had always loved the Frances Hodgson Burnett children's classic *The Little Princess*, and wanted to play the lead role of Sara Crewe, motherless daughter of a captain in Her Majesty's Army, who is placed in an exclusive girls' school when her father goes off to fight the Boers. Little Sara is treated like a princess until word comes that the captain has been killed in action and his fortune lost (at which time she is relegated to servant girl). Sara never gives up hope that he is still alive, and thereby hangs the suspense of the melodramatic but warming story. Zanuck read both the book and the play adaptation of it (the same play produced as an amateur production in which Nancy Majors had appeared). Agreeing with Gertrude that it would be a splendid vehicle for Shirley, he secured the rights. So solidly did he agree about the property's potential

---

*A year later in 1939, when Zanuck released *The Grapes of Wrath*, Nugent did a turnaround and declared this Zanuck film a screen classic. Two months later, Zanuck hired him at $750 a week as "a sort of resident critic and script doctor," Nugent later recalled. "Zanuck told me he didn't want me to write, that he just thought the studio would save money if I criticized pictures *before* they were made." He worked four years for Zanuck and never returned to criticism. He formed an alliance with John Ford and wrote, among other films, the screenplays of *Fort Apache*, (ironically, starring Temple), *She Wore a Yellow Ribbon*, *The Quiet Man* and *Mister Roberts*.

that he budgeted the picture for $1.5 million, double the cost of Shirley's previous film, and scheduled it as her first to be made fully in Technicolor.

The Little Princess went before the cameras in October 1938. Co-starring with Shirley were Richard Greene, Anita Louise, Ian Hunter, Cesar Romero, Arthur Treacher and ten-year-old Sybil Jason, who had been brought to Hollywood in 1935 from Great Britain by Jack Warner as his studio's answer to Shirley Temple. Most of Sybil's films for Warners had been clones of Shirley's movies.* Young Sybil, a beautiful dark-haired child, had a quaint charm. She sang, danced and did imitations. But although vastly talented, she failed to ignite the degree of popularity Jack Warner had anticipated. Aware of Shirley and "envious of her beautiful golden curls," Sybil had not been permitted by Warner to see Temple's films "just in case she started to copy her." After she made *Comet Over Broadway* with Kay Francis in 1938, Warner Brothers did not renew her contract. She was nine years old, about the same height as Shirley, and Zanuck hired her to appear in *The Little Princess* as Shirley's friend, the servant girl, Becky.

Sybil Jason remembers the day that she was scheduled to shoot her first scene. "It occurred to Anita [her older sister and guardian] that in the book, the character of Becky was a Cockney girl. Well, no one had mentioned that I was to talk with an accent. But Anita thought she should check it, anyway. You never saw such panic in your life. The studio assumed that since I was British [she had been born in Capetown, South Africa, and moved to Great Britain as a small child], I could speak in a Cockney accent. First of all, I had never heard a Cockney accent in my life, and by this time I had been in America for five and a half years. No time to get a dialogue coach in, and they couldn't change the schedule due to the fact that the sets were already [built]. We had a real problem. However, my sister, knowing that I had a good ear, asked if they could run a movie

---

*Jason's *The Little Bigshot* (1935) was patterned after *Little Miss Marker*. "Shirley's name was Marker, mine was Gloria Gibbs," Jason recalls, "otherwise the two pictures are interchangeable . . . *Changing of the Guard* was *Wee Willie Winkie* . . . *The Captain's Kid* [1936] bore a striking resemblance to *Captain January* and even had Guy Kibbee in a role as a New England sea captain." Jason also made *The Singing Kid* with Al Jolson; *The Great O'Malley* with Pat O'Brien and Humphrey Bogart and *I Found Stella Parish* with Kay Francis.

where someone spoke with a Cockney accent. Before I knew it, I was rushed into a projection room and was watching the wonderful Wendy Hiller in *Pygmalion,* and by the next morning I was all ready with the accent."

Also cast in the film was Marcia Mae Jones, who had played the crippled Clara in *Heidi.* This time she was to portray the mean girl in the story. "I remember that I received as much [fan] mail as Shirley did from *Heidi* because I received mail from crippled children everywhere. They felt if I could walk, they could walk. People said that Mrs. Temple probably would not let me do another movie with Shirley because of [my popularity] in *Heidi.* But I was told that Mrs. Temple did request me for *The Little Princess.*

"The scene I remember filming most vividly was when Shirley dumps ashes over me. They had made two dresses for me and two dresses for Shirley, in case the scene could not be done in one take. After Shirley dumped the ashes on me, I screamed and they yelled, 'Cut!' Shirley stood there for a moment, and then she walked over to the director [Walter Lang] and she said, 'Can we do that again?' She just loved doing the scene, and I was scared to death that they would do it again. The ashes were made out of [ground] corn flakes and flour and were not very pleasant to be covered in."

The Little Princess ran twenty days over schedule and, to Zanuck's distress, this required costly additions to the original budget. But the film, when it was released in 1939, was successful, and Shirley's performance in it—her curls drawn back in a new, more mature hairstyle, the petulance tempered, her acting never better—gave Zanuck new confidence that she would be able to make the transition from child star to adolescent performer.

About the same time that *The Little Princess* was released, Metro-Goldwyn-Mayer was preparing *The Wizard of Oz.* Mervyn LeRoy had been so impressed with Shirley's most recent film that he offered Zanuck double her salary to star her as Dorothy. For weeks, he held out hopefully, raising his offer to the absolute limit that the budget could afford. LeRoy's enthusiasm only convinced Zanuck that Shirley had made it over the most difficult time in her career and that she would "go on endlessly." He turned LeRoy down, and the role went to Judy Garland, while *Susannah of the Mounties* was prepared for Shirley.

The choice of this story, which had Shirley, as the lone survivor of an Indian massacre, rescued by the Canadian Mounties (led by Randolph Scott), was a miscalculation on Zanuck's part. The story was banal, and Shirley's character the least sympathetic she had ever played. Despite the popularity of *The Little Princess,* Shirley went from number-one box-office favorite in 1938 to number thirteen the following year, while Judy Garland zoomed from nowhere to number five after the release of *The Wizard of Oz.* Zanuck interpreted this as a sign that children's fantasies were "hot." Shirley's next film, he announced, would be an adaptation of Maurice Maeterlinck's play *The Blue Bird,* and would be photographed in Technicolor.

What Zanuck had not anticipated was that the summer of 1939 would see the advent of war. For a decade, the rhythm of daily life had been set by a depression whose grip seemed unbreakable. Complete recovery appeared remote. Over ten million workers were unemployed, and many had so succumbed to despair that they no longer bothered to seek work. In this atmosphere, the movies thrived. For fifty cents, a man or woman could be transported for at least ninety minutes by Astaire's and Rogers's nimble feet into a world of ocean liners, bouncy music and designer clothes, with the airiest problems solved in the happiest fashion by the final scene.

Shirley's films, too, had offered the quintessential escape. The plots were simplistic. No one went to see her movies expecting to be intellectually stimulated. People went because they knew they would be guaranteed a view of a naïve world where happiness and fortune could come with a little girl's dimples. If Shirley's ability to appeal seemed "endless" to Zanuck, it was because the Depression, which, after all, had already endured a full decade, also seemed endless. Then, almost completely unexpectedly, the German-Soviet Treaty of Friendship and Alliance was signed on the night of August 23, 1939. On September 3, Britain and France declared war on Germany. The evacuation of women and children from London had begun. Americans wanted desperately for their country to stay out of war, but they knew that they would eventually be drawn into the fight. This war, the people were convinced, would be truly global, the worst that had ever been fought.

Like a sponge, the war absorbed every other topic of discussion. "Newspaper circulation soared . . . Street-corner orators thrived." Two of the most popular songs in the winter of 1939–40 were the World War I favorite "Hang Out the Washing on the Siegfried Line" and Jerome Kern and Oscar Hammerstein's nostalgic look at pre-Nazi France, "The Last Time I Saw Paris." People rushed to the movies to see the latest newsreel coverage of the war—the sinking of HMS *Royal Oak* in Scapa Flow, the German invasion of Poland, then Norway, Denmark and France. The war news was bad. The brutal reality America saw in the newsreels was in direct contradiction to the flippant, superficial films they had formerly enjoyed. They flocked to *Gone With the Wind* (the Civil War), applauded *The Dawn Patrol* (World War I), laughed at Charlie Chaplin's *The Great Dictator* (a satire of Adolf Hitler).

An unsuspected cause of the success of *The Little Princess* might have been the Boer War background and the scenes of Shirley searching frantically for her father among the survivors brought back to a London hospital. Unintentionally, Zanuck had struck a topical theme: trepidation that one's kin might be killed or maimed by war. *The Blue Bird,* which had a Grimms' fairy-tale setting, could not have been more inappropriate. The screenplay, by Ernest Pascal, was an imaginative and often chilling retelling of Maeterlinck's fantasy about the two children (Shirley and Johnny Russell) of a poor woodcutter who seek the bluebird of happiness in the past, the future and the Land of Luxury, but eventually find it in their own backyard. Far less human than *The Wizard of Oz* (which was really a variation on the same theme), lacking a musical score and with a role for Shirley that, unlike Dorothy in *The Wizard of Oz,* was necessarily unsympathetic (the story, after all, was about children with misplaced values), *The Blue Bird* was doomed from the start. With war in 1940 a daily reality, with British casualties and losses mounting, audiences had little patience for allegorical fairy tales. Happiness meant stamping out evil (successfully accomplished in *The Wizard of Oz* when, however accidentally, Dorothy kills the wicked witch), while the only scourge in *The Blue Bird* was a child's lack of wisdom.*

---

*The Blue Bird was remade in 1976 in the first widely touted Russian-American co-production. Despite a star cast (Elizabeth Taylor, Ava Gardner, Cicely Tyson, Jane Fonda, Harry Andrews and Mona Washbourne), the film failed—"a flabby script, unsuitable casting and unresolved production problems" were cited. But it might be added that too little emphasis was given to the children in the story.

On the release of *The Little Princess,* columnist Hedda Hopper snidely reported a rumor that because of Sybil Jason's outstanding performance in the film, the studio would not reunite her with Shirley again. She was, however, signed to play the one truly sympathetic child's role in the film—the crippled girl, Angela Berlingot. Sybil claims, "Everyone kept an eye out for an attitude or any sign of competition that might have arisen between us two little girls. But that's just what we were—two little girls [Shirley was eleven, Sybil, ten] who worked well together. No doubt about that."

She remembers Shirley being very supportive in their scenes together, presenting her with gifts of pastel-covered chocolates and colored chalks. They both liked to draw. Sybil sketched pictures of tropical islands, and Shirley made portraits of her Pekinese dog. Regardless of Shirley's overtures, a real closeness never developed between them. After a scene, Shirley would return to her bungalow, while Sybil remained in the small private area on the set that was reserved as her dressing room. "We rarely came in contact with each other outside the studio. I did get to meet and know her brother [Jack was working at the studio], adored her father [who came often on the *Blue Bird* set], but somehow or other could never make friends with Mrs. Temple." And it was Gertrude and the studio whom Sybil blamed for any unpleasantness she experienced during the filming.

"In preproduction tests, they made me read Shirley's lines while they tested for the other players," she remembers. "Even at that age, I knew it wasn't right for me to have to do that, but I did what I was told."

At the start of the film, Shirley's character, Mytyl, is obdurately selfish. When the crippled Angela asks her to trade a bird that Mytyl has caught in the woods for Angela's most prized possession, Mytyl refuses. By the end of the movie, through a series of dreams that she experiences, Mytyl becomes generous, and the very first thing she does after discovering that the bluebird of happiness has been in her backyard all the while is to take the bird and present it to Angela. The crippled girl is so happy that she determines she can walk and, rising from her wheelchair, succeeds. This sequence was Sybil's most dramatic in the film, and she and her sister Anita had great hopes that it would give Sybil's career a needed boost.

"About one week before the premiere," she recalls, "Walter Lang, the director of both *The Little Princess* and *The Blue Bird,* called Anita and me to his office and said he felt we should know something before the date of the premiere of the movie. He said it was very hard for him to tell us, because he personally felt it was one of the best scenes in the movie, but he had been made to edit out the sequence where I received the bluebird and got up from my wheelchair and walked. Mrs. Temple had said if it was not cut out, she and Shirley would walk out of the studio. He said, 'My hands are tied. I want to explain to you. It's cut out of the movie. I had to do it.'

"The finished film didn't make sense at all. One moment Angela is crippled, and the next minute, without explanation except for Mrs. Berlingot's amazement, Angela is pictured outside her house standing up and talking to Mytyl.

"Mrs. Temple had the right to say who was in the movie, how it was cast and to choose the director and the cameraman. But regardless of who was responsible for this decision, as an adult I can almost understand the studio's thinking in cutting the scene. Shirley had been the biggest money-maker at Fox for many years, and they were protecting their interest.

"Shirley never realized any of this. I knew something was happening. . . . The premiere was held at Grauman's Chinese Theater, but after hearing the sad news that most of my work would not be shown on the screen, the decision was made [by us] that Anita and I would not attend. Shirley and I were never to work together again."*

Gertrude's victory in protecting Shirley's stardom in *The Blue Bird* was Pyrrhic. Although Shirley's personal reviews were not bad, the film, termed "leaden" and "dull," failed at the box office. Shirley's next picture, a show-business saga called *Young People,* cast her as the daughter of ex-vaudevillians who have trouble resettling in a rural community. The picture fared even worse than *The Blue Bird.* Rumors circulated that Zanuck "would not stand in the way of Mrs. Temple if she wanted Shirley to

---

*Cut drastically for re-release a few years later, the only existing prints now open with confusing abruptness as well. Ironically, the cast of *The Blue Bird* included numerous former child stars in bit parts, each struggling through the nadir of careers; Dickie Moore, Scotty Beckett, Juanita Quigley, Gene Reynolds and Ann Todd (not the English actress).

leave the studio." Nancy Majors Voorheis remembers George Temple about this time sitting in the Temple library bar and telling the Majors family that since Shirley, after taxes, was making only five cents on a dollar,* he and Gertrude thought they should pull her out of movies for a few years. Certainly he might well have suspected her career at Fox was drawing to a close. Several months went by without a script being developed for her. Under the terms of her contract, her salary and Gertrude's continued to be paid. Gertrude played a waiting game. Finally, a call came from Zanuck asking if she would meet with him.

"Zanuck didn't look at me once during our meeting," Gertrude later confided to Dickie Moore. "He carried on the entire conversation with a golf club in his hand and never looked up from the ball he was putting on the carpet. I told him if he wanted to get rid of us, he would have to pay off every penny that was called for in our contract."

Zanuck agreed only to continue to pay Shirley's salary for the unlapsed year, but flatly stated that with the losses on her last two films, he would not cast her in another movie. Gertrude was furious. After the dismal failure of *The Blue Bird,* if Shirley was kept off the screen for a year, her career could well be ruined. Two weeks later, her lawyers had exercised a right to buy back Shirley's contract from the studio. After a week of hard negotiation and for a figure in excess of $250,000, paid for out of Shirley's earnings, her contract with Fox was severed.

It was August 1940. Shirley had spent half her life at the one studio. She had made twenty-two films there, saved Fox from bankruptcy, and earned them over thirty million dollars in profits. Zanuck, the studio patriarch to the end, gave Shirley a retirement party in the Chez Paris and "presented her with an upright piano, a rack of her old costumes and some glowing speeches." Within a week, the famous Shirley Temple bungalow had been renovated, all traces of her tenure removed and the premises reassigned as a small office complex.

---

*George Temple was incorrect. The highest tax bracket for that year was 75 percent of earnings.

8 | ALTHOUGH THE STUDIO publicity department released a story to the effect that Mr. and Mrs. Temple had decided Shirley should retire and live a normal life, Gertrude apparently had no such plans for her daughter. She immediately set up meetings with several other studios. To her shocked surprise, the offers for Shirley's services were few and, by her standards, insulting. Without a home studio or even a film in sight, she was forced to review Shirley's future. There would be no private protector, no bungalow classroom. Shirley would have to attend school; and since fall classes had already begun, there was no time for an extensive search for a school. Marion and Nancy Majors, however, both attended Westlake School for Girls, as did John Boles's daughter, Janet, June Lockhart, actress daughter of Gene and Kathleen Lockhart, and Phoebe Hearst, granddaughter of William Randolph Hearst. Feeling Westlake was the right school, Gertrude went to see the headmistress, Carol Mills, and Shirley was enrolled.

The term at Westlake, which was located in Holmby Hills, only a short drive from Brentwood, was already in session when Shirley attended her first classes.

"Mom was sad," Shirley wrote, "because she was going to leave me at Westlake for the day and go away while I learned to get along by myself. But I felt wonderful."

The school took both boarding and day students. Shirley and the Majors sisters lived at home. Grif had been put on salary by the Temples, who still feared kidnapping, and drove the three girls to school in the morning, remaining close by until it was time for him to return them to their homes in the afternoon.

"Every morning the Temples' mile-long limousine pulled up to our home to pick up my sister and me," recalls Nancy Majors Voorheis. " . . . I remember that we were all prematurely boy-crazy, or maybe just plain crazy, for we laughed, giggled, whispered secrets about absolutely nothing but boys, boys, boys! There never was a conversation about school, classes or even other girls. It was really boys—all the way! An example: After my first year at Westlake, Shirley wrote in my school yearbook:

'To Nancy, you know the most interesting people. Lil Bug'

[Lil Bug was Shirley's favorite nickname, given to her by the girls at Westlake.] She meant when she said 'people,' boys—boys to whom I could introduce her."

Shirley later added, "Because I was the only student in my class until I went to a real school, I learned a lot quickly: sex, and all the things people did that I'd never known."

"Westlake was a beautiful, serene campus," Nancy Majors Voorheis reflects, "more like a lush green estate than a school. Classes were small, and thus intimate. On sunny days, lunch from brown paper bags was eaten on the lawn. There were only forty-eight or [forty]-nine girls in each grade. When Shirley entered, I was in the eighth grade, Shirley in the seventh and Marion in the sixth. Harold Lloyd's two daughters were classmates. But Shirley was the only real celebrity, not the daughter of someone. Everyone knew everyone else. It was a sheltered, cloistered, perfect little world. We wore uniforms, flat shoes and no makeup so there could be no one-upmanship.

"We had chapel every morning before classes, and after chapel we had to file by a senior inspection line. If anyone was caught wearing makeup, demerits were given, and the penalties were stiff. You had your special privileges taken away. [Study hall was substituted for elective classes like dancing, or the girl was confined inside during lunch hour.] For the longest time, Mrs. Temple put rouged lipstick on Shirley. I can still see an officious senior scrubbing it off with a piece of Kleenex. Mrs. Temple did Shirley's hair and got her ready in the mornings, but finally, after Shirley had been restricted a few times, she took care of these things herself and so passed inspection.

"Miss Mills, our beloved principal, was also our English teacher. She became very, very close to Mrs. Temple, and she adored Shirley. My recollection is that she thrived (more than we kids) on the celebrity of Shirley's fame.

"I remember the thrill of Shirley's twelfth birthday, which turned out to be her thirteenth [April 23, 1941]. This was a dinner for about thirty girls held on a Saturday night at the Bel-Air Country Club a few days early. This was the *first* time any of us wore a long party dress. I vividly remember Shirley's, and how perfect it was . . . white *peau d'esprit* with an accent of dubonnet velvet ribbon. [She wore] tiny white satin shoes, (she always was much smaller than the other girls) and dainty real pearls. Her famous curls were pulled back, giving her a new look of sophistication. She was particularly excited because her biggest birthday surprise was being told she was one year older! That made her a teenager. She was really thrilled."

Shirley's retirement was short-lived. Before her first year at Westlake ended, Gertrude had completed negotiations with Louis B. Mayer at Metro for Shirley to star in a film called *Kathleen,* at twenty-five hundred dollars a week. The terms were low when compared to her former Fox remuneration. But Gertrude was also to receive one thousand dollars a week, and the contract carried the stipulation that if Shirley's option was picked up for a second film, a 30 percent increase would be put in effect. Gertrude must have believed that at Metro, which had a host of teenage stars, Shirley had a chance to make the transition from child to juvenile lead. It is now apparent that Mayer was using Shirley's name to make a better package for a low-budget film.

"It seems to me," one of Shirley's co-stars in the film, Laraine Day, reflects, "that considering the kind of production given *Kathleen,* Mr. Mayer wasn't expecting too much. The film did not have a top cast with big-name stars to support Shirley. The budget was small. It was just an ordinary picture, and heaven knows, MGM had a lot of top stars who could have been in a picture with Shirley Temple and have provided her with a better background and a better vehicle."

Kathleen was being shot at the same time as, but on a budget less than one third that of, the Judy Garland–Mickey Rooney musical *Babes on Broadway,* which featured Virginia Weidler in a role that Shirley had previously been offered by Mayer, who had originally felt Shirley could not carry a major film. It could not have made Gertrude feel better that back at Shirley's home studio, Fox, Jane Withers had been starred in the successful *Her First Beau*, and thirteen-year-old Roddy McDowell had been cast in the John Ford film *How Green Was My Valley*. Universal was grooming fourteen-year-old Gloria Jean to replace the maturing Deanna Durbin. In two years, a twelve-year-old Elizabeth Taylor would startle movie audiences in *National Velvet*, and she and Margaret O'Brien (*Journey for Margaret*) and Natalie Wood (*Miracle on 34th Street*) would become Hollywood's reigning child stars. The vogue for young actors, either tots or teenagers, was far from over. The special charisma Shirley had as a child had not survived into adolescence. Still somewhat chubby, she possessed a budding bosom and features that retained their cherubic innocence. In these qualities, she much resembled Judy Garland. With its low budget and the Temple name, Mayer believed *Kathleen* would recoup its cost and at least make a small profit. To his surprise, it did neither.

"I think it would have been a better picture for Shirley," Laraine Day suggests, "if she had someone other than Herbert Marshall and me [as co-stars]. I had just finished playing Herbert Marshall's daughter in *Foreign Correspondent*, . . . he was too old [fifty-three] to be playing a sweetheart or a love story with me, and I felt I was much too young [twenty-four] to be playing a psychologist for Shirley." In the film, Kathleen was a lonely girl whose father (Marshall) was too engrossed with business and his personal life to realize that his daughter needed him. To compensate for this lack of affection, Kathleen lived in a dream world. Psychologist Day is hired to move in and study her. The obvious happens: Marshall and Day fall in love and the three live happily ever after.

The plot was predictable, the characters over-familiar. Still, that had seldom hindered the success of a Temple film. Judy Garland's earliest movies, made when she was about Shirley's age—*Pigskin Parade* and *Thoroughbreds Don't Cry*—also had weak, predictable scripts and low budgets. But Garland as a teenager had an appealing child-woman vulnerability, and the roles she played underscored this quality. The young woman in *Kathleen* was willful, confident and often stronger than her adult co-stars.

Instead of Garland's tender expression, soulful eyes and tremulous voice that tore at your heart, Shirley resembled a spoiled but self-assured youngster, whose life had contained snags but no real pain. Roger Edens had written many of Garland's songs and made all her musical arrangements, and Mayer assigned him to the film. Edens gave Shirley "a Garlandesque and beautifully melodic" song, "Just Around the Corner." Shirley sang it in a dream sequence where Kathleen imagines she is a musical-comedy star, complete with a male chorus. Her performance rated good personal reviews,* yet the old box-office magic was missing. The picture was released shortly after the attack on Pearl Harbor. The country was at war. Film themes had taken a more serious turn. Mayer did not pick up the option, and Shirley returned to Westlake School for Girls.

Her grades in her first year had been barely passing. She now applied herself, although her main interest remained "boys! boys! boys!" Nancy Majors Voorheis says, "She had her own little private court consisting of Phoebe Hearst, very strong and very aloof, and [another girl] Minerva Floor. Perhaps they were the real rulers, the king-makers. I, being one year ahead, was always more like the big sister, though still very close. As far as I remember, Shirley never talked about her future in movies at school. She was always terribly interested in the present, and boys seemed to dominate that.

"Grif, Shirley's bodyguard, took us to and from school every day, and he stayed there to protect Shirley . . . [and] when the school had dances he attended, too, [but] we didn't like that much.

"The dances were held in what we called the Great Hall. Our partners were recruited mostly from local boys' schools such as Harvard and Black Fox [both schools are Los Angeles military academies]. I remember Shirley was about fourteen and I was probably fifteen, and I was very smitten with a handsome Black Fox cadet, a blond boy by the name of Bill Curtin. Our dances were heavily chaperoned by parent volunteers. I remember Mrs. Temple was on duty that night. At certain points in the evening,

---

*"Miss Temple . . . is ingratiating" (*Variety*, 11/12/41). "No emotion is too difficult for this child to convey" (*Hollywood Reporter*, 11/11/41). "There is a new dignity and poise in her acting" (*Los Angeles Times*, 3/27/42).

we would have intermission and were allowed to go outside and to walk on Westlake's beautiful grounds.

"I got Bill outside, and as we walked along he leaned over to kiss me. At just that point, Grif sprang out of the bushes, got into our path and halted the action. I was humiliated, and I'm sure my date was, too, as Grif led us both back into the Great Hall. But Shirley was far smarter than I. She was always able to get away from Grif's heavy scrutiny."

Gertrude had become tremendously involved in Westlake activities. "Mom did more than I did," Shirley later confessed. "She was a Mothers' Club officer. I sang in the glee club and wrote a secret gossip column for the school paper [her name did not appear on the masthead], and I had small parts in the various school entertainments."

Shirley's second year at Westlake was interrupted when Gertrude signed a contract for her with Edward Small Productions that guaranteed her $65,000 for her first film under their aegis,* star billing and a dressing room on the set. The picture was to have an eight-week shooting schedule. An independent producer who released through United Artists Films, Small had made many successful commercial films, including *The Man in the Iron Mask, My Son, My Son* and *The Last of the Mohicans,* and was best known for action and adventure films. Shirley's contract gave Small a two-picture option with a pay increment of ten thousand dollars for the second film. No sooner had Gertrude signed, using an agent to represent Shirley for the first time, than Shirley revealed her strong desire to remain at Westlake. The Temples' agent, Frank Orsatti, was forced to telephone Small stating Shirley "had no intention of appearing on January 5th [the starting date] . . . unless the director was satisfactory to her . . . and unless certain other details concerning the production were approved [by her.]"

Shirley and the Temples were notified by Small's attorneys† that either Shirley would advise them in five days that she would live up to the terms of her contract or a suit for considerable damages would be filed. Shirley began work on

---

*Designated to be one of the following stories: *Little Annie Rooney, Secret Garden, Lucky Sixpence* or *Stella Marris*

†Swarts and Tannenbaum, then located at 650 South Spring Street, Los Angeles

Miss Annie Rooney on February 16, 1942. The screenplay, a fairly free adaptation by George Bruce of Mary Pickford's silent film *Little Annie Rooney*, presented Shirley as a teenager, attracted to boys and "hep to the jive" of her peers. The plot leaned heavily on the old Temple formula: the motherless daughter who must save an adult from misfortune and unhappiness. Annie's father (William Gargan) is jobless, and conjures up a crackpot idea for brewing synthetic rubber out of milkweed. Both Shirley and Gargan live with his father (Guy Kibbee), who fortunately has a pension. Annie meets the teenage scion of an aristocratic family (Dickie Moore) and he invites her to his sixteenth birthday party with all his rich friends. Just when Annie wins over the snobbish group, in walks Gargan, who takes the opportunity to display his rubber process to her beau's millionaire father (Jonathan Hale). The chemical procedure gasses everyone present and mortifies Annie. Nonetheless, she stands behind her dad, and in the end his invention turns out to have credibility.

The film's publicist managed to obtain far-reaching press coverage on Shirley's first screen kiss. Former child star Dickie Moore, for whom this film was also a comeback, was to bestow the kiss. "Photographers from every major wire service, newspaper, and magazine visited the set to record the event," he recalled. "My suit was soaked with sweat. Also, the script called for me to jitterbug with Shirley . . . [who] was a superb dancer, while I stumbled over curbs.

"In a last desperate bid to keep the film on schedule, the studio [United Artists] made a rubber mask of my face, and put it on a real dancer, who doubled for me in the musical numbers . . . when I kissed Shirley I hoped the world didn't know my secret; I had never kissed a girl before . . . let alone the Princess of the World. What if I got an erection while Hymie Fink and a wall of other cameramen recorded my first sin?

"Adding to my consternation, Shirley's breasts pressed hard against the party dress . . . her legs, firm and round, covered in this scene but well-remembered from the days preceding, were suggestively outlined beneath the skirts she wore . . . I was seized by a paralysis of fear . . . Edwin Marin, the director, called me over. He wore a tight little suit and tight little collar, with a tight little knot in a tight little tie. 'You seem very self-conscious,

Dickie. Have you any inhibitions about kissing Shirley?' " he asked. Moore lied and said he did not. The kiss ended up being no more than a peck on the cheek.

Moore added, "I liked Gertrude Temple, I wondered why she was so nice to me when I knew I was so terrible in her daughter's picture. . . . She treated Mother and me cordially and invited us one day to their home.

"There, after lunch, we toured the grounds and inspected the Doll House, a bright, farmhouse-style pool-side bungalow larger than our home. Entirely separate from the main house, it held Shirley's vast doll collection, which reposed inside glass cases."

The Doll House that Moore refers to was not the glass-brick building presented to Shirley as a playhouse when she was a child. In 1940, the Temples had built a two-story dwelling styled after an English cottage, half-hidden by trees and shrubs on a steep slope behind the main house, as a place where Shirley could relax, find privacy, entertain friends and display her dolls and other memorabilia. When the Majors sisters or Mary Lou Islieb visited on Sundays, they played there. The cottage also contained a movie theater complete with projection booth. The upper floor housed a little theater (decorated in scarlet red and chartreuse), complete with stage and dressing rooms, as well as a bath and kitchen. Downstairs was a full drugstore-style soda fountain (Shirley's pride), a small bowling alley, a room filled with racks of all of her film costumes, and the doll room (her collection now contained fifteen hundred dolls in glass cabinets that lined the walls of this huge room, which also displayed a fine array of doll houses and miniature furniture).

When Moore met Shirley many years later, she told him that *Miss Annie Rooney* "was a terrible picture." Critic John Mosher of *The New Yorker* described it as "not much, about not much." *Variety* reported, "Shirley is still a conscientious worker in any role that comes her way, even though her appeal remains limited to less sophisticated tastes." Not only was the script inane, the movie was outdated. Teenagers in 1942 did not use the argot employed in the film (closer to 1930's slang), and a fourteen-year-old girl would not have tied a ribbon in a bow around her hair. Young audiences did not identify with the movie. The film fared no better at the box office than had *Kathleen.* Edward Small did not pick up Shirley's option. Shirley, delighted to be back at Westlake, was unconcerned, and when no offers for her services were forthcoming, she settled in to become a real—not a movie—teenager.

"By her sophomore year," Nancy Majors Voorheis recalls, "she was going steady with Hotch, whose name was Andy [Andrew D.] Hotchkiss, from a boarding school nearby. Then he transferred to Thatcher in the Ojai Valley . . . and we would drive up [a ninety-minute ride] for a big dance in her car with Grif [and Gertrude] and we would spend Saturday, and Saturday night [at a nearby hotel], and come back Sunday. This was the biggest thrill in our lives."

Shirley recalled having her "first real dates" when she was a sophomore. "They didn't seem terribly thrilling . . . because I'd been going to our [boy-girl] school parties." Her most vivid memories were of a hop at West Point, June 1943. "There were four hundred or five hundred stags and they cut in on me so fast that finally they all just lined up and had me go down the line and dance a few steps with each one." Five formal Westlake cotillions were given each year, sponsored by the Mothers' Club, each class taking turns as hostesses. In the spring, every girl in the school would look forward to a new dress to wear at an upcoming cotillion, always held in the school's impressive "Great Hall, a big beautiful ballroom with two staircases. I always envied girls who lived at school, because they could float down those stairs so effectively in their evening dresses while I and the other girls who lived at home just had our dates call for us in the usual manner and came in wearing our wraps."

Nancy recalls that Shirley "dressed exquisitely. Her mother had the bulk of her wardrobe created by the then-famous designer Adrian. Needless to say, none of the rest of us wore three-hundred-to-five-hundred-dollar creations. Shirley seemed extremely sophisticated boy-wise, or perhaps ready or eager. Why she was so much more worldly than the rest of us I don't know. She smoked [when she was about fifteen], very sophisticated, we thought. She just seemed to *know* what she wanted, while the rest of us hadn't a clue. What she wanted [at fifteen] was to get married and go to some far-off romantic place. . . . She was always strong-willed. . . . There wasn't a passive bone in her body. Whatever she did she did with gusto. This was catchy, so when you were with Shirley you found yourself [following her lead].

"She was not athletic, but she was very well-coordinated. During the war years, we had military drill and Shirley prided herself on becoming a sergeant, and boy! she marched herself and others strong and hard!"

The athlete in the Temple family had always been her brother Sonny. When he joined the marines in March 1941, he was over six feet tall, weighed two hundred ten pounds and had aspired to be a professional football player. Before sending him to the South Pacific, the marines had turned him into a highly competitive amateur wrestler. After years of feeling like the nonachiever in his family, Sonny had been proud of his new accomplishment. He had fought at Pearl Harbor, and his subsequent war record was viewed by his family with great pride.

Jack had graduated from Stanford in 1937. After three years as a production assistant at Twentieth Century-Fox, he had returned to Stanford in the fall of 1940 (at the same time that Shirley had severed her Fox contract) to work for his master's degree in their School of Speech and Drama. A few months later, he married Miriam ("Mimsy") Ellsworth of Los Altos, California, but continued his studies. Shortly after America entered the war, Mimsy gave birth to a son.

The absence of her brothers from home did not affect Shirley's life. The vast age differences, the demands of her career and her overwhelming closeness to Gertrude had always distanced them. Now, Westlake made a strong impact upon her. Suddenly, she was aware of what Gertrude and her child-star status had caused her to miss. This experience was to alter dramatically her perspective of her future. "My heart was at Westlake, not in the movies," she wrote of the years she attended the school.

For the eighteen months that followed the filming of *Miss Annie Rooney*, Shirley was allowed to be as normal an adolescent as her celebrity permitted. Never had she been happier. Although Gertrude was always hovering close by, Grif was in constant surveillance and Miss Mills and a few others at Westlake treated her as "Shirley Temple," she discovered her own identity. She developed a surprising interest in medicine and science, her grades improved and she juggled her dual fascination with books and boys. One of her new friends was Robert "Bobby" Haldeman,* and she would go with Nancy and Grif to his San Fernando Valley estate to swim, ostensibly visiting his sister Betsy. Young men found her attractive. She had slimmed down and bloomed. She had also attained, on her own, a measure of independence from Gertrude and a sense that her life could one day belong wholly to herself. Then, almost unexpectedly, she was signed to a seven-year contract by David O. Selznick to begin work immediately in *Since You Went Away,* his first production since his Academy Award-winning classics *Gone With the Wind* and *Rebecca.*

Most of Selznick's recent female discoveries had become international stars in his films; Vivien Leigh in *Gone With the Wind,* Ingrid Bergman in *Intermezzo,* Joan Fontaine in *Rebecca.* He had been anxious to sign Shirley for *Since You Went Away* to play the younger sister of his most recent discovery, Jennifer Jones, because they bore a strong resemblance that would lend credibility to the film. Gertrude made no secret of her hope that Shirley was on her way to adult stardom. She had good reason for her optimism. Selznick agreed to financial terms about equal to her old Fox contract, and Gertrude was retained by the studio for her former salary of one thousand dollars a week. Selznick talked about starting Shirley in roles "that were young and light," and grooming her for future romantic parts while keeping her from becoming typecast. Also, Selznick's films were made on large budgets, were given the most lavish productions and employed the finest technical and artistic talents available. Whether or not it was Shirley's decision to interrupt her newfound happiness at Westlake, she nonetheless returned to work in the fall of 1943 in the full glare of a massive studio publicity campaign.

"Please be careful," Selznick instructed his publicity department, "to . . . use the casting [in releases] as stated . . . i.e., (Claudette) Colbert first, (Jennifer) Jones second, (Monty) Woolley third, and Temple fourth. . . . I'm anxious to get the accent off this as a Temple vehicle and start hammering away at its tremendous cast."

Since You Went Away was a simple, direct, contemporary story

---

*The same Robert Haldeman of the Richard Nixon Cabinet and of Watergate

of an American family living from day to day under the restrictions and dramatic effects of the war. Like *Gone With the Wind,* it dealt mainly with the homefront and women whose men were away fighting. But unlike Margaret Mitchell's classic, the picture contained no real spectacle.

Selznick had been so successful with his press campaign for *Gone With the Wind* that he dealt with this new film in much the same way. Publicity releases went out with the casting of even the most minor roles, along with announcements of the large budget and the uniqueness of the movie.* There were 205 speaking parts in the picture. Selznick adapted the script himself from a book by Margaret Buell Wilder.

Claudette Colbert portrayed the mother, Anne Hilton. Jennifer Jones and Shirley were her two daughters, Jane and Brig. The absent serviceman father was represented on the screen only by a photograph (of actor Neil Hamilton†). A brilliant bit of casting was Monty Woolley as the family's acid-tongued boarder. His shyly courageous grandson, Robert Walker, is killed in action, a tragedy that reveals Woolley's sentimental side and Jennifer Jones's love for the young man. Hattie McDaniel (Mammy in *Gone With the Wind*) was once again the jovial, understanding black servant. Joseph Cotten was cast as the devoted family friend. In telling vignettes were Lionel Barrymore, Agnes Moorehead, Lloyd Corrigan, Guy Madison, Dorothy Dandridge, Ruth Roman, Albert Basserman, Nazimova, Keenan Wynn, Craig Stevens, Jonathan Hale and one of Shirley's early co-stars, Theodore von Eltz *(Change of Heart, Bright Eyes).* Wounded veterans portrayed themselves in the hospital and rehabilitation-room scenes.

"Mrs. Temple was always on the set, of course," one of the crew remembers, "but she remained in the background. John

---

*Invited guests at the premiere were given elaborate printed programs that had been patterned after those made for the premiere of *Gone With the Wind* and the large cast had been delineated in the same manner, according to their family, location or wartime affiliation.

†Hamilton was a stalwart American leading man of silent films who had not made a successful transition to talkies. He had played small character parts in low-budget movies. Although his character in *Since You Went Away* was never presented in person, the plot revolved around his absence. He received no credit. He did very little film work over the next twenty years. In the 1960's, he was cast as Police Commissioner Gordon in TV's *Batman* series.

Cromwell was not the kind of director who would have allowed otherwise. And if he had been, Mr. Selznick would have fired him just as he had done with George Cukor on *Gone With the Wind* when [Vivien] Leigh and [Olivia] De Havilland began to run the show."*

To Gertrude's despair, and in the face of Shirley's tears, Selznick insisted Shirley have her hair cut and shaped after he claimed she looked like "an O-Cedar mop." He also insisted she wear no makeup; in fact, that she should scrub her face until it shone. "He said that if I didn't do it," Shirley admitted, "he'd come on the set with soap and a washcloth and scrub it himself." She kept in daily contact with her school friends during the filming of *Since You Went Away*. Arrangements were made by Miss Mills for her studio tutor, Mrs. Choate, to be sent all her school assignments so she could keep up with her class. The film was previewed at the Carthay Circle Theatre in Los Angeles on July 11, 1944. Shirley was escorted by Andy Hotchkiss, now Private Andrew D. Hotchkiss, Jr., of the U.S. Army.

"Selznick placed a big bet on Shirley Temple's comeback," the *Time* reviewer wrote, "and she pays off enchantingly as a dogged, sensitive, practical little girl with a talent for bargaining . . . chief reason U.S. cinemaddicts have breathlessly awaited *Since You Went Away* was to see Miss Temple in her first grown-up role. She is charming."

Selznick felt confident about Shirley's performance as soon as he saw the early rushes. He cast her in *I'll Be Seeing You* (originally titled *Double Furlough*) with Ginger Rogers and Joseph Cotten. The picture went before the cameras only six weeks after the end of photography on *Since You Went Away*. Her role in *I'll Be Seeing You* was that of a seventeen-year-old girl with romantic yearnings for the much older Cotten, who played a returning shell-shocked veteran. Rogers and Cotten meet during a ten-day furlough they each have, Cotten from an army hospital, and Rogers from prison, where she is serving six years for manslaughter (a crime committed while defending her honor).

Dore Schary, who had recently left MGM, was engaged by Selznick as producer. "Some of the MGM executives cautioned

---

*Cukor had been replaced on *Gone With the Wind* by director Victor Fleming.

me that Dore was more interested in trying to sell his causes than in making pictures. Dore was a big message man, but I thought more of him as a picture man than apparently they did at that time," Selznick wrote.

"He made *I'll Be Seeing You* for me. It sounded like a good idea and I told him to buy it. After a few months he sent me the script. I dictated all day long on it. (My criticism was as long as the script!) Dore came to see me and told me we had reached the crossroads, and this would prove whether or not it was possible for me to leave anybody alone . . . he felt he could not agree with . . . half of the comments; that perhaps . . . we were both right . . . but unless I was prepared to leave the details as to how the story would be told to him, it would be my picture and not his. He was so reasonable and made such good sense, that I told him to go ahead and make the picture."

After he saw the first rough cut, Selznick had doubts about this decision. He asked Schary for permission to re-edit. They reached another impasse, but Schary finally won the major control of the print. The film was not to gain the artistic or commercial success of *Since You Went Away*, but Shirley did well in her role.

"Shirley is exceedingly hot at the moment," Selznick wrote Reeves Esny, a studio executive, at Christmastime, 1944. "We can't commence to fill demands for interviews and other press material on her. . . . At the preview of *I'll Be Seeing You** . . . Shirley's name was received with the biggest applause of all three [stars] despite the fact that the Gallup Poll shows that Cotten is the great new romantic rage and that Ginger is one of the top stars of the business. . . .

"Shirley's coverage in the New York press both in connection with this appearance and in connection with her prior trip East to sell bonds [this appears to be the time of her invitation to the West Point dance] received more publicity—including, astonishingly, big front-page breaks in the middle of a war— than I think has been accorded the visit of any motion picture star to New York in many, many years . . . her visit received more space than that of General de Gaulle! . . . her fan-mail is greater than that of any other star on our list—actually exceeding by a

---

*The preview was held at the Fox Wilshire Theatre on December 15, 1944.

wide margin that of Ingrid Bergman, Jennifer Jones and Joan Fontaine, who are the next three in that order.''

At this juncture, the Temples had confidence that Shirley was in the second phase of a career that just might eclipse her celebrity as a child star. Two factors would dash those hopes.

Unlike Twentieth Century-Fox, Selznick International was a small studio that operated mainly as a one-man company. Only two films a year were made under Selznick's direct supervision, not enough to feature Bergman, Jones, Fontaine and Shirley, who were all under personal contract to him.* Therefore, outside films had to be found for whomever he could not cast in his own work. The majority of such pictures were not equal to the quality of Selznick's productions.

Second, Selznick had fallen deeply in love with Jennifer Jones. He had discovered and renamed her (she had been Phyllis Isley) and had guided her career. Jones divorced her husband, Robert Walker, also under contract to Selznick in 1945, and she and Selznick formed a liaison that would, four years later, lead to marriage. Soon after Shirley completed *I'll Be Seeing You,* Selznick became obsessed with establishing Jones as one of Hollywood's immortals. Most of his energies and talents were channeled into developing and producing her films.

If Selznick picked up Shirley's option for the next year, he would be obligated to pay $185,000 (including Gertrude's salary) even without the two pictures called for in her contract. The best alternative was to loan out Shirley's services to a major studio for a lead role in a suitable film at an equitable if not equal fee. This way, the momentum of her career would continue, and her next film could then be under the Selznick-International banner.

Columbia Studios had recently purchased the movie rights to the Broadway hit comedy *Kiss and Tell,* by F. Hugh Herbert. Selznick, who had a strong instinct that the role of the teenage Corliss Archer was ideally suited for Shirley's talents, approached the film's producer, Sol Siegel. Columbia had already signed a young New York actress, Patricia Kirkland, who had been brought to Hollywood expressly to star in *Kiss and Tell.* But

---

*Vivien Leigh was also under contract to Selznick, but had returned to England and was at the time attempting to break her legal ties with his company.

Siegel, who was regarded as a low-budget producer, could see the potential of casting Shirley in his film. After Selznick agreed to take over Kirkland's contract, which was only a fraction of what he was committed to pay Shirley, he signed an agreement to loan Shirley to Siegel for a fee of seventy-five thousand dollars. A heated controversy arose between the two men when Selznick prematurely announced to the press the proposed casting of Shirley as Corliss Archer along with the claim that he had been "accorded the privilege of approving the screenplay and the rushes [photographed scenes] each day."

After reading F. Hugh Herbert's screen adaptation of his own play, Selznick had found it "in part too sexy, and therefore unsuited for the sixteen year old Miss Temple." The script was rewritten to meet Selznick's approval. Negotiations began anew. When the contract was signed on January 20, 1945, Selznick retained the right to view the rushes. Shirley had been farmed out, but she was still under Selznick's protection. *Kiss and Tell* turned out to be Shirley's best film as a young adult. Selznick's involvement had contributed to the upgraded budget that gave her superb backing: an excellent supporting cast (including Walter Abel as Shirley's father, Katherine Alexander as her mother, Porter Hall, Robert Benchley, Tom Tully, Virginia Welles, Darryl Hickman, and Jerome Courtland as Shirley's youthful boyfriend, Dexter Franklin), a literate script and a well-photographed picture.

The plot was outrageous but reasonably probable. Corliss lets her parents and just about everyone else in the film believe she is about to become an unwed mother to guard the secrecy of the marriage of her soldier-brother to her best friend. The friend, two years older than Corliss, discovers shortly after her husband has gone back to his base that she is pregnant. Corliss's visits with her to her obstetrician cause the plot's complications. *Kiss and Tell* abounded in sophisticated adult comedy and double entendre.

"I've about decided the picture's superiority to the average Hollywood affair can be traced to the fact that . . . every situation, each line, has been tooled and refined . . . until hardly a dead spot remains," wrote the *Los Angeles Times* critic Philip K. Scheuer. Howard Barnes of the *New York Herald Tribune* lauded Shirley's performance as "quite extraordinary . . . the film is

delightful, pertinent and hilarious . . . [and she] has no end of know-how." *Variety* added, "In case you've had any doubts regarding Shirley Temple as an adult star, you can dispel them now. For Shirley's very curvaceously in the groove in *Kiss and Tell,* and she's a luscious sight for laughter. As the precocious Corliss Archer almost sixteen and frequently kissed, she gives a performance that the most veteran comedienne might well envy."

After they catch her kissing her boyfriend, Dexter, at a booth she is running at a USO charity bazaar, twenty-two soldiers line up to buy kisses from Shirley as Corliss. Shirley announced on the set, "of course I'll kiss them on the mouth. That's the only kind of kisses worth paying for. Kisses on the cheek are gratuities." Gertrude insisted the young men being kissed by Shirley be checked by a doctor and have their throats sprayed with disinfectant. (One participant was rejected "for garlic on his breath.")

Shirley filmed *Kiss and Tell* during her last term at Westlake. The pressures upon her were enormous. Here she was back to a six-day-a-week grind at a studio while attempting to keep up her grades and to take and pass all the tests required for graduation with her class. Inevitably, she was missing all the events and good times associated with being a high-school senior. Secretly, she thought she was in love with a handsome soldier (John Agar) whom she had recently been dating (which certainly added a touch of realism to her role), a situation she knew would bring her mother's disapproval. Strong resentment began to build from the start of *Kiss and Tell.* Within six weeks, it took the form of inner rebellion. With the upward surge Shirley's career had taken, Gertrude's dedication had become more intense, and Shirley, now sixteen and far more worldly about such things, knew her mother was not likely to loosen her hold or to push less. Gertrude was determined to prove that Shirley was not just one more child star who had outgrown her usefulness. Once she had completed her high-school studies, Shirley could be expected to devote herself full time to her career.

One reason Shirley, as a child, appeared natural on the screen was her own similarity to the characters she portrayed. Buoyant, fun-loving and bossy by nature, she adored her father and could relate to all her adult leading men. Because most of her films presented her in the role of a motherless child, her co-stars were usually father figures, and she played winningly with them. Seldom was there a great rapport between Shirley and the women cast in her pictures as her mother or as a mother-substitute. In *The Little Colonel, The Littlest Rebel* and *Wee Willie Winkie,* she had a mother. But in each film her attachment was to the men—Lionel Barrymore, Bill Robinson, John Boles, Victor McLaglen and Cesar Romero, and her scenes with them were her most memorable. How many people could recall her mothers in the same movies (Evelyn Venable, Karen Morley and June Lang)?

Gertrude was always right there by her side, at home and at whatever studio at which they were employed, and she believed that "being a good girl" meant that Shirley did exactly as she told her. On her part, Shirley loved and resented Gertrude, who represented both extreme loyalty and devotion while holding the key—guilt—that kept the young woman from ever really being free. Gertrude was never one to discuss sacrifices. But it was clear that she expected Shirley to make the most of her mother's consistent help to her. Shirley's time at Westlake had given her a taste of what true freedom could be like. Yet even there, Gertrude had the power to pull her out at the signing of a contract, and her watch guards, Grif and Miss Mills, were ever-present. Shirley joked and romanticized about marriage with the Majors sisters and with Phoebe Hearst. But as Christmas, 1944, approached, leaving only six months until her graduation, marriage loomed as her one escape. She was only sixteen, which meant Gertrude could control her life for another five years. Marriage would change that, for it would prove she was adult, and if her husband was older, he would be able to take command. "What I wanted more than a career [at sixteen] was marriage and children," Shirley told an interviewer many years later, "because you can get awfully lonely with scrapbooks. . . . I made decisions . . . one of them was to get married when I was seventeen."

The age she chose—for what she thought would be her liberation—had been selected because Gertrude had married at seventeen and Shirley believed her mother could not, therefore, rationally stop her from doing likewise. After all, her parents had been married over thirty years—a good record for a marriage—and there was no evident hostility between them. Shirley attributed the Temples' marital compatibility to her father's five-year seniority to her mother and to his lack of involvement in the film industry, where divorce was prevalent.

Her school friends say that at fifteen Shirley would look at each young man she met as a potential husband. She was searching for someone who was not in movies, at least five years older than she, good-looking, smart, and someone who didn't care about—or better yet, had never even seen—Shirley Temple in a picture.

Joyce Agar had entered Westlake in Nancy Majors's class in the fall of 1943. The daughter of an affluent Chicago meat-company executive, John George Agar, Joyce had moved with her mother, Lillian Rogers Agar, to Beverly Hills, California, that previous summer, shortly after Mr. Agar's death. Beverly Hills had not been a random choice. Lillian, who was a great beauty and a woman of exceptional taste, had many friends there, one of whom was the Temples' neighbor, ZaSu Pitts. Shirley had met Joyce at ZaSu's and liked her so well that she had persuaded her to attend Westlake. One day Joyce brought her oldest brother, John, to Shirley's to swim along with her two younger brothers, James, thirteen, and Frank, twelve.

Shortly after this meeting, John Agar enlisted in the Navy Air Corps and was sent to Texas for basic training for seven months before being transferred as a physical-training instructor to March Field, California. On a Sunday afternoon in the summer of 1943, ZaSu's daughter, Ann Gallery, held a small swimming party at her home. Agar, home on leave, attended, as did Shirley. Agar claims he thought Shirley was "very pleasant," but recalls that he gave her very little thought. At the time, he was twenty-three and she was only "a fifteen-year-old kid, although quite pretty." Immediately after this meeting, Shirley began to romanticize about the six-foot-two-inch Army (he had transferred from the Navy) Air Corps private with the all-American physique, charming manners and auburn-haired good looks, and managed to be at ZaSu's house when she was told that John (or Jack, as he was also called) was to be there.

Shirley confided to a friend that they seemed to be fated. Agar carried both her brothers' first names—Jack and George— and he was exactly one foot taller than she, which was also the difference between her and her six-foot-two-inch brothers. And Agar and George, Jr., both had attended military schools and were good athletes. Agar's father had been his role model. The senior Agar had held a record for the fifty-yard dash and had been on the football and track teams at the University of Chicago. The younger Agar's athletic coach at Lake Forest Academy, Illinois (which he had attended from 1935 to 1937), Emerald "Speedo" Wilson, has remembered that "[h]e was a tough kid who used to pester me to let him play with the older boys. When I let him, he'd often get banged up but always came back for more."

After Lake Forest, Agar had gone to Pawling Preparatory School (1937–39) in Dutchess County, New York. Upon graduation, he returned to Chicago. He was eighteen, and did not have good enough grades to enter college. Wishing to stand on his own, he took a job as a messenger for a chemical laboratory. Women found his square-jawed, blue-eyed good looks, easy charm and athletic bearing irresistible, and he concentrated on the social side of his life. Then came the war and his enlistment in the Naval Air Corps. Two years later, he had transferred from the Navy to the Army Air Corps.

Another of Agar's attractions for Shirley was his seemingly total disinterest in movies. This certainly could have been the case in 1944, when films meant little more to him than a display screen on which to view a parade of beautiful women. Agar says their meetings were "infrequent" during the year that followed. At the time, Shirley was working in pictures with a strong patriotic flavor (*Since You Went Away* and *I'll Be Seeing You*), and attending wartime school classes; a relationship, no matter how tenuous, with a serviceman was romantic.

"War reached down into the most exalted private schools and had the preppies learning close-order drill, motor mechanics, navigation, map reading and aeronautics," historian Geoffrey Perrett has chronicled. Westlake did not go quite that far, but the girls formed corps, drilled, and the focus of their education was quite definitely the war: "Spelling lessons mixed military terms with everyday words. English classes [stressed war themes for compositions], arithmetic problems used airplanes where once they used apples." There was one scrap drive after another. And air-raid drills occurred two and three times a week.

Los Angeles is on the coast and had strategic naval and air bases flanking it. At night there were blackouts. After the assault on Pearl Harbor, the fear of a Japanese air or submarine attack was constant.

Military schools, whose enrollment had languished in the thirties, became popular as boys prepared for a service in the armed forces. Shirley and her classmates at Westlake were guaranteed sufficient escorts for all their cotillions. But these young men were only playing at war. Most of the older girls had boyfriends in the services with whom they corresponded, a letter to a soldier being a patriotic as well as a romantic gesture. Shirley wrote to John Agar, and he replied. He obtained a ten-day furlough for Christmas, 1944, and during that time they did meet often. Agar felt that, at sixteen, Shirley was less experienced but a great deal more sophisticated than the majority of young women he had been dating. By the end of the furlough, they were very much in love.

Shirley confided her feelings for Agar to her parents, and his for her. Gertrude insisted the couple wait until after the war to make any plans. "You were married at seventeen," Shirley replied. "I promise we won't get married before I'm seventeen." That date was less than four months away. In Europe, the fighting in the Ardennes raged on, taking a toll of American casualties "that eclipsed the Battle of Gettysburg and the bloodiest encounter in the history of American arms; 55,000 killed or wounded, another 18,000 taken prisoner." In the Pacific, the struggle at Iwo Jima "seized people's imaginations as no other battle of the war had done, largely thanks to a memorable photograph of a handful of Marines raising the [American] flag on Mount Suribachi." But the cost of that "victory" in terms of American casualties was painfully high. "Please, for God's sake, stop sending our finest youth to be murdered in places like Iwo Jima," one distraught woman wrote her congressman in February 1945. "It is most inhuman and awful—stop, stop!" That same month, Agar was transferred to a base near Spokane, Washington, from which he was scheduled in the very near future to be shipped overseas.

With each passing month, events filled with so much sadness and fear and horror took place that to see anything in its proper perspective was difficult for those left at home. The Russians took Warsaw; Roosevelt, Churchill and Stalin met at Yalta to make postwar plans; Shirley's old friend and one of America's most memorable presidents, Franklin D. Roosevelt, died of a cerebral hemorrhage at Warm Springs, Georgia, shortly after his unprecedented reelection to a third term. The hardly known Harry Truman took office. Buchenwald was liberated and the bones of thousands of gassed and murdered inmates were found in open graves; Mussolini and his mistress were executed in Milan; the Germans surrendered; and Hitler and his mistress, Eva Braun, committed suicide. How were the people on the home front to react to this frantic acceleration of historic events? Everyday happenings seemed almost embarrassing to relate in letters to the men at the front or in hospitals, or preparing to be sent to the Pacific, where the Japanese doggedly fought on. In this climate, simple lives took on a drama they would not have assumed in peacetime. Women married men they knew little about, and servicemen became responsible for families from whom they would be separated.

In mid-April 1945, shortly before Shirley's seventeenth birthday, the senior class at Westlake held a luncheon for their forty-three members. The previous night, Agar, in Los Angeles on a three-day pass, had presented Shirley with a two-and-a-half carat, square-cut diamond ring. His first night in town he took her dancing to Freddie Martin's Orchestra at the Cocoanut Grove. The next evening, they went for a drive. "There I was, in a parked car, out on Sunset Boulevard. Nothing was elegant and we weren't all gussied up," she recalled. "Do you know where we were? . . . Midway between Engels Drugstore and the Eastern Star Home, just kitty-corner from a gas station . . . [when Agar proposed]."

Gertrude had insisted that they keep the engagement a secret, and Agar promised they would not marry for two or three years at least. Nevertheless, Shirley wore the ring to the luncheon the next day. ("Somehow, I wanted them [the senior class] to know, so I told them all about it.") Her mother reproached her for not holding to her word. Realizing that the newspapers would find out soon, Gertrude notified Selznick, who called a press conference at the Temple house with Agar and Shirley present and holding hands. "Shirley and John have promised not to get married for two years, possibly three," Gertrude told the reporters, adding that what she liked best about the newly promoted sergeant was his "sincerity." She did not, of course, mention what might have displeased her.

Lillian Agar had been left as a widow with large family responsibilities and too small an estate to care for her family as she would have liked. Realistically, she could not count on her oldest son to contribute amply to the Agars' support. He had always been a rebel, his preparatory-school grades had not been of college caliber, and except as a physical-training instructor he had no job qualifications. He was a good athlete, a talent immediately put to good use by the Air Corps. He could have found a place for himself in his father's meat-packing business in Chicago, but as he says, "The war interrupted no future plans." Gertrude and George could not help but wonder how Agar was going to support a wife. They made it sufficiently clear that her money would not be available to Shirley before the age of twenty-one, and then it would not come all at once, but over specified periods of time. If the couple chose to marry early, they would have no funds except those that the two of them could earn, and even then, the court would be obligated to set aside, until her majority, fifty percent of Shirley's earnings.

Gertrude was more concerned over Shirley's contract with Selznick. Despite her tremendous showing in the two films under his supervision and the good word that was spreading on the soon-to-be-released *Kiss and Tell*, Selznick had no immediate plans for her, no scripts that he was developing; nor was a major-studio loan-out being considered. With *Spellbound*, starring Ingrid Bergman, now completed, he was totally committed to Jennifer Jones's next film, a huge Technicolor spectacle titled *Duel in the Sun*. Suddenly, after Shirley's career had moved into high speed, a boulder had rolled into its path. With no film to occupy Shirley's time and energies, Gertrude feared her daughter would concentrate on her romance with Agar, who had just been notified that he was soon to be sent into the South Pacific theater. And Gertrude was right. After her graduation from Westlake, with no commitment to either a film or college, in late July 1945, Shirley insisted her parents give her permission to marry. Fearing that Shirley might elope, the Temples must have felt they had no alternative. Agar requested and was granted a ten-day furlough.

In less than two weeks, on August 6, the United States dropped an atomic bomb on Hiroshima, and on August 9, on Nagasaki. Japan surrendered five days later. The Second World War had ended. Agar learned he would not be sent overseas, but it was too late to stop or postpone the wedding, which was slated for Wednesday evening, September 19, news that received major national coverage. Shirley appeared deliriously happy. And the world, after so many years of death and casualties, found some small release in the daily coverage of the approaching marriage of America's princess to her Prince Charming, who now would not be wrenched away to go to war. After all, which of us does not enjoy a happy ending to a fairy tale?

AT THE VERY OUTSET, Shirley had put down her foot and said firmly, "I want an old-fashioned marriage. I don't want a Hollywood circus." In the end, it turned out to be an "intimate" wedding with five hundred of the two families' "closest friends" invited to see the couple married by Pastor Willsie Martin in the vast sanctuary of the Wilshire Methodist Church before a reception on the grounds of the Temples' estate. During the six short weeks between the day she had set the date and the wedding, Shirley was caught up in a frantic schedule of prenuptial preparations and parties. There were fittings for her gown, being made by the celebrated Hollywood couturier Howard Greer, his bridal design for "the wedding of the decade" a guarded secret. With Joyce Agar and Gertrude in tow, Shirley shopped for her trousseau. The wedding service was carefully planned and the bridal party chosen.* Many gala, glittering affairs were given in her honor.

"I gave my first big party, a bridal shower for Shirley," Nancy Majors Voorheis recalls. "I had just completed my first year in an eastern college and came home to spend the summer. When Shirley asked me to be a bridesmaid, I extended my stay. There was also a wonderful party that the two Lloyd sisters, Harold Lloyd's two daughters, gave in their palatial palace in Bel-Air.

---

*Temple's bridesmaids were: Joyce Agar, Katharine Ferguson, Phoebe Hearst, Mary Lou Islieb, Betty Jean Lail, Constance Webb and Nancy Majors. The ushers were James Agar, Thomas Gallagher, Ernest Greff, John Hereford, John McNeill, George Temple, Jr., and Sergeant Frank Walters. Jack Temple was Agar's best man, and his wife, Miriam Temple, matron of honor. George Temple gave his daughter away in marriage.

Our bridesmaids' dresses were made by designer Louella Brantingham, and they were an absolute dream. They resembled
shepherdess costumes and were a periwinkle blue [renamed by
the press "Temple blue"] gathered up in little puffs, each puff
with a small blue velvet ribbon in its center. We wore open-
crowned cartwheel hats of blue, shirred net, with scatterings of
the same tiny blue velvet ribbons, and we carried old-fashioned
bouquets that were just out of this world. The dresses were
really, really beautiful, and each one cost a bundle. I recall being
staggered by the price. But the nicest thing was that the Temples
presented the dresses to the bridesmaids as a gift along with
handsome leather-bound books depicting the wedding with our
names, Shirley's and Jack's and the date engraved. The whole
thing was like a fairy tale except for the terrible crush of the
crowds."

On the afternoon of September 19, the public started gathering at three o'clock in the afternoon in front of the Wilshire
Methodist Church. The wedding was scheduled for 8:30 P.M.,
and by then nearly twelve thousand people lined the streets,
held back wherever possible by Los Angeles policemen assisted
by a military motorcycle squad. Traffic down Wilshire Boulevard
was so hopelessly snarled that the service had to be delayed
fifteen minutes until all members of the wedding party (who had
been scheduled to arrive two hours earlier) were there. Just as
Darryl Zanuck had been seated, and David Selznick came in late
and out of breath, Shirley stepped out and into the aisle on her
father's arm and paused momentarily under one of the church's
massive crystal chandeliers. An audible gasp from the gathered
guests accompanied her appearance. From the small crown
made of corded satin loops that topped her long ash-blond hair,
to the very full, twelve-foot-long white satin train of her gown,
Shirley looked like the most regal and beautiful of royal brides.

The round low neck of her gown was edged by a looped cord
of satin studded with seed pearls, which also decorated the
tight-fitting bodice. The "Little Infanta" skirt was held out at the
side by panniers. From the coronet atop her head a silk-net veil
billowed behind her as she walked. She wore wrist-length white
satin gloves, also trimmed in seed pearls, and she carried a
spectacular bouquet of mixed white flowers with trailing seed-
pearl ribbons. (For "something borrowed" she had tucked into

her floral display a sheer lace handkerchief given to her by Nancy's mother, Helen Majors; for "something blue" she wore a blue garter; for "something old" her own small diamond cross around her neck; and for "something new," her wedding ring. In her shoe was a penny for good luck.)

On cue, the lights dimmed and the organist began to play Mendelssohn's Wedding March. The procession made its way in slow rhythm down the center aisle, which had blue satin ribbons stretched along each side. The altar and church bloomed with thousands of pink roses and daisies dyed to match.

Shirley performed her role "with the deftness of an Academy Award winner." She knelt gracefully at the altar beside her handsome bridegroom in his specially tailored Army Air Corps uniform, and rose again to her feet without his assistance. Her "I will" could be heard in the rear of the huge church. Neither of them missed a cue or muffed a line. At the conclusion of the ceremony, the sergeant gave his bride "a long, resounding kiss which brought a ripple of laughter from the audience." (Selznick commented that it "was longer than the movie censor would allow").

With eyes only for each other, Shirley and Agar walked back up the aisle of the church. The front doors were thrown open, and the couple stood in the aperture. To the guests' horror, as the mob outside caught their first glimpse of the wedding couple, they broke through the cordon of police who "were tossed helter-skelter like ninepins," and rushed toward the church doors, clambering over about fifty photographers, who went down in the melee. Women inside the church screamed as the crowd drew close to Shirley and Agar, who stood stunned in the bright lights of the flashing cameras of the remaining erect photographers. For a moment, it looked as though the mob would reach the Agars, then the groom pulled his bride abruptly back and into the shelter of the church. The doors were slammed shut, but not without some minor injuries to a few of the front members of the advancing throng, who fell and were almost trampled.

Added police arrived, but it was a while before enough order had been restored for the church doors to be reopened. Even then, the danger had not passed. The police had roped off a three-foot-wide lane to where the cars waited to take the newlyweds and the wedding party to the reception at the Temples' house.

Shirley, held close by Agar, her train caught up over her arm, made a rush for their car, a police guard of twelve men moving with them. Although tousled, they made it to their vehicle safely. The bridesmaids did not fare so well. They were pushed around and mauled by the mob.

"There seemed to be tons and tons of policemen trying to hold back the crowds, but they somehow could not get them in control," Nancy vividly recalls. "We [the rest of the bridal party] had to work our way down steep steps from the church into the waiting limousines. People grabbed at our dresses; they were actually shredding us. They tore off pieces of mine and others. I think that was one of the only times in my life that I felt true panic—when you absolutely have no control, when you are a victim of what's happening. [The police] finally got us into the limousines, and miraculously no one had been seriously injured. But it was scary. We had been roughed up, our hair was in disarray, our gowns torn, our bouquets pulled apart. We were all shaky, but grateful to be safely in the cars even though people ran alongside of them for a part of the way."

When the wedding party reached Rockingham Road, they were greeted by another milling mob. Now forewarned, the police had managed to cordon off a pathway for the procession of limousines so that they could reach the steel gates safely. Though shouting and pressing forward, the crowd offered no danger. Once safely inside, Shirley and her bridesmaids repaired themselves as best they could and then joined the reception line.

Huge canopies of green leaves attached to canvas had been raised. A myriad of lights had been strung between trees and buildings to turn night into day. Nancy remembers "particularly that the rose garden, which was right before the arbor where the wedding party stood to receive guests [along with California Governor and Mrs. Earl Warren, who were honored guests], had thousands of beautiful pink roses wired to the rose bushes so that there was just one mass of blooms." Although some famous Hollywood names appeared in the guest list, they were relatively few. Most of Shirley's co-stars were conspicuously missing. No other former child performers were present. In fact, ZaSu Pitts was one of the few actors invited. Movie folk were represented mostly by producers and a large contingent from the technical crews—cameramen, designers, wardrobe people—who had worked on Shirley's many films. The entire senior class at West-lake was present, as well as teachers and Miss Mills.

The wedding gifts were arranged on tables in Shirley's play-house, "sparkling like a million dollar display at Tiffany's." A large table glittered with more than two hundred silver pieces—trays, bowls, candlesticks and cigarette boxes. There were several sets of sterling-silver flatware, one containing two dozen of each formal ten-piece setting, and there was crystal enough to serve the wedding guests. Cookbooks, waffle irons and electric cookware—many given by fans—were also on display.

French champagne, which had been in short supply since the war, was served. The resplendent buffet was watched over by three large, gracefully sculptured ice swans. Strolling Spanish troubadours strummed their guitars. Not until midnight did Shirley and Agar cut their five-tiered, three-foot-high wedding cake. Agar drank a champagne toast, but Shirley consumed lemonade in a champagne glass. Finally, she tossed her bouquet (caught by Nancy Majors), and then left to reappear fifteen minutes later dressed in a dove-gray wool suit trimmed in soft blue velvet. A blue velvet beret with a gray veil completed her outfit. The bridal couple made a dash through a shower of rice, only to discover that one of the policemen on duty had inadvertently locked the keys inside their car. Two officers finally managed to break the lock, but the hinges of the door came with it. "The first ride of Mr. and Mrs. Agar," Shirley remembered, "found me unable even to sit close to my husband. I was on the far side of the seat straining every muscle to keep the car door from falling off its broken hinges."

A suite for the first night of their honeymoon had been reserved at the Bel-Air Hotel in the names of Emil and Emma Glutz. When the night clerk came on at midnight, long past the time reservations were held, he gave away their accommodations, not knowing the Glutzes were the famous couple. They got an ordinary room, not the bridal suite. The next morning, their departure was held up two hours while they waited for a repair man to fix the broken hinge on the door. A quiet ocean-side hotel in Santa Barbara, California, was chosen for their five-day honeymoon. No one was told where they would be. This quest for privacy caused still another unpleasant incident attached to the wedding. Shortly after their departure from Los Angeles, a fatal automobile accident just outside the city involved the same model car as theirs. The occupants were a soldier wearing sergeant stripes and a woman in a gray suit, both dead and unidentifiable. The Temples, Lillian Agar, police and newsmen were convinced the dead couple were John and Shirley. Not until twenty-four hours later did they find out the newlyweds were alive.

Agar returned to a new post in Kerns, Utah, directly after the honeymoon, and Shirley went back to Brentwood to oversee the conversion of her playhouse into an elegant two-story home for them. Agar's discharge from the service was expected on January 1, 1946. They began their married life in a borrowed one-bedroom guest cottage on the estate of a friend of the Temples, and they remained there for three months until their own residence was ready.

The reconversion had been extensive. The theater had been stripped of its stage and dressing rooms, and was now an enormous living room with the formerly chartreuse walls repainted a pale aquamarine. Large, rose-splashed chintz couches dominated. The room with the soda fountain had become the Agars' bedroom and was decorated a sunny yellow. The kitchen had been enlarged, a dining room had replaced the bowling alley. But the cavernous doll room with its glass display cases and the wardrobe room where racks and racks of her childhood clothes and costumes hung on overhead poles remained. Shirley had not been willing to let go completely of the past. Most difficult of all, at least for Agar, was the proximity to his in-laws—especially the "strong" and competitive Gertrude—who were less than fifty yards away. The necessity of sharing a common driveway meant that the Agars' comings and goings could be monitored. The independence Shirley had thought she had won with her marriage was short-lived. Gertrude still hovered over her. She found herself now caught between two forceful personalities, Gertrude and Agar.

Like so many returning veterans, Agar had no idea of what he wanted to do, although he was certain he did not wish to be associated with the meat-packing business. Shortly after his marriage, his mother, Lillian, had opened a Beverly Hills boutique, which did well from the start. No longer having to worry about assisting his family, he talked about attending Harvard Business School. But Shirley enjoyed a life-style that required a good income, and college took many nonearning years. Expenses were many: a maid's salary to be paid, two cars to maintain, dinners at the best restaurants and rumba dancing at the Cocoanut Grove and other exclusive nightclubs and bistros. Gertrude had been straightforward. Since Shirley was unemployed, she had only a modest "allowance." Her personal wealth was held in trust funds that she was not allowed to touch for almost four years. Shirley talked about quitting films, about John getting a job removed from the industry and Hollywood. She was fond of the San Francisco Bay area where Jack and Mimsy lived. She repeated to friends, "Thank God, he didn't marry me because I was Shirley Temple." She wanted to put Shirley Temple into mothballs, like the costumes in her wardrobe room. She called herself "Shirley Agar," and made sure everyone else did as well. Close friends believed she was trying to convince herself that the fairy-tale wedding had evolved into "they lived happily ever after." Her attraction to Agar was evident to them, but within a very short time they sensed a growing and unfamiliar nervousness in Shirley's demeanor. It was no secret that Agar could be moody (but wasn't this the case with many veterans?), that he drank and that he had not lost his appreciation of a pretty girl.

Although Shirley was still under contract to David O. Selznick, rumors now circulated that she was being considered by Jack Warner for a co-starring role in *Life with Father,* an adaptation of the hit Howard Lindsay–Russell Crouse play. On February 21, 1946, Michael Curtiz, the director, and Robert Buckner, the producer, telegraphed Selznick:

DEAR DAVID: WE UNDERSTAND FROM J.L. [WARNER] THAT YOU THINK WE CAN GET TO-GETHER ON TEMPLE FOR *LIFE WITH FATHER.* WE GREATLY HOPE THIS WORKS OUT AND ARE ANX-IOUS TO GIVE YOU ANY FURTHER INFORMA-TION OR ASSURANCES YOU WISH. WE PLAN TO START AROUND MARCH TWENTIETH. TEMPLE WOULD NOT BE NEEDED UNTIL FIRST WEEK IN

APRIL AND WE CAN DO MUCH TO CONSOLIDATE
HER WORK TO FIT YOUR NEEDS. MARVELOUS
CAST SET [WILLIAM POWELL, IRENE DUNNE, ED-
MUND GWENN AND ZASU PITTS] EXCEPT FOR
THIS PART WHICH IS MOST IMPORTANT AND
YOUR GENEROSITY WOULD BE LONG REMEM-
BERED.

By now, *Duel in the Sun* was being called *Gruel in the Sun* by
all concerned. The project had taken over a year of Selznick's
constant attention, and because of the script's demands and its
harsh outdoor locations, the filming had given Jennifer Jones
"the most terrific physical beating ever administered to an actress." For the better part of a year, she had worked fifteen-hour
days and had been exposed for hours to the intense heat of
Arizona wearing thick Indian half-breed makeup, with a good
deal of bare flesh exposed as she climbed mountains and
crawled over rock boulders. Selznick had to cajole, nurse and be
in attendance almost constantly. Shirley's career was far from
his mind, and when, in February 1946, RKO requested her
services for a loan-out for a low-budget film pertinently called
Honeymoon, he was only too happy to oblige. He recommended
the script to Gertrude. It had been written by Michael Kanin,
who had received an Academy Award for his co-authorship of
Woman of the Year, and was to be directed by William Keighley,
who had done *The Man Who Came to Dinner.* It also would reunite
Shirley with Guy Madison, who had been in the cast of *Since You
Went Away.* Nonetheless, Shirley might not have agreed to make
it except for one major consideration: She and Agar needed the
money to live comfortably. When the offer came from Warner
Brothers for her to play the key role of the daughter in *Life with
Father,* the ink had not even had time to dry on the RKO deal.
Selznick had no other recourse than to tell Warner that Shirley
was unavailable. The role went to Elizabeth Taylor.

Honeymoon (*Two Men and a Girl* in Great Britain) was the kind
of film comedy that needed the right director's "touch" for it to
work. Michael Kanin's screenplay from a story by Vicki Baum
contained many elements that could have had an amusing sparkle. That the finished product was "more labored than bright"
could well have been the fault of William Keighley's surprisingly

heavy-handed direction. In a scatterbrained role that required the expert comedic timing of a young Jean Arthur, Shirley was lost and lackluster. One reviewer even wrote, "When Temple was a tot, legend has it, before every 'take', her mother would admonish her, 'Now sparkle, Shirley, sparkle!' Well, either Mrs. Temple was nowhere near the sets of *Honeymoon* or her admonishments have lost their sting."

Gertrude had not been on the set, by Shirley's request. She was married and had celebrated her eighteenth birthday by the time she made *Honeymoon*. A co-worker had overheard her say to her mother, "You can't boss me anymore." Being regarded as a mature person was more of a prime objective in her personal life than in her career, which had suddenly taken on a new meaning—a job. She had never really thought much previously about money. Her work had always been equated by Gertrude to "play." Now it was her husband's and her livelihood. Agar had the money he had saved from the service, but after their own honeymoon and his contribution to their living expenses during their first months together that was now almost gone. She understood and sympathized with his inability to find an immediate career for himself, but her worst fears, that she would have to remain "Shirley Temple," with all that the name implied, had taken hold of her. Her initial act on arriving on the set on the first day of shooting *Honeymoon* was to take down the SHIRLEY TEMPLE sign on her dressing-room door and replace it with one that read SHIRLEY AGAR.

Gertrude's contribution to Shirley's performances as a child cannot be dismissed. Her assistance went much deeper than her admonishments to "sparkle." Gertrude had discussed the psychological and physical action in every scene. She had, in effect, become Shirley's drama coach and interpreter. When a scene called for Shirley to cry, Gertrude had taken her off to a corner before the cameras rolled and told her something sad enough to cause tears (remembering the death of her pet Pekinese was one stimulant). Gertrude had taught Shirley her lines and played out all her scenes with her. She had helped her memorize lyrics of songs with the proper inflection and, with her steady and confident (if pedestrian) piano accompaniment, worked out the tunes. And Gertrude had fought for the most advantageous camera angles, the most flattering wardrobe, and had run interference when she thought another performer was moving in too close (as with Sybil Jason in *The Blue Bird*). She had also acted as an ear and as a buffer to any criticism of Shirley, so that the child was never distressed when things were not going well. Money or contractual problems were simply not discussed.

Without Gertrude, Shirley was unsure, and her lack of confidence showed. Other disturbing factors existed. Young, stage-trained actresses like Anne Baxter, Teresa Wright and Phyllis Thaxter were being brought to Hollywood from New York. Drama coaches proliferated as youthful film actors strived to learn technique. Talent and natural intelligence had been all Shirley had ever needed. In *Honeymoon*, she had to create a character foreign to her own personality, a light-headed character more in the style of the 1930's screwball comediennes. Her role was that of a frivolous young woman who takes a train to Mexico City to meet and elope with a corporal (Guy Madison) stationed in the Canal Zone, but she somehow misses him and dumps herself, almost literally, into the lap of the much older, suave American vice-consul (Franchot Tone), nearly destroying his own romance (with Lina Romay). If the movie was to succeed as madcap comedy, the older man had to become titillated by the young woman and she had to *almost* become seduced by his charms before both of them realized where real love dwelled.

Otis L. Guernsey, Jr., the film critic of the *New York Herald Tribune*, wrote, "Shirley Temple is not likely to gain adult cinema stature on the basis of this effort. *Honeymoon* is too clearly a strained attempt to make an antic film without sufficient wit. . . . The erstwhile child star works just a little too hard for the quality of fresh allure." Bosley Crowther of *The New York Times* chided, "The friends of Shirley Temple must be getting a little bit tired of seeing this buxom young lady still acting as though she were a kid." Obviously, *Honeymoon* was an attempt to capitalize on Shirley's recent marriage.

Career problems, the difficulties of trying to place her new relationship with Gertrude in proper perspective and the pressures of a too-youthful marriage distracted Shirley, and Agar himself was wrestling with his own confusion over a career choice, adjustment into civilian life and to his marriage.

In the beginning, the glamour and excitement of their marriage had been enough for him. But once out of uniform, he realized he had not returned to freedom but to new responsibilities and restrictions. Where he had formerly relaxed over a few drinks "with the guys," now male camaraderie was missing from his civilian life. His physical desire for Shirley had overridden any consideration of their compatibility. He found that they differed in most of their likes and interests and that their basic personalities were at odds. He had no patience with her petulance. He was straightforward and believed in saying exactly what he was feeling, which could be anything from criticizing Gertrude's oppressive nearness to Shirley's sometimes immature, often prim responses to discussions of their problems. Her quick wit, good clothes sense, strong will and appreciation of the male sex before they had married had lent her an aura of sophistication. Now, he wasn't sure if she was child or woman, and, he suspected, neither was she.

Snow fell for the first time in seventy-five years on San Francisco the winter of 1947. The atomic bomb received the blame. So it was with most untoward happenings or malaise during the first years of peace. The war, or the end of it, was said to be behind each failed business or marriage. "What the veteran doesn't want," reported *Fortune* magazine, "is risk. . . . Security has become the great goal. . . . They want to work for somebody else—preferably somebody big." Security and identity were equally important to Agar, who did not want to be "Mr. Shirley Temple" any more than she wanted him to be.

When David O. Selznick had met Agar for the first time at the wedding reception, he had been taken by his rugged good looks and the assured way in which he moved. Published photographs proved Agar was incredibly photogenic, and convinced Selznick that with training, he had potential as a film actor. A few months later, while Agar was still in the service, Selznick had telegraphed him at Kerns Field, Utah, asking if he would be interested in making a screen test upon his discharge. Shirley had not encouraged this idea, but while *Honeymoon* was being filmed, Agar decided to accept Selznick's offer. Selznick was pleased with the outcome, and Agar was signed to a contract at a starting salary of six hundred dollars a week, and was immediately given intensive coaching in diction, acting and voice.

No one in the Temple family was overjoyed at Agar's decision to become an actor. Two acting careers in one household were seldom a solid basis for a marriage. Shirley had adamantly declared she would never marry anyone in films. But the Temples had their own returning veteran to worry about. After two years of action as a marine in the South Pacific, and many months of floundering after his discharge, Sonny had decided to become a professional wrestler, a career that was not generally looked upon as being respectable. Wrestlers played to their wild "grunt-and-groan" fans. They often dressed in bizarre costumes and were accused of throwing a match for the large stakes that were bet. Weighing 210 pounds, barrel-chested and muscular, Sonny wore nothing outlandish and used his own name (George Temple). "Why shouldn't I?" he demanded. "This is my game and it's what I want to make my name in. Shirley's a swell kid, but I'm not riding along on her name, thank you!"

"He's good looking enough to be a picture star and smart enough to be a professor," Shirley declared. "But wrestling's what he wants. He doesn't need me to get along either. He's good. If I could possibly get there I wouldn't miss one of his bouts for anything." Not much time was left on her schedule to attend Sonny's matches. Selznick loaned her to Dore Schary for another RKO film, this time a more promising vehicle, *The Bachelor and the Bobby-Soxer* (*Bachelor Knight* in Great Britain), to co-star with Myrna Loy and Cary Grant.

Though the film was produced at RKO, where Schary was the new head of production, Selznick did oversee some part of its early development. "Dore . . . convinced me to do the film," Myrna Loy later admitted. "The two roles were really Cary Grant's and Shirley Temple's but the script [written by Sidney Sheldon] amused me, the pay was good, and playing a judge for the first time seemed like fun." Shirley was cast as Loy's younger sister, and her responsibility since the death of their parents. Grant was a famous artist whom Loy had set free when he was charged with assault and battery. When he gives a lecture course at Shirley's high school, she becomes (unknown to him) infatuated. In some "wild manipulations of the plot" Loy sentences Grant to keep company with her sister until her crush is over. During Grant's frequent visits to the judge's house, he and Loy fall in love, and after several "reasonably funny scenes," Shirley realizes the middle-aged Grant is more suited for her sister than for her.

"The 'fun' picture got off to a miserable start," Loy has recalled. "Cary was uncomfortable with the young director, Irving Reis, whose previous output consisted mostly of B pictures. In those days Cary was very persnickety about such things, wary of newcomers lacking proper credentials . . . The fact that I liked and worked well with our director threatened my insecure co-star even more. When I asked Irving to redo my first scene twice, Cary got his back up and left the set to phone Dore. . . . Dore came down on the set and Irving walked out."

Schary told her that Grant had suspicions that she and Reis were "trying to put one over on him." This was smoothed out, but Schary played intermediary throughout the production.

"Playing [Shirley's] older sister wasn't easy because I had to treat her rather severely on the screen," Loy complained. "You had to be careful in pictures about being too hard on dogs, children and Shirley Temple; otherwise you could really alienate audiences. Perhaps I was too convincing in the role, for the little devil began to needle me. Among her tricks was blocking the movie-camera lens with the still photographer's used flash bulbs during my close-ups, which ruined the shots . . .

"She was eighteen on our picture and already married to John Agar—not very happily married, I suspected."

Myrna Loy was right: Trouble had brewed in Paradise; but then, Paradise has always been an imaginary location.

With Cary Grant's charm and box-office magic and his meticulous sense of timing in comedy, *The Bachelor and the Bobby-Soxer* could not have failed, but without his presence, it is doubtful if Myrna Loy or Shirley could have salvaged this contrived and often implausible story.

While filming *The Bachelor and the Bobby-Soxer,* Shirley was also having to cope with Agar's "surprising decision" to take up an acting career. Shirley was always to attribute her marital troubles to this. The public, fed by Shirley's interviews to the press, were to take her side in the matter. Agar remained silent. He admits his own transgressions, drinking and a roving eye, but says, "I was taught to be a gentleman, and a gentleman does not discuss his wife in public." In truth, his problems at home were not the sort that were easy to discuss. Shirley had led a uniquely protected existence. She was used to getting what she wanted and being the center of attention. Material comforts were expected as part of her everyday way of life. She smoked (but never in public), dressed smartly, carried herself with authority and had met some of the most famous and interesting people in the world. Shirley equated this with maturity, and before they had married, so had Agar. Now, he discovered he was wed to a willful teenager with overblown and romantic storybook notions of marriage.

In her family, Shirley had not seen disharmony because George took Gertrude's lead almost from the time of his daughter's birth and had never challenged her decisions. Shirley wanted life two ways: to be Shirley Agar, wife of a dominant, masculine man, and for that man and herself to live an idealized life as she saw it. Had she and Agar been cut from the same cloth, that might have worked. He might then have found a job in a large firm—manufacturing, research, securities—through any number of her parents' friends. And he eventually could have established himself and left her free to quit films. Westlake had prepared her for the country-club, Junior League sort of life. Her classmates had mainly been the pampered daughters of rich, influential men, and were expected only to marry well and conduct themselves with dignity. Being who she was singled Shirley out as "different." This same situation existed in her working world. Gertrude's insistence on Shirley's aloofness from other child performers had alienated many in their ranks and left Shirley with a sense of not belonging. Of the two life-styles, she had chosen the world of the Westlake debutante. According to her interviews at the time, Shirley thought Agar's seven-year age advantage compensated for her inexperience and meant that he was ready to settle down.

Her husband's background might well have supported this theory. He had been brought up in an affluent household, his father had been a successful business executive and his mother was a socially prominent matron. He had attended private schools. Had the war and his father's death not disrupted Agar's life, he might very well have followed Mr. Agar into the meat-packing business after a normal period of rebellion. But during his years in the service, he had lived, worked and spent his off-time hours with men from all walks of life. He had not been an officer and had quickly become "one of the guys." He had resented not having been sent overseas. The air force had believed his athletic and physical-fitness skills could be best used to train others for harsh fighting conditions. With the war's end, his four years of vocational training seemed useless.

So much has been written about Agar's drinking problem during and just after his marriage to Shirley that his character has been distorted. Agar was, and remains, a well-bred, innately good-mannered man. People who knew him then and those who have met him fairly recently portray him as soft-spoken, polite and respectful of women and the elderly. He had much charm, but very little talent for self-promotion.

An early friend says, "Johnny was inhibited, uptight. Alcohol helped to free him. The tighter Shirley bound the ties, the more he had to struggle to get loose. I don't think he ever wanted to be an actor, but that was one way of showing Shirley—and Mrs. Temple—that he wouldn't let them lead him around with a ring through his nose. Making money, lots of it, right away, was also very important. He had to prove that he could take care of Shirley, that he would not be looked upon as a fortune hunter. I don't believe he considered the repercussions—that very soon—and without wishing for it to happen—he would be placed in the position of competing with Shirley for public attention, that with his good looks, once he became a movie star (and he was certainly as big as Reagan was in his early films, bigger, because he appeared in class productions), women would make fools of themselves over him. Also, a funny thing happened. Johnny began his career just as Shirley was reaching the end of hers. He was looked at as 'a star of tomorrow,' and she was considered a has-been."

Once again, Shirley fell prey to the overwhelming demands of David O. Selznick's personal life. He was now involved in the unpleasantness of securing a divorce from his wife, Irene (Louis B. Mayer's daughter), to marry Jennifer Jones. *Duel in the Sun* had not met with good critical notices (although Jones's performance had won her an Academy Award nomination), and their present venture together, *Portrait of Jenny* (for which he had once considered Shirley), demanded all his creative skills. He therefore continued to welcome loan-outs for the performers who were under personal contract to him.

"Jack Warner called me in one day," Alex Gottlieb, a former Warner Brothers producer, recalls, "and told me that some agent had pawned off a property on him [a novel by Edith Roberts] and he wanted me to have a screenplay prepared. I read the book, which was about an adopted, illegitimate child taunted by the people in the small town in which she was raised and who ended up, at seventeen or so, in the arms of a man old enough to be her father—in fact, believed by the town to be exactly that. It was a lot of soap for an audience to swallow.

"Well, Warner was the boss, and so I got Charles Hoffman to do the screenplay, which everyone thought was pretty good. I went back to Warner and asked him who he thought we should cast in the picture. He said, 'Well, the guy is easy, we'll get Ronnie Reagan or one of those guys. The girl is tough. Who do you have in mind?'

"I said, 'What about Shirley Temple?'

" 'Shirley Temple!' he said.

" 'Well, she's eighteen or nineteen now.' He seemed to like the idea.

" 'I understand she's under contract to Selznick. I'll let you know tomorrow what happens.'

"The next day Jack [Warner] told me that Selznick would loan us Shirley Temple at a sizable profit [to Selznick], but we also had to take Rory Calhoun, who was also under contract to Selznick. So we wound up with both of them [in the picture].

"Shirley had not done much real acting lately, and Selznick's supervision had not turned her into a good actress. I was surprised to find she was frightened and very nervous when I first met her. She just couldn't face the camera. We got her without any hitch or trouble. Her acting capabilities were quite limited. The director of the picture, Peter Godfrey, felt the same way, but he did what he could. We needed a trained actress like Anne Baxter, who had recently done *Guest in the House,* or someone like Teresa Wright, who had just played the daughter in *The Best Years of Our Lives.* I, somehow, had thought that all those years in films meant Shirley could act. She never really understood the character she was playing. I had made a terrible error in judgment, and all through production I knew it would turn out a terrible picture and, boy, was I right."

When Ronald Reagan read the script, he went to Jack Warner and asked not to be cast in the film. Warner insisted, and since Reagan's wife, Jane Wyman, was five months pregnant at the time,* he could not afford to risk suspension (off-salary) by refusing. Production began June 4, with a seven-week shooting schedule. Problems plagued the company. Reagan took seriously ill with pneumonia and was hospitalized. For three weeks, he was out of the cast. Scenes had to be shot around him. By now, Shirley knew she was pregnant, and her more active scenes had to be either curtailed or played by a double.

Gertrude was recalled to Shirley's side to help her through this difficult period. "I love to have mother with me when I'm working," Shirley explained. "It's always been that way and I'm lost without her. She's a wonderful influence. We're really like partners and work like a team . . . she's hyper-critical . . . She doesn't believe in flattery. I have to earn her praise."

Gottlieb dryly recalls, "Mrs. Temple maintained quiet vigil on the sidelines, always within calling distance of her celebrated child, who was a child no longer."

Gertrude's vigilance did not help the fortunes of *That Hagen Girl,* which probably destroyed any chance Shirley might have had to move from child to teenage performer. "To add to the awfulness of the film, Reagan and Temple had no chemistry together."†

Alex Gottlieb states that "Shirley was ladylike, always cooperative, knew her lines and was very easy to work with, but the picture turned out as I predicted, badly." How badly could be measured by the deadly tone of the reviews, which called it "uninspired soap opera," "wooden . . . monotonous" and "a foamy dud." Reagan's premonition of disaster must have been equally obvious to Shirley. He, at least, was cited for "struggling valiantly in a thankless role" and doing "his level best under the worst of circumstances." But never had Shirley received such dismal notices. "Balderdash isn't helped a bit by the wooden acting of Miss Temple," "Shirley's acting is, to say the least, 'restrained,' " "Miss Temple smiles so winsomely in most of her

---

*This child, a girl born prematurely, died shortly after birth, while Reagan was still filming *That Hagen Girl.*

†Two years later, in a dispute over a role in *Ghost Mountain* he wanted that Warner gave instead to Errol Flynn, Reagan telegraphed Warner: [HOW COULD YOU DO THIS] WHEN I'VE ALWAYS BEEN GOOD AND DONE EVERYTHING YOU'VE ASKED—EVEN THAT HAGEN GIRL.

appearances [in the film] that she rarely makes one believe in her predicament."

Shirley did not publicly announce her pregnancy until she had entered her fifth month. By that time, *That Hagen Girl* had been sneak-previewed and she had begun work on *Fort Apache,* co-starring not only John Wayne and Henry Fonda but John Agar. The film was to be directed by John Ford. "Mr. Ford knew I was going to have a baby more than a month before I announced it," she told one reporter. "I had informed him, naturally, in discussing his picture. But he did not tell a soul. He has assured me that he will have me 'carried around on a feather cushion' if necessary. I won't have to ride horseback or do anything else that could possibly hurt me."

Selznick happily loaned her out once again to RKO. John Ford had agreed to pay one hundred thousand dollars for her services, which gave Selznick a 25 percent profit. Agar was also on loan-out for this, his first film. *Fort Apache* was based on *Massacre,* a short story by James Warner Bellah, "a romantic chronicler of the cavalry during the American-Indian Wars." Ford had been drawn to it because "it seemed to articulate all his wartime emotions, his fascination with the American military tradition, and the special nobility he felt was born of combat." But Ford was knowledgeable enough about box-office returns to know that pictures needed a love story, and that films with all-male casts were usually doomed to failure. Frank Nugent adapted the screenplay, and under Ford's direction he added two characters: Philadelphia Thursday (Shirley as Henry Fonda's daughter) and Lieutenant Michael O'Rourke (John Agar), a West Point graduate whose father is the post sergeant major (Victor McLaglen). Ford wanted *Fort Apache* to be a big, commercial picture, and to get the $2.5 million budget required, he loaded the cast with major stars. He hired Shirley not just as a sentimental gesture, but because he believed she and Agar would supply the necessary romantic "glow" while adding considerable publicity value.

Fort Apache was filmed in Monument Valley, "a spectacular region of desert plateaus and majestic rock formations" located on the huge Navajo Indian reservation in southern Utah, where Ford had also shot *Stagecoach* and *My Darling Clementine.* Conditions were rough. The Agars were housed at Goulding's Lodge, a comfortable ranch-style inn. But since the lodge could only accommodate a fraction of the huge location company, most of the cast and crew had to live in tents pitched outside. The August temperature reached 115 degrees at midday, cooling only to 90 degrees at night. The period of the film required a pregnant Shirley to wear uncomfortable, long-sleeved, floor-length dresses with numerous underskirts. She was not feeling well, and the strain of working in the same film as her husband was telling on her. Agar was nervous and unsure of himself and needed encouragement for his first film, which was not easy at this difficult time for her to give.

Matters grew worse. High winds and desert storms continually delayed shooting. The film went behind schedule, and Ford's mood turned "brittle, his temper short, and his sharp, barbed tongue spared no one. His principal target," claimed his grandson, Dan Ford, "was . . . John Agar. [Ford] chastised him for his halting delivery and his awkwardness on horseback, and delighted in calling him 'Mr. Temple' in front of the cast and crew.

"At one point, Agar rebelled and stormed off the set, vowing to quit the picture, but John Wayne took him aside and convinced him to stick it out. He explained some of the pressures [Ford] was under and said, 'You're the whipping boy now, but give him time. He'll get around to the rest of us soon enough.' Agar didn't have long to wait." A few days later, actor Ward Bond was flown up to Monument Valley. He announced his arrival by having the pilot buzz the company, which was set up out in the middle of the valley. He destroyed one take and forced Ford to wait until he landed before he could resume shooting.

Wayne turned to Agar and said, "Well, you can relax now, he's found another whipping boy."

Agar had found something himself—the burly Wayne, a good buddy and hearty drinking companion. His ill-treatment at the hands of Ford had also brought him the sympathy and instant friendship of the men in the company. A Ford film set always had a strong clubby, masculine atmosphere to it. For Agar, it took him back to his happier days in the Air Corps. He fit in well. Shirley, on the other hand, was pretty much excluded from most location activities.

"Every night the company gathered outside the dining room at Goulding's," Dan Ford wrote, "and waited for [Ford] to enter. Then the dinner bell was rung and everyone obediently filed in. After dinner [Ford] and a select group of actors and stunt men adjourned to his room, where a green felt cover was spread over the table and they had their game of pitch."

Fort Apache was "a vigorous, sweeping Western adventure drama done with the eye for shocking dramatic effect and spectacular action sequences." Some reviewers found the film more entertainment than art. It was a resounding commercial success, returning its $2.8 million final cost in six months, and eventually grossing double that amount. The personal reviews went to the veteran male actors—Fonda, Wayne, McLaglen and Bond. The Agars' romantic qualities were noted in the *Los Angeles Times,* which stated that "Shirley Temple and John Agar do not find much scope for their talents here," but predicted "fans will want to witness this pairing which will eventually become a permanent screen team." But their lack of acting skill was not glossed over by *The New Yorker,* whose critic wrote, "In a picture like *Fort Apache,* which consists mostly of gallops up and down a remarkably good-looking mesa, lovemaking, unless conducted at an implausibly brisk clip, seems boring. . . . The romantic doings in the piece feature the acting—and I'm using the word loosely—of Shirley Temple and John Agar."

Shortly before dawn on January 29, 1948, in Santa Monica Hospital, where Gertrude had given birth to Shirley not quite twenty years before, Linda Susan Agar was born.* Two weeks earlier, Jack and Mimsy Temple had become parents of their second son. The birth of Linda Susan should have elated George and Gertrude, but Shirley's marital problems were of great concern.

The last five months of Shirley's pregnancy had been fraught with situations that her naïveté and youth made even more stressful. Still under contract to Selznick, Agar continued his acting and singing lessons. His appearance in *Fort Apache* had not generated much industry excitement, and no film offers came his way. His ego was at low ebb, and Shirley made it clear that perhaps he had chosen the wrong profession. Within a short time, "[John] began not coming home for dinner," she later confessed. "First he would start coming home around 8 o'clock. After a couple of weeks, it became 10 o'clock. . . . [Then]

*The attending physician was Dr. William C. Bradbury.

. . . he stayed out nights until 2, 3, even 6 A.M. and . . . so intoxicated that he fell downstairs."

Since their return from Monument Valley five months earlier, John had been drinking steadily. His association with John Wayne on *Fort Apache* had encouraged his growing reliance on alcohol. Wayne had taken him under his protection, and soon the Duke, as Wayne was called, and John were "drinking buddies." Agar says defensively, "I didn't drink any more and probably a lot less than John Wayne, Ward Bond, Victor McLaglen, Clark Gable, Spencer Tracy, Bing Crosby and others." Quite likely, that was true. All these men were prodigious drinkers. Tracy's, Gable's and even Wayne's drunken escapades were legend in the industry. These men, however, were major film stars who made millions of dollars for their studios. Any one of their names insured the success of a picture. They had publicity departments to cover up their drinking forays, and payoffs to keep away unfavorable press were common. Had Shirley still been big box office, either Selznick or RKO might have covered up for Agar to protect her name. But Agar was not a star, and was fair game to the press's vociferous appetite.

With his drinking, the situation on Rockingham Road became even more difficult, as Gertrude once again took charge of her daughter. Gertrude announced the selection of her granddaughter's name to the reporters waiting at Santa Monica Hospital the night Linda Susan was born, and then she added cautiously that, of course, "Shirley and John will have to talk that over a little first, I guess."

John had been by Shirley's side when the baby was born, and for the next few months managed to curb his appetite for liquor and seemed especially happy to be a father; it was quite evident that Shirley enjoyed motherhood.

By that summer, a year had passed since either one of them had worked. RKO had bought an original story by Lesser Samuels and Christopher Isherwood,* a variation of the old story of the teenager whose individuality brings trouble to her conservative family. Robert Young had been cast as the minister father. Shirley was offered the role of his daughter, and Agar the part

---

*Isherwood was the author of a series of stories that were the basis for the John Van Druten play *I Am a Camera*, which was itself later the basis for the Broadway musical and film *Cabaret*.

as a young man she is constantly getting into trouble. Neither one wanted to work together. Shirley was resentful that she had to work at all. She could have refused the film loan-out; but because that would have meant Selznick had acquitted himself of his contractual obligation for one film, her decision was to accept the assignment. There was also one other, strong consideration—Agar's role in the film was better than his part in *Fort Apache,* and it seemed logical that his career might benefit. She talked about retiring soon from the screen altogether and having two more children.

The picture, titled *Adventure in Baltimore,* proved to be a pleasant working experience. She enjoyed being reunited with Robert Young (who had last played her adopted father thirteen years earlier in *Stowaway*) and with Richard Wallace (who had directed her in the successful *Kiss and Tell*). Robert Young found her "as confident and professional as she had been as a child." A member of the crew who had also worked with her on *Kiss and Tell* adds that "Young and Shirley had a great rapport, and Dick [Wallace] played to it. Also, she was treated like a princess by both these men. I think she felt very comfortable. Agar worked like a son-of-a-gun. Always asking people for opinions of the way he played a scene. I thought of the two, he had the better chance at the time and probably needed to get away from working with her. He had a leading-man quality about him. Maybe he was a bit too good-looking, but he had the kind of square-jawed William Holden good looks front face and a really striking profile. He was a better light-comedy personality than a dramatic actor. But I remember thinking then that with the right pictures he could be a star. He liked the camera, smiled easily, wasn't stiff— and the camera liked him. Fact is, I thought he seemed more comfortable [on] than off-camera."

No sooner had photography ended on *Adventure in Baltimore* (which would be received coolly by critics and moviegoers) than the Agars were each offered separate film assignments. Agar was re-teamed with Ford and Wayne in *She Wore a Yellow Ribbon* and returned to location at Monument Valley. Shirley was to make *Mr. Belvedere Goes to College,* with Clifton Webb in the lead as a character that he had made famous in *Sitting Pretty.* Shirley was to find *Mr. Belvedere Goes to College* a traumatic experience: The picture was to be made at Twentieth Century-Fox.

 WHILE SHIRLEY and Agar were waging their own private war, the people of the United States "were engaged in a conscious attempt to become the greatest nation in history." The ambition was breathtaking "—to outshine Greece in its glory, Rome in its grandeur, France in its various phases of greatness, and Britain at the height of its power." Americans at Christmastime, 1949, dreamed of being "the richest, the most powerful, and, were it possible, the most accomplished people in history." And they attempted to take the lead in almost every important human endeavor. This pursuit of the American dream had three major objectives—"liberty in a world of tyrannies, peace in a world torn by wars, abundance in a world of scarcity." In the wake of the nuclear age, with atom-bomb drills at schools and bomb shelters an accepted fact of life, films dealt with man's—and woman's—need to secure their own, and their nation's, loftiest dreams, and with his will to destroy any obstacles in the way of that goal.

This was the year of Ayn Rand's *The Fountainhead,* of *Pinky, Champion, All the King's Men, Adam's Rib, Home of the Brave, The Great Gatsby, On the Town, The Heiress* and a great number of excellent English films made in 1948 and released in the United States the following year—Olivier's *Hamlet* and Carol Reed's *The Fallen Idol* among them. *All About Eve, Sunset Boulevard, The Men, The Third Man* and *The Asphalt Jungle* were all in some phase of production. Independent producers were gaining footholds. The big studios were beginning to lose their power, and television had reared its channeled head. The Depression era, which had given rise and royal trappings to little Shirley Temple, was ancient history.

In this atmosphere of aspirational fallout, Fox's *Mr. Belvedere Goes to College* was made and released.

Zanuck still "ruled supreme" at Twentieth Century-Fox. Of the films made there in the late forties, Zanuck said, "Every creative decision was either authorized, or okayed, or created by me. Every script! There was no individual, no executive between me and the back lot. I was The Executive. I decided whether we made something or didn't make it." Which indicates he must ultimately have been responsible for the decision to borrow Shirley from Selznick for *Mr. Belvedere Goes to College.* Shirley's return to the studio where she had gained worldwide acclaim was marked by a "Welcome Home" party attended by many actors and crew members with whom she had worked. Zanuck breezed in and departed a few minutes later after a photo had been taken of him and Shirley.

She had asked if she could have the use of her old bungalow. "The studio couldn't oblige. Only a year before . . . a dentist moved in," publicity head Harry Brand recalled. "But Shirley managed to get some use out of the place, anyway. She visited the bungalow and had a wisdom tooth extracted."

She was to play a young war widow with a three-year-old son who returns to college. Once she was signed, Samuel Engel, the producer, began to worry that she looked too immature for the role. Speech lessons to lower the pitch of her voice were begun, and her hair was cut in a short bob.

The first scene was shot on the same stage where sixteen years earlier she had made her Fox debut in *Stand Up and Cheer,* and Mary Lou Islieb Hurford (who had recently married) had been signed as her stand-in for the new picture. Some exterior scenes were shot on the University of Nevada campus.* But for most of the picture, Shirley was at her old lot, with Clifton Webb receiving the star treatment. The script had been written around him, and directed toward his earlier, brilliant interpretation of Mr. Belvedere, the middle-aged genius who knew all about everything in the wildly successful *Sitting Pretty.*

Margie and *Mother Was a Freshman* were also shot on location at the University of Nevada.

"Our main objective," explained producer Engel, "is to make the two Belvedere stories so completely different, except for the amusing idiosyncracies of the character, that exhibitors could show both films on a double bill without lessening the entertainment value of either." Clearly, from the outset, this was to be Clifton Webb's movie.

Film comedy sequels are seldom as good as their originals, and *Mr. Belvedere Goes to College* was no exception. The screenplay by Richard Sale, Mary Loos and Mary McCall, Jr., was bright, "fast-paced; the lines witty, the situations amusing." The plot, which was too obviously contrived, presented the problem. "Our hero, somewhat overage for a freshman, finds it necessary, for some complicated plot reason, to get his college degree—a slight matter he had neglected to attend to in his youth," one reviewer began his synopsis of the story. "In characteristic fashion, he sets about acquiring his B.A. in one year instead of four. Whereas this might be a formidable challenge to most people, Mr. B. takes it in stride—with enough time and energy left over to straighten out the college president and board of trustees on the proper method of running a college, the local editor on how to gather news, and the sorority mentors on how to teach their bobby-soxers manners, music, proper English and civilized cooking. Along the way, Mr. B. also gets into a number of scrapes, lands in jail, and patches up a romance between young war widow Shirley Temple and her undergraduate admirer Tom Drake."

While Shirley was caught up in the emotional situation caused by her altered status at Fox, Agar was involved in the exciting day-to-day "combat" and creativity of working on a John Ford film. This time, Ford treated him with the same mixed brand of camaraderie and tough-mindedness he used on Wayne. The picture was made at breakneck speed—in thirty-one days—and was brought in at half a million dollars under budget. All the elements seemed to mesh. The picture was filmically magnificent,* and Wayne's portrayal of the cantankerous but kindly Nathan Brittles established him as one of Hollywood's top mature leading men. He would, in fact, play a variation of

---

*Winton C. Hoch, the cinematographer on *She Wore a Yellow Ribbon*, won the Academy Award.

this character in almost every picture over the next twenty-some years. In this film, Agar was Wayne's young sidekick (and adjutant) and received co-starring credit. He handled himself well, he and Wayne had some moving moments together and his romantic scenes with Joanne Dru were most believable. Wayne liked to work with a younger man as he had with Montgomery Clift in *Red River*. But he never could have the same rapport with the sensitive and moody Clift that he could with Agar. Their work on a second film had further cemented their friendship. Like Ford, Wayne was most comfortable acting with performers he knew well.

She Wore a Yellow Ribbon was released about the same time as *Mr. Belvedere Goes to College*. It proved to be an immediate box-office success, and though not generally well received by the critics of its day, became one of the most profitable movies that year and later was revered by film buffs as one of Ford's and Wayne's best and most-remembered films. Its release and popularity created a new tension in the Agar marriage. Agar was now regarded as a movie star. He had his own fan club and was recognized and besieged for autographs wherever he went. And in social situations, women became more aggressive. When he and Shirley went out, he drew the stares, and often warm overtures, of women. Suddenly, the prince consort had become the power figure, and the royal princess fell back into the shadow. Agar did not handle the new situation between them well, and neither did Shirley.

He sometimes did not return home until dawn, and then he was often inebriated. According to his friends, Shirley was to blame for his distraction; according to hers, Agar provoked her hostility. But seldom is there only one injured party when marital differences occur. Agar did drink heavily; he had philandered; and his marriage to Shirley had been responsible for his career. On her part, Shirley had wanted things her way. Always a despot with her childhood and teenage friends, she had adopted the same attitude to her marriage. Childhood friends formerly had to swim or not swim when she wanted, come to her house, not she go to theirs—and on specified days—and play the games she chose. And so it was with Agar, who was expected to live within sight of Gertrude and adhere to Shirley's rigid rules of demeanor, one of them being never to be seen drinking or smoking in public.

Both did a lot of unpleasant backbiting. Though Agar chose never to discuss it publicly, Shirley had reverted to her teenage flirtatious ways as soon as he began to flaunt his liaisons. At this time, she was also, according to one close acquaintance, "a little predatory where other girls' men were concerned," which was said in reference to a flirtation she was rumored to have had with actress Kathryn Grayson's husband, Johnny Johnston.

Her contract with Selznick reached an unpleasant impasse. He obviously had no intention of casting her in one of his films, and the pictures she was offered were low-budget potboilers. Her career was on a down curve. She had done very little to change her image or to improve her acting technique. She was, in fact, exploiting her own past celebrity, appearing in lackluster roles that normally would have been played by a lesser-known and less expensive actress. Producers had felt that her name would add to the budget and box office of the pictures in which she had been recently cast. By the spring of 1949, even that inducement had begun to pale. "Shirley Temple" now became a pawn in the hands of inexperienced promoters.

Colin Miller, a young man with great ambition but without any previous film-production experience (he had been a newspaper reporter and an investor in Enterprise Films, a company that had swiftly gone under), applied the old three-way shell game to make a picture deal. Starting with an idea (in this case, to do a sequel to the successful *Kiss and Tell*), you approached a director (Richard Wallace, who had been at the helm of the original movie) and told him you could put together almost the original package; director, star (Shirley Temple) and release (United Artists). The director then agreed that if that was so, he was in, but, of course, for a major percentage. The star was next and was informed the director was already part of the package. The star would usually hedge and agree to make the picture (also for a sizable percentage, as well as salary) *if* a major release could be obtained. With star and director "under the shells," the independent met with the distributors (United Artists), telling them he had the other members of the package secured.

Miller had to give away about seven eighths of the picture. The film's partners were Milbak Productions, his own corporation, in which Marcus Loew II, his associate producer, and Richard Wallace were participants; Strand Productions, the organization that owned General Service Studios and was pro-

viding the studio's physical facilities as their investment;
Berthugh, Inc., owned by F. Hugh Herbert, creator of the character of Corliss Archer, who was sharing his interest with Howard Dimsdale, writer of the scenario; and United Artists. Shirley
had been "given" a percentage, but was not a partner. The
picture would have had to be a huge money-maker before Shirley could have received any additional revenue.*

After six months of work, Miller, despite bringing together
all these factors, was asked to supply a male star to back up the
investment before being given the go-ahead by the distributor.
With no more points to trade, Miller had to find a name actor
under contract to another producer, not an easy task with such
a slim project. That he managed to sign David Niven was more
luck and timing than ingenuity. Niven and his boss, Samuel
Goldwyn, had been engaged in a battle of two strong wills for
several months. Niven had been forced to do a picture (*The
Elusive Pimpernel*) that he had not wanted to do, and had exhibited what he called "spoiled-brat behavior of the worst sort
. . . idiotic, conceited, indefensible and unforgivable . . . Goldwyn, of course, had no further use for me and all the direst
predictions came true . . . upon the completion of *The Elusive
Pimpernel,* I was immediately loaned out to play the heavy in a
Shirley Temple picture, a disastrous teen-age potboiler."

The movie was called *A Kiss for Corliss,* and even while it was
being filmed, Shirley recognized the folly of her judgment. The
picture concerned the temporary love of an adolescent girl for
a much married-and-divorced older man. The production-code
administrators took exception to the extremities of the comedy,
and demanded that the number of marriages in Niven's past be
reduced from six to three. What was known to the code men as
"a disclaimer" was also introduced. A speech was written in
which Shirley had to explain that despite her emotions, she
"could never think of marrying a man [Niven] with all those
wives."

Selznick now loaned her to Warner Brothers for a two-pic-
ture deal, for which he received $100,000 upon the execution
of his agreement and an equal amount upon the start of the

---

*The corporation formed for this film was eventually to file for bankruptcy. In 1952,
a permanent injunction was placed on its release to television.

second film. Additionally, during the twelve-week term of each picture, Selznick was to be paid $4,166.67 "on Thursday for services rendered during the week which ended on the immediately preceding Saturday." He, in turn, issued a weekly check to Shirley for her original contract figure of $4,000.*

Six weeks after the completion of *A Kiss for Corliss*, Shirley drove out to Warner Brothers Studios in the San Fernando Valley to begin *The Story of Seabiscuit* (originally titled *Always Sweethearts*), with one of her early directors, David Butler, at the helm. Her role in this "biopic" about the famous racehorse Seabiscuit was that of an Irish colleen—the first time she ever had been required to use an accent for a character. As the niece of Seabiscuit's trainer (Barry Fitzgerald) and the fiancée of the horse's jockey (Lon McCallister), Shirley "rode the movie into the loser's circle."

But *The Story of Seabiscuit* seemed in the conceptional stage to fuse a number of proven box-office ingredients. Barry Fitzgerald was a popular star; equine Horatio Alger stories had always had great appeal; and Seabiscuit was one of the greatest horses ever to race in the United States. Jack Warner still had faith in the Temple name and believed that by reuniting her with David Butler, the man who had directed her in four of her most successful childhood movies—*Bright Eyes*, *The Little Colonel*, *The Littlest Rebel* and *Captain January*—her former magic would be rekindled. But in the Fox years, Butler had always relied on Gertrude to bring out the sparkle in Shirley. Warner had not guaranteed Gertrude either expenses or salary as he had when Shirley had filmed *That Hagen Girl*. She was, perhaps, never aware that the team element of their relationship so instilled by her in her daughter had made it difficult for Shirley to interpret a role on her own. David Butler admitted

---

*Selznick's contract with Temple guaranteed her four thousand dollars weekly for forty weeks in each calendar year. She had to make $160,000 yearly in outside films to reimburse his legal obligation to her. The contract covered a seven-year period (1944–51). Selznick no longer had his studio, and Selznick International was now owned by Vanguard Films, which, however, remained in his control. Selznick's loan-out agreement for Temple with Warner gave him the "right from time to time . . . to discuss such aspects of the production of each picture and to make such suggestions in connection therewith . . . with [Jack] Warner, the producer, the director, the artist and the cameraman." Warner was not "obliged to adopt them." However, Selznick never went on record as having monitored the contracted films in any stage of their production.

that she had no animation in her performance. Recalling the films they had made when she was a child, he "found occasion to have Mrs. Temple called to the set" once he realized Shirley was not giving him the performance he needed. "With the mother there Temple and Butler seem to work with more confidence and speed," Carlisle Jones, a Warner staff member, noted. Other members of the company, however, thought that Gertrude's influence brought out a saccharin quality in Shirley's performance. The woman who was able to bring sparkle to a small child simply did not have the resources to enhance a grown woman's performance.

The opening sequences of the movie, supposedly set in the Kentucky bluegrass country, were actually filmed near the studio at Northridge Farms, a 110-acre establishment, originally developed and owned by Barbara Stanwyck and her agent, Zeppo Marx, and called Marwyck Farms. There, on April 23, during the second week of shooting, Shirley was given a party, primarily for press and newsreel coverage, for her twenty-first birthday. But Agar, Gertrude and George joined in the celebration, as did her old friend Mary Lou Islieb, who was working once again as her stand-in, and David Butler, who could recall her birthday parties at Fox. "I always work on my birthdays," Shirley told Harry Brand. "I cut a cake, they take lots of pictures, and then I go back to work." Agar, who had the day off from filming *I Married a Communist* at RKO (co-starring Robert Ryan and Laraine Day), smiled lovingly down at her as she cut the cake, and the cameras whirred.

Shirley had no problem picking up the Irish brogue required for her character (Arthur Shields, Fitzgerald's brother, was her coach). But she seemed unable to bring any depth to her part. After the first cut of the film was seen by Warner and the staff on August 7, John Taintor Foote, the scriptwriter, memoed Warner immediately: "The weakest part of the picture . . . are the love scenes. They needed a sensitive *capable* actress. In the hands of Shirley Temple . . . they are insipid . . . Any legitimate shortening of them will help."

Shirley's contract called for a second film, *Pretty Baby*, to follow. A few weeks after the completion of *The Story of Seabiscuit*, she was notified that Betsy Drake had been cast in *Pretty Baby*. *A Kiss for Corliss* was released on October 19, 1949, and *The Story of Seabiscuit* on December 7. Both received devastating reviews. C. A. Lejune, the film critic for the *London Sunday Observer*, responded in imperfect rhyme:

> Sometimes I think that David Niven
> Should not take all the parts he's given.
> While of the art of Shirley Temple,
> I, for the moment have had ample.

Her marriage had reached an impasse by the end of the summer. Agar refused to recognize that he had a drinking problem. A few days before Thanksgiving, Shirley's lawyer, Grant Cooper, greeted Agar when he returned home late one night. Shirley and the baby were with George and Gertrude. "He [Cooper] told me to leave the house with my personal posessions only," Agar recalls. "I wanted to see Shirley but he refused to allow it. . . . I tossed some clothes in a suitcase and left." Agar spoke to Shirley on the telephone, but she would not see him, and on December 5, after a five-day thinking-through period in Palm Springs, she went to court to testify in the divorce action.

Agar was in Buffalo, New York, on a publicity tour to coincide with the release of *I Married a Communist* when—her hair coifed perfectly, her makeup discreet but artfully applied—Shirley Temple Agar entered the courtroom of Superior Judge Roy L. Herndon, wearing a chic gray suit, a small navy-blue veiled pillbox hat, impeccable white gloves and, about her collar, a silk scarf looped through a lucky-coin charm. Tears rimmed her eyes as she took the oath and glanced over to her father, who had accompanied her.

"When I was two months pregnant, he came home intoxicated at 2 A.M. He had lipstick on his face. When I was five months pregnant, he came home with a group of people, brought another girl into my bedroom, and asked me to go to a party with them. He left without me and didn't come back till 4 A.M." She told her lawyer, Grant Cooper, "After the baby was born he brought another girl with him [to their home] and danced with her in our playroom for two hours, kissing her many times." She added that he often became "very drunk and belligerent," and then tearfully admitted to a shocked and crowded courtroom that one night he had come home so drunk and abusive that, terrified, she had "jumped" into her "car and was going to drive over a cliff or something."

Agar's attorney, Clore Warne, rose to his feet at this point. "I feel I should say that when the differences arose—and they did arise—[Mr. Agar] acted at all times and has acted as a gentleman . . ."

Judge Herndon replied, "The court views your remarks as not inappropriate." He then granted the divorce, and the right for Shirley to revert to her maiden name, but not before delivering a short speech to the packed courtroom.

"This court cannot fail to take notice of the well-known fact that this plaintiff occupies a special place in the hearts and affections of millions of people . . . throughout the country. Therefore, this appears to be a peculiarly fitting and appropriate reason upon which to reassert and re-declare the vital public concern with the problem of divorce and the urgent need for giving serious study to the environmental and sociological factors which contribute to it.

"We all know that the integrity of the family lies at the very foundation of the welfare, tranquillity and good order of our society. Accordingly, this court is faithful to the declared and established policy of this state, that no divorce shall be granted except upon grounds which our law recognizes as sufficient.

"Fairness to this plaintiff . . . requires this court to declare that the evidence which has been offered here, the plaintiff's demeanor, and the very evident sincerity with which she testified have convinced the court the grounds . . . are serious and substantial . . . but also that the plaintiff has made every reasonable effort to save her marriage and to avoid necessity for this proceeding."

Shirley was given custody of Linda Susan, twenty-two months old, together with one hundred dollars a month child support. Under an out-of-court property settlement, Agar had agreed to pay over his half of all community property in a trust fund for the child. The house had always been in Shirley's name. But, in effect, this meant that Agar would be left without a cent. Shirley would have 50 percent of all their bank accounts, investments and property, furniture and household goods, and Linda Susan would have, in trust, the remaining half. Agar went out of the marriage as he had entered it—with no money and a car.

He did have a career, some good and bad publicity and a small daughter.

"As usual," Agar told reporters in Buffalo in a low voice, "there are two sides to the controversy. There is much I might have said and might say now. However, as I see it, no constructive purpose could be served by recriminations or airing our respective sides in public." He did add that Shirley's testimony in winning the divorce "reflects incorrectly our real differences."

He returned to Los Angeles for Christmas, staying at his mother's home. He saw Linda Susan (whom the Temples now called Susan), but Shirley would not discuss the divorce or a possible reconciliation with him. "She had a way of walling herself in, of being indifferent to all sides but her own, of simply *being,*" one friend comments.

The new year appeared bleak and empty. Her marriage had ended. The devastating reviews and financial failure of her last two films made her future in pictures doubtful. However, she was, at twenty-one, the enormously wealthy woman Gertrude and George had promised she would be. But had Gertrude also realized that such a large, lifetime income of her own would finally permit Shirley the freedom she had always wanted, enabling her to leave Rockingham Road, the converted playhouse, Hollywood and little Shirley Temple behind forever?

On Her Own

"YOU CAN TAKE all the sincerity in Hollywood, place it in the navel of a fruit fly and still have room for three caraway seeds and the heart of a producer," dour-faced comedian Fred Allen once proclaimed. To which columnist Erskine Johnson added, "Hollywood [is a place] where everyone is a genius until he's lost his job."

Shirley's contract with Selznick was still in effect. A compulsive but gentlemanly gambler, Selznick would never welch on a wager. When he had signed Shirley at the time of *Since You Went Away,* the odds favored a good return for his investment. The year to come, the last of Shirley's contract with Selznick, would cost him $160,000 unless he could cast her in one of his own pictures or a loan-out, but no offers for her services were forthcoming. Nor were any likely, after her recent disastrous movies. Yet Selznick had still maintained his early enthusiasm for her more mature career, although he was far too involved in his private life to concentrate on finding a property for Shirley. The previous July, he and Jennifer Jones had been married, and throughout the year had been "seeing" Europe. "I was tired," he wrote. "I had been producing . . . for more than twenty years. I wanted to do some of the traveling that I had completely denied myself during my long concentration on work in Hollywood."

More than his own pleasures were at stake. Although it had been responsible for the successful American distribution of both *The Fallen Idol* and *The Third Man,* Selznick's company owed twelve million dollars in bank loans, and he feared that if he "continued to produce for a rapidly declining market [caused by competition from television] the debt would grow." As he toured Europe, he negotiated to sell foreign distribution rights on the pictures he had already made, the only avenue he saw to raise the money to pay off his huge debts.

Shirley's salary was a minor liability compared to his other commitment.* He urged Shirley "to take her daughter to Europe, to study the culture, the repertory companies, become a mature actress, and even change her name." But Shirley had neither curiosity about Europe nor a desire to continue as an actress. She had worked almost steadily for eighteen years, had made fifty-seven movies, and had been on display and photographed without much relief on a nearly consecutive daily basis over that long span. The divorce suit against Agar had been the killing blow. The codes Gertrude had taught her were strict. In the way of British royalty, family privacy was to be guarded assiduously. Public exposure of her marital problems and Agar's drinking were as close as she had ever come to scandal. Shirley, like Selznick, was "tired" of gossip, work, pressures and the unpleasant memories Hollywood represented. Aware of Shirley's restlessness, Gertrude suggested a compromise with Selznick's advice: a trip to Hawaii—dear vacationland of her daughter's childhood—just Gertrude, George, Shirley, the baby and her nanny. Not one to brood on the past, Shirley agreed.

The Temples flew (Shirley's first air flight) to Hawaii, departing on Sunday, January 30, 1950, Susan's second birthday. Los Angeles was deluged by seasonal rains on the day they left, but the skies soon cleared. More than three thousand "shouting, pushing persons" at Honolulu Airport "roared a welcome." When Shirley disembarked with Susan in her arms at 9:05 that night, they were greeted with "the most enthusiastic 'Aloha!' in the airport's history." The traditional *leis* were hung about their necks and Shirley shouted back "Aloha!" with a broad smile. Not one reporter asked about the divorce. Shirley fielded innocuous questions about her vacation plans and recalled her earlier visits. "I feel," she said, "as if I've come home." Four Honolulu

---

*Selznick wrote, "While I was not personally involved in the obligation [outstanding loans] the sole ownership [of the stock in my company] imposed upon me—according to my lights—I had a personal moral obligation." Selznick repaid the loans with interest in full within five years time.

Airport policemen had to fight a path through the terminal to reach a waiting green Buick. The huge crowd surrounded the car, and it was ten minutes before the officers could make a clearing to permit her vehicle to depart.

A familiar landmark of the Honolulu skyline was the gigantic towering steel-and-cement pineapple, three stories high, that sat atop the Hawaiian Pineapple Company Building, owned by white-haired but spry James (Jim) Dole, who had entertained the Temples on earlier visits. Jim Dole employed a young assistant, Charles Black. Two days after Shirley's arrival, Dole gave a dinner party in her honor, and the suavely handsome Black was one of the invited guests. "I really wasn't very interested in meeting Shirley Temple," Black recalled. "I was living a very full life of my own and—well, I just didn't care. I had never seen a Shirley Temple movie in my life." But Shirley countered, "It's corny, but it's all true. You know, some enchanted evening across a crowded room." They were to meet again the following night at another dinner, this time at the home of novelist James Norman Hall, co-author of *Mutiny on the Bounty*.

Within two weeks, she knew she was in love. The Temples returned to Los Angeles as previously planned, and Shirley, Susan and the nanny moved into a rented beach house for an additional month.

Nine years Shirley's senior, Charles Alden Black was born on March 6, 1919, in Alameda County, California, the second son of Katharine McElrath and James Byers Black, whose rise in the utility field had been spectacular. The senior Black had been born in Sycamore, Illinois, in 1890, and came to northern California with his parents when he was ten. After graduating from the University of California at Berkeley with a degree in mechanical engineering, he took a job as a service inspector for the Great Western Power Company. Within ten years, he had become vice-president and general manager. Moving quickly on the wheels of corporate takeovers, Black retained his position with Great Western, along with the vice-presidency of the North American Company, which had acquired it. When merged, these firms became the nation's largest utility, Pacific Gas and Electric Company, and Black became its president.

The Blacks were wealthy and socially prominent. Their sons, Charles and James, Jr., as well as their daughter, Kathryn, had been brought up on San Francisco's elegant Nob Hill and in a palatial summer home in Del Monte (an estate section of the seaside community of Monterey) and been given every advantage—education, travel and prestigious contacts.* Charles Black, with his tanned good looks, black hair, tall, aristocratic presence, monied position, social background, connections and his disinterest in films, embodied all the qualities Shirley desired in a man.

"When she fell in love with Johnny, Shirley thought he was everything that Charlie [Black] ended up being," one friend comments. "I don't think Johnny ever misrepresented himself. Shirley was an overly romantic kid and she saw what she wanted to see. Gertrude said you have to marry someone not interested in your fame or your money. But without that, she wouldn't have been *who* or *what* she was. And when she met Johnny, she had just made a pretty sensational comeback [in *Since You Went Away*]. And Johnny's family *had* known better times. Naturally, he was attracted to her success and all that went with it.

"Charlie? Well, he was the real thing where Johnny had been a facsimile—at least in Shirley's eyes. . . . There was something Scott Fitzgeraldian about the whole thing. When Johnny entered Shirley's life, he was kind of all-golden, but he didn't know how to deal with the exigencies of fame. Lots of Shirley's friends saw him as a tragic figure. He did not have a lot of personal resources. Charlie, on the other hand . . . was loaded with them. He was quite brilliant, decisive and, well—I guess you'd say—*manly*. Anyway, he had no trouble standing up against Gertrude. And maybe that's what Shirley was looking for all along."

Charles Alden Black had prepared at the select Hotchkiss School, received his B.A. from Stanford and an M.B.A. from the Harvard Business School. He enlisted in 1941 in the navy as an apprentice seaman, but was sent directly to Officers' Training

---

*Among his many public and social associations, James Byers Black (1890–1965) was also chairman of the board of management at the San Francisco Golden State International Exposition, a director of the New York World's Fair Corporation (1939), an appointee on Harry S Truman's Advisory Board on the Merchant Marine and to the National Labor-Management Panel (1947); he was a director of the San Francisco Symphony Association and of the San Francisco Ballet Association for twenty-three years. His younger son, James Byers Black, Jr., was a partner in the San Francisco branch of the investment banking firm of Lehman Brothers. Kathryn Black, his only daughter, married Joseph Burk of Gladwyn, Pennsylvania, the crew coach for the University of Pennsylvania.

School. He saw action in some of the toughest campaigns in the
Solomons, New Guinea, the Dutch East Indies and China.
Awarded the Silver Star and a presidential citation for bravery,
he emerged from the war a lieutenant commander in the Naval
Reserve. He spoke French, Malayan and several Tahitian dia-
lects. A keen sportsman, he also enjoyed classical music. Shirley
"was snagged," as one friend put it. Black must also have been,
for, two weeks after Shirley had returned with Susan to Los
Angeles, he flew to meet her and the Temples in San Francisco
to attend an annual society event, the Bachelors' Dance (April
16, 1950).

The new romance was reported in the press. With her divorce not yet final, Black, who possessed a strong sense of pro-
priety, was careful not to be seen with Shirley in public. Over the
next few months, he was to fly to see Shirley several times, but
their meetings were kept private—visits at the Brentwood
house, drives to the beach, picnics on the sand. In what free time
he had, he met with local television executives. In August, he
resigned from Hawaiian Pineapple to join KTTV as an account
executive, a job that had him commuting between their offices
in Los Angeles and San Francisco. "I couldn't compete for her
hand 3,000 miles away," he later commented.

In August, Shirley received a call from the offices of Peter
Lawrence and Roger Stevens, the Broadway producers of *Peter
Pan*. The revival of the James Barrie play with music and lyrics
by Leonard Bernstein, starring Jean Arthur, had been a huge
success that year. Arthur had taken ill, and Shirley was asked if
she would read for the role. Not since her early years had she
had to audition for a part. But the idea of appearing on the stage
intrigued her. Accompanied by Gertrude, she flew to New York
on August 15 on the "hush-hush" expedition that could have
marked her theater debut. The reading did not go as well as
anyone had hoped. Jean Arthur possessed a fey quality that
brought a fresh approach to the play. Shirley did not have the
necessary lightness, and, dispirited, she retuned to the Coast
the following day. The turn-down on *Peter Pan* convinced her
that her acting career was over.*

---

*Anne Jackson understudied the role, but she was soon replaced in the part by
Barbara Baxley. When the show went on tour, the role was played by Joan McCracken,
who had scored a great success in *Oklahoma!*.

Once Black had entered the scene, however, the idea of remarrying became her prime consideration. Shirley carried Charles's picture in her wallet next to Susan's. They saw each other daily, and though it was not publicly announced, they planned to marry shortly after December 5, when her divorce from Agar would become final. In November, the adjoining houses on Rockingham Avenue were listed privately with a realtor. The couple did not want to live in the converted playhouse, and the Temples had decided the expense of maintaining the estate was too costly for them alone.

During this same year, Nancy Majors had fallen in love with Richard R. Gros, a public-relations executive from the San Francisco area, and the two childhood friends were once again drawn close together.* Nancy was married in the spring of 1950, and Charles, who knew Gros well, was best man. "Shirley wasn't a bridesmaid because I only had my sister as attendant," Nancy explained. When Shirley came to San Francisco to be with Black, she would stay in the apartment of the newly married Groses. "The reason for that," Nancy comments, "was that the Black family was extremely conservative, and they did not think it proper for Shirley to stay with Charlie or even alone in a hotel. She arrived with these huge medical text books—each one of them must have weighed twenty pounds. Now, Shirley never did go to college, but she was always very interested in medicine. And she read these books with a great deal of attention—making notes, that sort of thing. She always had an intellectual curiosity and was attracted to the real and concrete."

Another friend adds, "At Westlake, Shirley excelled in biology. When it came to dissecting frogs, 'Lil Bug' was a standout!" An unconfirmed story that circulated at Westlake had her donning a surgical gown to watch while a young veteran had his leg amputated shortly after she had visited his bedside on an army hospital tour. "Medicine, and especially surgery, always fascinated Shirley. And I don't think she was morbidly curious either—just drawn to the professional skills of a surgeon. If the cards had fallen differently, I think she would have gone on to study medicine."

---

*Robert R. Gros was Nancy Majors's first husband. She was later to marry Phillip Voorheis.

During the year she had been separated from Agar, and as her feelings for Black deepened, her interest in medicine did intensify, and she considered the possibility of associating herself in some way with the medical profession. "I know now the kind of person I am," she was quoted as saying in November 1950. "Normal home life appeals to me, the same as normal school life used to, with maybe a little medicine thrown in on the side, if there's a hospital nearby."

As a single parent, she had become closer to her daughter. With no work commitments, she spent her days watching over, entertaining and eating with the child, which meant having dinner at six.

Shirley owned three acetate records of songs she had sung at Fox. Every night before the child's bedtime at eight, she would play them for her. *Dreamland Choochoo,* a lullabyish song, was the final number and meant lights out for Susan. Even when Black was with them, the routine seldom varied. Nightclubs were not to his liking. When they went out, it was usually to the home of friends.

"Charles was definitely part of San Francisco's upper strata, but I don't think he ever saw himself that way," Nancy Majors Voorheis says. "He was not really social. He was stunningly handsome but very quiet . . . and as far as I could see, he did not mix well with people. He was a solid person, a man of great integrity . . . but . . . he was not easy to get to know. Being as handsome as he was, it perhaps didn't matter much. He cut a distinguished figure, and when he did enter into a conversation, you were struck by his tremendous intelligence."

Another friend added, "He's calm and conservative—a solid-citizen type."

They were married in his parents' Del Monte home in the high-beamed living room before a fireplace covered with pine boughs and flowers at 4:30 P.M. on Sunday, December 16, 1950. Superior Court Judge Henry G. Jorgensen of Salinas performed the ceremony in the presence of only the immediate families— the Blacks, the Temples, Jack and Mimsy, and the bridegroom's brother James, Jr., and his wife and three children. Shirley wore a simple gray suit with matching hat, and Black a dark business suit. They left immediately following the ceremony, with Black at the wheel of his late-model gunmetal convertible. They managed to lose the reporters who were waiting outside for them by entering the vehicle in the attached garage while a member of the wedding party started the motor of a similar car parked out front. They remained sequestered at a family friend's home, which had been loaned to them for their six-day honeymoon, while reporters searched the Monterey Peninsula for a sight of the bridegroom's convertible.

Wednesday, dressed informally—Shirley in "a snug red turtleneck sweater and slacks, Black in sports trousers and a gray open-necked polo shirt"—they ventured out for a "mid-afternoon breakfast" on Monterey's Fisherman's Wharf and were spotted just as they were leaving.* "Acting as though his bride needed protection," her bridegroom stepped in front of her as the reporters moved in. With Shirley laughing behind him, he met all questions with a tight-lipped "No comment." The following day, a press conference was called in the San Francisco apartment of Charles's parents, after the honeymooners escaped injury in a minor automobile collision. Shirley announced that her contract with David Selznick had just expired, and that she was quitting films after nineteen years.

"That's long enough," she said. "My only contract is to Mr. Black." With that, she gave her new husband a hug, and the press a knowing wink. "And it's 'exclusive,' " she added. But her obvious happiness was not without an approaching cloud or two.

Throughout the spring of 1950, tensions had risen in the United States over the buildup of a threatening situation in Korea, a peninsula that sat between two stronger and belligerent countries, Japan and China. Historically the battlefield of invading armies, Korea was now divided into Communist-controlled North Korea and the anti-Communist government of South Korea. At the end of World War II, the United States signed an agreement with the United Nations to withdraw all American military forces. On June 25, the North Koreans crossed the boundary—the 38th parallel—of their province and swept the South Korean Army before them.

Political pundits believed President Truman would find a

---

*The *Los Angeles Times* went so far as to report that Shirley "had bacon and eggs. Black had a cracked crab and two seafood cocktails."

way to appease the North Koreans and the Russians and Chinese
and that he would not risk World War III for the fate of South
Korea. However, he surprised "them even more than he did on
Election Day, 1948."* His order, given at 12:07 P.M., Tuesday,
June 27, "directed American forces to resist the North Korean
attack by air, by sea, and on the ground." Once again, the nation
was at war.

Charles Black was a trained officer in the Naval Reserve.
Unless the Communists were pushed back swiftly by the South
Koreans, he most certainly would be recalled to active duty. In
September, General Douglas MacArthur launched "a brilliantly
successful" campaign that "caught the North Koreans by surprise." By November, all South Korea had been regained, and
since Black had not yet been put back in uniform, he and Shirley
could be optimistic about their immediate future.

But on the same day as their marriage, December 16, a state
of emergency had been proclaimed in the United States following a staggering reversal. Three hundred thousand Chinese soldiers had infiltrated deep into MacArthur's rear forces. Had the
Chinese been better equipped, they might have "turned the
[resulting American] defeat into a rout."

On January 4, 1951, North Korean and Chinese Communists
took Seoul. The newlyweds, in Los Angeles with Susan, knew it
was only a matter of weeks, at most months, before Black would
be recalled.

This already bleak start to their marriage was given added
stress when, on January 13, Agar was arrested on a charge of
driving his car down the wrong side of Wilshire Boulevard while
intoxicated. With him at the time was fashion model Loretta
Barnett Combs. He requested a trial by jury, and it was set for
February 5. Agar was already on probation on a reckless-driving
charge from the previous April. With each of these offenses, Los
Angeles newspaper headlines referred to him as "Shirley's Ex."
Agar's trial was postponed until March 16. A month before this
date, he was again arrested for drunk driving, and after a night
in jail ("This will ruin my life," he told the judge) was released
a second time on bail. He faced a maximum six-month prison

---

*The morning papers had announced that Thomas Dewey had won the election.
When all the votes were in, Truman emerged the winner.

sentence if found guilty. When the case was finally brought before the court, his attorney, standing up to question a police witness, fainted. A mistrial was declared, and a new date, July 20, set.

Agar's escapades made frequent and somewhat sordid newspaper reading. He and Miss Combs eloped to Las Vegas on May 17, but the nuptials were delayed an hour because the county clerk believed Agar was not sober enough to know what he was doing. After downing six cups of black coffee in a nearby café, Agar led his bride-to-be back to the courthouse, where they were married. Found guilty on both charges of drunk driving at his trial in July, he received a six-month county jail sentence, thirty days of which were suspended. On the stand, he blamed his drinking on the failure of his first marriage and attributed some of his difficulties to unfavorable publicity instigated by Shirley at the divorce trial.

"Don't blame this on Shirley Temple," the judge warned, before sentencing him. When he later appeared before the court to shorten the time of his incarceration, the same judge complimented him "on taking his medicine like a man."

His wife, his mother and many members of the industry stood by Agar. He had co-starring roles in several action pictures despite his drinking problem. Some producers apparently felt it toughened his image, and he seemed to drink between pictures, not during their production. But to Shirley, his behavior brought constant embarrassment and fear that Susan would somehow be adversely affected. During Agar's troubled post-Temple years, father and daughter were mostly separated. Agar had lost more than a famous wife when Shirley divorced him. Without realizing it, he had relinquished his position in his daughter's life. With the new Mrs. Agar's dedicated help, medical assistance and a redefined belief in "God and religion," he eventually pulled himself back up.*

---

*Agar's film credits from 1950 included *The Magic Carpet* with Lucille Ball, *Along the Great Divide* with Kirk Douglas (1951), *Bait* (1954), *Frontier Gun* (1958), *Johnny Reno* (1966), *The St. Valentine's Day Massacre* with Jason Robards (1967), *The Undefeated* (1969), *Chisum* (1970) and *Big Jake* (1971), all with John Wayne, and the remake (in a small role) of *King Kong* with Jessica Lange (1976). He also engaged in several business enterprises, from insurance to vending machines, and was well known in television for a series of commercials he did as Mr. Clean, with head shaved and a gold earring in one ear.

In April, Black was ordered to report for duty in Washington, D.C. Shirley decided she would accompany him and remain there as long as was possible. The newlyweds set off with Susan on a cross-country car journey, stopping in Phoenix, Arizona, to leave her for a time with Jack and Mimsy and their sons while they continued on to find a home at their destination. They departed Phoenix early on Saturday morning, May 5. Late in the afternoon of the next day, while driving through Tulsa, Oklahoma, Shirley was stricken with an acute appendicitis attack. Black drove directly to Hillcrest Memorial Hospital in that city, where she was operated on three hours later in an emergency appendectomy. Gertrude arrived a short time later, while Black continued on alone to Washington, where he had been assigned to the Pentagon staff, an indication that he might remain in Washington and not be sent overseas.

Once Shirley had recovered and joined him, they purchased and settled into a comfortable forty-eight-thousand-dollar seven-room home situated on River Road in fashionable Bethesda, Maryland, near Chevy Chase, a fair commute to the Office of Naval Operations, where Black was stationed.* The house, small by her previous standards, was set on a rise and surrounded by slim dogwood trees, and Shirley set about decorating it with verve, scouring the local antique shops for items of interest. Two massive ship's lanterns were mounted on the outside gateposts. The good-sized living room and the library had fireplaces back to back. But the master bedroom had just enough space for their double bed, the California sun lamp they both enjoyed using, and the hair dryer that occupied one corner—"mute testimony that Shirley does her own hair (no longer golden, but a surprising black)."† A barn in the back of the house had been built by the previous owner as a stable. The area was fox-hunting country, and Bradley Farms, the subdivision where the Blacks owned property, was surrounded by many large and imposing estates. Because they considered their house too close to the main road to keep a horse, they turned the barn into a small guest cottage. Shirley claimed she just wanted

---

*A comparable house in that area in 1988 would cost from $500,000 to $550,000.
†As Shirley had matured, her hair darkened. While she made films, it had been tinted ash blond. She no longer camouflaged the natural color, which was not black but dark brown, still a shock to anyone who recalled the fabled golden-haired child.

to be a housewife and mother. The excitement of Washington's politically charged atmosphere, however, was soon to overtake her.

Black's politics were conservative, and very much in accord with the principles of Republicanism to which Shirley and the Temples subscribed. As a young woman, Shirley had not taken an active interest in politics. Now, she stepped forward and publicly supported General Douglas MacArthur when, in April, shortly before the Blacks' move to Washington, President Truman had dismissed the general because of his campaign to recoup his losses in Korea by a plan to attack China. Her statement to a reporter that "General MacArthur is a great man and would make a great president" does not seem too adventurous. Truman's action in recalling MacArthur had thrown the country into "shocked indignation. Flags were flown at half-mast. The Los Angeles City Council adjourned, too sick at heart to conduct the city's business that day." The Michigan legislature passed a resolution that began, "Whereas, at one a.m. of this day, World Communism achieved its greatest victory of the decade in the dismissal of General MacArthur . . ." and polls showed that two-thirds of the nation believed Truman had made a grievous error.

Washington society found the near presence of Shirley Temple and her handsome navy husband irresistible.

"Louis Parsons, a vice-president of United States Steel, took the Blacks under his wing socially," one friend recalls. "They attended and gave small dinner parties where government officials and foreign diplomats discussed the Cold War, Korea, nuclear armaments, the economy, the United Nations and the future of the world.

"For Shirley, this represented a whole new area, although Charles had long been interested in politics and world affairs." Among the many leading Washington politicians they met were Senator Richard M. Nixon and Secretary of the Navy Dan Kimball. The energetic and colorful "Big Dan" Kimball, grandson of a steamboat captain, towering and with a deep voice in keeping with his large size, became a good friend and golf buddy of the Blacks. As former director of the General Tire and Rubber Company, he had lived many years in Hollywood. A close crony of Bing Crosby and Bob Hope, Kimball had a fund of stories, laughed a lot and was never seen without a cigar stuck in his mouth.

"During the two years we were in Washington," Shirley reflected, "I had meant to get involved only in local politics, but of course in Washington local politics are national and international politics."

Although they knew many high-placed government officials, the Blacks were not included in the greatest Washington social event of the year, the visit of Princess Elizabeth and her husband, the Duke of Edinburgh, in November 1951, an ironic oversight, for as a child the princess had doted on Shirley Temple movies.* Shirley was at that time in the early months of her second pregnancy. The decision was made that, like most other navy wives, she should have the child at the Bethesda Naval Hospital. On the morning of April 28, 1952, five days after Shirley's twenty-fourth birthday, a son, Charles Alden Black, Jr., was born by Caesarian section.

"They had me get up the second day and walk," Shirley has recalled, "and the stitches broke and I eviscerated. It wasn't discovered until my bandages were changed eight hours later." An embolism developed in her bloodstream and entered the pulmonary artery. Shirley's condition was critical.

Black immediately telephoned Dr. William C. Bradbury in Santa Monica, who had delivered Susan, and he boarded a navy plane and was by Shirley's side in twelve hours. "I found her frightened," Bradbury said, "but she was getting the very best of care, and she began to improve at once. I stayed [five days] just to give her confidence." Daily bulletins were issued in the newspapers. Her progress was slow. On June 13, seven weeks after her son's birth, Shirley was finally able to leave the hospital and return home.

Domesticity now occupied the center place in her life. Days as well as evenings revolved around the two children. For a few weeks after her grueling hospital experience, she employed a

---

*"We've just had a visit from a lovely young lady and her personable husband," wrote President Truman to King George VI. "As one father to another we can be very proud of our daughters. You have the better of me—because you have two!" Also duly recorded was the meeting of Truman's mother-in-law, the elderly Mrs. Wallace, and the royal couple. Mrs. Wallace reportedly said to Princess Elizabeth, "I'm so glad your father's been reelected."

nurse to help with little Charlie. But then she proudly proclaimed that she had no maid or nanny and cooked, cleaned and
cared for the children herself. Susan, now nearly five, continued
to eat with the family and any guests. "Adults do have some
adjustments to make with small fry at dinner," Shirley wrote in
an article about raising her children, "but it is an invaluable
moment for our family get-together." In a most revealing passage, she admitted, "When discipline is necessary, I use the
same chin-and-hand-holding method my mother used on me.
Very gently I cup her chin in one of my palms and grasp her
hands with the other. This obliges her to give me her undivided
attention while I explain the cause of my displeasure."

Her daughter was "intrigued by horses and their care," and
had a natural grace and talent for the piano. She had inherited
her mother's dimples and flashing eyes. But Shirley was strong
in her desire that Susan have a normal childhood, which meant
no career. Susan had seen only one of Shirley's pictures, *Rebecca
of Sunnybrook Farm* and, according to her mother, she was "unimpressed." In October, Shirley entered her in the private Honeywell Foundation School in nearby Sky Meadows. As the holiday
season approached, Susan was cast as a fairy in her kindergarten
class's Christmas pantomime play of *Cinderella,* to be given in the
American University's Glendenen Gym. Shirley herself made
her daughter's crepe-paper costume with tinsel ribbon and gos-
samer wings.

The morning of the performance, Tuesday, December 16,
the *Washington Post* sent photographers to take pictures of the
children in their costumes. Dr. Honeywell, the headmaster of his
school, claimed later that Shirley "very charmingly helped pose
the children," that she knew in advance that the photographers
were coming and that she went home "apparently perfectly
happy," an assessment that seems correct, since Susan appeared
in the play that afternoon with the Blacks in attendance. The
next morning in the *Washington Post,* a photograph of Susan in
her costume appeared beside a picture of Shirley at the height
of her fame. A short article by drama critic Richard L. Coe
accompanied the photographs: "Shirley Temple's four-year-old
daughter made her stage debut yesterday afternoon . . . The
young lady is programmed as Miss Susan Black. Susan was born
Linda Susan Agar, the daughter of Mrs. Charles Black and her

first husband, John Agar. The Honeywell Foundation's Christmas Pantomimes are an annual event, a reminder of the big 'pantos' which are underway by the score throughout the British Isles this time of year. . . . Mrs. Black is restrained about the future of her daughter's career and observes that no record of the debut should overplay her daughter's appearance by ignoring other children in the play." Coe then listed the names of the twelve other children appearing in the pantomime, an invitation-only affair for parents and friends, and ended by noting the performances would be repeated at seven-thirty that Thursday evening, December 19.

Upon reading the coverage, an "incensed" Shirley drove directly to the school and pulled Susan out of her class. Charles then telephoned Honeywell to confirm that Susan had been removed. Later that afternoon, Shirley issued a statement to the United Press that "My only desire is to be retired and left alone," and that she was "appalled that the Honeywell school would attempt to capitalize on Susan's presence in a childish class exercise." She added, "I consider the action of the school authorities a break of faith and am withdrawing Susan immediately from any association with the school.

"It's a sad commentary that Susan must be parted from her good little friends at Christmas time, but I have not and will not allow anyone to commercialize on my daughter's presence."

Both Coe and Honeywell were "staggered" and "baffled" by Shirley's dramatic action and her statement. "To me," Coe said, "it was going to be a nice little story. I don't see anything sensational in it and can't see why anyone else would either." Honeywell replied to Shirley's accusations, "If we were trying to commercialize on Linda Susan's appearance we would have given her a leading part . . . Can I help it if the newspaper played up the appearance of Mrs. Black's daughter?"

The entire incident seems to have been blown out of proportion, but it revealed some of Shirley's fears and emotions, the possibility that the Honeywell establishment might have benefited from the publicity given Susan's "stage debut" being the least of these. Although there was a minor charge for tickets, the pantomime performance was "invitation only," and the presence of Shirley Temple's daughter could not greatly have affected its attendance. In government-conscious Chevy Chase, the enrollment of an offspring of a politically powerful parent was far more prestigious to a school than the daughter of a former film star. Clearly, the newspaper had seen "a human interest story" and was simply catering to a reading audience curious about Shirley Temple's daughter.

The ever-present fear of kidnapping (she had maintained a bodyguard for Susan at the time of the divorce) was a main reason why the article incensed Shirley, for the *Washington Post* story pinpointed the child's identity and her whereabouts at certain hours. Agar was also to be considered. Susan had been registered at school as *Black,* and that is how Shirley wanted it. Agar was to have no part in the child's life. Within a few weeks of this time, he would be sentenced (January 21, 1953) in a new splash of adverse publicity to 120 days in jail for yet another case of drunken driving and violation of probation.

Shirley was not the only one of the Temple family involved in problems dealing with a child from a previous marriage. Sonny had married twice, first to Florence Bruce, a ballet dancer and the mother of his son, Richard Temple. When they divorced two years later, "little Butch," as the boy was called, was adopted by his maternal grandparents, Virginia and Howard Bruce. His second marriage, to Patricia Ruth Temple, ended in a bizarre divorce action that named another man as the father of the estranged Mrs. Temple's five-month-old daughter, Kelly Ann. About this time, Sonny began to show the classic symptoms—double vision, unsteady gait and problems in coordination—of multiple sclerosis, a chronic, often progressive disease of the central nervous system.

Along with then-Senator John F. Kennedy, Grace Kelly and Frank Sinatra, Shirley pitched in to help raise funds for the National Multiple Sclerosis Society. This was the first time she had become involved with a national campaign of any sort, and she discovered how good she was at it. Life became more stimulating; and as the 1952 presidential race accelerated, the Blacks worked for the success of the Republican ticket headed by General Dwight D. Eisenhower and his running mate, Senator Richard M. Nixon.

THROUGHOUT THE FIRST THREE MONTHS of Dwight D. Eisenhower's presidency, his major effort was drafting an acceptable plan for an armistice to halt the Korean War. Six weeks before his election, he had visited Southeast Asia and proposed to end the hostilities through the introduction of tactical nuclear weapons, "even if it led to making atomic attacks on military bases inside China." But by now, Russia and China were as war-weary as the United States, and the president put forth considerably more moderate terms to end the Korean conflict: "a restoration of the status quo ante-bellum and the return of prisoners of war."

Peace might yet have been delayed many months had Stalin not died in March 1953. Three weeks later, an agreement had been reached on the exchange of sick and wounded prisoners. An armistice was finally signed on July 27 at Panmunjom, and Lieutenant Commander Charles Black, along with thousands of other reserve officers, was relieved of active duty. The Blacks would have to leave Washington, a place Shirley had come to love. "It has such a small-town air about it. Everyone whispers and looks so important," she confessed, adding later, "I was pregnant most of the time, or so it seemed. When I look at pictures of myself at Embassy parties, I get bigger and bigger and bigger."

Black was offered a position as business manager at ABC-TV Los Angeles, and the family returned to California as soon as was feasible. With the two children, and a car packed with those things they considered too valuable to send by truck, they set off on the long drive cross-country, staying at small hotels and eating picnic lunches on the roadside.

Shirley's parents had recently sold the large house on Rockingham Avenue and had bought from their daughter the converted playhouse, which they now occupied.* The Blacks, shortly after their arrival in Los Angeles, moved into a mountaintop house at 2200 Bowmont Drive overlooking Beverly Hills, larger than the Chevy Chase house and with just the right combination of privacy and space. Shirley set about decorating it herself. The children, the house, her work on behalf of the National Multiple Sclerosis Society, and a course she was taking in interior decoration kept her well occupied. Sorely missed, though, were her Washington activities and political involvement.

Life in Los Angeles was unsettling. Agar, out of prison and now happily remarried, wanted to see his daughter. The court had given him visitation rights, but Shirley did not welcome his presence in either her own or Susan's life.

"On [January 30] Linda Susan's sixth birthday," Agar says, "I made an appointment to take her a gift. When I arrived, Shirley met me at the door and said Linda Susan was asleep. I could hear a little girl and a man giggling in the background. I called that night to wish Linda Susan a happy birthday. When she came to the phone, she said, 'Hi, Agar! I am sorry I didn't see you, but I was completely exhausted after my birthday party.' Quite a vocabulary for a six-year-old." Shirley, he implies, was bitter and vindictive about their failed marriage and his troubles, although his personal problems had not altered the regularity of his support payments.

"When Shirley divorced me," he adds, "my half of the community property went into a trust for Linda Susan. As a matter of fact, the only things I took when I was asked to leave by Shirley's attorney were my personal belongings. Wedding gifts

---

*227 Rockingham Avenue was transferred from Shirley Temple Black to George and Gertrude Temple on April 20, 1951. It was sold a few days later to Colonel George Phelps. The Temples moved into the converted playhouse (209 Rockingham Avenue). Shirley Temple Black held the deed until it was sold to Albert Braslaw in 1963, when the Temples moved to Palm Desert. The Blacks' home on River Road (Bradley Farms) in Chevy Chase was sold for $60,500 on March 23, 1954, after the Blacks had returned to Los Angeles.

from my family and friends were all left behind. After we both remarried, I thought about the sterling-silver flatware my mother had given us. I called Shirley and asked if I could have it, since the initial A was on the silver and Shirley's last initial was now B. Shirley said no, that she had changed the initial."

The previous September, she had learned she was pregnant again. Lori Alden Black was born on April 9, 1954, at Santa Monica Hospital, by Caesarean section. Dr. Bradbury was in attendance. This time, Shirley had a normal recuperation. But neither she nor Charles was satisfied with life in Los Angeles. Agar's nearness remained disconcerting. Susan considered Black her father, and that was how Shirley wanted it to be.* It seemed providential therefore that Charles preferred the more stable environs of San Francisco to Los Angeles.

California has always been a polarized state, divided into North and South almost as the nation was once. Historically Republican, northern California held more to conservative politics and Old World values. Black was hired as head of business administration for the Stanford Research Institute in Menlo Park, California, a short distance from San Francisco. Within months after Lori's birth, the Blacks packed up again, this time heading to Atherton, "an aggressively upwardly mobile, upper middle-class area" twenty-eight miles south of San Francisco, which boasted some palatial estates along with newer homes on one-acre subdivisions. The house the Blacks purchased for fifty thousand dollars was one of the latter and still under construction. This gave Shirley free rein on the decoration, and since her family was domiciled in small quarters at a local inn while the work was being undertaken, she proceeded at a whirlwind pace.

The result of her marathon project was a handsome Japanese-modern (known as "Pacific style" for a number of years after the war) redwood ranch house with furnishings of Oriental

---

*"From our divorce in 1950 until 1964, I paid Shirley child support," Agar says. "In 1964, Loretta, my wife, and I were in the process of adopting our son John III, and the court required that I show proof from Shirley that I paid that support. Before I received that proof, I was served with a summons telling me Charles Black was going to adopt Linda Susan. Now I had through the years sent presents which were never acknowledged, and though I have tried many times to contact Linda Susan, I have not seen nor talked to her since she was six years old. The thirtieth of January [1988], she will be forty years old. Yes, I authorized the adoption . . . [but] I would still like to see and know my daughter."

design. The house spread out in T-formation from a center hall floored in sand-colored tile. An enormous tropical planter stood on either side of the ceiling-high glass pane beside the front door. A sliding glass wall in the living room looked out on a beautiful little Japanese garden, complete with stream and small bridge. A monochromatic decorative plan was followed: floors, carpets, walls, the stone fireplace and ceilings were beige; natural raw silks were used for the upholstered pieces, with jewel-toned pillows added for color. A brilliant five-foot silk canvas depicting Oriental mythology hung over the fireplace. Framed vivid antique *obies* (pieces of Polynesian fabric) decorated the other walls. The ships' lanterns Shirley had brought with her from Washington had been converted into two massive lamps that stood on large, square off-white marble tables. Often, in the evenings, Shirley and the children would don Japanese robes in keeping with the general decor. "The children love dressing-up, just as I loved my costumes when I was a little girl," Shirley commented.

When asked about the professionalism of her decorating, she recalled, "I've been interested in decorating since I was a child in the studios. They used to have miniature sets of all the pictures I worked in, and for each film there was usually a different period set. While other little girls were playing with doll's houses, I was playing with these authentic miniature sets, prepared by some of Hollywood's greatest decorating talents."

The house reflected only a few reminders of her glittering past. She had leased half of her doll collection to the California State Exposition Building—a state museum.* "The funny thing is I didn't like dolls," Shirley had confessed when Susan was small, "and neither does my daughter," yet the remaining half of her collection was kept in glass cases in the girls' rooms. The white Steinway grand piano, autographed personally under the lid to her from one of the Steinways—given to her at the age of seven—occupied a prominent position in the living room. On a bookshelf in the same room, a neat row of "reddish-brown leather albums were lined up with the title of one of Shirley's

---

*For many years, Temple moved her doll collection from museum to museum, adding to it with each new exhibit. She did not receive remuneration, but the expenses of packing and transporting the collection were borne by the institutions involved.

movies lettered in gold on each. The albums contained stills from and clippings about the films." Only one photograph of her as a child was exhibited, and that was hung on the wall of little Charlie's room.

The work Shirley had done on the house so impressed her new friends in Atherton that for a time she associated herself with a local interior-decorator's shop. "I enjoy color psychology. But I can't work for strangers," she confessed when this did not turn out well. "They just want to ask me about Elizabeth Taylor." Much of her time and energy continued to be given over to fund-raising for the National Multiple Sclerosis Society (of which she was now national director) and other charities, including the Allied Arts Guild, which supported a children's convalescent home and a rehabilitation center for the physically disabled. One day a week was spent at Stanford Hospital taking blood samples to the laboratory and wheeling out new mothers and babies when they were ready to go home. "Once," she admitted sheepishly, "I forgot the baby." With Charles, she joined the conservationist Sierra Club, which dealt with problems of ecology. On clement weekends, they picnicked at the ocean with the children, went snorkeling, skin diving, or played golf. She was a fair golfer, and her score ranged from 100 to 110 for eighteen holes.

She had become "a fearless conversationalist," and since her Washington years had developed an insatiable interest in world affairs.

Television and film work had been offered her. But she refused to play roles that cast her as an alcoholic or a "fallen woman," parts that had been submitted to her, "because of the reaction it would have" on her "children and husband. Besides," she added, "I have no burning desire to act." Selznick had called once to ask her to take part in a television special he was producing. "I accepted on the telephone," she remembered, "and then little Charlie got sick and I called back and said 'I guess I'm too much of a mother.' But I would have done it if I had only realized that my father-in-law's company was one of the sponsors." James Black, however, would not have been pleased with that decision, for he made it clear to those close to him that he did not approve of Shirley returning to films.

Susan once asked her mother what she had missed in her

childhood and Shirley had replied, "Darling, only the mumps!" Those came in 1955—on both sides—when little Charlie caught them and passed the disease on to Susan and Shirley. Gertrude came up to Atherton to nurse her ailing daughter and grandchildren and promptly made it a foursome by catching the mumps herself.

George had recently retired, and the Temples were considering a move to Palm Springs. The "winding down" of her formerly active life and the absence of Shirley as a central force had not been easy for Gertrude. Among her friends, it was no secret that she had not wanted Shirley to quit at a time when her popularity was at such a low point. For her part, Shirley still refused to discuss the past. "It's senseless," she had once said, "like talking about an operation. The sooner you stop the sooner you start feeling better." The last years of her career obviously remained a painful memory.

Shirley was approaching her third decade. The normal life she had touched upon when she had attended Westlake School now seemed fully hers. The closest she came to movies was as a board member of the San Francisco International Film Festival. Mostly, she lived the life "of the wealthy suburban matron, caught up in a busy round of teas, balls, fashion shows and entertaining." She had the "perfect" husband, and three children to love, mold into adults and discipline, but it had not proved to be enough. She kept adding responsibilities—demanding charity, hospital and fund-raising work and mounting involvement in campaigns to preserve the environment.

Though she could well afford live-in domestics, she insisted on hiring only part-time household help. Family dinners, which she cooked herself, remained sacrosanct. She wanted everything perfect—the happy ending to the fairy story of the little girl who was princess of the world. One relative thought she had become driven, that she was trying to prove her worth, her ability to take care of not only her own family, but *all* the needy.

"Somehow [among former child stars] the defense mechanism breaks down around the age of thirty. They no longer seem able to suppress their outrage at the abuse and exploitation of their childhoods," Diana Serra Cary claims. "This [rebellion] takes different forms: erratic behavior (Patty Duke), self-destructive death wish (Jackie Cooper and race cars!), mental blackouts

(Edith Fellows). In my case, I experienced unbearable mental anguish—conflicting feelings of guilt and rage." Shirley's guilt was at having failed in her first marriage and in the adult years of her career.

"I think it comes down to the fact that a breadwinner child feels *so* responsible. They can't remember when they weren't the family's meal-ticket. One's first reaction is having 'let others down.' You put off thinking how ill-treated *you* may have been, because your own sense of failure keeps the monkey on your back, and you're so busy dealing with that, you haven't got time to think about yourself as a victim. That keeps getting postponed until one day it's Mount St. Helen time!" Mrs. Cary concludes. But Shirley kept right on going, with no apparent explosion.

Always the linchpin of her circle, Shirley had retained her closeness to her family, including her in-laws, whom she saw frequently. Her two marriages and the miles that separated their homes had not distanced Shirley from Gertrude. When Gertrude took ill about this time, she came up to San Francisco to have major surgery. Shirley felt responsible for and closely identified with Gertrude, who—with Sonny's illness added to her own—was under tremendous stress. But George was in good health, and Jack was now working for the FBI.*

Shirley's life was filled, but not complete. The Blacks ate their dinner with the children, and Charles retired early. She never got to sleep before 2:00 A.M., which gave her a very long evening alone. ("I inherit that from mother," she admitted. "She sits in her dressing room, so as not to disturb daddy, and knits and reads and dozes far into the night.") Her once-avid interest in medicine had faded, interior decoration had not satisfied her, her charity work did not fulfill her and the children were no longer babies.

Coincidence could have been involved; but as Shirley neared her thirtieth birthday, she decided to reactivate her acting career. Charles had recently left Stanford Research Institute and taken a job as director of financial relations for the Ampex Corporation in nearby Redwood City. Ampex, makers of both

---

*Jack Temple would soon associate himself with hospitals as a professional fundraiser.

home and professional tape-recording equipment, was responsible for many technical advancements in television, and the
Blacks watched more than their share of broadcasts on their set.
Four of Shirley's early films—*Heidi, Wee Willie Winkie, Captain
January* and *Rebecca of Sunnybrook Farm*—had been released to
television. Along with her own children, millions of people were
seeing her as the child she had been, not the woman she now
was. Shirley began to put out "feelers." Perhaps "she couldn't
resist wanting to bring herself up-to-date publicly," one friend
explained.

Another old-time Hollywood acquaintance comments, "I
think she did it [picked up her career] to finally exorcise her
feelings of failing Gertrude. This guilt always was a shadow on
her present happiness. To 'quit at the top' meant she had to get
back up there again. Then there was Charlie's family. They
didn't think much about her Hollywood years. They would have
been more impressed if she had been a Nob Hill debutante.
They weren't really snobs. In fact, they were good, intelligent
people. But I suspect anyone connected with the making of
movies or television—excluding the kind of research and scien-
tific work Charlie's company did—seemed demimondaine to
them. Shirley more than likely chaffed at this and needed to
prove that she could be a star *and* a lady.

"Then, too, I think the 'exurban life' as she called it, was
beginning to bore the hell out of her. Charlie is what one might
call 'a quiet type,' very solid. Life in Washington had been exciting. Atherton was a whole other ballgame."

Work was all Shirley had known for her first twenty-one
years, and it had given her tremendous self-control and self-
discipline and a keen, well-trained memory. As a child star, she
had learned how to concentrate on several things at once. "We
had to memorize lines, go to school, and shoot scenes almost
simultaneously with hammers and ringing bells and lights being
set up and all the usual confusion of a movie set," Diana Serra
Cary recalls. This ability to succeed on several levels under the
most pressing conditions had become part of Shirley's life.

By 1957, she had been "retired" for eight years. The Blacks
lived well, but modestly and within Charles's income. Shirley
had a great reluctance to use the money that had been invested
for her by George and Gertrude and the court's decree. And

even though she wished to return to work, of one thing she was certain—she would never go back to Hollywood full time.

Lori, at three, seemed to have inherited her song-and-dance talents and prattled about "being a movie-star."

"Yes, Lori is crazy about acting," Shirley told an interviewer, "but because she is *my* daughter she is not going to lose the *whole* life she is living now, the love and joy and fun of being part of a warm family group, for the one-sided life of being a celebrity. Not until she is old enough to know what she is doing, anyway." The determination behind these words glaringly exposed Shirley's feelings of pain and deprivation in her own childhood. Why then would she want to subject herself to more of the same, only in reverse—the parent being torn away from the family circle?

Shirley's will had always been formidable. She was convinced a Hollywood production company could be made to employ her services in Atherton, just as in her youth the Majors' girls and Mary Lou Islieb had been induced to come to play at her house. When she was actually approached, a compromise was achieved. But she still managed to protect her active role as homemaker at the same time that she picked up the reins on her career.

At a testimonial dinner given by AFTRA,* which she attended because of Charles's association with Ampex, she met the honoree, Henry Jaffe, a producer of *Producers' Showcase,* a series of television specials that had known five years of continued critical acclaim. One of Jaffe's most successful shows had been a production of *Peter Pan.* Shirley mentioned that she had once been considered for the role of Tinkerbell. They discussed the impact of fairy tales on the lives of children.

"After all," she later mused, "as a child I lived in a storybook world; it was like living in books instead of just reading them. I was Heidi in Switzerland, Wee Willie Winkie in India, the Little Princess in England, and [in *The Littlest Rebel*] I got to sit on Abraham Lincoln's knee."

The meeting spurred Jaffe; and he and the executive producer for his company, William Phillipson, put their heads together and came up with an idea for a weekly one-hour playhouse that would retell classic children's stories and star

---

*Associated Federation of Television and Radio Artists, an actors union

Shirley. Phillipson, a man of considerable persuasive charm, was on the telephone almost daily to Shirley trying to convince her to sign with them. "I had other TV offers, lots of them," Shirley claimed, "but Bill Phillipson just kept after me until I had to at least give it serious consideration." The idea "really appealed" to her because, as she admitted, she was "a pushover for fairy-tales."

Family councils with all the children present were a continuing feature of life in the Blacks' Atherton household. Usually, the subject of these sessions had to do with the younger Blacks' recent behavior and their individual and current wishes. This time, the topic posed was: "Does Mommy go to Hollywood and stay there to act in a lot of television shows?" The decision was: "No, Mommy goes there once a month and *only* tells the story. She can only act herself in a couple of them." Shirley claimed that Lori's vote first went for her acting in all the stories; but when she explained this would mean her absence from home all week long, the little girl promptly reversed herself.

Shirley relayed her decision to Jaffe: She would narrate a series to be called *Shirley Temple's Storybook* and would appear in no more than one of the stories every four months. Her other stipulation was that the narrations should be done in San Francisco.

Henry Jaffe dispatched another of his associates, Alvin Cooperman, to Atherton to convince her that all segments of the show had to be shot in Hollywood. "I told Shirley what we had in mind," Cooperman recalled. "It was just the kind of show she approved of and we just sat there and talked it over." Cooperman finally agreed on a monthly format that simulated *Producers' Showcase*. Seven shows a year would be telecast as "specials," preempting scheduled programs. Her narration would be filmed in three days, her acting parts would be separated by four months. Approval of these scripts and a generous percentage of the gross would be given her. To Cooperman's amazement, "she got out her typewriter. We worked out a one-page contract. Shirley didn't have an agent, and she laughingly suggested maybe she should call her lawyers. When one page sounded right to her, she just sat right down and signed it on the bridge table in her living room."

"I'm a lawyer," marveled Jaffe, "but if I needed a lawyer I'd take Shirley." The final deal called for her to receive one hundred thousand dollars per episode, plus 25 percent of the profits.

Even with their mother working, the children's lives changed very little. A live-in housekeeper, Margaret, who "did just about everything, except plan the menus," was added to the household. Susan attended private school nearby and Lori and Charlie a local nursery school. Except for her days in Hollywood, Shirley drove them to school and Charles to the office and fetched her family later in the day. She continued her charity work and entertained as frequently as before, with buffet dinners that she supervised. Added to her former schedule were the reading and selection of stories for the series. Once the show got under way, there were fittings for the gowns Don Loper designed, the memorization of her lines and fan mail to be answered. Inclined to be a bit chubby, she had to slim down 15 pounds and maintain her weight at 102 pounds.

From January 1958 through December 1958, in a revised format, Shirley narrated sixteen and acted in three segments of *Shirley Temple's Storybook* for NBC, some of which were taped while others were filmed live. "Dreams Are Made for Children," the theme song, written by Mack David and Jerry Livingston, was sung by Shirley to open and close the programs. For each segment she wore a different fanciful ball gown—suitable for Glinda the Good Witch in *The Wizard of Oz*—while poised on a movable bicycle seat hidden by her dress and anchored on a pole in the center of a platform designed to resemble a floating cloud.

Backed by a comfortable mixture of sponsors (Sealtest dairies, Hills Brothers coffee and Breck shampoo), Jaffe mounted the opening show, "Beauty and the Beast," in color and with opulent care. The production starred Claire ("the Old Vic's delicate") Bloom and Charlton Heston. "Shirley felt that Beauty did not change character enough as the show progressed, so we did quite a lot of rewriting [of Joseph Schrank's adaptation]," said Norman Lessing, the story editor. "We sent [the script] to her as a matter of course. But . . . she came up with some good ideas; I don't know whether they were intuitive or the products of her measured thinking, but they were always incisive. She had such good taste and such a sense of fitness of things that [thereafter] we consulted her on many things that didn't concern her."

As a television series debut, the enduring moral fable had been a critical success, lauded for its faithfulness to the original and its "disarming simplicity."

Shirley's first acting role was in the third show of the series— "The Legend of Sleepy Hollow"—as the flirtatious Dutch woman Katrina Van Tassel. The show was shot live, which required ten days' preparation, and Shirley had her lines memorized on the first day of rehearsal. Her narrations won her more praise than her performance, which received negative reviews. Several critics pointed out the poor judgment employed in her use of a low Dutch dialect. But Cooperman countered, "She had all the warmth and laughter in her voice that the series needed. She was the story-teller telling stories to her children. Nobody [could have been] better."

Jaffe thoughtfully added, "There were unexplored depths in Shirley as an actress, dancer and singer. But to plumb those depths would take time, and Shirley didn't want to be tied up in her new career for more than a few days a month."

In the Christmas 1958 presentation of "Mother Goose," Elsa Lanchester starred and Shirley appeared, pleasantly enough, as Polly-Put-the-Kettle-On. This show also provided an opportunity for her three children to make their professional acting debuts, directed by Mitchell Leisen.* These appearances turned out to be their last. Little Charlie had one line as a lookout on top of a Maypole: "I see him coming. It's the Prince, the Prince." There wasn't enough excitement in his voice to please Leisen, and he asked Shirley if she could get a little more projection from him.

"You've got to act *excited*, Charlie," she called out to him.

The six-year-old looked down from his position on the pole and said, "I'm getting tired sitting up here, Mamma."

"You're the one who wanted to be on TV," Shirley archly replied.†

After several more wooden repeats of his line, "a pathetic, forced round of applause was led by his mother." Gertrude, still referring to Shirley as "Presh," hovered close by in a brief re-

---

*More notable television debuts in "Mother Goose" were made by the young Joel Grey (as Jack of "Jack and Jill") and Rod McKuen (as Simple Simon).

†Charlie was paid $570 for his part; Lori and Susan each the minimum $80 for one day's work as extras.

turn to "stage motherdom" and was more critical, her hands remaining by her sides. During the rehearsals for "Mother Goose," "a stagehand said the word 'shit' . . . and Shirley had him fired. 'This is a show for children,' she explained to a dumfounded cast—since no children including her own were present at the incident."

The show was extremely successful and prompted one critic to write, "It proved once again that [Shirley Temple] could, if she wanted to, steal Christmas from Tiny Tim."

Her renewed popularity presented her with a rare business opportunity. She persuaded the Ideal Toy Company to manufacture a new version of the old Shirley Temple doll. When a visitor was shown one of the new dolls, she said proudly, "That was *my* deal."

"She drives a hard bargain," said one business associate. "She is frugal almost, but not quite, to the point of being cheap." B. F. Michtom, president of the Ideal Toy Company, remembered receiving a call from Shirley in 1958. "Hello, Mr. Michtom," she said in a clear, warm voice. "This is Shirley Temple Black. Do you remember me?" She then informed him of the series she was doing for television and of the release of her old films for TV. "This strikes me as a good time to bring the doll out again," she told him. Michtom agreed, and within six months the company had sold over three hundred thousand dolls. On behalf of her "doll interests," Shirley made personal appearances in department stores, autographing dolls for those who bought them. Her presence in Macy's New York store was a near riot. She also made a deal with Rosenau Brothers, a manufacturer of children's clothing, to put out a new version of the Shirley Temple "Baby, Take a Bow" dress, and with Random House publishers for three books of collected fairy tales that carried her name.* She made two West Coast appearances

---

*The first Random House book, *The Shirley Temple Storybook*, sold over 125,000 copies between publication date, October 6, 1958, and Christmas of that year. The two other books, *Shirley Temple's Fairyland* and *Shirley Temple's Stories that Never Grow Old*, sold one hundred thousand copies each over that same period. In addition to the books, the Shirley Temple dolls made by the Ideal Toy Company and the dresses by Rosenau, there were also a Shirley Temple coloring book, published by Saalfield; Shirley Temple hats (manufactured by Richard Englander); coats (Brambury); handbags for children (Pyramid); doll-clothes patterns (Advance and Simplicity); and a toy Shirley Temple TV theater. Shirley controlled the licensing rights in all these product enterprises.

in book departments of the Emporium in San Francisco and the May Company in Los Angeles. Both scenes were mayhem, with mobs of between four thousand and six thousand "hysterical fans lining her route from her car to the book department where some stood on counters just to get a look at her." After autographing about thirteen hundred books in each store, she was escorted through the crowds by several burly detectives.

"I think Shirley's hobby is business," commented an admiring NBC official. Her attorney, Deane Johnson of Los Angeles, shared this view. "You only have to tell her once," he observed. "She retains and understands everything."

Her interest in politics returned, and in the 1960 presidential campaign she became precinct captain for San Mateo County in Richard M. Nixon's race against John F. Kennedy. She was extremely adept at getting out the vote. Nixon won the county and California, but lost the election.

Her codes were strict and simple. Her life was led in "Quaker black and white." When she took Lori's third-grade class to a movie, *My Dog Buddy,* touted as suitable for children, she marched them out of it after ten minutes. "Right off," she explained, "the parents of the family were killed in a head-on auto collision, their little boy seriously injured, and Buddy took off for the hills. I was furious. I blistered the manager, and wrote a letter to the producer."

Dinner at the Blacks remained a six o'clock ritual, with all children present. "You have to arrive at five-thirty to count on a drink first," one dinner guest commented. "We all talk together about *any* subject," Shirley said, "taking turns as chairman. Puppies, politics, religion or Bach. We want our children to know the art of old-fashioned conversation."

The well-disciplined life was natural to her. "Even as a baby," Gertrude recalled, "Shirl had an unusual seriousness about her. I always have to ask her permission to talk to interviewers and she sizes everybody up very thoroughly." Shirley acknowledged, "I have a mean eye. I don't like people who read stories about me to know where the children go to school or what day the maid is off. Mixed-up fans still come around. . . . A man came to the door the other day [1961] and said he'd married me in 1940 and sold his stamp collection to get here. One of my brothers [Jack] is an FBI agent and when we called

him [after the stranger had been dispatched coolly by Shirley]
we found he had been a child molester."

The last television segment she filmed for Jaffe* was completed in March 1961 and shown later that year. She made a
guest appearance on *The Red Skelton Show* the following year
singing "By the Beautiful Sea" and a few bars of "Side by Side"
with Skelton, appearing opposite him as a snobbish society girl
in a comic sketch. "Skelton held back his usual ribald antics
during Shirley's appearance because she seemed so poised and
ladylike. I don't think he was very comfortable," observed one
stagehand. A more successful variety-show appearance was her
guest spot on *The Dinah Shore Show* a few months later.

Christmas, 1963, found the Blacks in a new, larger and more
expensive English Tudor house that they had built on Lakeview
Drive in Woodside (an area one journalist called "a hotbed of
rest"), a short distance from Atherton. Shirley had brought the
Oriental contents of the old house with her, and since her color
schemes remained the same, the transition to the new house had
not been jarring. Woodside was an elegant community, a
"haven of rolling hills and shrouded woods." The well-to-do
were originally attracted to Woodside by the woodlands and
hundreds of vineyard acres. In the early nineteenth century,
Woodside's old La Questa Winery exported its famous cabernet
sauvignon to many of the major cities in Europe. By the turn of
the century, the small town contained the mansions of coffee
millionaire James Folger, spice baron August Schilling and William Bourne, heir to the Spring Valley Water Company. For the
Blacks, Woodside's narrow and private country lanes, where the
children could safely ride bicycles and horses, had been a tremendous attraction. With under five thousand inhabitants, the
town lay on the eastern slope of the Santa Cruz Mountains,
halfway between the Pacific Ocean and San Francisco Bay, and
was without industries except for several commercial orchards,
farms and boarding stables with riding schools.

Shirley's last foray into television was made in January 1965,
at Twentieth Century-Fox. Steel-and-glass skyscrapers had re-

---

*After the sixteen *Shirley Temple Storybook* segments had been made, Jaffe had
changed the title to *Shirley Temple Theater*. Nine more programs were filmed with a
broader format that encompassed more than adaptations of classic children's stories.

placed the old Shirley Temple sound stages, as a new generation of film executives ground out "more footage for television than for theaters." Her bungalow had gone through many transformations, and was now the studio dispensary. Shirley shot a television pilot, *Go Fight City Hall,* a situation comedy in the format of the successful *Mary Tyler Moore Show* featuring Shirley as a social worker employed by the Department of Public Assistance, a young woman fighting equally for her own independence and the rights of others. Her co-stars were Jack Kruschen and Bill Hayes.

When Shirley arrived at the studio for the first day of filming, she was greeted by a huge red-and-gold-lettered "Welcome home, Shirley" banner furled across the front gate. A champagne party was held in the commissary "with old friends and studio executives." Klammie, her former tutor, was present, but, in fact, there were not too many familiar faces. Zanuck, after a boardroom war, had lost his position as head of production to his young son, Richard. A spokesman had choked out the painful truth: "If there had not been a Shirley Temple, there would not be a Twentieth Century-Fox today."

Somebody else had stood up to remember "the party given in 1935 to celebrate the sensational merger of Fox and Twentieth Century. At one point," the old-timer recalled, "I happened to pick Shirley up in fun, and a horrible silence fell on the room. The bankers from New York turned white. Here I was holding practically all the assets of the company in my two hands. I was so scared I nearly dropped her."

Returning to the studio proved most difficult for Shirley, who, in face of the drastic changes, was a complete stranger.

Since the show was unable to attract a sponsor, only one episode of *Go Fight City Hall* was filmed. Gertrude stood by on the sidelines during the last day of shooting. "[I could see Shirley] was so tired and anxious to get home—Charles always meets her. But she said, 'Mom, I loved it. I loved it all,' and you could see it in her eyes. Why, her eyes were dancing." The light Gertrude detected could well have been generated by a new source of energy.

With the popularity of her television series, Shirley had been in great demand as a guest speaker at various fund-raising affairs for the National Multiple Sclerosis Society and for the Republican party, as well as at college graduations, where a good, upright person—highly visible, of strong moral character and intelligence—was a requisite. At the start of this new public side of her life, she accepted only engagements close to home. But by the time *Go Fight City Hall* failed, she was traveling as far as Texas. The issues she chose to discuss had more to do with conservative politics than with homely matters or the subject of women's careers: Waste in government spending and saving the environment were two of her favorite topics. Her two years in Washington had been a fine training ground for what she now considered her calling—politics. The desire came to her, she claimed, on a flight home from a speech given in Houston, Texas. She felt she had something important to say and an ability to put her ideas into action.

In October 1964, Ronald Reagan had come to San Francisco during the key days of the Republican presidential nominations to give his famous "A Time for Choosing" speech in support of Barry Goldwater. Reagan's own political viability was attracting a great many supporters among Republican party leaders, and another of Shirley's old co-stars, George Murphy, had successfully made the transition from actor to senator from California. The notion that she could join them as actor-turned-politician greatly appealed to her. Now, she had to sell Charles and the children on the idea. Then she had to look around for a *modus operandi*—a bit like an actor in search of the right role.

SHIRLEY HAD MET Soviet Premier Nikita Khrushchev at a reception in San Francisco during his second visit to the United States in the autumn of 1960, which perhaps had ushered in a more amicable relationship between the two powers. She remembered that after a "teary" recognition of who she was, he had roared, " 'I'll have you kidnapped.' He grabbed my arms and pulled me against his chest. I told Dick Nixon, his chest was so hard—it felt just like steel—he must have had on a bullet-proof vest." Khrushchev had gone on to inform her that Shirley Temple films had been popular in Russia and that her name was still known there.

American-Soviet relations took a remarkable turn for the better in 1963. The new spirit was known as detente, and was born in the afterglow of the Moscow Agreement signed by President John F. Kennedy and Premier Khrushchev, which banned nuclear testing in the atmosphere, in outer space, or under water, and was hailed as a major step toward those goals.

Through her work with the National Multiple Sclerosis Society she had heard that the Soviets had developed advanced techniques for treating the disease. Sonny's condition was swiftly deteriorating, and by Christmas 1964 he was confined to a wheelchair. Khrushchev was no longer the Soviet premier, but her meeting with him in 1960 had made Shirley confident that she would be well received if she ever chose to visit Russia. Plans were put into motion, visas applied for. Her aim was to find out if the Soviets had a medication not available in the West that could reverse Sonny's illness or at worst prevent his further decline. She and Charles would travel under the auspices of the

National Multiple Sclerosis Society, their main goal being to interest the Russians in sharing an international research program for the disease.

A week before the Blacks were to depart, Charles's father was taken to Presbyterian Medical Center in San Francisco when the cancer he had been valiantly fighting for over two years reached a critical stage. Shirley and Charles were set to cancel their trip, but Mr. Black insisted they not do so. They departed on March 14 for London, where they planned to spend a week before continuing on to Moscow. Shirley had never been "east of Bermuda," and she hoped to do a little sight-seeing. To her amazement, she was greeted at the Tower of London by sixty girls in school uniforms who had seen her early films in recent reissue. Wherever she went, she was mobbed, causing her to cancel many of her planned outings. But she did have the opportunity to collect the money, and the considerable interest that had accrued on it, from her successful childhood libel action against *Night and Day* magazine and Graham Greene.

Moscow was like no other city she had ever visited—a great metropolis and at the same time an overgrown village—its ornate skyscrapers dwarfing its onion-domed churches, its grand-scale avenues trailing off into muddy lanes. In March, the city was bitter cold. The great walls of the Kremlin—a city within a city—emerged "like phantoms from the mist and snow."

Khrushchev—now removed from office and replaced by Premier Aleksey Kosygin—may have recognized her name, but from the moment Shirley set foot on Russian soil, she knew winning over the Russians would not be easy. In the United States, Mr. Khrushchev, jaunty and plebeian, had seemed approachable. But in Russia, several days of attempting, through diplomatic channels, to arrange a meeting with him brought no results. Taking the matter into her own hands, Shirley, with a translator's help, prepared a card telling him of her presence in Moscow, her reasons for being there, and her wish that they might be able to exchange a few words. Then, escorted by a member of the American embassy staff, she drove to the ex-premier's apartment building. As she started up the stairs, she was stopped by a caretaker-guard. Eventually, an English-speaking Russian appeared and promised to deliver her card to Khrushchev. She waited for a reply, but was finally asked to leave.

She fared better in contacting the Russian neurologist who was said to have a new method for treating multiple sclerosis. The mission, however, was disappointing; for the same methods had been used in the West for years. However, the neurologist did promise to join in an international research program for the disease.* After a visit of one week (which included a tour of a Moscow film studio), the Blacks flew to Amsterdam, where they learned that James Black had died on January 20. Since he had requested there be no funeral or memorial service, they remained abroad for a few days as planned before continuing home.

When Shirley returned from her Russian pilgrimage, she increased the number of her speaking engagements at fund-raising rallies, many of them out of state, on behalf of the Republican party. Her travels seemed to have heightened her patriotism and made her more aware of her country's "uniqueness." Lori, her youngest, pert and inclined to mimicry, was eleven. Charlie, tall and lean at thirteen, was attending military school. Susan (now legally Susan Black, having recently been adopted by Charles), looking very much a stylish young debutante, had graduated from high school and been given a splashy coming-out party, covered by *Life* magazine. Shirley gave this event much personal attention, supervising Susan's hairdo, the selection of her gown and all details of the celebration. The children were now more self-reliant. Shirley's visibility and interests broadened, as she decided the time was right for her to embark again on a career in public life.

Decorating no longer held the same charm for her. And although her work on behalf of multiple sclerosis had not slackened, she was now drawn to activities and committeework inside the Republican party. Charles, she mused proudly, "is the kind of husband who pushes me out the door. He likes me to get involved. He urges me on." A witness adds, "While Charles certainly encouraged her to get involved in politics, international affairs and diplomacy, Shirley was strong-willed enough to want to make it on her own."

With the Vietnam War accelerating, crude, hard-fisted Lyndon Johnson in the White House and large-scale student vio-

---

*The program was eventually called the International Federation of Multiple Sclerosis Societies.

lence (which had begun at Berkeley in the summer of 1964) practically in her backyard—Shirley had a wealth of material to draw upon for her speeches. She attacked monolithic government with its "disastrous cycle of tax, spend, inflation and deficit," and declared that "private will has been eroded and personal initiative derided . . . and much of the rising cost of government [is the result of] back-filling the holes it has dug with public largesse." Assailing lack of leadership at the executive level, she contended that in Washington "problems aren't solved; they're subsidized." She would use statistics to make her point: Five times as many people were now on welfare as during the Depression; the Vietnam War was more than quadrupling the number of bombs dropped by the Allies in all of World War II, with every enemy killed costing three hundred thousand dollars; major crime had increased 62 percent in six years; riots had accounted for a quarter-billion dollars property damage in 1966; and federal spending had risen 14,000 percent in the last fifty years. Her arguments, delivery and impressive figures bore an amazing likeness to those of Ronald Reagan.

Reagan had run successfully for governor of California in 1966, and Shirley had been a diligent worker in his campaign. (Once, in her childhood, she had remarked, "God is the most important person in the world and the Governor of California is second.") Out of moral conviction, she had resigned from the San Francisco Film Festival Committee's 1966 presentations in protest of the entry of the Swedish film *Night Games*, * which she called "pornography for profit." Early in 1967, she became a vigorous advocate of charging California students tuition at the state university because she believed "they would appreciate their education more if they paid for it."

She was a speaker in search of a platform, and when a congressional seat was vacated by the death of Representative J. Arthur Younger of California's Eleventh District, San Mateo County, of which she was resident, she found it.†

Younger had seen Shirley, a long-standing acquaintance, at

---

*A naturalistic film about children's covert sexual explorations

†Jesse Arthur Younger was born April 11, 1893, in Albany, Oregon, and did not move to San Mateo County until 1937, as executive vice-president of Citizens Federal Savings and Loan Association in San Francisco. He had been elected as a Republican to the Eighty-third through the Ninetieth Congresses (January 3, 1953–June 20, 1967).

the Woodside Country Club on Easter Sunday, March 26, 1967. The elderly conservative was suffering from leukemia, and was aware that he had limited time. During the course of the afternoon, he sought Shirley out for a few private moments of conversation. Shirley later said that Congressman Younger had asked her to run for his seat in the event of his death. On June 21, less than three months afterward, Younger died.

Shirley had been a member of Governor Reagan's Finance Committee and one of his appointees to the state's Advisory Hospital Council, a top-level job. The council made recommendations about which communities would receive state hospital funds, and Shirley considered this a toehold into California's Republican politics. Very soon after Younger's death, she intimated that she might enter the race for his congressional seat, in a special primary election slated for November 14. She quickly drew back from this idea, and not until August 29, after four local Republican leaders had already declared themselves and obtained pledges of support, did she confirm her candidacy.* From that moment, Shirley's life and that of her family were overtaken by election fever. Not since seventy-one Texans had ponied up fifty dollars each to file for Lyndon Johnson's vacant Senate seat in 1961 had American politics seen anything like the congressional contest of California's Eleventh District. By the close of filing, twelve candidates—seven Democrats and five Republicans—"representing every shade of [the] political spectrum, were in the race." One Republican candidate, clergyman Gregory K. Sims, revealed a sense of both humor and how the race would be run by arriving for the filing ceremony in a brightly colored hot-air balloon called "Good Ship *Gregory*" (he later withdrew from the race). The contest was to be conducted as eleven male candidates against "The Good Ship *Lollipop*." Jest though they might, Shirley's presence in the race presented an awesome challenge to her opponents.

Still held dear to the hearts of movie-going millions, her ability to fund-raise well established, Shirley, from the start,

---

*The other Republican candidates to declare were: Paul N. McCloskey (thirty-nine), Portola Valley lawyer and decorated Korean War veteran; Robert Barry (fifty-two), Woodside businessman and former two-term Congressman from New York; William H. Draper III (thirty-nine), Atherton investment executive; and Earl B. Whitmore (forty-nine), San Mateo County sheriff.

seemed "the odds-on favorite to become the third former movie star to win high office in California in the last two years."* A close observer added, "She is also smart as paint, tough-minded and highly professional, with the devilish charm of a cunning Lucifer-child asking to stay up till nine."

She announced that she would run for Congress at "one of the biggest gatherings of newspaper, radio and TV reporters in the Bay Area since General Douglas MacArthur's return." Sixteen television cameras, twenty-five microphones and over fifty reporters from all over the country recorded the announcement made in the meeting room and restaurant of the Villa Chartier Motel. In a smart linen suit worn with striking jade accessories, she stood poised and cool before the battery of newsmen while a barrage of tough questions was shouted at her. When asked if she believed her movie background would give her an unwarranted political edge, she replied, "Not all actors should be in politics and not all haberdashers should be President," a pointed reference to former Democratic president Harry S Truman. She referred to Lyndon Johnson's Great Society as "a pretty bad movie which has become a great flop," and blamed Johnson for "a lack of leadership in preventing Negro riots."†

Discussing the war in Vietnam, she insisted that the United States had to honor its commitment: "We have to keep the Communists of North Vietnam from taking over South Vietnam." She added that she believed the president should rely more on the Joint Chiefs of Staff in conducting the war "and less on Defense Secretary Robert S. McNamara . . . It is not progress for the largest, strongest military power in the world to be mired down in an apparently endless war with one of the smallest and weakest countries in the world." She was not above using her acting technique to make a point when she then glanced over to young Charlie, dressed in his military-school uniform and seated beside his sisters and father, and remarked, "and I am the mother of a 15-year old boy who will soon be eligible for service in Vietnam."

She appeared unthreatened by her aggressive inquisitors,

---

*Reagan and Murphy were the two obvious others, although John Lodge, who had played Temple's father in *The Little Colonel*, had also gone into politics, to become governor of the state of Connecticut (1950–54).

†That year had seen a rash of violent eruptions in the black ghettos of Detroit, the Watts section of Los Angeles and in Cleveland.

and her mature beauty should have put an end to the taunts that "little Shirley Temple was running for Congress." But the nation would not allow her to divest herself of the past.

At the time Shirley started on the campaign trail, *Curley McDimple,* a theatrical spoof of her most famous roles, opened off-Broadway, and a three-foot poster showing Little Miss Marker garbed in a leather jacket sold in the tens of thousands across the country. A satire of her as a child, performed by Carol Burnett on television, was to become a classic comic sketch. Shirley was in danger of progressing from living legend to high-camp heroine. She had every right to be "half-mad, alcoholic and suicidal with the obsessed, narcissistic arrogance of the once-adored," but she was doggedly none of these. She had never surrounded herself with sycophants nor lived on memories of times gone by; she had taken her life into her own hands.

Nothing in Shirley's career had prepared her for the utter ruthlessness of an American political campaign. Her mother, the studio, her financial security and her own celebrity had all shielded her from harsh reality. Even at the time of her unhappy marriage to Agar, her lawyer had gone to her house to ask her husband to leave while Shirley awaited his departure in her parents' home. The press, always anxious for any story she might give them, was often relentless, but not until she entered politics had the media ever been unkind. Even the controversial Graham Greene article had been directed at the studio's *use* of her nubile seductiveness, and not at Shirley herself.

That spring, she had discussed with Reagan the possibility of her running, and he had intimated his support. But by the time she had announced her candidacy, he was hard on the campaign trail for the 1968 presidential elections and had left the state and his office almost entirely in the hands of his attorney general. Richard Nixon was revving up his forces to beat Reagan for the Republican nomination. Neither of these men could afford to get involved in a party contest that promised to be controversial, since the San Mateo Republican candidates represented all factions of their party. For Reagan, there was the added danger of associating himself perhaps too closely with his motion-picture past. Congress had convened, and George Murphy was busily occupied in Washington. Even had he been available to extend his help, he might well have been reticent, for Shirley had refused to endorse his candidacy (on grounds that she was not a politician) at the time of his own campaign.

That Shirley had no close friends or advisers with practical political knowledge would seem to have demanded she hire one of the several California public-relations firms that specialized in election campaigns. But by custom, she was against the use of outsiders in all business and career matters. During Shirley's last years in films, Gertrude had blamed her daughter's decline in popularity on the theatrical agency that represented her. Retired now with George to Palm Desert, Gertrude could not have helped her daughter in the political arena even if she had been available. Shirley turned to Charles, who, after all, had encouraged her to toss her hat into the ring. The choice was unfortunate. Charles was no more savvy about the chicanery and demands of politics than Shirley was, and no one could quite believe she had been foolish enough to make him her campaign manager.

"Just a few days after Shirley entered the race," a Woodside lawyer recalled, "I saw Charlie and strongly advised him to get professional help. I even recommended a firm with a solid reputation for this sort of thing. But he was determined to keep the campaign a family matter. I believe he thought it was a better choice for Shirley's image, that she would have more voter appeal as a woman out there on her own, except for her husband's support. As I recall, there were no other women running congressional races at that time. At least not in northern California. This could only help her chances. And at the start, she damned well stood a good chance. I know she scared the hell out of the Democrats when she announced.

"The general public has this concept of her drawn from her film and television career. I mean [as a child], she had been a most compassionate and loving figure, much put upon by conservative and reactionary forces. And it had been a few years since they had seen her [on TV as host of The Shirley Temple Theater] as a grown woman. In the intervening years, she had greatly matured. The fairy godmother look had suddenly become a bit jowly. It was going to take some doing to convince the voters that this lady was Shirley Temple, or to prove to them that her lack of experience as a politician in no way diminished her ability to represent them with spirited rightness.

"Well, she marched right into this lion's den certain that she could tame the opposition and win the hearts of the crowd. But everything she said and did was all wrong. Voters who had been brought up on little Shirley Temple didn't like to face the fact that she had grown up to become a member of the same reactionary forces she had so valiantly fought [in her movies] as a child. To add to this stumbling block, her credibility was successfully attacked by her opponents—both Republicans and Democrats—in the earliest days of the campaign."

When Shirley publicly stated that Congressman Younger had asked her to run, Mrs. Younger immediately stepped forward. "If he did encourage her, he did so in jest," the widow asserted. A former Younger aide was quoted as saying, "She's trying to get an endorsement out of a dead man." Then, after Shirley's vehement declaration that "little Shirley Temple" was not running for anything, she turned around and changed the name on her voter's registration from Shirley Jane Black to Shirley Temple Black.

Further trouble plagued her when she alleged that former President Eisenhower had said he "was all for Shirley Temple" (a comment made much earlier and in relation to her work on Reagan's campaign.) Shirley proudly added that his endorsement was "a great honor." Eisenhower's aide, Brigadier General Robert L. Schulz, replied to the press that "General Eisenhower has no intention of getting involved in California politics. He is perfectly certain that voters of the 11th District need no outside advice in selecting their candidate for Congress."

For the primary on November 14, the voters of California's Eleventh District were to choose one Democrat and one Republican candidate. The runoff between the two party winners was to be held on December 12, and whoever the Republican might be, one thing was certain. He or she had to swing enough registered Democrats to the Republican side to carry the election, for Democrats outnumbered Republicans in this contest by twenty thousand registered voters.* Of the four men in her party that

---

*San Mateo County's Eleventh District had in 1967's registration 117,862 Democrats, 96,972 Republicans and 7,127 miscellaneous registrants, making the total 221,-961. Though the district was historically Republican, student voters registered heavily as Democrats—and this was the time of student revolt in nearby universities.

she had to overtake, Paul "Pete" McCloskey was a most formidable opponent.

"Well," laughed one resident of California's Eleventh, "here you had Shirley Temple on one hand and Jimmy Stewart on the other. Of course, Pete McCloskey was Irish, and in fact, looked a little like John Kennedy. But he had the kind of dedicated humbleness that the characters Stewart portrayed in pictures had—*Mr. Smith Goes to Washington*—that sort of thing."

Pete McCloskey was a self-styled country lawyer with a scholarly bent. His great-grandfather, an Irish immigrant, had landed in San Francisco in 1853. Pete was the first McCloskey born in southern California (in 1927 in San Bernardino). By Depression standards, the McCloskeys were not poor, but they could hardly have been called rich. At age eight, Pete became critically ill with nephritis. His two-year recovery was a drain on the family's finances, and he felt responsible for their subsequent pinched circumstances.

His illness had set him behind other boys his age both athletically and scholastically. When finally able to return to school, "too awkward to make the [baseball] team," he persisted at batting practice for hours after classes each day and eventually "wound up as the team's best hitter." The same perseverance marked his studies. When war came, he joined the navy's V-5 Pilot Training Program. To his great disappointment, he was not sent overseas. Upon his discharge, he attended Stanford University on the federal and California G.I. Bill, which instilled in him a sense of obligation to the taxpayers who had made his education possible. He continued on at the Stanford Law School, augmenting his G.I. Bill by working hard at a variety of menial jobs.

About this time, he joined the Marine Reserves and, shortly afterward, he was married. With the advent of the Korean War, he requested and was granted overseas service, much to his pregnant wife's distress. On February 16, 1951, the day his daughter was born in Palo Alto, Second Lieutenant McCloskey of the 5th Marine Regiment, 1st Division, landed in Korea. Three months later, while commanding a mortar platoon, he was wounded. Nonetheless, "he continued to lead the assault and personally attacked enemy-held bunkers, knocking them out." For his "daring initiative, aggressive determination and inspiring leadership responsible for the success of the attack," he was awarded the prestigious Navy Cross (outranked only by the Congressional Medal of Honor). And still he remained at the front. In June, shortly after he recovered from his injury, he led a rifle platoon in support of a tank patrol. Eight of his men fell: "McCloskey put the balance of his platoon under cover then crawled through fire to administer first-aid to the wounded. In the process he was severely injured in the leg, but continued to treat his men." For this act of bravery, he was awarded a second medal, the Silver Star, and returned to Palo Alto at Christmas a true local hero.

Admitted to the State Bar of California in 1953, he became what he claimed had always been his dream—"a small-town lawyer." An observer noted, "McCloskey loved the law. He had always nursed defensive feelings on behalf of the underdog and increasingly he sharpened an old and fundamental view of himself as a righter of wrongs." To the despair of the partners in his law firm,* he consistently "handled no-fee cases for juveniles, the indigent, and impoverished groups." His popularity in San Mateo County burgeoned. He became president of the Palo Alto Bar Association and the Stanford Area Youth Club. He was named Young Man of the Year by the Chamber of Commerce in 1961, an honor closely followed by his election as president of the Conference of Barristers of the State Bar of California.

The McCloskeys had been Republicans for generations. Pete was "devoted to the concept of private enterprise and fiscal conservatism. But in terms of humanitarianism and the role of government in society, his brand of Republicanism clearly stemmed from that of the nineteenth-century abolitionists . . . and the Theodore Roosevelt Progressives of 1912. . . . In a very real sense [he] was a manifestation of the progressive liberal Republicanism that [had always been] a part of California's political heritage." He had considered contesting the more conservative J. Arthur Younger in the 1966 G.O.P. primary, but was asked by party members not to do so. Instead, he decided to fight Younger in 1968, which meant organizing a campaign in 1967, before anyone knew about Younger's terminal illness. By the time Shirley declared on August 29, McCloskey's campaign had been in motion for nearly five months. Large sums of money had been raised in his behalf, and hundreds of persons were

---

*McCloskey, Wilson, Mosher and Marten

already actively involved in his campaign, which was being managed by one of the most experienced men in the business, Sanford Weiner, who had guided the successful election of George Murphy and more than sixty other California campaigns, winning 80 percent of them.

Weiner shifted gears in his handling of McCloskey after he watched Shirley's original press conference on television. "In the few seconds allotted [McCloskey] on the network coverage, Pete had violated every tenet of television . . . his head was characteristically cocked to one side, he scratched his ear, he looked alternately amused and disdainful, and he was magnificent! Whatever the camera angle, it was impossible to obtain a bad shot. McCloskey's natural restraint and manner and speech were superb for that medium." Weiner now moved from his original "grass-roots" concept (door-to-door visits, trips by the candidate to factories and supermarkets) to presenting McCloskey on televised debates and in prominent public appearances that would draw the attention of television newscasters.

Weiner immediately drafted a memo to McCloskey and the executive committee of his staff advising them not to attack Shirley Temple for being a movie star, and to remember that George Murphy's and Ronald Reagan's "good-guy" images on-screen had helped them. "If Shirley Temple was allowed to become a political princess, she would win." Therefore, her lack of qualification was the area to be attacked.

He went on to suggest they "exploit the female jealousy factor," further noting that "the female voter is apt to resent a glamorous figure doing and accomplishing things she would like to do herself." His other directives included:

1. "The image of McCloskey as the only moderate Republican in the race should remain."
2. "McCloskey should corner Shirley Temple on the issues of Vietnam, Civil rights, riot control, juvenile delinquency."
3. "McCloskey should be cast in the role of the underdog."
4. "All press releases . . . should stress McCloskey as the number one challenger [including Democrats] to Shirley Temple."
5. "She should be hit hard with the ultra-conservative label."

6. "Finally, in all planning it should be remembered that whereas Reagan and Murphy still looked and appealed to people as the actors they once were, Shirley Temple no longer looks like 'The Good Ship Lollipop.' "

Weiner's intent was to portray her as a rich, moralizing society matron. His next move was to hire a full-time press representative with media contacts outside the county and to raise an additional fifty thousand dollars in campaign funds. McCloskey already had secured one hundred thousand dollars in pledges, while Shirley at this juncture had about half that amount. Though she certainly could have managed to finance part of the campaign herself, Shirley was determined that all funds would come from pledged support.

With no personal experience of the scruffy tactics of a political campaign, and surrounded by a well-meaning but uninformed staff, Shirley began her congressional race hip-high in troubled waters. Charles did not so much run his wife's campaign as back her up and carry through her ideas while balancing the campaign budget. Based on the premise that her film career not be recalled to the voters' minds (the Shirley *Temple* Black being her only concession), her literature and brochures "depicted a glacial-faced, black-haired, austere clubwoman. Her red, white, black and blue color theme had her name superimposed with the slogan, 'Let us work to create, to build, to inspire.' " Weiner had been absolutely correct. The personality she projected to voters was not the effervescent, loving golden-haired child they fondly remembered. That image had been replaced by a wealthy society woman who "lectured people on immorality."

In her speeches and brochures, Shirley emphasized four main issues—escalation of the Vietnam War to ensure a swift victory, an end to crime in the streets, reduction of taxes for homeowners and a halt to the spread of pornography. She launched her campaign in something less than main-line splendor by appearing at local supermarkets and shopping centers and simply shaking hands. Her presence did not draw crowds, but Shirley was unconcerned. She had one advantage the other candidates lacked—instant recognition. Seldom had a congressional race received such broad-scale national coverage even though no new or revolutionary issues were at stake. The mere fact that Shirley Temple was a political aspirant was newsworthy enough to elicit major coverage in leading national weekly magazines, with photographs old and new of Shirley abounding. Along with the local *San Francisco Chronicle, The Wall Street Journal, The New York Times,* the *Chicago Tribune, The Los Angeles Times* and newspapers abroad all reported on the campaign. The Hub, a San Francisco movie house, ran a month-long Shirley Temple festival, Shirley's old films occupying just half of a nightly double feature. The second show each evening was *Night Games*—a choice that raised arch editorial comment in the press and on television. A San Francisco toy store displayed a window of the newest vinyl version of the Shirley Temple doll with the sign: "You wind it up and it runs for Congress."

By the end of September, Pete McCloskey's local TV spot commercials were being shown with frequency. The tall, dark, lean, good-looking candidate scratched his ear and smiled winningly as he peered directly into the camera and accused "Mrs. Black of wanting to escalate the war." When he stepped forward, one detected a slight limp, a token of his war injury. "I seek a meaningful negotiation." Voters were reminded of his service record and his moderate Vietnam position.

In contrast, when interviewed by a reporter from *Look* magazine, Shirley expounded her views on the sums of federal funds spent for rat control. "Is rat control really a job for the Federal government?" she asked, and quickly noted, "I'd like to know who counted the rats, anyway. It would be a wonderful cartoon, a little man ticking off a procession of scurrying rats. One. Two. Three."

Protest letters came pouring into *Look*'s editorial offices, and the editor printed a number of the most condemning. "Shirley Temple Black seems quite concerned about morality. She might begin by questioning the morality of . . . making jokes about controlling rats that bite hundreds of slum-dwellers' children each year." Another reader bluntly wrote, "The children in our slums may still await a spokesman, but fortunately the rats have found one."

Despite her statistical cramming and her abiding interest in medicine, Shirley seemed not to know that some 12,500 Americans infants living in slum conditions had been bitten by rats, that many of them had died from those attacks, that an estimated four hundred million dollars worth of foodstuffs had been ruined by the vermin. The rat problem was a most serious and growing national concern.

Shirley's attitudes exposed "a basic indelicacy born of insulation that stood glaringly revealed." Something had to be done quickly. "Charles pushed for backing Shirley up with some famous and well-loved celebrities," one of Shirley's campaign staff recalls. "We all thought that was wise, and Shirley agreed."

Bing Crosby was asked to join her finance committee. The Crosbys were nearby neighbors and members of the same golf club. The fact that Bing was helping in her campaign was not likely to downplay Shirley's Hollywood connections, but wherever Bing publicly appeared, press photographers were also present, and journalists did not have to look hard for a humorous quote.

Crosby was "a freshly registered Republican." One of his first endeavors as such was to host a hundred-dollar-a-plate dinner for Shirley at the Thunderbolt Hotel in a San Francisco suburb. Attended by over four hundred supporters, the affair, called "A Party With Shirley," was nationally covered, with photographs of the old crooner, pipe in mouth, horn-rimmed glasses slung low on his nose. Crosby "sidled up for a solo turn at the microphone," and after removing his pipe cracked a typical Crosby joke.

"On the way in a guy asked me 'Why don't you do what Ronald Reagan and George Murphy and Shirley Temple are doing?' I said, 'You mean get into politics?' and the guy said, 'No, get out of show business.' " After he made some "mellow, serious, and sincere" comments about Shirley's accomplishments in and out of the entertainment world, Shirley, her hair lacquered in a towering bouffant coiffure, made her way to the podium in stiletto-heeled black pumps and declared, "John Public . . . is the forgotten man. But he's the one I seek to represent." Once again she espoused increased United States involvement in the Vietnam War and her belief that "the country ought to leave it to the military experts to accomplish what we have determined as our practical objectives."

She had written her own script and insisted on sticking to it. Though her coverage had been more than that of any other candidate and her fund-raising abilities once again proved (her campaign coffers were augmented by nearly fifty thousand dollars within three weeks time), she remained behind McCloskey in opinion polls. Convinced, finally, in the last week of September, that she had to find a professional campaign-management organization to take over her race, she settled upon Whitaker and Baxter, the most venerable of such firms.

Whitaker and Baxter had been in the business of selling candidates since the Depression, and numbered among their past clients Earl Warren, Eisenhower, Nixon and former California Governor Goodwin J. Knight. The firm had successfully spearheaded the American Medical Association's campaign against Truman's proposed public-health program. "Ideologically, as well as by reputation, Whitaker and Baxter appeared to be a perfect firm for Shirley . . . [they] had enjoyed [their] greatest success in the Joe McCarthy–early Richard Nixon era when the technique of personal attack was much fancied. After their entry into the campaign, Shirley's press statements and remarks toward McCloskey took on a more personal accusatory tone." Weiner could not have been more delighted. After October 13, when Charles had been replaced by Whitaker and Baxter, the contest became a head-on fight between Shirley and Pete. "Whitaker and Baxter had played right into our hands," Weiner recalled.

McCloskey challenged her to a debate, but she refused, which proved to be one of the most devastating decisions of her campaign. Her opponent accused her of placing herself above the main issues at stake. Still feeling confident that visibility was the key to her success, Shirley remained on the run seven days a week from early morning to late at night, going door-to-door, greeting workers as they came off night shifts and catnapping whenever possible during rides to and from engagements. Fashion had no place in her schedule; she carried "only a sweater, a coat, a pair of heels and a pair of flats ('because you have to move fast')." *Women's Wear Daily* reported her hemline was too long, her heels too high, her hair "too PTA conventional, [she is a] very proper matron in a very proper suburb," and added, "Hollywood's former baby princess accepts responsibility like true royalty . . . that's why she decided to run for Congress."

Nonetheless, she was always gracious and patient, and showed no sign of artistic temperament. She was assiduous about doing her homework. She read five papers daily and used statistics like "an old political pro." The rat incident would not recur.

Wherever she appeared, her views on Vietnam were questioned. Asked once how she thought the war could be shortened, she replied, "It would only take four hours and two planes to mine Haiphong harbor." She constantly stressed her expertise as a mother in the area of morals and inspirational leadership.

Whitaker and Baxter were trying to parlay her sex and maternity into a bid for the woman's vote, and her hawkish views (although she once said she was not "hawk or dove but owl") into an appeal to the ultraconservative bloc, and their plan did have an impact on her vote-getting ability. By the first of November, with only two weeks remaining until the primary, Shirley had risen in the opinion polls and was running on the Republican ballot only about five percentage points below McCloskey.

Weiner and McCloskey's executive staff set up a television interview between their candidate and the local press. The questions were tough, but the faster and harder they came, the more passionate and knowledgeable were McCloskey's replies. As the allotted thirty minutes neared its end, he was asked if he would support Mrs. Black should she win the election. McCloskey rubbed his chin, shifted his weight from his bad leg and stared unrelentingly across the space between himself and his questioner. Finally, he replied, "I don't know. I thought I would when this campaign started, but when you run for the great debating society of the United States and you won't debate your own opponents in front of the electorate, it gives me great pause, and I don't think I want to vote for any candidate until I can see her or him under cross-examination such as you gentlemen have put me through today."

A reporter had one last question: "Would not San Mateo county receive national recognition with Mrs. Black as its Congresswoman?"

McCloskey leaned in close to the microphone. His voice was intimate. "I think we shall draw a great deal of attention if we should choose to elect a lady who will not come forward and state her views and respond to questions."

"Whitaker and Baxter *almost* did something right," Weiner commented wryly. "They got her into a debate with nothing but Democrats." The event was scheduled for November 10, four days before countdown. Two days earlier, on her own initiative, she paid a surprise visit to the state capitol at Sacramento. An aide reported that she was there "to be briefed on congressional reapportionment plans before the state legislature. She was introduced to both houses. She gave the appearance of taking things for granted . . . that she believed herself [already] to be the winner." The visit brought her additional unfavorable press. Undaunted, Shirley prepared for her debate with the Democrats.

South San Francisco, where the debate was to be held, was Democratic party territory. Shirley was walking right into the enemy camp. Whitaker and Baxter made sure she did not go unescorted. Wearing a lacquer-red tunic dress, she appeared at the cavernous El Camino High School gymnasium, where two thousand persons had gathered. She entered on Charles's arm, while a band of cheerleaders, girls with red, white and blue sashes, led the way shouting their cheer: "S - H - I - R - L - E - Y, SHIRLEY! B - L - A - C - K, BLACK! SHIRLEY BLACK! GO! GO! GO! SHIRLEY!" As she mounted the podium, they raised placards with her photograph on them. In the audience, several hundred of her supporters held up red balloons with the same matronly picture of Shirley stamped on them. Noisemakers passed out to the audience by her staff made a cacophonous yowl.

Shirley's organization had approached the debate as if it were a political convention. None of the four Democrats she was to face had equipped their representatives with gimmickry such as balloons and baton-twirling cheerleaders. But Republicans were outnumbered three to one in the audience, and in response to Shirley's rallylike tactics, those attending began to stamp their feet. Outside, another Republican candidate, Sheriff Whitmore (whose chances were slim), campaigned by shaking hands as people entered, a sound truck nearby blaring, "Vote for Whitmore!"

The format had been arranged so that Shirley was to open

the debate and to speak for fifteen minutes. Each of the Democratic candidates then had ten minutes. Rebuttal time had been limited to five minutes for each participant, after which the debate would be thrown open to the press for forty minutes of questions to be answered by the candidates. Her four opponents were Edward M. Keating, a forty-two-year-old lawyer, a leading dove and former publisher of *Ramparts* magazine; Roy Archibald, forty-seven, a former mayor of San Mateo and the front-runner on the Democratic ballot; Daniel J. Monaco, forty-five, a lawyer and former Democratic county chairman; and Andrew Baldwin, a schoolteacher.

"The number one issue in this district and in the country is Vietnam," Shirley began her speech. Her view, she said, was that the United States was conducting an "off-limits, part-time war" and she then reeled off statistics about how much of the enemy's territory had not yet been devastated. Chiding her dove opponents, she asked, "How can you say stop the bombing when a case can be made that it hasn't really started?" At that point, boos rang out in the huge room, and people in the audience jumped up and started popping hundreds of Shirley's red campaign balloons.

She took the assault well, waiting a minute or so and then asking the chairman, "You are timing this, I hope?" Then she sailed right back into her speech. The audience quieted as she went on to stress that the country was losing the "war on pornography." When she said "the thing to do about drug pushers is to put them in prison and throw away the key," noisemakers were shaken and shouts of "Go, Shirley, go!" rang out from her supporters.

"I feel Mrs. Black and I live in two different worlds," Keating said when his turn came. Proclaiming himself "the only genuine peace candidate," Keating ranked high among student voters, and this statement was met with a loud roar of approval. Smiling, Keating nodded toward Shirley and said, "Sorry about that, Mrs. Black."

When all the candidates had finished their speeches and rebuttals, Shirley appeared clearly the loser. Undeterred, her staffers, just before the press was to have the question period, passed out copies of her speech and led a large group in cheering and applauding their candidate. At this point, one reporter rose to his feet and said, "This is no rally, this is a press confer-ence. Who are these people anyway?"

"I don't know," Shirley smiled, as she grabbed the micro-phone, "but I'm awfully glad to see them here!"

Asked if she thought she had enough experience to be in Congress, she replied, "No one is experienced . . . until he gets there." Her qualifications, she said, were that she was "an hon-est, hard-working woman who will do an honest job. I have lived [in this district] over thirteen years; people know what I've been doing since I was three."

On the following night, national television's most popular news team, Chet Huntley and David Brinkley, devoted a large portion of their NBC evening newscast to the San Mateo elec-tion. McCloskey was gaining in strength during the last days, but so was Shirley; and almost all the preelection media coverage on a local and national level was centered on Shirley's colorful appearance at the debate. Shirley obviously felt confident, for on election day not one of her workers, as was the usual rule, was dispatched to help get out the vote, while McCloskey volunteers assisted people in reaching the polls, providing car pools and baby-sitting services when required.

The polls closed at 8:00 P.M. Shirley waited at home with Charles, her children and her key staff members. Television crews had already set up cameras at the Villa Chartier, the desig-nated site for Shirley's "victory" celebration; McCloskey's head-quarters were at the Thunderbolt Hotel. The first figures came in at 8:15 P.M. With 50 percent of the precincts reporting, the three leading Republican candidates were McCloskey, 4,624; Black 3,046; and Draper 1,926. Archibald had the Democratic lead with 1,134.

The Blacks heard the initial returns on the television set in their living room. "A radio was turned on also, since results were broadcast faster by that medium and a telephone rang repeatedly as aides took down statistical information. Incoming returns were given to Charles . . . who compared them with a voter survey [they] had taken but never publicized." The poll had reversed Shirley's and McCloskey's percentages.

As the night progressed and more precincts reported, McCloskey's lead grew. Charles remained confident that Shirley had a good chance. The conservative north county vote, which included the Woodside-Atherton-Menlo Park areas, had not yet been tabulated. A short time later, this vote settled the issue. McCloskey led Shirley by six thousand votes. "Face drawn, handkerchief in hand," Shirley, along with Charles and the children, left for the Villa Chartier, where about two hundred of her supporters awaited her arrival. When she entered, Shirley made her way briskly to the bank of microphones. Television cameras whirred. She thanked her workers in a voice devoid of defeat. There was defiance in the lift of her head. "I will be back," she warned. "I am dedicating my life to public service because the country needs us now more than ever before, and I want to help. This is my first race—now, I know how the game is played." No tears were shed; her audience applauded. Over at McCloskey headquarters, as they watched Shirley's concession on television, McCloskey's followers burst into a chorus of "The Good Ship *Lollipop.*"

The next day Shirley conceded, "I've always supported the Republican party and of course [I] will support Mr. McCloskey." But to Weiner, whom she met a few days later at a so-called G.O.P. "peace meeting," she complained, "Well, you certainly know some cute tricks." She remained bitter about the campaign for years. "If I had had two more weeks I could have won," she later claimed. Although she had been gaining toward the end of the campaign,* so had McCloskey, who went on to win the runoff against Archibald by a wide margin of votes, and was reelected to represent the Eleventh District in Congress for several terms.

Her opponent's primary triumph was a product of intensive precinct work by three thousand volunteers and sufficient funds to buy radio and television exposure that counteracted the avalanche of free publicity she received. But McCloskey's Vietnam position ("She wanted to bomb more heavily; I urged gradual withdrawal," McCloskey says) and his own heroic past drew the needed Democrats to the polls for him.

Looking back, McCloskey feels that Shirley was "truly desirous of serving her country. Most of the national issues were new

---

*The final votes cast were: McCloskey (R) 68,920; Black (R) 34,521; Draper (R) 19,566; Archibald (D) 15,069; Keating (D) 8,813. Total Republican vote, all candidates, was 120,263. Total Democratic vote, all candidates, was 33,671. Black lost Woodside to McCloskey 793 to 397, and Atherton 1,465 to her 830.

to her, however, and I'm not sure her campaign advisers were competent or served her well. She should have won, given first-class campaign direction. [I felt that she had the edge] until a September poll showed that her seventy percent name recognition still didn't give her more than one in three of the people who knew her name and that one-half of the twenty percent who had learned my name were going to vote for me."

Charles's inexperience and the tactics of Whitaker and Baxter helped sink Shirley's chances; and the debate had lost her votes, as had a letter sent by her staff to fellow Republicans alleging, in McCarthyite rhetoric, that McCloskey's stand on Vietnam would lead to "a slaughter unparalleled since the days of Nazi Germany" and that McCloskey's sentiments were aligned with Red China.

Privately, Shirley was a "warm, interesting person with impish humor," a campaign veteran commented. "[But] on the political stump she could be jarring and intemperate. Running into negative reactions on questions or issues, she became intractable and refused to acknowledge her own errors." She had overestimated the power of her celebrity, guessed badly on Vietnam, and hired the wrong advisers. But even McCloskey found her enthusiasm impressive.*

When he arrived in Washington, McCloskey was given the label "The man who sank 'The Good Ship *Lollipop.*' " But Shirley was more buoyant than anyone suspected.

---

*By 1988, McCloskey and Black would work together in George Bush's presidential campaign. "She is far more politically astute and sophisticated today," he says, "and she is a pleasure to work with."

FOR THE ESTABLISHMENT, 1968 was to be "the cataclysm that nearly happened." Flower children would be replaced by street-fighting youths, and army gear would overtake crushed velvet. Revolution was in the air. Young radicals appeared in the United States and all over Europe. The Old Guard had become the enemy, and the year was to bring a monthly calendar of activist horrors, assassinations and challenges to authority. Shirley was regarded as a symbol of the status quo, and her forthright espousal of her views on Vietnam served to label her right wing.

SHIRLEY SAYS DECLARE WAR appeared as a headline in the *San Mateo Times* on February 20, 1968. "I feel quite strongly that we should rescind the Gulf of Tonkin Agreement and Congress should declare war [on North Vietnam,]" she had stated in an address at an "Abe Lincoln Dinner" sponsored by the Waukegan [Illinois] Young Republicans, and had added: "If war were declared we would be able to blockade Haiphong. . . . There's a great danger in escalating the war without a declaration. But I would not want to see the bombing cease until Hanoi sets a date for the negotiating table."

Three weeks earlier, she had announced her decision not to challenge McCloskey when he was to stand for his first full term later that year. But her bitterness was underscored by her remarks to the press the day she ended all speculation as to her future plans: "Congressman McCloskey may have been nominated by less than one third of the Republican party (on November 11) and elected by less than one half of the electorate (on

December 12). However . . . as he lowers himself into our [Eleventh District] chair in Washington, I intend to provide him time to show his true political colors." She then concluded, "If he develops those qualities of mind and principle which warrant our trust, he will deserve to stay. But if his actions are erratic . . . he should be duly replaced by one who puts public trust above political self."

With Susan away at Stanford University and Charlie and Lori fairly independent teenagers, Shirley had even more time to devote to her political ambitions. She was a most desired speaker and was invited to be mistress of ceremonies at political rallies and dozens of social, civic and charity affairs. Although her concern for Sonny and her dedication to the National Multiple Sclerosis Society had not dimmed, she was not yet ready to settle for becoming "a lady of charity." More speaking invitations streamed in from the conservative wing of the Republican party. She accepted these now, hoping to have some small influence on the coming presidential election.

With the unpopularity of the Vietnam War, student rioting on over two hundred campuses and blacks "putting some of the biggest cities to fire," Johnson's presidency seemed to have failed. The country had taken his decision not to seek reelection "as an admission of defeat." The election appeared wide open, and Shirley was vehement in her wish to see her old friend Richard Nixon win the Republican nomination, certain he could then carry this victory on to the White House. Coordinating her ideas with the Republican National Committee, she traveled to forty-six cities in twenty-two states and gave over two hundred speeches in support of her candidate in the six months between February and July 1968, raising well over a million dollars for his campaign.

After the Richard Nixon–Spiro Agnew ticket was chosen at the Republican Convention, she headed an effort to organize American voters living abroad, planning to "barnstorm" foreign countries where large numbers of Americans resided and taking advantage of her European trip to help set up a new branch for the International Federation of Multiple Sclerosis Societies ("I call the Federation my little U.N."), of which she was vice-president.

Worldwide violence had erupted in the last months before

she was to leave on her tour. In London, on March 17, one hundred thousand protestors had crammed Grosvenor Square outside the American embassy screaming, "Hands off Vietnam!" In the United States, the Reverend Martin Luther King, Jr., leader of the black Civil Rights Movement and winner of the 1964 Nobel Peace Prize, was assassinated on the balcony of a Memphis motel on April 4; in May, tens of thousands of Parisian students hurled themselves on police and army with a vengeance that startled both sides; Senator Robert F. Kennedy was shot down on June 5 in a Los Angeles hotel directly after delivering his victory speech upon winning the California presidential primary; a steamy summer brought disruptive sit-ins at the Pentagon and the brutal clubbing of protestors by the Chicago police during the Democratic Convention in that city.

Czechoslovakia, where Shirley was going in order to organize a federation branch, had been a Soviet satellite since 1948. Under President Ludvík Šoboda and First Party Secretary Alexander Dubček's recent regime, many liberalized reforms had taken place. Stringent censorship had been eased, and relations with the West and with humanitarian organizations encouraged. But not long after the Czechoslovakian Central Committee won government endorsement for its policy of resisting pressure from the U.S.S.R., the Soviet Union announced that maneuvers were under way in areas near the Czechoslovak borders. Dubček had refused to abandon his country's sovereignty, and as Shirley was readying herself for the journey, Yugoslavia's President Tito arrived in Prague, the Czech capital, to show his support for the liberation drive. Shirley expressed no untoward concern about the prospect of going there at a time of such unrest.

She arrived in Vienna, the home of the federation's secretary, on Wednesday night, August 14. On the weekend, she was in Prague, where a meeting of the organization was to be held the following Tuesday, August 20. She was then to continue to Copenhagen, London and Paris to campaign for Nixon before returning home. The meeting in Prague between Shirley and a group of neurologists and biochemists had been arranged through the joint efforts of the minister of health and the president of Charles University in Prague, himself a physician.

Shirley was met late Saturday afternoon, August 17, at the Prague airport by a Czech driver from the American embassy and taken directly to the Alcron Hotel on Štěphánská Street. At the hotel, a once-grand establishment whose elegance had long since dimmed, she was given a rear room, number 21, which looked out at "a bleak stone wall across a light well." Since she was to leave in four days' time, the accommodations did not seem to matter. Her original plans had included a courtesy visit with Dubček on Monday, but a message canceling the social call because of "an emergency" was waiting for her upon her arrival. She dined that night at the American embassy. Conversation was light (the ambassador made no mention of any serious concern about Czech-Soviet relations), the food rich and delicious, with plenty of slivovic poured as a further relaxant.

Her schedule included a tour of the "hundred-towered" ancient city with its avenue of statues, its looking-glass view of the Vltava Valley and its numerous bridges spanning the beautiful Moldau River. She observed the people, whose native gaiety had been subdued by years of war, occupation and struggle for personal freedom. Their obdurate will could be detected in their brisk pace as they came and went with purpose.

On Tuesday morning, she was taken directly by car to the university, with its superb Gothic oriel. The meeting was held in an anteroom of the seventeenth-century, two-story-high assembly hall. Attention was focused entirely on the matter at hand—bringing Czechoslovakia into the International Federation of Multiple Sclerosis Societies. By the end of the discussions, Shirley "had been charmed out of" her boots by the group, whom she found "friendly" and "intelligent." The long day and evening had gone well, ending with the Czechoslovakians' agreement to work with the federation.

Her departure for Copenhagen was scheduled for early morning. The midnight news was broadcast over Radio Prague shortly after she returned to her hotel, but since she did not understand the language, she had no idea of what was being said. A few hours later, she was awakened by the telephone. The operator told her a man who had "just come from the airport . . . was there, speaking excitedly." He asked to see her immediately. Shirley, unable to ascertain who he was, told the operator to take a message. The man, apparently her driver, had wanted to inform her that Prague was under siege by the Russians and that the airport had just been closed.

Unaware of the events that would soon endanger her life, Shirley fell asleep again, but was soon awakened by a hammering at her door. Outside, there was "the shriek of a low-flying jet plane . . . distant shouts in the street and a rattle of gunfire." A member of the hotel staff had come to warn her of the invasion. "Tanks and troops are entering Prague!" he shouted. He also confirmed that the Russians had control of the airport and that it was closed. She dressed quickly and packed her suitcase in readiness, although she was not sure for what. Down below in the stark lobby, people milled nervously about. A number of other Americans and British, though strangers to each other, spoke and speculated. They knew little more than that their embassy or consul had told them to stay put and await directions. Štěphánská Street rumbled with the weight of massive, oil-streaked, dark green tanks with red Soviet markings, their crews staring "grim-faced" from the turrets as "they fired over the heads" of the disbelieving street crowds. The hotel manager insisted the guests move away from the front doors and windows.

Rumors proliferated in the Alcron; 250,000 Soviet troops were already in the country, hundreds had been killed or injured. The hotel management informed the guests that a "dark-to-dawn curfew" was in effect. But with the false cheer of an August sun streaking its way through the black smoke from planes and gunfire, the crowds had not dispersed. A knot of hotel guests remained close to the hotel's only television set in the dry bar. At noon, a newscaster, unable to control her sobs, announced that all public broadcasting had been ordered halted. A moment later, the screen went blank.

Lunch and dinner were served as usual in the dining room, the sound of distant machine-gun fire a steady accompaniment. The Alcron's two telephone operators had remained on duty, but outgoing calls were impossible, and incoming ones limited to local exchanges. By now, the guests had been augmented by several dozen East German plain-dressed "monitors" stationed on the landings and in all the ground-floor reception rooms.

A few of the new Czechoslovakian federation members came by the hotel to see how Shirley was managing. And shortly before dusk, a woman she had met at the meetings entered, drew her aside and cautiously told her, "The American Embassy cannot help you. We [the federation members] can get you out safely. It is all arranged. You must come immediately." But Shirley could not get herself to countermand embassy orders, and from the talk in the lobby, she knew "the nearest border was [over] one hundred kilometers away, through a darkened countryside presumably teeming with Russian men and armor." She refused the woman's offer as gracefully as she could.

At nine o'clock the following morning, a man appeared in the lobby, claiming to be the driver from the American embassy. He insisted Shirley and several other Americans come with him. Shirley could not recall if this was the man who had picked her up from the airport and taken her to the embassy dinner. But he did look vaguely familiar, and the station wagon that he had parked before the hotel bore a diplomatic license plate. She decided to accompany him and hurried to her room to collect the few odd bits not already packed. A bellman helped her to the car, and a chambermaid presented her with a bouquet of the country's national flower, red carnations, wrapped in a crumpled old news sheet that bore a photograph of Ethel Kennedy swathed in widow's weeds attending her husband's funeral. It did not seem a very good omen.

Two other American women were waiting in the car. After a ten-minute, fear-filled wait, they and Shirley were joined by two more women. A tank with four soldiers, weapons poised, came abreast, stopped and then moved on. Their car's driver started up Štěphánská Street. They were headed, he informed his passengers, for the American embassy. He could tell them no more than that. A ride that would normally have taken ten minutes stretched into nearly an hour as the station wagon encountered one roadblock after another before reaching the arched entry of the walled embassy, where ten other cars were lined up. The curb was crowded with American officials, embassy families and travelers. Shirley was asked to move to the front seat of a Mercedes sedan parked before a black station wagon draped with an American flag. "It reminded me of a hearse," Shirley recalled.

A young embassy worker slipped behind the wheel of her Mercedes. They were to lead the convoy of cars to the checkpoint, he explained. Then the flag car behind them would take over the lead. They were headed for the West German border, a trip of 115 kilometers through dense forests and occupied areas.

The convoy moved forward at a snail's pace, having to halt every few minutes for roadblocks of Russian tanks and armored vehicles. After five hours of this stop and go, Shirley's driver got out of the car to talk to Russian officers about letting them through a roadblock, and she was commanded to drive on and pull up ahead. This was the checkpoint. After her driver returned, three more Americans joined their car, and the flag car, as planned, took the lead. By now, there were nearly one hundred cars in the convoy.

Their progress was slow. Nightfall was approaching when they finally reached the border. An hour later, with only about half the members of the convoy allowed to cross the line,* Shirley and her fellow refugees were being given coffee and C rations by the U.S. Army serving with NATO. A special train then took the group to Vienna, where they arrived at 5:00 A.M. the following morning, exhausted and showing the strain of the last forty-eight hours. Canceling her previous arrangements, Shirley returned home the next morning via Lufthansa to San Francisco, where her family and nearly a hundred newsmen met her.

Dressed crisply in a navy-blue suit with starched white collar, a white cloche hat topping her outfit, she looked surprisingly chipper. With a blazing bouquet of red carnations in her arms, she faced microphones and television cameras. Then she handed the flowers to Susan and held up a record. "It's the Czech national anthem," she said. "They are not playing it any more."†

Undeterred by her grim experiences in Czechoslovakia, Shirley set out once again for Europe on September 4, just ten days after her return. Her national press coverage had been decisive

---

*Many Czechs had joined the convoy, hoping to reach the West. Thirty-seven of their number were known to succeed. They were mostly in cars with Americans and British.

†The Soviets justified the invasion of Czechoslovakia by claiming that the Czech government had requested assistance. NATO declared the invasion illegal and demanded withdrawal of Soviet troops. In a Moscow meeting, Czech leaders acceded to Soviet demands to abolish liberal policies and agreed that Soviet troops remain indefinitely. In April 1969, Dubček was forced to resign, and a pro-Soviet Czechoslovak government was installed. Dubček was assigned a job as a forestry worker. Historians and scientists were turned into night watchmen and stokers; theologians became street cleaners. That the battle for liberalization had not been entirely lost was shown in January 1977, when a manifesto was smuggled out of the country proclaiming the antitotalitarian convictions of a large bloc of Czechs.

in the Republican National Committee's immediate creation of European branches in France, Germany, Belgium, the United Kingdom and Italy. To help get out the absentee vote for Nixon among Americans living in Europe and to raise money for the Republican party, Shirley spoke at meetings and rallies in Rome, Paris, Frankfurt, Brussels and London.

After Richard Nixon was indeed elected, Shirley's efforts were turned toward the task of maintaining a Republican majority in Congress. She traveled wherever the Republican National Committee thought her presence was needed. Despite a rumor that she might be appointed chief of protocol, an offer of the position did not materialize.

"There is no doubt in my mind," a co-worker says, "that Shirley hoped for . . . a Cabinet post—Department of Health and Welfare, preferably—or as an ambassador to a major country. She had paid her dues, worked hard, and really was responsible for getting out the vote abroad. She still had this amazing magnetism, an ability to charm the hell out of an audience, to hold their attention. She was never good at [extemporaneous] press conferences. . . . But with a memorized, rehearsed speech, she was really a wow. . . . Most speakers look over their audiences heads or down at their text. Shirley almost never did. Before she got to the podium, she had selected various scattered members of the audience and spoke from time to time directly to them. I never saw another political speaker able to do this. And, of course, there was that dimpled smile—easy to come, flashed often and so winning."

Not until August 29, 1969, seven months into his presidency, did Richard Nixon give Shirley an appointment, naming her as a member of the United States delegation to the United Nations. Charles had recently become president of Marine Development Associates (Mardela), and at the time of the announcement the Blacks were on a deep-sea fishing boat off Oahu in Hawaii, where Shirley had spoken at a testimonial dinner for Republican Senator Hiram Fong of that state. Contacted by the press on ship-to-shore telephone, she said she had not yet been officially notified, "but I'll take your word for it. It's the thrill of my life." She added that the United Nations was "a great hope for peace in our world." This was in contrast to an earlier statement made during her congressional try. At that time, she had been quoted as saying that while the UN serves "as a means of communication," it conveys "mostly communist propaganda."

At the Western White House (Nixon's home in San Clemente), Press Secretary Ronald Ziegler commented that he was "not aware" that "Mrs. Black had made such statements, but nonetheless, the White House has confidence in her. We're sure she'll do a good job. That's why she was appointed."*

On September 16, the United Nations convened in New York. Shirley had only two weeks to prepare for the session. Charles decided to accompany her to New York and would commute to and from San Francisco during the thirteen weeks of the General Assembly sessions. Shirley's parents had recently moved from Palm Desert to Woodside, and Gertrude, although ailing, could keep an eye on Lori, now a lovely fifteen-year-old with hopes for a future career in some phase of music. Shirley and Charles took a suite of rooms at the Barclay Hotel, a short walk from United Nations Plaza.

Autumn had come to New York. Days were turning crisp, the East River a grayer hue, and the leaves on the sturdy trees along the bank that sloped down from the Plaza were in flame. When Shirley stepped off the plane at Kennedy Airport, she carried "a vivid red patent-leather briefcase decorated with a blue 'N' for Nixon—a souvenir of the victorious election the year before." Whatever else, Shirley's new adventure was to be colorful.

---

*Named with Black as principal representatives for the next United Nations session were Charles W. Yost, permanent U.S. representative to the U.N.; William B. Buffum, deputy permanent representative; Congressmen Dante B. Fascell (D., Florida); and J. Irvin Whalley (R., Pennsylvania).

15

THE BARCLAY, Shirley's home in New York, was built in 1926 as an opulent fourteen-story apartment hotel catering to the very rich. Harold Stirling Vanderbilt lived for sixteen years in an apartment of seventeen rooms on the top floor. A circular staircase of onyx and marble led to the hotel roof, where Vanderbilt had his private squash court and gymnasium. Perle Mesta occupied an even larger apartment comprising an entire floor, where she gained her pre-ambassadorial reputation as the "hostess with the mostes'."

After World War II, the Barclay became known as a frequent residence for United Nations representatives. Shifting fortunes and "the lingering aftermath of bankruptcy" (when the hotel's owner, the Penn Central Railroad, failed) had sent the hotel into "genteel decline." When Shirley moved into a suite once kept by Mary Pickford, the Barclay was not only old-fashioned—despite renovations in the mid-1950's, it was "downright seedy."*

One night, a creature Shirley "took to be a mouse brushed up against her leg. She called the hotel operator and said, 'There's a black mouse in my room.' The operator answered, 'There are no black mice in the hotel, it must be a rat.' A hotel employee with a flashlight arrived in time to see the rat run off into its hole."

Like a once-splendid dowager who has seen better days, the Barclay also had its charms. Compared to the cavernous mir-

---

*The Barclay became the Hotel Inter-Continental in 1978 and was "lavishly restored."

rored and glittering lobbies of more modern hotels, the Barclay lobby, with its great skylights, wrought-iron gates, decorative plaster work, wood beams, leather sofas and dark wood furniture, offered a clubby atmosphere. Permanent guests remained in the majority, and half of the third floor was rented by the Manhattan Club, a powerful organization of New York's legal and political community whose members included Mayor John Lindsay and Senator Jacob Javits. Shirley arose early to prepare her breakfast on the hot plate in the small kitchenette of her suite, which overlooked the heavy traffic on Forty-eighth Street.

The United Nations, its more than one hundred brilliantly hued flags snapping in the brisk October wind, rose over verdant gardens and marble statuary beside the East River. In its enormous, gilded assembly hall, the delegates met, hoping to bring forth miracles. Across the broad thoroughfare of First Avenue was the mission, which contained the offices of the delegates; Shirley's was situated on the seventh floor.

To walk from the Barclay to the United Nations complex took no more than ten minutes even at a leisurely stroll, but Shirley had received a series of life-threatening letters soon after her arrival. A New York City police detective, paid for by the UN, was hired as a bodyguard, and she was driven by chauffeured car wherever she had to go.* The writer of the letters was never found, nor was a reason ever given for the threat to her life.

The few days that she had before the start of the sessions were spent acquiring a knowledge of parliamentary procedure and an instant background in intricate international problems. Whatever her politics had been before, her appointment to the UN would permanently affect her thinking. She was to become, from this point in her life, involved and well informed in foreign affairs, the Third World and environmental matters. Suddenly, people began to take her seriously.

International travelers (almost everyone in the United Nations) had been plagued throughout 1969 by a Swissair ad campaign whose punch line was "Heidi wouldn't lie." The week Shirley was to be sworn in, a British diplomat deadpanned to a

---

*The UN post paid thirty-eight thousand dollars per year, plus a living allowance for out-of-city delegates.

group in the UN delegates' lounge, "You know that old saying about diplomats being sent abroad to lie for their country, well, you Americans have got the perfect answer with Shirley Temple on your delegation. You can use the slogan 'Heidi wouldn't lie.' "

The Briton's drollery was a harbinger of the prejudice that might be awaiting Shirley. Former U.S. delegations had contained stars from various fields of entertainment: In 1957, Irene Dunne had served on the Third Committee (where social, humanitarian and cultural matters are debated and voted upon before they are reported to the floor for plenary sessions); Marion Anderson had been an appointee in 1958; and throughout that decade Myrna Loy had served on several special committees.

"A certain faction of the U.S. delegation resented me," Loy admitted. "There existed an obvious division between the down-to-earth people who understood my reasons for being there and the intellectual snobs who looked down their noses at the movie star invading their ranks. This ivory-tower mentality . . . infuriates me. I certainly do not think we [actors and entertainers] are second-class citizens . . . I entered [the meeting she was to speak before] scared to death but prepared and dressed to the nines. Women should never be intimidated in dressing down to strengthen their professional image. . . . My speech emphasized the difficulty in selling peace. . . . Well, [at the finish] the place came down; they just kept applauding. One [man] came up, took my hand and said, 'You belong.' That meant a lot to me. Despite my unruffled exterior, I was afraid, unsure of my abilities. . . .

"[Shirley's] appointment caused general skepticism. 'What have we got here, Myrna?' Ralph Bunche [undersecretary-general to the United Nations at that time] asked. 'What have we done now?' They doubted her capability. . . . Our politics differ—she is a confirmed Republican—but I really applauded her accomplishments in the United Nations."*

Clad in a poppy-red suit, her high-heeled, ankle-strapped shoes buckled in rhinestone, her hair lacquered into a beehive,

---

*Loy did not serve with the United Nations the year of Black's appointment, but she maintained her interest and relationships in the organization.

Shirley was sworn in along with the other members of the United States delegation on Tuesday morning, September 16, at 11:00 A.M. Although officials stressed that the delegation would serve as a team, the press corps made it evident that "the spotlight at the oath-taking" was on Shirley. "I'm all goose-flesh," she commented as cameras recorded her genuine excitement.

The delegation discussed the day's agenda, ate lunch together in the delegates' lounge and then "mingled on the floor of the huge Assembly Hall for about half an hour." All around them, other delegates (approximately 600 from 126 countries) shook hands, slapped backs and "generally [behaved] like the members of any other club gathering for an annual event." At 3:00 P.M., Shirley took her seat behind the arc of desks assigned to the United States in the great blue, gold and pale green assembly hall, its gilded decorations dazzling in the warm light. Shortly after the session opened, the five-man delegation from Swaziland marched barefoot to its seats, strikingly attired in off-shoulder togas of bright red and red-orange with bold black-and-white geometric designs. Massive bone necklaces adorned their costumes. The chief delegate wore four feathers in his hair; the other members, according to their rank, three, two, one or none.

The first order of business was the election of the president for that session. The statuesque, ebullient Angie E. Brooks of Liberia, who had served as chairman of many UN committees dealing with decolonization and was the adoptive mother of nineteen refugee children in addition to her own two, was the overwhelming choice. She had been the unanimous nominee of the African states—it was Africa's year for the presidency—and the other members never questioned her selection. Mrs. Brooks "sailed unhurriedly up the aisle of the Assembly, resplendent in flowing blue and white robes, and a tall silken turban. Swinging an enormous red and black handbag, she climbed the stairs to the podium, heartily embraced a surprised U.N. official who guided her to the chair, and took her place next to the beaming Secretary-General U Thant. Then, after acknowledging the ovation of the delegates, Angie Brooks—the first African woman to serve as Assembly President—let them have it." Last year, she said, the assembly had shown, "the opposite of dynamism," that "advisably or by default" they had "either sidetracked or ignored important world problems and thus contributed to the gradual decline of the United Nations in the eyes of public opinion."

When asked later how she felt about taking on the demanding role of president of the General Assembly, Mrs. Brooks replied, "I am proud of my continent, my country and my sex." Then she winked. "Not bad for a woman, eh?"

The delegates of the twenty-fourth session of the United Nations faced a long list of major issues, which included: "resolutions concerning arms control and United Nations peace making machinery; treatment of prisoners in the Vietnam War; Chinese representation in the U.N.; the situation in the Middle East; and the need to promote fiscally sound U.N. budgetary policies, including reduction of U.S. assessment." Congressman Dante B. Fascell, a member of the American delegation, recalled: "One of the sessions's most positive accomplishments, which I remember well, since I helped lead the struggle, was to secure passage of a resolution calling on nations to take the necessary steps to punish hijackers. This was the first time the UN had taken such a firm position on this issue, and was a major success in marshaling world opinion against the hijacking epidemic of that time."

He also remembered that shortly after the delegation had arrived in New York, a press conference was held. This was Shirley's first exposure to the issues confronting the UN. "She had not had an opportunity to read the first cable or position paper. So, when a particularly troublesome question was raised by a reporter, Mrs. Black—without blinking an eye—said, 'Dante Fascell, as a member of the important Foreign Affairs Committee, will answer that question [what the U.S. should do about Vietnam]. . . .' Her tone and manner did not raise any feeling that she was evading the question or that she perhaps was not sure of the answer. It was an adroit handling of the question. . . .

"She immediately became an integral part of the U.S. delegation . . . they were aware, of course, that her fame and popularity would bring considerable attention to [their] work and the U.N. . . . That is exactly what happened.

"During disarmament talks with the Russians . . . Shirley

unexpectedly found herself alone, without advisers, facing a highly technical question about 'airborne-sensing techniques.' " Unwilling to admit to a full Soviet delegation that the United States representative was unprepared, she filibustered, telling them everything unclassified she knew about outer space and avoiding having to answer the question, "a most clever diplomatic ploy," a colleague commented.

As far away as Taiwan, banner headlines heralded "The Beloved Lady Delegate."

She had hoped to be assigned to a position on one of the health committees. Instead, she was placed on the Third Committee to work on social, educational and cultural activities and problems—a position called "the performer's chair" by Myrna Loy. Shirley took the appointment with grace, but after she spoke with Charles Yost, the delegation's permanent representative, he assigned her to several interassociated committees dealing with the problems of youth, social progress, environment, peaceful uses of outer space and refugees.

Congressman Fascell states that he "appreciated her strong stand and determination with regard to issues which she supported and which were in conflict with conventional wisdom (and even official policy) at the time. Mrs. Black, for instance, believed that the U.S. had to move away from our policy of opposing the admission of Red China to the U.N., which she recognized as unrealistic. . . . I recall that it seemed to Mrs. Black that by opposing the entry of the People's Republic of China, we were in fact helping the Soviet Union, since the Soviets were very unenthusiastic about the PRC being admitted. Subsequent events proved Mrs. Black's instincts were on the mark."

"Everybody has the impression that I'm such a right wing conservative," she told one reporter. "I am a conservative . . . when it comes to fiscal planning and the use of taxpayers' money. But I'm very liberal on international affairs."

In view of her stand on Vietnam and her get-tough attitude toward the Soviets, this statement was open to debate. However, Shirley was genuinely dedicated to, and conversant with, environmental problems, and she took the lead within her delegation in this area, as well as in youth-related conferences. Her first statement before the General Assembly dealing with world problems of young people was delivered from her seat on Tuesday, September 30, just two weeks into the session. Usually, it is difficult to spot a seated speaker among the sprawling concentric horseshoes of UN desks (the speech itself is carried throughout the assembly hall via a powerful public-address system.) But on this occasion, almost everyone turned around to look at Shirley, dressed in a vivid green suit and banked by the American delegation positioned in the very back row.

"I had never seen that happen," a veteran Swiss journalist commented.

She had written the address herself, and her audience could feel her pride in her own words. The style was journalistic—short, snappy sentences delivered in a punchy manner "and a kind of housewifely enthusiasm for genuinely worthy causes." Eyebrows may have been raised among her American colleagues, but in a world assembly reeling under the weight of hundreds of speeches and documents every day, the absence of "governmentese" in her language and her unorthodox simplicity won the admiration of the assembly hall. She spoke dramatically, her text almost entirely committed to memory, and she employed some colorful metaphors.

"In Ancient Rome, the two-faced god Janus stood at the door of time. One face was of an old man looking to the past, the other of a young man with visions of the future," she began. Her view was that youth would be better served if it had a say in the work of the United Nations, and she made six proposals for the participation of young people:

1. The formation of an International Voluntary Service Corps to collaborate "with a country's own national service corps in development projects."
2. The formation of an International Youth Assembly.
3. The appointment of young delegates to the 25th General Assembly in 1970.
4. The recruitment and placement of promising young people on the staff of the U.N.
5. The formation of a U.N. Information Center on Youth Programs.
6. The formation of a Conference on Youth and the Second Development Decade [youth aged ten to twenty] in 1971.

She also urged that the age of majority be lowered from twenty-one to eighteen, a request that drew "a barrage of irate letters" when it was reported in the press.

After she had finished her speech, Saudi Arabia's garrulous
sage and longtime ambassador, Jamil Baroody, crossed the auditorium and congratulated her. This admiration coming from
such an unlikely source set the tone for the rest of the assembly.
Like Myrna Loy, Shirley had been accepted. Socially, she had no
problem. Entertainers had always been an integral part of the
UN social scene. Many international movie, stage and recording
stars were regular guests at parties given for delegates during
the session. The official residence for American ambassadors
returned home for the assembly was a tremendous suite on the
42nd floor in the Waldorf Towers. Here, the ambassadors
would bring together diplomats, Broadway stars, movie idols
and assorted intellectuals for late-night gatherings, usually buffet suppers that ended with "the guests sitting on the floor
clapping to a singing group." During the period of Shirley's
appointment, Peter Ustinov (goodwill ambassador to UNESCO
in 1969) would appear in the delegates' lounge "telling stories
and studying the inexhaustible store of national accents to add
to his repertoire of mimicry."

Shirley swiftly became the ranking celebrity of the UN social
scene. ("Do you realize that Shirley Temple films have just come
to Bulgaria?" a member of the delegation reported.) Before any
reception or party, there was a great deal of "buzzing" as to
whether she would attend. She was very selective, not out of
snobbishness, but because the work ethic had always been
strong in her. There were difficult briefs and transcripts to study
at night, as well as speeches to write. To her surprise, when she
did attend these UN affairs, foreign delegates asked for her
autograph. Visitors to the United Nations stared and pointed at
her from the spectators' galleries when she was sitting in committee meetings. (If she observed them, she flashed the younger
ones the V-for-Victory sign.) United Nations employees stopped
her as she came on and off escalators or walked along the marble
corridors, introduced their children and snapped pictures of her
with them. At first, she resented this celebrity, although she took
it graciously and in her stride.

Her penchant for brightly colored clothes and her exag-
gerated high heels, which seemed only to emphasize her dimin-
utive size, became her UN trademarks. Her round face had
remained "remarkably youthful, except for a few tiny lines that

* crop up around her eyes whenever she smiles. And she is almost *always* smiling." For most people, the fact that Shirley Temple was little more than forty was a shock, since they considered her films so far back in their own pasts.

The United Nations Ball given that year on October 16 was the social highlight of the season.* The previous Saturday, Shirley had escorted some children of delegates to an ice-skating rink, taken a nasty fall and broken her left hand, which had to be set in plaster. The injury did not deter her from attending the gala. With Charles, suntanned and handsome, by her side, she entered the ballroom of the Waldorf Astoria, wearing an eye-catching pink and green halter-top satin gown "that emphasized her . . . curves," sporting her cast on the injured hand. Her reddish-brown hair was drawn back into a French-twist hairdo. Together, she and Charles "looked like [the famous dance team] Marge and Gower Champion as they dipped and twirled their way through bouncy fox-trots and bumpy rumbas," her cast nestled safely on Charles's shoulder. After one such set, Merle Oberon, looking spectacular in emerald green with matching jewels, applauded loudly as the Blacks came off the dance floor.

"A party such as this gives us a possibility to change the environment," said Yakov A. Malik, head of the Soviet mission to the United Nations. "Here we meet our friends in another place . . . and we laugh and we talk."

Yakov Malik had already sat across from Shirley at dinner at a party given by the Jordanian delegation. "I presented to him what I call 'my jovial idea'," Shirley remembered. "I suggested that there be only women on the Security Council. So far he hasn't expressed himself on that idea." At the same dinner, Shirley almost faced sudden disaster when a pine nut in a rice dish lodged in her throat. "I started to black out," she recalled. "But then I thought to myself, 'I'm a representative of the United States, and I'm the only one here, and I can't die. If I do, nobody will believe that somebody didn't do something to me on purpose.' Finally, the nut went down."

---

*The United Nations Ball in 1969 was attended by 950 guests representing 102 countries. Tickets were one hundred dollars per person. The proceeds went to the United Nations Association, an educational organization that sponsored foreign student exchange.

During her baptism into the world of diplomacy, Shirley did make "a few faux pas—impetuously speaking out without consultation with allied governments, sitting stubbornly, arms folded, through a vote, contrary to her government's instructions, overstepping and having to improvise a filibuster on disarmament." Ambassador Glen Olds, the number-two man at the mission, eventually dubbed her "the U.S.'s *Secret Weapon.*" In relations with delegates and at UN social affairs, "where personal impressions directly influence policy decisions," she excelled as "a genuinely well-informed negotiator."

"People were surprised at the toughness of her position," Ambassador Olds confirmed, "but she prepared; that's what made her tough-minded." He added, "She'd take home some of my books [on current international politics] in the evening and the next morning say, 'I've outlined these, do you have anything else?' "

As the session progressed, Shirley's familiar voice was more frequently heard. Her refreshing frankness impressed her audience. On the occasion of a speech on refugees, she opened in Zane Grey-ish fashion, "In the autumn of 1830 a contingent of blue-clad American Cavalry galloped into an isolated Cherokee Indian village." What followed was "an indictment of her own country's record in expelling the original inhabitants from their land and making them refugees." When complimented later on her defense of the Indians, she was quick to reply that she believed "deeply in social justice [and her own] children had Indian blood in their veins," a reference to a distant ancestor of Charles's, General John Sevier, the first governor of Tennessee (1796–1810), who married a Cherokee princess, one of the great romantic episodes in the Black family history.

Many visitors found their way to her mission office. Always one of the earliest to arrive, she was usually at her desk by half-past eight in the morning. But it was in her committee work rather than in her public addresses that her abilities were tested and proved.

Her admiration for Angie Brooks developed into a meaningful friendship and a desire to learn more about the African countries. Coming so soon after Prague, the UN experience and her meeting with Brooks would leave an indelible mark. Her vision had widened, sharpened. Her tolerance for people and ideas outside her ken had expanded. One day, as she left the mission, she was confronted by a group of "agitating" Black Panthers. "I'm not afraid to extend my hand to anybody," she boasted, "although sometimes it hangs there for a long time. So I put my hand out and said, 'Hello, I'm Shirley Temple Black,' and the fellow said, 'Hello, I am a Black Panther.' And the very brutal-looking man got tears in his eyes and said, 'Oh, I remember.' "

During the last week of the session, Shirley flew to Washington to address the National Conference on World Refugee Problems. Because of a severe rainstorm, her plane was delayed several hours. On arrival, she went directly to the East Room of the Mayflower Hotel, where her anxious audience had remained waiting for her. "I'm sorry I'm still in my work-day outfit [the familiar bright red suit she wore frequently at the UN] and wearing boots," she apologized. "I did bring a pretty dress, but it's still at the airport."

On the dais with her were Prince Sadruddin Aga Kahn, United Nations high commissioner for refugees, and Graham Martin, U.S. ambassador to Italy. "Cherokee Indian blood flows proudly in the veins of my son and daughter" she once again announced, and then in "a down-to-earth manner . . . plunged into the issue at hand: the world's eighteen million refugees." Knowledgeably, she rattled off the alarming increase in the world's refugees in the last decade. The major point she made was that "refugees are people and not just statistics. . . . The situation we face is not only of empty stomachs or vengeful hearts; it is a witches' broth of degradation, destruction, and death."

The same week, she was presented with the Sarah Coventry "Woman of the Year" Award, honoring her for "dedicated public service to the world community." Her humanitarian work did not diminish her political fervor. Before leaving Washington, she was interviewed on *Meet the Press,* a national TV program geared to Capitol matters. In the closing minutes, she urged Americans to ask their U.S. senators to restore cuts made by the House of Representatives in President Nixon's foreign-aid bill. "The American foreign aid program is not a give-away, it is a partnership. Contact the U.S. Senate not to allow this cut to happen," she entreated.

Her last speech, delivered on December 15, centered on one of her favorite topics—the human environment. "As Apollo 12 was half way back to Earth," she began in her characteristic storytelling style, "one of the astronauts peered out the window and saw the planet Earth. Millions of us heard him say, 'It's a beautiful world.'

"From his perspective it's true. Down here on earth we are not so sure."

She presented an eloquent plea for the need of a UN Conference on Problems of the Human Environment, one in which she wanted very much to be a participant. She now hoped that Nixon would reappoint her to the next session, deemed—because it was the twenty-fifth anniversary of the United Nations—to be an especially important year. "I'd like to come back," she told reporters as she sorted through papers in her mission office for the last time. "I'm going to recommend to the State Department that appointments to the Delegation be made for at least two years—with the appointee the President has in mind for the third year entitled to sit behind the delegate during the second year in preparation for his job. . . . We need more continuity."

Although other nations often reappointed nonprofessional diplomats several years in a row, the precedent was, and remains, for American presidents to name a different set of non-professionals (along with career diplomats) to the UN delegation each year. This policy offers a president more chances to pay political debts and reward distinguished citizens with a seat.

She joined her family in Woodside for the Christmas holidays. "My children told me when I got home that I seemed much more serious than when I left in September," she commented. "I think it's because I got used to giving thoughtful answers all the time." She added with a big smile, "Oh yes, and something else. If you want to make a statement at the U.N. you say, 'I want to make an intervention.' That's gone over very big at the [family] dinner table." She was not home long. Early in February 1970, she traveled to Iran and the Mideast. On February 26, she was a witness before a Subcommittee on International Organizations and Movements in the House of Representatives, where an attempt was being made to appraise the United Nations' place in the field of social programs and of human rights.

In welcoming her to the subcommittee, one of its permanent

members, Columbia University Professor Felix Frelinghuysen, commented, "I note we have a very large, and I would say predominantly youthful audience, so it is quite obvious that you have a fan club. I am sure it is not the nature of our hearings that brings out this crowd. It is encouraging as one of the older members here to realize that fame has a continuing effect, at least in your case." Whereupon the subcommittee chairman, Congressman Cornelius E. Gallagher of New Jersey, quipped, "I hope it doesn't get back to Ambassador Yost that you outdrew him." The remark brought stilted laughter.

Shirley gave an impassioned, well-received address that emphasized "the potential" of the environment and pleaded that we not "wring our hands at the shortcomings." Looking poised and confident in a knee-length navy and white dress, her long hair swept up in the back, she answered questions fully and without hesitation on the UN's progress on issues in which she had been involved. Nonetheless, the subcommittee seemed incapable of letting go of their own past where she was concerned.

"Mrs. Black, I want to welcome you here," Congressman J. Herbert Burke of Florida added to the welcoming statement by his colleague. "I feel that you are the type of person that just never does grow old. You grow more beautiful [this before about one hundred House spectators and to be recorded in a government document] and while this sounds flattering, I think most of us here have seen you grow to be a very beautiful woman. For instance, I think my younger daughter still believes you are a very beautiful little girl, and while this might embarrass you, I would like to say that I have probably seen *The Littlest Colonel* [sic] so many times that I expected to see you walk in with the military uniform of the Old South." This statement met with open laughter, and Shirley replied, "Mr. Congressman, [even in movies] I did grow a bit more than that."

CONGRESSMAN BURKE: Yes, you did. [And I might add] you have grown in beauty in many ways . . . your humanitarian efforts in the fight on multiple sclerosis and with your hospital work . . . and now your work in international programs for the benefit of mankind. But . . . [in] your statement, you talk about nationalism . . . and where I agree it is fine to support the principles of nationalism . . . it is difficult to rein in nationalism, when it gets

started, and I am sure you remember the nationalism
that swept Europe, prior to World War II, and the
nationalism that resulted in Fascism, and the military
nationalism of Japan.

MRS. BLACK: Mr. Congressman, when I spoke of nationalism, I was speaking . . . of the developing countries.

CONGRESSMAN BURKE: Yes, I know, but that is what both-
ers me. . . . We [have] found every nation getting more
nationalistic and yet we in our country find people from
various organizations telling us that we are imperialistic
. . . I ask [another] question . . . with regard to the refugee
problem . . . What would you think would be our contribution to . . . the smaller countries looking to the more
wealthy countries to do the job for them?

MRS. BLACK: Mr. Congressman, . . . I don't think the
nations of the world want to be told by any individual
country how they are to live, how much money they are
to be given. I think those days are past. In the refugee
camps . . . I feel it is most important that we help in
education and training, because 18 million people need
our help, need our assistance, and if I may interject
something, I would like to mention that I think we must
do a lot more about our own American Indians.

After her testimony, Representative Dante Fascell, a member
of the subcommittee and of the UN delegation, announced, "I
want to say something now to your face that I have been saying
behind your back, so that the record will be clear that it was not
only just a pleasure to work with you [at the UN] but you certainly carried your share of the burden and made our work
immeasurably better and easier, as an entire delegation. . . . You
presented [before this subcommittee] a very forthright statement as you always do. It is on one hand ideological and on the
other hand very practical, which I learned in three months is the
kind of person you really are, and I commend you for that."

Fascell then turned to Congressman Abraham Kazen, Jr., of
Texas, who had been less than agreeable in his questions earlier
to Shirley, and said pointedly, "Mr. Kazen, you will be happy to
know that one of the real benefits that—despite some critics and
some skeptics, who thought it was useless to appoint Mrs. Black

to a position of that importance—that she not only served ably, and made preparations of substance in behalf of the U.S. position, but . . . she was able to get coverage when the rest of us couldn't find our way out of the dark. [Laughter.] You know the men with the cameras didn't even know where I was unless I happened to be standing next to Mrs. Black."

"Mr. Chairman," Shirley interjected, "if I could respectfully suggest that Congressman Fascell might, if he goes back [to the UN] wear a red suit. [Laughter.] A *bright* red suit."

16

A FEW WEEKS LATER, she was appointed to serve as deputy to Christian Herter, Jr., head of the U.S. delegation to the United Nations Committee on the Environment. Shirley was propelled into the complex preparations for an international conference on world environment problems to be held in Stockholm two years down the line, in June 1972. The assignment had come in response to personal letters she had written to President Nixon and Secretary of State William P. Rogers, asking to be given a further appointment.

"I don't think there is any question now that people are finally taking me seriously. Those who have always been close to me, those who know me well, have never doubted that I was a hard worker. [The others] didn't know me at all, or were thinking of Shirley Temple, the movie star," she reflected.

The first meeting on environment was held in April 1970 in New York, and lasted ten days. Periodic sessions were conducted after that. "It's very lonely to have a nice big family and a nice home in California and not be there," she said wistfully. "But [the work I do is] most important, we all agreed. They've always supported me and urged me to be productive."

The children were grown: Susan was twenty-two and had recently graduated from Stanford with an A. B. in art, Charlie was eighteen and Lori was sixteen. Charles remained close at hand, and Gertrude and George were always available. Her family understood that not only were Shirley's abilities being channeled into serious commitments, but that she was driven by her need to free herself from her screen image. Her work on behalf of the Republican party, the United Nations and multiple sclerosis were all regarded with respect. However, the press still referred to her as "the former Shirley Temple," or worse yet, "the one-time child star," or even more contemptibly as "the once fabled curly topped dimpled moppet of yesteryear." Her press interviews were more likely to appear in the women's sections of newspapers than on the political pages.

Ronald Reagan had not had Shirley's problems in ridding himself of his Hollywood past, but he had not been a star of Shirley's magnitude. Perhaps downright snobbishness, prejudice or envy caused members of the press to regard her as "an overqualified board member and professional volunteer . . . searching for some larger purpose for her instantly identifiable name." She could, of course, have deleted the Temple, or reduced it to a slim and dotted initial. She did not, a fact that could well indicate her awareness that, like it or not, "little Shirley Temple" could play an important role in the selling of her causes, whatever the political or committee post.

To her great disappointment, she was not returned as a UN delegate in 1970, although she remained a productive member of the environmental committee. In October, Governor Reagan asked her to serve as chairman of the state's community meetings, called to "implement national reassessment of environmental goals." According to Shirley, the purpose of the California program was also "to increase the knowledge of all Californians in respect to the United Nations and to peacekeeping . . . and to present dramatic evidence of informal California concern and opinion to those who represent us in Washington." A series of one-day sessions in various sections of the state were held with Shirley as moderator; the transcripts were then sent to President Nixon and to the United Nations. But her activities were not limited to the United Nations.

"Shirley Temple Black, one-time child movie-star . . . arrived [in Bucharest] last night to meet men of art and culture and see cultural objects and establishments in the Romanian capitol," *The New York Times* reported on November 15. For the next two days, she toured the country as a guest of the Communist government. She had become America's goodwill ambassador. The charm, the smile were always in evidence when she traveled—and she seemed to be everywhere during 1970 and 1971: Japan,

Her 21st birthday. April 23, 1949. The occasion was celebrated with John Agar at Universal Studios where she was filming. *University of Southern California*

Hand in hand. Mr. and Mrs. John Agar walk around the grounds of their home, once Shirley's playhouse. Six months later Shirley filed for divorce. *Mark Wannamaker private collection*

Not like old times. *Left,* Darryl Zanuck greets Shirley on her return to Twentieth Century-Fox to make *Mr. Belvedere Goes to College* in 1949. *University of Wisconsin*

Early political stirrings. *Above,* she was a guest at President Harry Truman's Inaugural Ball, January 1949. But her allegiance was to be to the Republican party. Here, with Chief Justice Fred Vinson. *Life*

Hawaiian love song. On a visit to Honolulu in 1950 she met San Francisco social scion Charles Alden Black. The attraction was immediate and mutual. *AP/Wide World Photos*

Wedding bells. Childhood friend Nancy Majors married Charles Black's buddy, fellow San Franciscan Robert Gros, in 1950. Shirley and Charles were married later that year. *Nancy Majors Voorheis private collection*

Dinner at the Stork Club. *Above,* Shirley and Charles celebrate the recent birth of Charles Alden Black, Jr. The happy father was now a lieutenant-commander in the Navy, stationed in Washington for the duration of the Korean War. The diamond star necklace was an early gift to his Navy wife. *The Bettmann Archive*

White House guests. Before leaving Washington in 1953, the Blacks and Susan called on President Eisenhower. Later, Shirley was to seek his help in her political career. *The Bettmann Archive*

Housewife and mother. Helping son, Charles, mount a pony in 1955. The Blacks were living in Atherton, California, and Shirley declined all career offers. *Life*

Public announcement. Two years later, Shirley agreed to host and appear on television in a series of special programs titled *Shirley Temple's Storybook* after her children, Susan (10), Lori (4) and Charles (7), gave their votes of approval. *San Francisco Chronicle*

The storybook lady. Her gowns were designed especially for the show, but she wore her own jewelry. *The Bettmann Archive*

Traveling. In 1965 she went to Russia on behalf of the International Federation of Multiple Sclerosis Societies, stopping en route in London where she was surrounded by fans. Foreign travel soon became an integral part of her life as her activities broadened. *B.B.C. Hulton Picture Library*

Sharing secrets. Lori, age 11, accompanied her parents to London, later that same year. *B.B.C. Hulton Picture Library*

En route. With Charles (side to camera) leaving London and

arriving in Paris. *Rex Features, B.B.C. Hulton Picture Library*

Graduation Day. Charles gives his adopted daughter, Susan, a fond embrace. *Life*

Susan's debut. The event was preceded by an afternoon reception attended by family and friends. Susan is pictured here with Nancy Majors. *Nancy Majors Voorheis private collection*

Final touch. Right, Shirley adjusts her daughter's gown in a reception room of San Francisco's Sheraton Palace Hotel before the new debutante makes her entrance. *Life*

A moment to be remembered. Susan walks onto the stage of the hotel ballroom as her name is called. *Life*

The congressional candidate. *Above,* September 8, 1967, Shirley Temple Black announces she will run in the primaries of California's 11th District. Charles, standing behind her, was her campaign manager. Her children, Lori, Charles (in military uniform) and Susan (far right), supported her decision. *Life*

In her own backyard. Shirley enjoyed the casual aspects of California life—the pool, the barbecue, the sun-filled days. Young Charles is on the grass. Woodside, 1967. *Life*

August 1968. She had been caught in Czechoslovakia during the Soviet invasion, but arrived safely a few days later in Vienna. The bouquet of carnations was given to her by a Prague hotel employee as she started out on her dangerous return to the West. *B.B.C. Hulton Picture Library*

United Nations delegate. President Richard Nixon appointed her to the American delegation in September 1969. Shirley rides up to her office in the Mission for the first time. She is carrying her famous briefcase with the "N" for Nixon boldly displayed. *Rex Features*

Settling in. It did not take long for the U.S. delegation to accept Shirley as one of them. She was always prepared, articulate, and incisive in her views. *The Bettmann Archive*

Speaking out. She evolved as the U.S. delegation's spokesperson on environmental issues, refugee problems and youth-oriented matters. Her speeches, delivered in a lively, journalistic style, were well received. *The Bettmann Archive*

Home away from home. Her suite in the Barclay Hotel was a short walk from the United Nations. However, a threat on her life forced her to be driven to and from work. *Rex Features*

A diplomat's life. Though often alone, she always traveled with family photographs she could display. *Rex Features*

Stockholm, 1972. As a member of the U.S. delegation to the United Nations Conference on Human Environment, she made one of the closing speeches, delivered in her usual charismatic manner. *Rex Features*

Arrival in Ghana. Her appointment as ambassador to a Black African nation was accepted with enthusiasm on her part. Charles and Susan accompanied her. *Ghana Information Services*

A royal welcome. Twenty thousand Ghanaians cheered as she was lifted "like a side of beef" by four strong men and carried through the streets. *AP/Wide World Photos*

Market Day. Ambassador Black, wearing Ghanaian clothes, makes her first official visit to the Makola Market in Accra, where most of the stalls are run by women. She soon became their good friend. The uniformed man is Lieutenant Colonel B. T. Okai. At the far right, the city treasurer, Nii Quaye-Mensar is in a business suit. *AP/Wide World Photos*

A presidential handshake. President Gerald Ford congratulates her on becoming the new United States ambassador to Ghana. George Bush, far right, applauds her choice. Bush had just been made ambassador to China. *Gerald R. Ford Library*

Ambassadrice de charme. Shirley is greeted by a French dignitary at the formal ball she hosted on January 20, 1981, in Paris to celebrate the inauguration of President Ronald Reagan. The guest list included French and foreign diplomats and distinguished Americans living in France. *Rex Features*

Reunited. Three former child stars—Marcia Mae Jones, Jane Withers and Sybil Jason— appear on stage with Shirley at the Samuel Goldwyn Theatre in Hollywood. The occasion was a special tribute to Shirley given by the Academy of Motion Picture Arts and Sciences, May 21, 1985. The moderator is Robert Osborne. *Marcia Mae Jones private collection*

Hollywood tribute. A full-sized Oscar was presented to Shirley by Gene Allen, president of the Academy, to replace the mini-statuette she had been given fifty years earlier. *Rex Features*

Iran, Yugoslavia, Greece, Egypt—almost always on behalf of environmental programs. She had become one of her country's leading environmentalists. Wherever she went, she won not only converts to her views on ecology, but friends for Richard Nixon.

"Once," she recalled, "at a White House dinner commemorating the U.N.'s 25th Anniversary [December 1970] Henry Kissinger requested that I sit next to him. . . . I tried to persuade him to bring the Vietnam War before the Security Council by having him read the worn miniature U.N. Charter that I carry every place I go, [and that night] had in my evening purse. He had to stop eating to look over the marked pages. 'If we paid attention to these articles we could avoid wars,' [she told him] 'or get out of those we are in.' Henry obliged, jesting, 'here I wanted to sit next to the youngest woman invited [she was forty-two] and what does she have me do, read a *book!*' "

Charles added, "If Shirley Temple Black can persuade a man like Henry Kissinger to read a book at a White House dinner, who can tell what her future in politics will hold." One cannot tell from this remark if Charles was joking, or if he had more ambitious hopes for his wife's political future. Meanwhile, Shirley concentrated on the task at hand.

"All of us who have in one way or another, helped to begin to shape this vast mound of environmental dough into something more manageable . . . have reason to hope that the pudding to be served up in Stockholm next June may truly be worth eating," she metaphorically told the UN General Assembly on September 20, 1971. "But I confess to a creeping apprehension that if the priceless ingredient of public understanding and public commitment is slighted, that wonderful pudding may end up tasting like glue."

Taking up residence again at the Barclay, she spent the autumn at the United Nations preparing for the two-week Stockholm Conference the following June. "Imagine, only two weeks?" she said to *Washington Post* reporter Richard Coe, the same writer with whom she had once done battle over Susan's stage debut at age four. "That's a job people could spend months just talking about. Some things have got to be realized by nations who aren't joining the Stockholm meeting. No country can be aloof from pollution. The air just sweeps everything around the world with no attention whatever to boundaries."

With President Nixon's planned trip to China the big news at this time, Coe asked her if she would also like to go. "Of course," she replied. "A fourth of the world's people live in Communist China. *Detente* with the Soviets would mean nothing if China was not brought into the international community." Then she wondered aloud, "Would someone tell Dr. Kissinger that I learned to speak Chinese at the age of eight? It was for a movie called *Stowaway,* and for it the studio gave me lessons for six months."

The dates for the United Nations Conference on the Human Environment were set for June 5 through June 16. Including Shirley, who was the only woman, there would be thirty-five members of the United States delegation. The scenario for Stockholm had been laid out eighteen months earlier by the conference's designated secretary-general, Maurice Strong, a dapper Canadian tycoon "wise in the ways of industry." Twelve thousand representatives of the world's people were to attend the conference. Yet the Soviet Union and most of the other European Communist countries would not be present. The Russians, active in the early preparations, were staying away in protest against the exclusion of East Germany, not a member of the United Nations and so ineligible to take part in the conference.

June is the best of all times to visit Stockholm. The weather is mild, and the brilliant midday sunlight casts a golden warmth. Most representatives arrived on Monday, June 5. The first full assembly was to be held the next day, which was also "Swedish National Day," with parades and exuberant celebrations throughout the city. Shirley's hotel, the elegant Grand, faced the waterfront and the royal palace, where at 12:10 every afternoon, the colorful changing of the guard took place. Located just across the bridge from the royal palace was the royal opera house, where the delegates gathered for a welcoming ceremony.

King Gustav VI Adolph, attired in a plain dark blue business suit, appeared with aides in the royal box, and Secretary-General Kurt Waldheim of the United Nations, Maurice Strong, and other conference dignitaries sat in an opposite box. Sweden's Premier Olof Palme (long a critic of the United States policy in Vietnam) set the tone of the conference in his opening speech. Without mentioning the United States by name, he condemned "the indiscriminate bombing by large-scale use of bulldozers and herbicides," as an outrage "which required immediate international attention." Mr. Palme asked that the United Nations Conference on the Human Environment "unequivocally proclaim" that the presently enormous channeling of resources into armaments should be stopped. The American delegation was deeply disturbed. Its members exchanged muffled comments, and their body postures grew considerably stiffer.*

Following Premier Palme, Kurt Waldheim left his box and mounted the stage to describe armaments as the "ugliest of all pollution." The subject was not on the agenda, but he called on the world to reduce "and ultimately suppress" armaments. After several more speeches, the delegates broke for lunch, and then reconvened in the auditorium of the Folkets Hus, a modern trade-union building in the heart of Stockholm. During the intercession, there was great speculation as to whether the United States would walk out to protest Mr. Palme's statement. Reporters rushed around the delegation as it entered the auditorium for the afternoon session. Speaking on behalf of his colleagues, Russell Train made it very-clear the United States had no such intention, and expected "to work within the conference and make it a success."

Subjects tackled during the eleven days of actual talks ranged from the "cry of the vanishing whale" to atmospheric monitoring to ecocide (ecologically destructive acts such as the use of defoliants in the Vietnam War). Four days into the discussions, China denounced the United States and other "imperialistic superpowers" as being "primarily responsible for global environmental problems."

"Our conference should strongly condemn the United States for their wanton bombings and shellings, use of chemical weapons, massacre of the people, destruction of human lives, annihilation of plants and animals, and pollution of the environment," Tang Ka, chairman of the Chinese delegation, told the 114-nation assemblage. The vehemence of the Chinese attack coming so soon after President Nixon's visit to China again took the

---

*The following day, the United States State Department officially commented, "We find it incomprehensible that a head of government of the host state should have interjected the Vietnam issue, which we consider extraneous at the United Nations Conference."

U.S. delegation by surprise. That day, Russell Train asked for rebuttal time. Five hours later, the hefty Christian A. Herter "puffed to the platform to report that the rebuttal was not yet ready." It was deferred for three days, giving the State Department time to assist with a reply.

An observer at the conference said longingly "that it needed a Thomas Jefferson—someone who could lift the delegates above their parochial concerns and rally them behind a contemporary call for life, liberty and the pursuit of happiness." The reply given him was that "even a Jefferson would find it hard to make ennobling history with delegates from 114 countries." Nonetheless, the conference did weather "the political squalls that repeatedly threatened to swamp it," and the U.S. delegation came through intact.

Walter Sullivan, covering the Stockholm meeting for *The New York Times,* deemed the United Nations Conference on the Human Environment a success, for "beneath the polemics ran a groundswell of unanimity. Most of the final decisions were made without a dissenting vote.* It was as though the nations comprising the family of man had become aware, as never before, of the vulnerability of their planet and how essential it is that they work in concert to preserve it. [And perhaps] the conference was more important for the change in national attitudes that it symbolized than for what it did."

Shirley sat silent and attentive through all the plenary sessions, but spoke up strongly in her delegation's private meetings. Not until June 16, the last day of the conference, was she asked to address the assembly. Given only ninety minutes to prepare her speech, she quickly scanned the continuing notes she had made throughout the conference and wrote a short address, which she read, urging "the acknowledgment of our kinship as human beings working together for the rational management of our common resources." Her words were well received.

---

*The concrete results of the conference were: approval of an action program to monitor climate change and oceanic pollution; promotion of birth control and preservation of the world's vanishing species; the approval of an environment fund to cover the part of the international effort not paid for by specialized agencies and national governments; establishment of administrative machinery to coordinate worldwide environmental efforts; and an agreement on a declaration of principles.

The day she flew back to the States, June 17, a task force known as the "the plumbers" broke into Democratic Party Headquarters in the Watergate Building in Washington and was arrested. At the time, no one perceived what this might lead to. The presidential election was five months away, and Shirley continued to work on behalf of Richard Nixon's campaign.

"Some presidential aspirants seem to be pandering to our frustrations, mouthing vague programs which suggest a withdrawn, isolationist fortress America," she told the United Nations Association of San Mateo County upon her return. The statement was a pointed jab at the Democratic presidential candidate, George McGovern.

"America's Little Sweetheart," the *San Mateo Times* reported, "warned against the stirring winds of isolationism blowing across this country." The paper quoted her as saying, "Has twenty-five years of history since the isolationist days of Senator Robert Taft taught us so little? Politics does indeed make strange bedfellows."

A few weeks later, she was in Geneva to attend a United Nations meeting concerned with "the law of the sea, debating such remote matters as ocean-dumping, territorial seas, continental shelves and marine pollution."

In late August, President Nixon appointed Shirley special assistant to the chairman [Russell Train] of the American Council on Environmental Quality. The council had been organized by Nixon following an agreement he had made with Soviet leaders to cooperate in fighting pollution. She was sworn into her new post on Friday, September 1, at the Executive Office Building in Washington. Her first assignment would take her to Russia for U.S.–U.S.S.R. meetings for the Joint Committee on Cooperation in the Field of Environmental Protection. As she dressed in her Jefferson Hotel suite for the swearing-in ceremony, she routinely examined her breast, a daily task her gynecologist had recommended after the birth of her first child and which she had religiously maintained. To her chilling incredulity, she found a lump at the position of twelve o'clock on her left breast.

Directly after the ceremony, she made arrangements to fly home to Woodside, where Charles had remained, to see her doctor. A mammogram was done. Her doctor assessed the chances at sixty to forty that the detected tumor would be benign, and he urged that she make an appointment at Stanford Medical Center for a biopsy. Shirley, latching on to the optimistic 60 percent odds, assumed there was no immediate danger and set the date for November 2, allowing her time to make the Russian trip and to participate in an environmental symposium in Cincinnati, Ohio, directly thereafter.

She was the only woman on the twenty-six-person Council on Environmental Quality. The group was met in Moscow by Soviet Culture Minister Eketerina Furtseva. Shirley's previous trip to Russia and her close work with the Soviet delegation at the United Nations served her well. As always before attending a convention abroad, she mastered words and phrases of the host country, extremely helpful preparation in terms of diplomacy. Her excellent phonetic ability gave authenticity to her pronunciation and made an added impression. On the second day of the conference, she sat in the distinguished guests' gallery of the Supreme Soviet Parliament while Vladimir Kirillin, chairman of the State Committee on Science and Technology, described capitalists as the world's major polluters.

The next morning, speaking to the American press in Moscow, Shirley rebutted with, "There is no difference. Pollution can be accrued just as easily whether [the polluters] are Communists, Socialists or Capitalists or whatever." She became the spokesman for the American delegation, and the talks went well enough for her to conclude later that "[b]oth countries will cooperate in matters concerning water pollution, air pollution, agricultural waste, misuses of agricultural land, Arctic and sub-Arctic ecological systems, genetic and biological problems resulting from pollution. They also will cooperate in studying earthquake prediction and a team of Soviet scientists will be coming to about ten minutes from where I live in California to investigate the San Andreas fault."

As the press was taking its leave, she turned to them and pleaded, "Please do not refer to me as the former child star. I prefer to be identified with my present job or my work with the United Nations."

"How about 'a former actress,' " one man asked.

"Alright," she smiled, "but not in the lead paragraph." The reporter, who was with United Press International, included the entire exchange at the end of his release. He had cannily won his point through her own quote and yet satisfied her request.

As she prepared for the homeward journey, the U.S.–U.S.S.R. treaty on pollution having been signed, she steeled herself for the medical procedure she was about to face. Her breast had become sensitive to her touch, and occasionally she awoke in her Moscow hotel room with a burning sensation in the area around the lump. She later recalled telling herself, "I bet this isn't going to be so good." She arrived home three weeks before her appointment at the Stanford Medical Center. Her parents, who now lived with her, were a grave concern. Gertrude had not been well, and Shirley did not want to alarm her. She also "could not bring herself" to talk with Charles about the suspicions she had about the possible outcome of the procedure.

She engaged in what she called "surreptitious" research, reading all she could on breast cancer, including the pros and cons of the various kinds of mastectomies. She asked her brother Jack, who was now working in the field of hospital administration, to send her pertinent material, and did a thorough job of researching all the options open to her if a malignancy was found. To make the subject easier to broach with Charles and the girls (Charlie was on a deep-sea fishing trip off the coast of Central America), she began to leave news articles about breast cancer around the house. "We discussed the clippings and were sobered by what we read," she recalled. Her fears were not eased by the grim knowledge that three of her close friends had died of breast cancer. She had also known women who had gone in for a biopsy and, without realizing the importance of a medical release they had signed, awakened from the anesthesia without a breast. Determined this would not happen to her, Shirley signed papers agreeing only to an excisional biopsy, which meant the final decision would be hers if the tumor was found to be malignant.

On the afternoon of November 1, the day before the procedure, she drove alone through strong wind and overcast skies to the hospital. The next morning, Charles was beside her when she came out of the anesthetic. He told her as gently as he could that one section of the tumor was malignant. She went back to sleep, not yet able to absorb the full impact of what he had said.

"When I came out of that sleep, out again of the haze of anesthesia wearing off, and faced it, I cried. My daughters came and we held on to each other and we all cried," she admitted. She soon pulled herself together and was ready to make her decision.

Her surgeon, Dr. Frederick P. Shidler at the Stanford Medical Center, recommended a modified radical mastectomy.* Requesting and receiving from the hospital a detailed report of her biopsy and reviewing what she had studied about her options, Shirley refused to undergo this procedure but "signed a release paper giving . . . permission for a *simple* mastectomy, plus, if necessary, the removal of a few lower nodes." From her medical reports, she felt optimistic that the malignancy had not spread. Her choice would lessen the cosmetic deformity of the original recommendation. "I felt . . . if the tumor *had* spread so far that more drastic surgery was necessary, it probably would be too late to save my life," she explained.

The operation was successfully performed on Friday, November 3. She admitted there had been "some intermittent weeping." She owned up bravely to the truth—the operation had been an amputation. By Monday, she had formulated plans to turn her "adversity into some help for [her] sisters." In 1972, mastectomy was a whispered word. Fear, shame and doubts about their womanliness plagued those who had had the operation. No well-known woman had gone public about having had her breast removed.† Unlike with the loss of a limb, a woman can conceal a breast amputation with a good prosthesis and well-made clothes so that no observer need know. But as Shirley later stated, this only made the emotional pressures on the woman greater.

Once she had decided to speak out, a direct, widespread way of doing so had to be found. Four days after her operation, she called Dave Shultz, the editor of the local *Redwood City Tribune*. He came immediately to the hospital. She presented him with a well-prepared and very personal statement and asked him "to get it on the wires" to all the news services. Then, her hair held

---

*The removal of the breast, lymph glands and nodes located under the arm and in the armpit.

†In recent years, many women have courageously shared knowledge of their mastectomies with the public, including First Ladies Betty Ford and Nancy Reagan and American television personality Betty Rollins.

back by a becoming ribbon, she allowed pictures of herself lying in her hospital bed to be taken. The fabled dimpled smile and laughing eyes were caught easily by the camera.

With great candor, she discussed her uncomplicated recovery from "a simple mastectomy, the surgical removal of one breast . . . I am telling this because I fervently hope other women will not be afraid to go to their doctors when they note any unusual symptoms. There is an almost certain cure for this form of cancer if it is caught early enough." She acknowledged that she had waited six weeks from the time of discovering the lump until her biopsy, and she stressed that other women should not be that lax. She added that she had personally made the decision to have the whole breast removed when informed of the malignancy.

The public response was overwhelming. The telephone board of the hospital was jammed. Some fifty thousand letters arrived for her within a week. Flowers overflowed her room, and she distributed the many additional bouquets she received to the various wards in the hospital. More important, the American Cancer Society reported a 30 percent increase in women seeking information on how to test themselves for breast tumors in the month following Shirley's disclosure. Only three weeks after surgery, she wrote a moving and well-informed article about her experience for *McCall's* magazine.

"Coming out of a hospital is to breathe freely again," she wrote. "I could smile and have a few wry thoughts." She then admitted to being one of the few Hollywood actresses who had never needed falsies. She joked about learning some Hollywood tricks in getting used to a prosthesis. ". . . as I look in the mirror I feel quite unattractive . . . I will accommodate to the look and to the feel. My arm hurts less each day. And my mirror looks back at me more kindly." With these confessions came precise information about breast cancer, the choices women victims had and how they could obtain counseling as well as medical help.

While Shirley had been hospitalized, Richard Nixon had been reelected president. In a series of articles beginning on October 10, 1972, the *Washington Post* had made the Watergate break-in a major moral issue, a lead followed by the rest of the East Coast media. It failed to stop a Nixon landslide. Yet within twenty months, the electoral verdict of 1972 would be negated.

Richard Nixon was, however, riding high in January 1973, when Shirley's strength returned; and she was hopeful that the president she had so loyally supported would recognize her diplomatic potential and name her to a prestigious post. The wait was long, and the assignment—when it did come—was not what she had expected. By then, Nixon had tearfully resigned in disgrace, and Gerald Ford, his Republican replacement, made the appointment.

17

FOLLOWING THE WATERGATE DEBACLE and Richard Nixon's resignation on August 9, 1974, Vice-President Gerald R. Ford, who had also filled Spiro Agnew's vacated office when he had resigned after pleading "nolo contendere" to the charge of income-tax evasion, was approved by Congress to become the thirty-ninth U.S. president. No sooner had he moved into the White House than President Ford made his first three diplomatic appointments: George Bush, in the sensitive post of ambassador to China; Peter Flanigan (a former Nixon aide), ambassador to Spain; and Shirley Temple Black, ambassador to Ghana.

Under the Nixon administration, the curious American presidential custom of dealing out ambassadorships "as if they were party favors" had turned into something akin to tobacco auctions. During the House Judiciary Committee's presidential-impeachment inquiry, Nixon's personal lawyer, Herbert Kalmbach, testified that Peter Flanigan had asked him to "contact a Dr. [sic] Ruth Farkas in New York. She is interested in giving $250,000 for Costa Rica."

According to Kalmbach's testimony, when he met with Mrs. Farkas over lunch in New York, she said, "Well, you know I am interested in Europe, I think, and isn't $250,000 an awful lot of money for Costa Rica." Then Mrs. Farkas contributed three hundred thousand dollars, and became American ambassador to Luxembourg.*

---

*Farkas received her M.A. in psychology from Columbia University in 1932 and had been an instructor at New York University School of Education, 1949–55. She had been

About the nomination of Flanigan for the embassy in Spain, William Shannon of *The New York Times* wrote that "President Ford identified himself with the corrupt, cash-on-the-barrelhead practices of his predecessor." He added that "Mr. Bush . . . knows as much about China as the usual rich Texas tourist* . . . there are rare instances in which a President will reasonably appoint a distinguished outsider to a diplomatic post. But these should be persons so eminent and so uniquely qualified that their nominations would be immediately recognized as a stroke of imagination." President Ford's choice of Shirley, he stated, did not "fall in that category."

But there was much to be said in support of Shirley's appointment. Her work at the United Nations had given her a special understanding of African problems, and she had made many close friends among representatives from the Third World. Ghana was a strongly matriarchal society, where a woman would be well accepted, and a well-known American ambassador would help the nation's flagging self-esteem. Certainly, Shirley had proved her intelligence and diligence at the UN, and Africa held a great fascination for her.

When queried about Shirley's appointment, President Ford later replied, "I do not recall if there were other specific individuals who were under consideration. Most likely there were other career Foreign Service candidates but . . . Ghana was a very upward African nation during that continent's turmoil in the 1970's. It was important that the new Ambassador be identified as a personal choice of the White House. Mrs. Black was so recognized. Her appointment was a clear indication of Presidential concern for the problems in Africa."

White House Press Secretary J. F. terHorst commented that the president was simply carrying out former President Nixon's desire to name "Mrs. Black to the diplomatic post," a statement that did not blunt the barbs of the press.

---

personal consultant for Alexander's Department Store, New York City, 1955–72, president of Dolma Realty Company, Fort Lauderdale, Florida, 1955–70, a member of the U.S. Committee to UNESCO, 1964–71. Her husband, George Farkas, was chairman of the board of Alexander's Department Store, a multimillion-dollar organization.

*Though born in Milton, Massachusetts (1924), Bush had co-founded (1953) the Zapata Petroleum Company and the Zapata Offshore Company based in Houston, Texas, which was his main residence until his election as vice-president in 1980.

Ford's friendship with Shirley "was longstanding [and was] both social and political." They had been golf buddies, and she had compaigned for him in past elections. But Ford would prove right about Ghana's reaction to her appointment. Although her close ties to the president and her celebrity were to give Ghana a sense of "being favored," the American press continued to think otherwise.*

"As a developing country Ghana deserves to be treated as more than a dumping ground for political appointees," the *Washington Post* stated. "Black, like Bush, received a United Nations post after unsuccessful political pursuits; this career pattern is an unsatisfactory substitute for professional diplomatic experience, and will not enhance respect for the United States abroad."

Other newspapers implied that Shirley had purchased her new post with political contributions. At her request, the State Department arranged a news conference at which she told the journalists that she and Charles had contributed merely $1,167 since 1970 to various political organizations, ony $310 of which had gone to the Republican party. "I think that proves I didn't purchase the post," she said. "But if I could have picked a place to serve it would have been in black Africa."

Her friendship with Angie Brooks and other representatives of African nations at the UN had not diminished, and she had a great respect for, and interest in, the continent and its people. She sincerely believed she was qualified and that her work for the UN had provided her with "a good deal of diplomatic experience."

Diplomacy, she said, had been a business she had known since childhood, and spoke of the time when she was seven. On a publicity tour, a mayor had accidentally slammed a car door on three of her fingers. The door was immediately opened, and Gertrude whispered, "Don't cry!" "My mother put my fingers in her mouth. She was afraid to look. [The fingers were] cut . . . but not badly. It was an early [diplomatic] lesson."

She had been anything but inactive since her cancer operation. Her work in environmental matters had continued, and she

---

*Black was not the first former film star to become an ambassador. John Lodge, after his term as governor of Connecticut, served as U.S. ambassador to Spain (1955–61) and ambassador to Argentina (1969–73).

had entered industry and big business as a member of the boards of the Del Monte Corporation ("the largest canner in the world"), the Bank of America and the Disney Corporation. Plans were made for Charles to accompany her to Accra, Ghana's capital, and to conduct his marine-resources business from there during her two-year planned tour-of-duty. Charlie was at Stanford University, Lori studying music, and both would join them on holidays, but Susan was to come with her parents.

"In a big double feature at the State Department yesterday [Friday, September 20] Shirley Temple Black was sworn in as Ambassador to Ghana and John Sherman Cooper [former U.S. Ambassador to India] was sworn in as Ambassador to the German Democratic Republic," the *Washington Post* reported. "His ceremony drew a bigger crowd but hers was more of a show and included refreshments . . . Secretary of State Henry Kissinger told the former child actress and later U.N. Delegate that he had always wanted to 'get movie stars into a position where they had to come when I called them, and now that I've solved the problem, I'm married.' " The remark brought only a wry smile to Shirley's face.

In the two-and-one-half months before her departure, she attended fifty-five official State Department briefings on Ghana, studying pertinent material dealing with the people, their history, economic condition and relations with the United States. She took a "crash, brush-up course" in French (English is Ghana's official language; French is spoken in Ghana's neighbor Togo) and learned a smattering of the main African tongues spoken there. The family gathered in Woodside for Thanksgiving, and on November 28, Shirley, Charles and Susan flew to Accra.

Ghana was the birthplace of black Africa's dreams. Once a prime shipping point for slaves going to America and known as the Gold Coast during its years as a British colony, it was the first West African country to break from colonial rule, a feat engineered by the political skill of one man—Kwame Nkrumah. Educated in the United States, his early thirties spent in London, where he mixed with leftist friends, Nkrumah was a reformist rather than a revolutionary. He returned to his home in Accra at the end of 1947, and within two years formed the Convention People's Party (CPP). After leading a disruptive general strike, he was taken political prisoner by the British. Despite his incarceration, his power increased, and in 1951 the CPP won a general election. Released by his captors, Nkrumah was offered the leadership of a CPP government with internal autonomy. His achievement was seen "as a proof to all Tropical Africans that real progress against colonial rule was possible." Nine years later, the Gold Coast became a republic and was renamed Ghana, after an ancient country of the western Sudan. Nkrumah emerged as one of the most powerful African leaders and became the inspiration for many other African nationalist movements.

The grand visions for his country that Nkrumah implemented—new roads, expensive state buildings, the expansion of his personal guard into a regiment—led to reckless spending, unbridled corruption and unpaid debts to Western creditors. In February 1966, while he was in Hanoi on his way to China, the Ghanaian police and army led a coup that toppled him from power, and he never was to return to the country he had liberated.*

The military ruled Ghana for three years before leadership was handed over to the former head of the party opposition, the erudite, Oxford-educated Dr. Kofi A. Busia.† This government was overthrown in 1972 by a military coup headed by Colonel Ignatius Kutu Acheampong. Ghana's government was now a military dictatorship but not entirely a police state, for the press was tolerated, as were trade organizations.

Nevertheless, corruption and mismanagement plagued the Ghanaians under the despotic Acheampong. Most of the country's cash crops, particularly cocoa, were smuggled out of the country, and half the nation's foreign-exchange earnings were unable to be accounted for. Food shortages were desperate. Stores displayed empty shelves. The transportation system had broken down, and few buses were in service. Acheampong and

---

*Nkrumah lived in exile until 1972, when he died of cancer in Guinea, where he had held power as "co-president" with Sekou Touré for six years.

†Busia had been a visiting professor at Northwestern University, Illinois, 1954; professor of sociology, Institute of Social Studies, The Hague 1959–62; professor of sociology and culture of Africa, University of Leiden 1960–62; director of studies for World Council of Churches, Birmingham, England 1962–64; professor of sociology, St. Antony's College, Oxford, 1965; and had published many books, *The Challenge of Africa* (1962) and *Africa in Search of Democracy* (1967) being perhaps the best known.

his huge staff drove Mercedes-Benzes (flown into Ghana at a cost of $110,000 each plus shipping charges) for their personal use and squandered "so much money . . . there was no more foreign exchange." Widespread demonstrations against the government were rampant, and Acheampong retaliated with all the brutality at his disposal.

Ghana was not inherently poor. Had the money from cocoa exports remained in the country, it would have amounted to nearly one billion dollars a year. Diamonds, bauxite, gold and manganese remained to be mined. But there were no open mines or equipment. During Acheampong's regime, "Ghana had been stripped bare, cannibalized like a car whose working parts had been stolen by thieves," according to African historian David Lamb. "As the economic situation worsened [in the 1970's] the country produced its own version of boat-people, peasants fleeing not repression but poverty, moving north in little home-made boats to the Ivory Coast and Liberia. When the government offered free transportation home to the 50,000 Ghanaians [the country had a population of eleven million] living and working in Nigeria, no more than a handful accepted."

A rampant black-market system known as *kalabule* (meaning "to take away without looking") had replaced the legitimate economy, and inflation rose 50 percent in one year. People who "had talked about their ability to achieve, now [spoke] only of their capacity to endure."

The man Shirley was to replace, Ambassador Fred Latimer Hadsel, had held the post since September 1971.* He and his staff had to deal not only with the severe problems in their host country but with their own shaky financial and living conditions, because the State Department insisted that the embassy staff pay for food, shelter and other commodities in Ghanaian cedis. To do otherwise was against Ghanaian law, "a consideration," Shirley's future counselor for public affairs, Kenneth Bache, recalled, "the staff of the American embassy were almost unique in observing." He added ruefully, "Many foreigners, notably

---

*Hadsel was a career diplomat. From 1946–56 he served the Department of State as executive secretary on African affairs. He was first secretary in the American embassy in London, 1957–61; deputy chief, American embassy, Addis Ababa, Ethiopia, 1961–62; director of inter-Africa affairs, 1963–64; ambassador to Somalia, 1969–71. He retired from foreign service upon departure from Ghana.

Lebanese, who had arrived with suitcases full of dollars, pounds, Swiss francs, etc. (as well as many well-placed Ghanaians), were ready to trade in other currencies. The result was that as soon as landlords could find pretexts to get us out of their houses, they did so, and turned them over to people less concerned with such niceties of law." As a result of the State Department's decision, the American members of the embassy staff were forced to scrounge for decent living quarters and staples without resorting to the black market. Nor did the policy make it easy to find Ghanaian workers willing to fill the nondiplomatic jobs—both clerical and domestic.

"The economy simply was not functioning," Bache continued. "What little was produced was promptly smuggled out in search of virtually any currency other than the worthless Ghanaian cedi. Even gainfully employed Ghanaians spent much of the work day on lines to buy soap or cooking oil, during which time they did not produce even for the smuggling trade. Ghana, which had had the heady experience of carving out its own destiny under the charismatic Kwame Nkrumah, was now as badly off as any of its Third World contemporaries—indeed, worse off than some prominent ones such as its next door neighbor, Ivory Coast, which was in the process of supplanting Ghana as the world's leading cocoa producer.

"It's not much of an overstatement, if any, to suggest that the Acheampong regime's security lay in part in the fact that few potential rivals saw much to be attained by seizing power. Certainly there was very little wealth to skim off."

Those citizens who had some foreign currency at their disposal tried to obtain a visa for either the United States or Great Britain. "Every morning when we opened the doors to the American embassy, at least fifty people would be waiting to apply, and the numbers never seemed to dwindle," another staff member recalled. "They would line up at dawn."

Because students had a greater chance of obtaining visas, fraudulent educational documents were submitted by at least two-thirds of the applicants. Even so, two thousand Ghanaian students made their way to the United States in 1974.

"There's no country club life for an envoy in Accra," Robert Price, an American who had just returned from there, commented. "And when you leave Accra to go up-country there is no indoor plumbing. It's a rough job." Shirley had replied that she was quite capable of roughing it.

"There was keen anticipation of Ambassador Black's arrival in Ghana," Ralph H. Graner, economic/commercial counselor at the American embassy in Ghana remembers. "In fact, there was so much anticipation that . . . an American television network program [60 *Minutes*] decided to cover it.* [Along with the television personnel and camera crew] a protocol official from the government of Ghana was present at the airport, members of the embassy staff and their spouses were there with several other ambassadors assigned to Ghana from other countries . . . as I recall that crowded arrival scene, although she must have been tired from such a long flight, Ambassador Black carefully met and chatted with every person there to greet her."

"I want to see the embassy now," she requested as she was being led to a waiting car. The marine guards, she confided, "are all going to be waiting to see what the new Ambassador is like—is this going to be a working Ambassador or one who wants to play tennis all day?"

The sprawling city of Accra is on the Gulf of Guinea in Ghana's southernmost region. Sandy, palm-studded beaches extend along the gulf. To the east are the rain forests and high mountain ranges that form a natural border between Ghana and the small country of Togo. To the west are equatorial forests and the Ivory Coast. The massive Volta Lake is nearby, but one could not swim in the Volta or drink its water. Accra is humid most of the time, with the long, warm rains coming in two seasons—April to July and September through October. In August, the crowds reach maddening density at the two most popu-

---

*This segment of 60 *Minutes* was shown on television in the United States on Sunday, February 9, 1975. Judith Martin, television critic of the *Washington Post*, wrote, "The cheap, obvious, and hilarious trick [the producers] pull is to alternate film of Mrs. Black as U.S. Ambassador in Ghana with film of Miss Temple as li'l sweetums. Wee Shirley goes to bed with her ringlets all spread out on the pillow and lisps a song about growing up and going to a ball in a palace and meeting a prince. Mrs. Black then takes over with her hair stiffly teased, and a mother-of-the-bride type outfit on, walking on a red carpet through marble halls [the Ghana Administrational Building] to present her credentials to the head-of-state [Acheampong]. Another time Mrs. Black boards an airplane to fly to Accra, and then Miss Temple suddenly bounces up and down the plane's aisle singing about 'Good Ship Lollipop.' " Despite this, Martin concluded that "by the end of the program, the narrator is a fan, and the viewer will probably be at least wavering."

lar beaches—Labadi, which is frequented mostly by Europeans, and the coco-palmed Mile 13. The harmattan (a strong wind that often lasts from December through February) was momentarily due to arrive and cover everything in its path with a thick red carpet of dust.

The American embassy on Ring Road East was a strikingly designed neoclassic building, incongruously set among great coco palms and banana trees and squat, stucco neighboring buildings. "The Embassy was a security nightmare," Kenneth Bache recalled, "as it would be easy to be trapped inside; and it could not be expanded without radically distorting its design."* The ambassador's two-story residence, only a short distance from the embassy ("Ten minutes on a slow traffic day. If it was a heavy traffic day, it could take forever."), contained few of the luxurious features and bore no resemblance at all to the Blacks' Tudor-styled home in Woodside. "The downstairs looked like a cruise ship, large and open, and the upstairs was an amazing mish-mash of very small bedrooms, and very large adjoining bathrooms," Shirley said in describing the residence. "The garden was very pretty but airless. If only the British in the old Colonial days [when the house had been constructed] had built near the sea . . . but the British always seem to want to build inland and have lovely gardens." However, her new home did come with sufficient household staff. Since their wages could not be paid in foreign currency, Shirley soon learned the importance of *dash* (the Ghanaian word for a tip).

"Our first night," Susan recalled, "as we explored the garden of our official residence, the air around us was filled with a sound which resembled hundreds of creaking wheels . . . they were the cries of a large colony of fruit bats which roost in the trees about the house." The Blacks soon "accepted their dusk to dawn creaking as a friendly part" of their home environment as well as their "every-Sunday ritual: malaria tablets with breakfast," for Ghana has a variety of the disease that is "quickly fatal."

Malaria was not the only disease to fear. Measles was also "a killer . . . the water [in Ghana] carries many parasites," Shirley revealed, "and even a cold can almost take a life. So part of my

---

*Better security measures were provided for in renovations five years later.

work was to improve health conditions. We had this 'model kitchen' [in the residence] but it wasn't what you would think of as a model kitchen. It was a large plastic drum in which we kept boiled water. We had to boil water about twenty minutes to get out all the parasites."

Almost from the start of her tour of duty, she lived under a terrorist-group death threat. "I asked the State Department to ask [the terrorist group] why, and they said for the publicity." The explanation did not dispel the Blacks' concern for their well-being, but as a child Shirley had been aware of the constant danger of kidnapping. Caution had been observed, but had not been allowed to inhibit her normal routine. The Blacks had been used to the open spaces of California and the warm evenings when they could sit on the terrace; they continued this after-dinner ritual in Ghana, but under the watchful eyes of embassy-employed Muslim guards stationed at a discreet distance, and armed with bows and arrows.

One night, shortly after the Blacks' arrival in Ghana, their appearance in the garden startled the old Muslim guard on duty. Because snakes were more likely to move about in the open at night, Ghanaians seldom ventured into their gardens. Upon seeing the two figures outlined dimly in the shadowed moonlight, the old man drew back his bow string and aimed directly at Shirley, who was closer to him, obviously believing she was an intruder. Shirley froze as she caught sight of the man poised to shoot his arrow. "I thought back frantically," she recalled. Ghana had been a colonial state with allegiance to Queen Elizabeth. She waved her arms in an imperious gesture she had seen the queen use in a documentary, and then repeated the gesture rather widely. "He got frightened and dropped his bow, and took off with Charlie in hot pursuit," she remembered.

The new ambassador held her initial staff meeting on Tuesday afternoon, December 3, just two days after her arrival. "My first impression on meeting her," Bache remembers, "was how incredible—seemingly almost unnaturally—she had retained her well-known childish appearance. She was a little chubbier than perhaps a woman of her age would normally consider desirable, [which] created the illusion of . . . [her having] the same baby fat that helped make up her appearance as a child star. But it went beyond that. Her walk was clearly reminiscent of her [strutting] gait in the movies. Her intonation . . . was certainly recognizable from the old films. All this helped make me damn near incredulous when I was offered [at this first meeting] with a cup of coffee, a plate of Oreo cookies [brought with her from California]!

" 'Charming' is an inescapable adjective for Ambassador Black. She concentrated her attention heavily on you in any interchange. She obviously worked hard in making you feel good and being entertaining. By the same token, she did not like dealing negatively with anyone. She had her dislikes, but she usually relied on others to convey disapproval or other negative messages."

Shortly after this meeting, she presented her credentials to Acheampong in the grand reception room of the palatial Administrational Building built by Nkrumah (the cost of which had nearly bankrupted Ghana.) "It was probably the most thrilling moment of my life," Shirley remembered. "Standing alone in a little canopied setting with the Ghanaian Air Force band playing 'The Star Spangled Banner' was almost too much. I was covered in gooseflesh; then the talking drums of welcome really covered me with gooseflesh; the talking drums go all the way to the pit of your stomach. To me it was like *The National Geographic* magazine come to life."

Seated on a massive carved wood throne, dressed in an elaborate uniform embellished with a dazzling display of ribbons, gold-braid and medals, the large, dark-skinned Acheampong was an imposing figure. On cue, Shirley stepped forward from her canopy and walked toward him. He stood, towering over her as she handed him a leather portfolio. "Your Excellency," she said in a strong, clear voice, "I am deeply honored to present the letters by which the President of the United States, Gerald R. Ford, accredits me as Ambassador extraordinary and plenipotentiary of the United States of America to the Republic of Ghana. Thank you." Acheampong handed the portfolio to an aide, and with equal formality, in a grave, deep voice, welcomed her to Ghana.

Variously a Roman Catholic, an Animist, a Rosicrucian, Acheampong also "dabbled in black magic." He chain-smoked cigarettes and had an enormous capacity for whiskey. "He was very fearful that people were out to get him," Shirley commented. "He was a complicated man."

She settled right into a stiff routine of long hours and much commonplace drudgery. But the role of American ambassador to Ghana also involved a great many social events—with Ghanaians, with diplomats from other countries, and with members of the American community living in Ghana, which, apart from the embassy staff, included executives from the thirty-five American companies operating in the country, a few traders in African arts, Peace Corps volunteers, missionaries and a handful of Americans married to Ghanaians.* Well-known personalities did not often visit Ghana, and Shirley was sought out as a guest at all large events, either governmental or social, rapidly establishing herself as the most popular foreigner in residence.

Confirming President Ford's feeling that Ghana would be honored by Shirley's appointment, Kenneth Bache comments, "The presence of a celebrity ambassador . . . symbolized some sort of importance accorded them by the U.S.; and it drew media attention to them, which had some prestige advantages and could have helped with the tourist trade if they had been prepared to handle tourists. Unhappily, Accra's two hotels operated pretty much the way the rest of the economy did. [Nevertheless,] quite a number of American journalists who otherwise would not have included Accra on their itinerary did show up to do stories on the 'moppet ambassador.' "

Her ambassadorial style was a unique blend of show-business know-how and serious dedication to her job. She undertook her diplomatic chores in blithe disregard of protocol. Invited by Accra's Market Women's Association for an official visit to the city's teeming outdoor Makola Market, she wore a colorful African dress and matching head scarf, and greeted the "market mammies," as the women who ran the stalls were called, in the native Ghanaian languages of Fanti, Ga and Twi. "It was an exciting and heart-warming experience," she recalled. "They were all wearing local cloth and singing songs of welcome; they spread cloth on the ground in front of me. I didn't want to step on it until they explained it was a sign of welcome. So I stood on it and did a Highlife [a native dance] in my walking shoes. It wasn't hard to learn. The music is complica-

---

*The major American corporations with offices or plants in Ghana at the time were Firestone Tire and Rubber Company, Johnson's Wax and the Kaiser Aluminum Corporation.

ted, but the step itself is easy." After this accomplishment, she was "cheered, hugged, kissed and touched by literally thousands of the market women." From this time, Shirley, at formal state functions, frequently wore African dress bought from the stalls of the Makola.

"I can't imagine Princess Margaret making a better job of a royal stay than Ambassador Black accomplished in Ghana. And the Ghanaians treated her that way—as an American princess," a staff member recalls. "She was installed with regularity as an honorary member of the various native tribes. Within a matter of months of her arrival, scores of newborn Ghanaian babies were being christened with her name."

Kenneth Bache remembers the time when, soon after coming to Ghana, she was inducted as an honorary chief in a tribal community in Cape Coast, a town about two hours out of Accra.

"The event was part of a *durbar*, a lengthy and elaborate set of rituals involving dances, speeches, invocations, drumming and the like. The chief was seated on a raised platform at one end of an open field, where all the goings-on took place. She was on another platform at the other end. She had nothing to do but sit there—but she had to stay there for several hours without interruption, at least three, as I recall, probably more. She stayed the course, always sitting bolt upright, always paying full attention to what was going on, always smiling and appearing gracious and happy. The rest of us could sneak off and take care of the demands of nature. She could not. To this day, I don't know how she did it."

Of her earliest meeting with a Ghanaian chief, Shirley noted "my deputy chief minister [Jack Linehan, who was 6′4″] was very tall and always sitting with his legs crossed. Well, you never cross your legs in front of a [Ghanaian tribal] chief—it's an insult. And you never show the bottom of your foot either . . . I had [not been there very long]. I didn't want to tell someone to stop doing something. But I was kind of gesturing to him to put his foot down . . . when the chief asked me something. I didn't quite hear him and I tried to be very polite and said 'yes' to whatever he said. I had apparently agreed to marry him—my first diplomatic incident. He had several wives already and had very few teeth; he was an older man . . . that started me off [in Ghana]." Her first official job of diplomacy was getting out of this situation gracefully without insulting the chief, a feat she managed to accomplish.

"I had met her in the fall of seventy-four, as she was about to depart for her new post," Jack Linehan explained. "At the time, I was director of public affairs of the African Bureau in the State Department, and it was my job among other things to meet with all new ambassadors and talk with them about public relations and press and the like. With her, it was a different case, because she was certainly used to dealing with the press. [Three months later] she returned to Washington for consultations and at that time was looking for a new deputy—hers was on the verge of finishing his tour. . . . She asked if I would like to be her deputy, and I said yes.

"One of my most vivid memories is of the opening of an international trade fair which was held by the Ghanaian government in Ghana and in which many nations participated. The American exhibition was in the first of two international buildings and directly across from the East German exhibition. Shirley advised me that the Ghanaian chief of state [Prime Minister Kofi A. Busia] would come first to the American exhibition before he went to the East German." Shirley then went outside, returning a short time later with the prime minister. "I asked her how she managed it," Linehan continued, "and she said, 'Oh, it was simple. I wore my brightest dress, and as he came along, I stepped out and said, "Your Excellency, welcome to the American exhibition," and I backed in front of the East German ambassador, so I simply upstaged him.' I said, 'Well, that's pretty damn good,' and she said, 'Of course, I've been doing it all my life.'

"Whenever I saw her standing at attention at a government function, that spunky child in *Wee Willie Winkie* came to mind. She could hold a ramrod position *forever* it seemed. And she never walked but *marched* up onto a stage," a staff member adds. On another occasion, wearing a Ghanaian dress and several gold bangle bracelets, she was carried before a cheering throng of twenty thousand. "Four of them picked me up like a side of beef," she smiled. "Then they gave me my royal scepter and stool."

She saw as her main job the promotion of greater American business interests in Ghana and the encouragement of America's assistance in the development of the economies of African countries. She instituted monthly discussion meetings among the executives of the Ghana-based American companies, and worked to pitch Ghana's opportunities in the business of fisheries, construction and agriculture to Americans looking for foreign investments. She took an active part in programs to set up more child-care centers and to teach mothers how to improve their children's diets on little money and limited food supplies and was a familiar figure in Accra's large and influential Market Women's Association meetings.

Because Ghana is a matriarchal society, men are most often the laborers and women their overseers.* Women manage the farms, own the fishing boats and run the fleets of open-sided vanlike taxicabs, known as "mammy wagons." In such a country, Shirley had no problem being taken seriously as a diplomat. And she enjoyed her role immensely. "She's got these people right in the palm of her hand," one American remarked. Another was overheard to comment at a reception, "You've got to give it to her; she always manages to say exactly what they want to hear."

The least successful of her endeavors in Ghana was her relationship with some of the Americans on her embassy staff. "She wasn't used to the management of a group—least of all a group of individual professionals, each of whom was used to taking responsibility for an area of operation," Bache explains. "She did not know how to put her staff in positions where they could function with maximum effectiveness in support of her. I honestly don't think it ever occurred to her that by moving into the center of any activity and any contact with Ghanaian officials, she was making it more difficult for her officers to be continuously effective with those contacts."

"She had a pretty good right-hand man, the deputy chief of mission, Jack Linehan," William K. Rosner of the staff recalls. "She left most of the administering to him. Jack was a very capable foreign service officer." On Linehan's arrival in Ghana, Shirley told him, "You're the pro, I expect you to run the show, but I want to know what's going on." Linehan took her at her

---

*Ghanaian descent is traced and inheritance is passed on through the female rather than the male line.

word. "I found myself working with a person I admired and with whom I enjoyed working," he commented.

"The embassy staff was a sort of slaphappy crew," Rosner continued. "We got out and did just about everything there was to do in Ghana. We traveled to the neighboring countries when we had the time. In the evenings, we entertained almost every night in each other's homes or went to parties at the homes of other diplomats. Every national day called for a party and a reception. Quite a bit of drinking was done. There were no indoor movie theaters, they were all outdoors. The one I used to go to had a big tree off to the right of the screen, which usually cast a shadow on the picture."

With Shirley's talent for nesting, her family life was maintained along with her official duties. Construction was begun on a swimming pool (paid for by the Blacks), a Boxer pup was added to the household and Shirley learned how to cook Ghanaian food. Charles was away frequently on company matters, but Susan was at hand, and mother and daughter were often in each other's company. Susan attended many functions with Shirley and remembered an afternoon party at Peduase Lodge given by Ghana's commissioner for foreign affairs, Lieutenant Colonel Kwame Baah. The lodge is "an imposing white structure situated in the Aburi Hills. . . . Guests could swim, play tennis, billiards or ping-pong. . . . Lori, visiting us over the Christmas holidays, suggested [we] watch the table tennis games in the indoor pavilion . . . We found a large appreciative crowd and at its center a spirited match between mom and the Ambassador of the People's Republic of China. The play was rapid and a credit to both sides, but at game's end, the victory was Ambassador Yang's."

Later that same afternoon, Shirley played a losing game of chess with the counselor of the Soviet embassy. Relations were good among the various embassies. The Soviets hosted a film party for the staff of the American embassy; Shirley reciprocated by inviting the Soviets to view some of her old movies; the Chinese ambassador paid a unique courtesy call (to his surprise, instead of offering him tea or coffee, Shirley served hot bouillon soup); and within a month of her arrival Susan began to date an attractive young man, Roberto Falaschi, a first secretary at the Italian consulate and son of the Italian ambassador to Uganda.

Each embassy celebrated its national holiday with a large reception. To commemorate Independence Day, Shirley decided on holding two events: one, a picnic for all the Americans residing in Ghana (about twenty-five hundred at the time), and the other a formal reception at her residence for the staffs of her own and the more than forty other embassies.

William Rosner remembers "something really odd at the picnic. It was the ambassador standing up on a podium while [a recording of] a very patriotic talk she had made somewhere in the United States—probably at an Air Corps base, because in the background there was the sound of fighter jets zooming overhead—came over the loudspeaker system. The speech was about what it means to be an American—something you could probably not get away with on any day of the year except the Fourth of July, and it was rather well received by the American colony [about one thousand had attended]. But it was bizarre for her to stand there at attention listening to her own speech.

"The formal Fourth of July reception was held that evening. I remember being at several staff meetings with the ambassador to discuss preparations. Rather than serve the normal little French hors d'oeuvres and the things people passed around at cocktail parties, she wanted this to be an all-American party in every respect, with typical American food served. The menu was to include hamburgers, hot dogs, potato salad and corn on the cob, and she was insistent that peanut butter and jelly sandwiches—which she saw as a typically American snack—also be served. [Numerous jars of peanut butter duly arrived and were given to the Ghanaian kitchen staff.]

"I remember cruising down the buffet tables and picking up something to eat—a hot dog here, some potato salad—and then seeing a couple of large metal trays, almost like cookie sheets but a little bit deeper—great big ones. In them was this soupy green mixture and something murky lurking on the bottom. I didn't take any. I just sort of looked at it and shook the tray discreetly to try to figure out what it was. Some of the Ghanaians, to be polite, tried to spoon it out on their plates. I saw them staring down at the green globs which were swimming on their plates, running over on their food.

"Later, we realized that in a former British colony like Ghana, if you say *jelly,* you're referring to what Americans call a gelatin dessert. The kitchen staff had followed her instructions exactly and put down a layer of sliced white bread on the cookie tins, spread the peanut butter over them and then topped them with slabs of lime gelatin. When they put this out in the tropical climate of Ghana, the [gelatin] began to melt into a sort of green soupy mess thickened slightly by the oozing peanut butter. No one was really quite sure what it was, but I think they thought it was all typically American.''

Ralph Graner, who was assigned to the embassy during Shirley's entire term of office, felt that she "respected the professionalism of those who worked for her, thus—in my view—bringing out the best in them. . . . She kept herself carefully informed of all that went on. . . . She expected to and did take responsibility for major decisions, usually—but not as an automatic matter—accepting the advice of her staff. She read great quantities of briefing and other material, seemingly retaining all the detailed information for great periods of time. Most evenings she went home with a full briefcase of things to read there.''

She fell under grossly unfair attack when a widely publicized rumor accused her of seeking to purge her staff of blacks in key positions, notably Reginald Ingram, deputy executive director of the Agency for International Development. Shirley had in fact written to James Pope of the Bureau on African Affairs in the State Department to urge the department to "do what is possible to ensure that blacks and other racial minority groups continue to be well-represented in Embassy assignments. There are political advantages to our posture in Africa if our posts continue to include personnel drawn from minority groups." Pope, when asked to comment on Ingram's recall, said that it was the result "of an economy drive and had absolutely nothing to do with the Ambassador.''

Recounting her own experience in Africa with the race problem, Shirley told a journalist, "I don't think black Africans are racist. Within a week after I arrived in Ghana, I no longer noticed whether an individual was black or white. The blacks don't seem to notice color either." She also reminisced about a time when she was nine years old and vacationing in a cottage at the exclusive Desert Inn in Palm Springs, California. Bill Robinson came down to teach her a new dance number for the film *Rebecca of Sunnybrook Farm.* "When he arrived I asked Bill what cottage he was staying in. 'I'm staying across the road, above the drug store,' he told me. . . . It wasn't until years later that I understood why."

She went on record "as being strongly in favor of majority rule in both Zimbabwe and Mamebia," and added, "I'm for an end to apartheid in South Africa as rapidly as possible. . . . My hope is that by getting the black nationalists and the whites directly affected—plus the leaders of other black countries—to sit down and talk, they'll be able to avoid a bloodbath if the talks fail."

After a moment's pause, she commented, "One thing that upsets me about my own country, and may even trouble some black Africans, is that we Americans don't seem to have heroes any more. Everyone is being cut down. When I was little girl I had many heroes. I met Eleanor Roosevelt when I was nine years old and I think she influenced me, got me interested in human rights and human dignity for all people. I admired [aviatrix] Amelia Earhart for getting out on her own and doing something women hadn't ever done before."

Ghana had one woman hero, Justice Annie Jiagge, internationally known for her work in the fields of law and human rights. Ghanaian women held many senior government positions in medicine, journalism, the arts, finance and law. Besides Shirley, there were three other women ambassadors in Ghana. Her sex did not make her unique, but her personal style and charisma set her apart. Her success as a career woman was much admired in a country where "women's liberation banners draped the dusty streets of even the most remote village. . . . Liberation is not freedom from work—it is freedom to work," she was quoted as saying. In such a female-oriented society, Charles's role as the husband of the ambassador was fairly nebulous. As Shirley's tour of duty progressed, his business trips became more frequent, but, as Susan says, "he retained his love, support, and pride in mom's work."

"The only thing I ever saw [Charles Black] doing," William Rosner observes, "was cleaning out the swimming pool [at the residence.] He used to run one of those nets over the top of it and pull out insects and palm fronds and things like that."

In the summer of 1975, Susan, now twenty-seven and a neophyte author, and Roberto Falaschi announced their engagement. They were married October 8. The union received much coverage by the paparazzi in Italy and brought about a brief revival in that country of the sale of Shirley Temple dolls and dresses. A new Italian recording of "On the Good Ship *Lollipop*" was made, and it sold well enough to make the Italian charts.

Rosner, who dealt with all visas to the United States, remembered that shortly after their marriage "the Ambassador's daughter and her husband showed up at my office with their passports. Now, of course, Ambassador Black's daughter had an American passport, but at this time she also had an Italian diplomatic passport which she was entitled to as [Falaschi's wife.] She gave the passport to me and said, 'Would you please give me a tourist visa?'

"I explained that I could not issue her a visa because American citizens are prohibited from receiving American visas. It became evident to me that she was applying for [a visa] on her Italian passport so she could use [a diplomatic passport] to enter the United States. I told her very politely, 'I can't do this, it's against the law.' I [later] had a phone call from the Ambassador asking me to please issue her daughter a visa. I explained to her that it is illegal . . . [It was] a delicate situation [and] I phoned the State Department . . . She [soon] received a communication from the Department of State again citing the law. . . . The incident seemed to upset the Ambassador's daughter . . . whenever I saw her again after that she was rather cold."

But it was to be Henry Kissinger, not Susan, who would create Shirley's most difficult diplomatic problem in Ghana. In March 1976, she received word that the secretary of state was planning a tour of African nations in the following month. The most important stop on his tour was to be Zambia, where he was expected to make a major foreign-policy address in which he would advocate black-majority rule while warning against foreign intervention. Ghana had not been included on his itinerary, and Shirley was determined that this oversight be rectified.

However, Secretary of State Kissinger's presence in Ghana would have created a difficult problem of diplomacy for Acheampong's regime. Ghana, along with Nigeria, had opposed the United States' stand on Angola, and earlier, in protest, Nigeria had rejected the possibility of a visit by the secretary of state.* Now, this stronger, richer nation placed pressure on Ghana to back it up. Acheampong was in a quandary. On the one hand, he could not afford to offend the United States by refusing to welcome the secretary of state if he arrived in Ghana; on the other, he was not in a position to deny Nigeria's request. Although this situation was made clear to Shirley, she pressed on until Acheampong relented and offered a welcome for Kissinger, shaded in cool terms.

The secretary of state was to arrive in Ghana on April 29, on an itinerary that also included Kenya, Tanzania, Zambia, Zaire, Liberia and Senegal. At the outset of the tour, Kissinger believed that his ambassador to Ghana had cleared the way for a receptive state visit. But "[t]he Ghanaians . . . insisted that a mere cabinet member could not meet an exalted person [such] as [Acheampong]," Craig Baxter, the American embassy's political officer recalls. "Kissinger's insistence and Ghanaian stonewalling resulted in the cancellation by the Ghanaians of the visit." The secretary of state was in flight when he received his ambassador's notification that the Ghanaian government had withdrawn its invitation. Relations between the two countries were suddenly most delicate.

"The reason given is the poor health of General Ignatius Kutu Acheampong," Robert Funseth, a State Department spokesman, told reporters traveling with Kissinger aboard the plane. "However," he continued, "we recognize the many pressures that the government of Ghana has experienced from foreign sources. We regret that the visit has been cancelled." Later, another official said that "the United States had been aware that Soviet diplomats were agitating among Ghanaian officials and students against the visit and that the U.S. planned to make a formal protest" the next day.

---

*After Angola failed at an attempt at independence in 1974, twenty thousand Cuban combat troops and more than fifteen hundred Soviet and Eastern bloc advisors arrived on Angolan soil. "The choice Washington faced was to sit by and watch a Marxist government come to power or to step up its support of the rebel armies enabling one of them to make the final push that would establish a pro-Western government. Ford and Kissinger had taken the latter course. The rebels had been given 40 million dollars. The U.S. Congress, wary of another Vietnam-type involvement, was unwilling to confront the Eastern bloc . . . and after long debate it cut off funds [to the rebels]." Several of the African nations, fearing that Marxism would now be planted on their doorsteps, saw the discontinuance of financial support to the rebels as an American betrayal.

"Obviously, the climactic problem for Ambassador Black in Ghana," Kenneth Bache says, "involved the aborted visit of Secretary of State Kissinger. . . . She had personally pushed him to schedule that visit . . . and the Ghanaians to invite him. . . . In hindsight, it was an error of political judgment to recommend the visit at that difficult time in the shaky Ghanaian military regime, and it was unfortunate that she made the project a personal issue for herself."*

The secretary of state asked her to meet him in Monrovia, Liberia (a country the other side of Ghana's neighbor, the Ivory Coast), the next day, April 30. Ostensibly, she would be attending a dinner given by Liberia's president, William R. Tolbert. The secretary of state could not have been in too good a mood, for he had been ill with severe stomach pains following a Zaire state dinner of wild boar and leaves of manioc plants. At the end of her short stay in Monrovia, Shirley announced that she was being recalled to Washington "for consultations."

A few days later, she received a letter from the State Department officially recalling her, and with it one from President Ford requesting that she accept an appointment as chief of protocol. Bache remembers that she showed him the letter from the president "and remarked rather gloomily that it was not the kind of request from a president that one could decline. What she was really saying was that she was hurt at having been thought of for such an assignment rather than one dealing with substantive aspects of foreign affairs. . . . She had mentioned more than once, in gatherings with senior officers, that she thought she might be named the next assistant secretary of African affairs. . . . Whenever she made trips back to Washington, she saw a glittering array of the administration's top Cabinet officers, who always assured her of full cooperation in whatever she asked. But somehow the implementation nearly always fell through. I think she sensed, as we did, that she was thought of in Washington as too prominent to be snubbed, but not really to be taken seriously. It had to have hurt."

---

*Acheampong was overthrown by his chief of staff, Lieutenant General Frederick W. K. Akuffo, in 1978. The next year, Akuffo was overthrown by thirty-two-year-old Ghanaian Air Force Lieutenant Jerry Rawlings, who had Acheampong and Akuffo executed following a secret trial. " 'Action, action, finish them all!' yelled the crowd as the former heads of state and several other top officials were blindfolded and bound to execution posts."

Her last few days in Ghana were most uncomfortable for her and the Ghanaians. "I vividly recall a very awkward sort of vigil at the airport," Bache remembers, "when all of us saw her off. She made no secret of her pain over the matter. The Ghanaians gave her virtually no send-off."

Packed in her suitcases were her Ghanaian dresses, the head scarves, carved jewelry and gold bangle bracelets. But her kinship for Africa had grown truly deep roots. "Africa is calling out for understanding," she told a reporter. "It is trying to make its voice heard in the West, just as we are trying to make our voice heard in Africa. All of us should listen to what is being said. . . . We are bound together in a complex web of interdependence."

Charles was by her side as she boarded the plane. She stood erect and waved from the top of the stairs as she was about to enter the cabin. She smiled broadly enough for her dimples to show, but there were tears in her eyes. Susan, married to a diplomat stationed in Ghana, would remain. Her daughter waved back, and the former ambassador to Ghana disappeared into the U.S. Air Force plane.

18 IN 1937, President Franklin Roosevelt appointed George Summerlin, former minister to Panama, to the newly created office of chief of protocol. Until then, diplomatic courtesy still was based in large measure on precedents and tradition. To avoid the possibility of appointment on a political basis (an intent that changed in later years), the new position was to be filled by an experienced Foreign Service officer with the rank of minister or ambassador. Among many more technical matters, the Department of Protocol was "made responsible for presentation to the President of Ambassadors or Ministers . . . correspondence concerning their acceptability . . . questions regarding rights and immunities of representatives of foreign governments in the United States, arrangements for all ceremonials of a national or international character [at home or abroad] . . . questions concerning customs and other courtesies extended to foreign officials . . . as well as to American officials abroad . . . arrangements of visits of foreign naval vessels and military organizations, the preparation of medals to be conferred and of certain communications from the President to the heads of foreign states."

Serious complications arose for the Department of Protocol during the period of racial unrest in the early 1960's. Angier Biddle Duke headed the department during the Kennedy administration, when "about half of the Washington diplomatic corps from 110 nations came from Africa and Asia and could not travel to some areas of the country or look for an apartment safely in Washington without assistance from the Department of

339

Protocol." At that time, the department was moved to the offices of the secretary of state.

The office of the chief of protocol was now responsible for highly sensitive matters as well as social niceties. Shirley's job was not that of a social director or a mere minder of manners. With an election due, the chief would also function importantly in the plans for the inauguration.

Her hair trimmed into a smart short bob, she took the oath of office on a Bible held by Charles, on July 20, 1976. President Ford asked if she wished to be referred to as Madam Ambassador. She replied that just Ambassador would be fine, but never Ambassadress, "which sounds more like something a person would be wearing." From this ceremony, she went directly to her large Spartan office in the center of which stood a massive desk backed by the special blue-and-gold consul flag and formerly occupied by her predecessor Henry E. Catto, Jr., who had been appointed U.S. ambassador to the United Nations Organizations in Geneva. She was the first woman to hold the job, and told reporters she looked forward to "shaking up anything I see that needs shaking up." An hour later, dressed in a chiffon gown, she sped to the White House for her first official duty—to introduce members of the Washington diplomatic corps at a bicentennial celebration. To the amazement of her associates, not one person was misaddressed nor was any name mispronounced. She had read through the list of guests and memorized it.

Heading a staff of forty-four, she quickly realized the job would entail an enormous amount of administrative work. One of her first assignments was to charter an aircraft for one hundred members of the diplomatic corps to travel to Kansas City, Missouri, in August for a one-day trip to the Republican National Convention (being conducted at Kemper Auditorium). Each ambassador paid $176 for the day trip. "They came back [to Washington] the same night," Shirley confessed. "We couldn't find any hotel rooms." Shirley had whisked the ambassadors, their wives and first secretaries on a "low budget eleven hour tour [of Kansas City] that included a V. I. P. look at bleary-eyed convention delegates in their closing-night cacophony." It ended at President Ford's headquarters, where a toast was made with imported Russian vodka in iced shot glasses.

Shirley's charges departed before Ford's expected nomination was confirmed, but she and Charles returned to Kansas City the next day to join in the president's victory celebration. They were given a room for the night that "had a White House phone in it," she remembered. "I said, 'Oh Charlie, maybe he was going to ask me to be his running-mate and had the phone installed.' I picked it up and it was disconnected. I'd be curious to know who had the room before me."

The Democratic National Convention had been held in the mid-July heat of New York City, and the nomination was won by Jimmy Carter, a relatively obscure governor of Georgia who had risen meteorically in a matter of three short months. "We had won the nomination, but the general election was still three months away," future First Lady Rosalynn Carter recorded. "After the Republican Convention in August, our lead plummeted from a high of 25 points to 8 or 9 points. It was understandable, everyone assured me. Ford was the familiar figure; Carter the unknown . . . it brought everyone back from thinking about where their offices were going to be in the White House!"

When Shirley had accepted her new post, Gerald Ford's chances of reelection were good. Had this occurred, Shirley almost certainly could have looked forward to a long tenure in Washington. Travel on behalf of his company would keep Charles away a good part of the time, but Shirley had become used to these periods of separation. They sublet a spacious high-rise apartment on Massachusetts Avenue in northwest Washington and decorated it with California furniture and African artifacts. George and Gertrude remained in Woodside. Young Charlie was also at home, with plans to study international relations at a graduate school that fall.* Lori was continuing with her music studies.

Shirley ran her new home with a minimum of outside assistance. She lunched in the State Department cafeteria on cottage cheese, "the only thing she really missed in Ghana." Her most difficult problem was shared by other women in the Diplomatic Corps and Foreign Service. "They all need wives. The Chief of

---

*Charles Black, Jr., was employed in 1988 in Washington in the Commerce Department as confidential assistant to Joseph F. Dennin, the assistant secretary for international economic policy.

Protocol's wife is expected to assist her husband," Shirley explained. "During arrival ceremonies she is supposed to hold the flowers given to the visiting head of state's wife by the President's wife." She was also expected to take care of the staff and refurbishing of Blair House, the official residence of state visitors. "I have to be my own wife," Shirley admitted, although she delegated many such tasks to some of the other women on her staff and to the wife of the deputy chief of protocol.

Her attitude toward men straightforward and yet never overbearing, Shirley was especially qualified to be working in a male-oriented, high-executive capacity. She claimed in a proud tone that she had to work harder than a man in the same job—and could do it with more energy and grace, a statement supported by her staff. "Indecision is the thing that drives men against a wall," Shirley commented. And she was never indecisive.

After the disappointment and personal embarrassment of her last days in Ghana, she was determined to avoid any further such indiscretions. She admitted that one of her most strident critics was her boss, Henry Kissinger. But "I'm durable," she stated. "I don't damage easily."

Her current post precluded any active campaigning on behalf of Ford. As Election Day drew near, Ford's defeat was a real possibility. The president had lacked the mandate of election. He had held the office only two years, the first spent in a desperate effort to disentangle the administration from Watergate, the second "in a bid to put together a coalition to get himself elected." One observer notes, "Behind the orderly facade of the Ford White House, there were inconclusive battles for power among rival subordinates which Ford lacked the authority and savagery to end. As a colleague put it, 'Good old Gerry was too damned good for his own good.' Ford's views, on the rare occasions when they emerged, usually turned out to be sensible, but he lacked *gravitas*. In public, he developed an unfortunate tendency to fall over [a reference to the several times he tripped in public]."

Carter, on the other hand, beamed self-confidence and promised "not only new formulas but effective implementation." When he won the election by a narrow margin in November, Shirley had good reason to suspect her days as chief of protocol would be numbered because of her zealous connection to Nixon and Ford.

But she had always been more a nationalist than a Republican. To Shirley, it was America's image, pride and power that were truly important, and she believed that the Republican party was better equipped to achieve these ends. The political part of her nature that had surfaced in the 1960's had been satiated by the hundreds of campaign speeches she had given in support of her party's candidates. She had, in fact, made more speeches and appearances on behalf of Richard Nixon than had his wife, Pat, or either of his daughters. Her association with the United Nations, the Multiple Sclerosis Society, environmental committees and wildlife-preservation groups and her years in Ghana had given rise to wider ambitions.

"I don't think she liked working under Henry [Kissinger]," a staff member comments. "She had what she called an 'open-door' policy. We [the staff] were to go into her office and discuss all our problems and gripes. 'No calls for five minutes' she would tell her secretary if the subject appeared serious, and you knew she meant *five minutes.* She liked people to be straightforward with her and she would reply in that same manner, but she never betrayed her own problems or doubts. I never got over the fact that I was asking Shirley Temple for advice and that afterward I was often able to cope with a problem that had previously seemed insurmountable.

"You know, she had a way of chuckling—with her chin tucked in and her eyes wide—that suddenly dissolved the distance of years. There she was, little Shirley, telling gruff old Lionel Barrymore in simple terms how to be happy. It was very disconcerting. She is surprisingly wise and never wishy-washy. And she would never put you down.

"We used to call Charlie 'the consort.' He was terribly proud of being 'Mr. Black.' No one on her staff thought [her present job] would be the end of her career, least of all Charlie. I suspect he would have liked her to go on to a Cabinet post or even as a vice-presidential candidate."

Preparations for the Carter inauguration were begun immediately following his election. As tradition dictated for presidential appointees, Shirley had filled out a resignation form giving the new president a free hand to select those he wanted to assign key jobs. But with the arrangements for the inauguration facing her, she had little time to worry about the future. Her main duties were to be in charge of the diplomatic corps present at the ceremony. There would be 126 ambassadors and their spouses plus 25 representatives from the Organization of American States.

"We'll be putting them on eight different busses to take them to the inaugural ceremonies in the morning, then bring them to Blair House where I'll be hosting a luncheon," she explained. "Then we must deliver them to the various inaugural balls that evening." Laughing, she added, "There's no way that Mr. Carter will be able to relieve me of my duties before that time." In December, she met twice with the president-elect and found him "cordial."

"Sometimes I feel like the oldest living American," she told a reporter (a reference to the fact that she had worked forty-five of her forty-eight years) as she prepared to return to Woodside for Christmas.

The holiday season was not a happy one for Shirley. Gertrude's health had continued to fail in recent years, and she now suffered several related, deteriorating illnesses. She died at Stanford University Hospital with Shirley close at hand at 2:15 P.M. on January 1, 1977, at exactly the same hour and day she had been married to George sixty-three years earlier. The time was one of great introspection for Shirley. The imminence of Gertrude's death had not lessened its shock. Few mothers and daughters had been as close, and the bond had continued throughout the years despite the distances between them and the responsibilities of Shirley's own family and her career.

Shirley returned to Washington five days later. Less than two weeks remained before January 20, the date of the inauguration, the fourth she had thus far attended.* She threw herself into the demanding task before her. "I planned Jimmy Carter's inauguration," Shirley declared. "I was involved with the F.B.I., the Secret Service, the local police, the Military District of Washington and everything else, because the Chief of Protocol puts everything together. I think we did a good job. We didn't know he was going to walk down the middle of the street. We didn't have that planned. He did that himself."

This was a reference to President Carter's instructions to his secret-service driver during the inaugural parade to stop the car

---

*Shirley had been a guest at the inauguration of Truman, Eisenhower and Nixon.

so that he and his family could walk the remaining 1.2 miles down Pennsylvania Avenue to the White House. Carter explained, "I remembered the angry demonstrators who had habitually confronted recent Presidents and Vice-Presidents. Furious over the Vietnam War and with the revelations of Watergate, I wanted to provide a vivid demonstration of my confidence in the people as far as security was concerned, and I felt a simple walk would be a tangible indication of some reduction in the imperial status of the President and his family. . . . People along the parade route, when they saw that we were walking," Carter wrote in his diary that night, "began to cheer and to weep, and it was an emotional experience for us as well . . . there were gasps of astonishment and cries of 'They're walking! They're walking!' "

A few minutes before the walk had begun, Carter had taken the oath of office "on the bunting-draped, ornate temporary platform at the east front of the Capitol." Shirley had occupied a prominent seat. The weather was bitter cold, and she did not join the parade to the White House.

Numerous inaugural balls are held to accommodate the many divisions of government. Shirley's job was to oversee the arrangements for the gala celebration of the foreign diplomatic corps.

"I went over to look at the room in the railway station [Union Station] that was going to be [the site of the inaugural ball for foreign diplomats that evening] where we were all to wait for the President and Vice President to arrive. This was a big, drafty old place . . . and it had one bathroom. I had some 300 people [due to come]. . . . Well, I had them all meet me in the lobby of the Department of State before we went to the ball, and I said, 'Don't drink anything. Eat crackers.' "

Later, dressed in flowing chiffon, she returned to the colorfully decorated Union Station to make certain her diplomatic charges were well tended.

"All the ballrooms were packed," Mrs. Carter wrote. "There was virtually no breathing room, much less dancing room, and a human wall had to be formed down the aisle to hold back the cheering crowds as we made our way to the platforms.

" 'Are you having a good time?' the new President asked. 'Yes!' came back the cheers. 'Do you believe in America?' The cheers grew louder. 'Are you going to help me?' The response was a roar! . . .

"At each party Jimmy and I waltzed a turn under the spotlights while the band played a romantic piece; then it was time to move on to the next ball, and the next and the next. It was a night of pure magic. . . ."

Perhaps this was true for the president and the First Lady, but not necessarily for the ballroom guests at Union Station. "I'll tell you," Shirley reminisced, "we had the best behaved diplomatic corps in the world. Sober as can be. Thirsty, full of Fritos and potato chips. The President and his party came at about a quarter to ten, and of course, breezed right through in about 15 minutes. Then, I told everyone they could have a drink and they said, 'I think we'd rather just go home.' So everyone went home, and as soon as they left, I left."

A few days later, Shirley was invited to the White House for breakfast with the president's mother, Miss Lillian; the wife of the president of Mexico, Mrs. López Portillo (whom Shirley had been escorting during the inauguration); and a few other members of the diplomatic community. The ham-and-grits breakfast was to be one of her last official appearances as chief of protocol. On January 29, she received notification that President Carter had accepted her resignation. She was to be replaced by Evan Dobelle, former mayor of Pittsfield, Massachusetts, whose appointment, since he was a Republican, raised already arched eyebrows in Washington political circles.

The Blacks made immediate plans to return to Woodside. In an interview before departing Washington in February on a "leisurely" cross-country drive home, she praised Carter. "I like him. He's very personable, very direct. He had a good sense of humor. I would give the same description of his wife. And I like Miss Lillian very much." Then she added, "I would like another Ambassadorship to a third world country . . . I empathize with the third world people. I feel I can assist. I think it's just my nature."

Not long after Gertrude's death and Shirley's return to Woodside, Nancy Majors Voorheis, her sister Marion and their mother were visiting in the San Francisco Bay area, and on invitation drove down to see Shirley.

"Well, we arrived at their beautiful home, and Shirley greeted us very warmly," Voorheis remembered. "She was wearing the huge solid-gold jewelry that she had collected when she was ambassador to Ghana. Her help, whoever it might have been, was off for the day, so we had the simplest lunch—little sandwiches and soup—and I helped Shirley bring it out from the kitchen. We all sat down in her quite formal dining room, this small group, and Shirley said, 'Now wait a minute,' and she reached out and she took the hand of whoever was seated next to her, and she said, 'Let's hold hands. I would like to say a blessing.' She bowed her head and she just said, 'Thank you, God, for this time, this special time, for old and dear friends and for all your blessings. Amen.' I was absolutely astounded, because I had no idea that Shirley had a sense of [religion]. It was a very beautiful, moving moment, and we held it a very long time.

"We talked and talked for hours and hours about old times. Shirley kept looking at the door and looking at her watch. She was waiting for her dad to come home from playing golf. He must have been near ninety at the time, and she grew terribly nervous . . . Finally, George walked in and Shirley jumped up and her face just lighted. He was just as full of fun and as funny as he had always been."

Travel and seeing other cultures had become a way of life for Shirley. In April 1977, she and Charles left Woodside for a three-week trip through mainland China. Though traveling as a private citizen, Shirley was unable to leave her political curiosity at home. "We had plenty of solid political talk," she said a few days after their return, "but never an exchange. You can ask the Chinese anything you want. They were free in answering questions—sometimes clearly, sometimes inscrutably—but not in asking questions." She told a group of Chinese university students, "Conversation is a two-way exchange, like applauding with both hands. If I applaud with only one hand, you can't hear it. So please ask me a question." When no one responded, she began to quiz the audience. A few moments later, a guide stepped in and said, "That's enough, we have to move along."

Back home, she told the membership of the San Francisco Commonwealth Club on May 13, "I need not remind Washington that it faces formidable unfinished business in the Peoples' Republic of China. New developments and old enmities magnify the situation. Preoccupation with the rigidities of the past often obscures both problems and opportunities of the present. . . . If non-secrecy and public participation are indeed the new spirit of Washington, I detect less than a unified approach on matters related to China. . . . We seem to be losing U.S. initiatives . . . In effect, the conditions for our action have been stipulated by China. This is a poor way to play international chess.

"U.S. diplomatic recognition of China today is ill-timed. It sets the stage for miscalculation by the Soviet Union, produces only marginal incremental values for the U.S. and leaves unanswered the old hostilities of the Korean Peninsula."

She made no secret of her hope that Carter might give her a worthy appointment, but she did not allow herself the luxury of inactivity while she waited. She remained on the board of directors of several large American corporations, the World Affairs Council of Northern California and the United Nations Association, and was a member of the Council on Foreign Relations, Inc., the National Committee on United States-China Relations, Inc., the Sierra Club and the Commonwealth Club of California. And she never stopped working for the cause of multiple sclerosis.

By the end of 1977, George Temple had developed Bell's Palsy and required considerable personal attention. For the time, her foreign travel would be curtailed.

She received a few television offers for guest appearances. "I've done all that," she commented. In her view, her acting career was part of another life, although she found it amusing that she and Minnie Mouse would both celebrate their fiftieth birthdays in 1978. When she was asked if there was ever a moment when she wondered why her life had not turned out tragically, as had the lives of so many child stars, she replied, "When you start doing anything at age three, it doesn't seem to be different than what everybody else does. You don't get a big head, you don't get star struck, because this is the normal work pattern . . . [and] my mother was very wise. She made certain that when I came home every day from work, all the fantasy was left at the studio . . . she did not let me know I was a celebrity. How, I don't know, but she really managed beautifully."

The celebrity she had not recognized as a child had since, however, alternately shadowed and lighted her way. On December 8, 1978, the Masquers Club (Hollywood's oldest and most respected theatrical club) recognized her legendary status by awarding her their highest honor, the Order of George Spelvin* (presented to, among others, Fred Astaire, Humphrey Bogart, Judy Garland, Laurence Olivier, Mae West and Groucho Marx). It was given to actors not for the quality of their performances, but for their contributions to the profession.

Gathered in the large reception room to honor Shirley were many of her adult and child co-stars. Although he did not attend, the printed program was dominated by a double-page spread containing a rather ambiguous message from Darryl F. Zanuck reading, "Success has never changed you."

The master of ceremonies, Pat Buttram, observed that as a child performer Shirley had saved Twentieth Century-Fox and the industry in general. "I think the only thing you didn't save was the Republican Party."

"Just wait a while," Shirley rejoined.

And although U.S. Senators Barry Goldwater and S. I. Hayakawa did not make their scheduled appearances at the tribute, the event "frequently sounded like a Republican party rally as bursts of applause greeted repeated references to her party ties. At one point a man in the audience protested that he was a Democrat.

"There are no Democrats here," Buttram retorted. "Only Republicans can afford $25 a plate." When a congratulatory telegram from former President Ford was read, Buttram remarked, "I liked it when Gerald Ford was President. It was nice having a president that wasn't our fault."

On the dais with Shirley were David Butler, Alice Faye, Cesar Romero, Lois Wilson, George Montgomery and former child stars Jane Withers, Marcia Mae Jones, Sybil Jason and Jerome

---

*George Spelvin was an imaginary actor born (in the theater) in 1904 when a performer playing a policeman in the first act of a play adopted the name for a different role in the third act. In one 3-year period during the 1920's, "George Spelvin" appeared in 210 different roles. Many famous theatrical names were linked with his. William Gillette first used him as a "double" in *Secret Service*. Jacob Adler of the Yiddish Theatre frequently employed the pseudonym. The Moscow Art Theatre once listed the name "Gregor Spelvinovich" on their programs.

Courtland, giving the ceremony the appearance of a Twentieth Century-Fox alumni party. Later, they all signed each other's programs as members of a graduating class might do, writing short personal notes to one another. Shirley, using red ink, inscribed only "Shirley Temple Black" in her graceful left-slanted hand.

The next year was taken up caring for George. His palsy had progressed to a stage where he was unable to feed himself or swallow solid food. Shirley cooked his meals, pureed them and then spoon-fed him. She seldom left Woodside. On September 4, 1980, George took a sudden turn for the worse and was moved to a hospital in Menlo Park, where he died on September 30 at age ninty-three. A few weeks later, Shirley's first grandchild, Theresa Lyn Falaschi, was born. The press found Shirley Temple becoming a grandmother astounding.*

About this time, Dickie Moore, who had bestowed on Shirley her first kiss in *Miss Annie Rooney,* arranged to see her in Woodside. He was then writing *Twinkle, Twinkle, Little Star,* part memoir and part history of Hollywood's child stars. She greeted him at the doorway, "wearing a bright print dress made from fabric she had bought ten years before in Ghana . . . the impish gaze was still level and direct, the hazel eyes were even more knowing . . . She pointed to the left side of her face: 'Kiss me here on the cheek, like last time,' she said."

They talked, but Moore could not get her to speak freely about the past. He noted that she herself served him a sandwich and salad for lunch and that she had no maid. She told him she personally cooked and cleaned the house, which she remarked "looked like the kind you used to draw in school.

"I don't have many early memories of other [film] children or their parents," she confessed to him, "because I didn't socialize with my peer group at the studio."

"You were really isolated, weren't you? Far more than any of us," Moore remarked.

" 'Yes,' she said, after a moment of reflection, 'but I turned out alright.' "

He noted that on his departure she showed him the consul

---

*Roberto Falaschi had been re-posted to the United States, and the child was born at the Stanford Medical Center on December 21, 1980. The Falaschi marriage ended in divorce a few years later.

flag she had taken from her office in Washington. Being an ambassador, she told him, was the proudest achievement of her life.

With Republican President Ronald Reagan occupying the White House, Shirley's hopes were raised that she might yet be assigned a challenging government position. He did send her to Paris as his representative during the inaugural celebrations of Americans abroad. But—perhaps because Shirley had championed his then-rival George Bush in the early days of the 1980 presidential race—no ambassadorship or high-government office was offered to her.

When Lenore Annenberg resigned as chief of protocol in December 1981, rumors abounded that Reagan would reappoint Shirley. "Frankly, I don't believe in looking back," she said when the post went to Selwa Roosevelt, and then added, "It's not a substantive job." She did accept the State Department's offer for her to be named vice-president of the American Academy of Diplomacy, and to assist in the training of new ambassadors, a job that gave her a chance to spend considerable time each year in Washington and to keep herself attuned to the political climate of the country.

The house in Woodside that had once been decorated in 'Pacific-Oriental' was now a place for display of her souvenirs from her travels and diplomatic life, notably the time spent in Ghana. She remained outspoken about her convictions and opinions on foreign affairs, frequently voicing her views on the "abhorrent practice of apartheid." "I think she's one of the most unusual women who ever lived," Charles said of his wife of thirty-five years. "Her whole life has been spent in various types of public service, either by entertaining people or by serving them." Then, his voice growing softer, he added, "I think she's some sort of deity . . . and I support her in everything she does."

On the evening of May 20, 1985, the Academy Foundation of the Academy of Motion Picture Arts and Sciences gave "A Tribute to Shirley Temple" in Hollywood at the Samuel Goldwyn Theatre. Clips from many of her films were shown and interspersed with commentary from Jane Withers, Sybil Jason, Marcia Mae Jones, Darryl Hickman, Jerome Courtland, Cesar Romero and Shirley, with Robert Osborne as moderator.

The night was one for reminiscing. Cesar Romero remembered how he used to prevail upon Jane Withers to perform her Temple impression behind Shirley's back. At this point, Withers rose and stepped forward to do the imitation with her voice an amazing likeness to Shirley's in the years of her childhood stardom. The audience applauded, and Shirley quipped into the microphone, "That's why we only did one movie together."

Then the important moment of the occasion arrived. Gene Allen, president of the Academy, stood on the podium beside Shirley and presented her with a full-sized Oscar to replace the miniature she had been given in 1935. Shirley held it in her hands for a moment, and then, looking over the heads of the audience, said, "This is really for my mother, Gertrude Temple, and this evening a tribute to her."

Appendices

CHRONOLOGY:
SHIRLEY TEMPLE BLACK

1928, April 23	Born
1932, January	First short made
1934, February 9	Signed Fox Films contract
	Presented with miniature "Oscar" (Academy Award)
1935, February 27	Meets President Franklin D. Roosevelt
1940, Autumn	Enters Westlake School for Girls
	Twentieth Century-Fox contract ends
1943, Spring	Signs with Selznick International
1945, Spring	Graduates Westlake School for Girls
September 19	Marries John Agar
1948, January 30	Birth of Linda Susan (Agar/Black)
1949, January 20	Attends President Truman's inauguration
1950, December 5	Divorces John Agar
1950, October	Contract with Selznick International ends
1950, December 16	Marries Charles Black
1951, May	Moves to Maryland
1952, April 28	Birth of Charles Alden Black, Jr.
1953, June	Visits President Dwight D. Eisenhower
1953, July	Moves to Los Angeles, California
1954, April 9	Birth of Lori Alden Black
	Moves to Atherton, California

1958, January 12	First *Shirley Temple's Storybook* (television)
1960	Campaigns for Richard Nixon's losing presidential race
1961	*Shirley Temple Theater* (television)
	Moves to Woodside, California
	Co-founder of the National Federation of Multiple Sclerosis Societies
1965	San Francisco Health Facilities Planning Association (board member)
	Travels to Russia for International Federation of Multiple Sclerosis Societies
1967	California Congressional campaign
1968	Awarded Dame, Order of Knights of Malta, Paris
	Travels to Prague for IFMSS
	Campaigns abroad for Richard Nixon
1969	Director, Bank of California
	Director, Firemen's Fund Insurance Company
	Director, BANCAL Tri-State Corporation
	Director, Del Monte Corporation
	Member, California Advisory Hospital Council
1969–70	Representative to 24th General Assembly of United Nations (appointed by President Richard M. Nixon)
1972–74	Special assistant to chairman, American Council on Environmental Quality
1972	Representative, UN Conference on Human Environment in Stockholm (appointed by Secretary of State William P. Rogers)
	Delegate treaty on environment U.S.S.R.-U.S.A. Joint Committee, Moscow
	Breast cancer (mastectomy)

1973	Member U.S. Commission for UNESCO
1974, May 28	Elected Director, Walt Disney Productions
1974–76	Ambassador to Ghana (appointed by President Gerald R. Ford)
1975, October 8	Marriage of Linda Susan Black to Robert Falaschi
1976–77	U.S. chief of protocol (appointed by President Gerald R. Ford)
	In charge of arrangements for inauguration and inaugural ball for President Jimmy Carter
1977, January 1	Gertrude Temple dies
	Life Achievement Award of the American Center of Films for Children
1980, September 30	George Temple dies
December 20	Birth of granddaughter, Theresa Lyn Falaschi
1981	Member, U.S. Delegation on African Refugee Problems, Geneva
	Appointed to Board of Directors, National Wildlife Federation
	Member, UN Association, United States
	Founding Member, American Academy of Diplomacy
	Co-chairman, Ambassadorial Seminars
1985	Presented with full-sized "Oscar"

TRIAL TRANSCRIPT OF THE HIGH COURT OF JUSTICE

HIGH COURT OF JUSTICE
KING'S BENCH DIVISION
LIBEL ON MISS SHIRLEY TEMPLE: "A GROSS OUTRAGE"
TEMPLE AND OTHERS V. NIGHT AND DAY MAGAZINES,
LIMITED, AND OTHERS
Before the Lord Chief Justice

A settlement was announced of this libel action which was brought by Miss Shirley Jane Temple, the child actress (by Mr. Roy Simmonds, her next friend), Twentieth Century-Fox Film Corporation, of New York, and Twentieth Century-Fox Film Company, Limited, of Berners Street, W., against Night and Day Magazines, Limited, and Mr. Graham Greene, of St. Martin's Lane, W.C., Hazell, Watson and Viney, Limited, printers, of Long Acre, W.C., and Messrs. Chatto and Windus, publishers, of Chandos Street, W.C., in respect of an article written by Mr. Green and published in the issue of the magazine *Night and Day* dated October 28, 1937.

Sir Patrick Hastings, K.C., and Mr. G.O. Slade appeared for the plaintiffs; Mr. Valentine Holmes for all the defendants except Hazell, Watson, and Viney, Limited, who were represented by Mr. Theobald Mathew.

Sir Patrick Hastings, in announcing the settlement by which it was agreed that Miss Shirley Temple was to receive £2,000, the film corporation £1,000, and the film company £500, stated that the first defendants were the proprietors of the magazine *Night and Day*, which was published in London. It was only right to say that the two last defendants, the printers and publishers, were firms of the utmost respectability and highest reputation, and were innocently responsible in the matter.

The plaintiff, Miss Shirley Temple, a child of nine years, had a world-wide reputation as an artist in films. The two plaintiff companies produced her in a film called *Wee Willie Winkie,* based on Rudyard Kipling's story.

On October 28 last year Night and Day Magazines, Limited, published an article written by Mr. Graham Greene. In his (counsel's) view it was one of the most horrible libels that one could well imagine. Obviously he would not read it—it was better that he should not—but a glance at the statement of claim, where a poster was set out, was quite sufficient to show the nature of the libel written about this child.

This beastly publication, said counsel, was written, and it was right to say that every respectable news distributor in London refused to be a party to selling it. Notwithstanding that, the magazine company, with the object no doubt of increasing the sale, proceeded to advertise the fact that it had been banned.

Shirley Temple was an American and lived in America. If she had been in England and the publication in America it would have been right for the American Courts to have taken notice of it. It was equally right that, the position being reversed, her friends in America should know that the Courts here took notice of such a publication.

"SHOULD NOT BE TREATED LIGHTLY"

Money was no object in this case. The child had a very large income and the two film companies were wealthy concerns. It was realized, however, that the matter should not be treated lightly. The defendants had paid the film companies £1,000 and £500 respectively, and that money would be disposed of in a charitable way. With regard to the child, she would be paid £2,000. There would also be an order for the taxation of costs.

In any view, said counsel, it was such a beastly libel to have written that if it had been a question of money it would have been difficult to say what would be an appropriate amount to arrive at.

Miss Shirley Temple probably knew nothing of the article, and it was undesirable that she should be brought to England to fight the action. In his (counsel's) opinion the settlement was a proper one in the circumstances.

Mr. Valentine Holmes informed his Lordship that the magazine *Night and Day* had ceased publication. He desired, on behalf of his clients, to express the deepest apology to Miss Temple for the pain which certainly would have been caused to her by the article if she had read it. He also apologized to the two film companies for the suggestion that they would produce and distribute a film of the character indicated by the article. There was no justification for the criticism of the film, which, his clients instructed him, was one to see which anybody could take their children. He also apologized on behalf of Mr. Graham Greene. So far as the publishers of the magazine were concerned, they did not see the article before publication.

His LORDSHIP.—Who is the author of this article?

Mr. HOLMES.—Mr. Graham Greene.

His LORDSHIP.—Is he within the jurisdiction?

Mr. HOLMES.—I am afraid I do not know, my Lord.

Mr. THEOBALD MATHEW, on behalf of the printers, said that they recognized that the article was one which ought never to have been published. The fact that the film had already been licensed for universal exhibition refuted the charges which had been made in the article. The printers welcomed the opportunity of making any amends in their power.

Mr. LORDSHIP.—Can you tell me where Mr. Greene is?

Mr. MATHEW.—I have no information on the subject.

His LORDSHIP.—This libel is simply a gross outrage, and I will take care to see that suitable attention is directed to it. In the meantime I assent to the settlement on the terms which have been disclosed, and the record will be withdrawn.

REVIEW OF
WEE WILLIE WINKIE IN
NIGHT AND DAY
OCTOBER 28, 1937

The Films by Graham Greene

Reprinted Courtesy of Chattow and Windus

The owners of a child star are like leaseholders—their property dimin-
ishes in value every year. Time's chariot is at their back; before them
acres of anonymity. What is Jackie Coogan now but a matrimonial
squabble? Miss Shirley Temple's case, though, has peculiar interest:
infancy with her is a disguise, her appeal is more secret and more adult.
Already two years ago she was a fancy little piece (real childhood, I
think, went out after *The Littlest Rebel*). In *Captain January* she wore
trousers with the mature suggestiveness of a Dietrich: her neat and
well-developed rump twisted in the tap-dance: her eyes had a sidelong
searching coquetry. Now in *Wee Willie Winkie*, wearing short kilts, she
is a complete totsy. Watch her swaggering stride across the Indian
barrack-square: hear the gasp of excited expectation from her antique
audience when the sergeant's palm is raised: watch the way she measures a man with agile studio eyes, with dimpled depravity. Adult
emotions of love and grief glissade across the mask of childhood, a
childhood skin-deep.

It is clever, but it cannot last. Her admirers—middle-aged men
and clergymen—respond to her dubious coquetry, to the sight of her
well-shaped and desirable little body, packed with enormous vitality,
only because the safety curtain of story and dialogue drops between
their intelligence and their desire. "Why are you making my Mummy
cry?"—what could be purer than that? And the scene when dressed
in a white nightdress she begs grandpa to take Mummy to a dance—
what could be more virginal? On those lines her new picture, made
by John Ford, who directed *The Informer*, is horrifyingly competent. It

363

isn't hard to stay to the last prattle and the last sob. The story—about an Afghan robber converted by Wee Willie Winkie to the British Raj—is a long way after Kipling. But we needn't be sour about that. Both stories are awful, but on the whole Hollywood's is the better. . . .

MOVIE CHRONOLOGY: SHIRLEY TEMPLE

1. THE RUNT PAGE, Educational Films Corp., subsidiary of Educational Pictures, Inc., 1932, 10 minutes.

> CAST: *Shirley Temple* .... Lulu Parsnips
> *Georgie Smith* .... Raymond Bunion
> *Unknown* .... Bears Bugs

Directed by Roy LaVerne; *Produced by* Jack Hays.

2. WAR BABIES, Educational Films Corp., 1932, 11 minutes.

> CAST: *Shirley Temple* .... Charmaine, French girl
> *Georgie Smith* .... Soldier boyfriend
> *Eugene Butler* .... Soldier boyfriend

Directed by Charles Lamont; *Produced by* Jack Hays.

3. PIE COVERED WAGON, Educational Films Corp., 1932, 10 minutes.

> CAST: *Shirley Temple* .... Captive
> *Georgie Smith* .... Rescuer
> *Cowboys and Indians*

Directed by Charles Lamont; *Produced by* Jack Hays; *Written by* Jack Hays; *Photographed by* Dwight Warren.

4. KID'S LAST FIGHT, Educational Films Corp., 1932, 10 minutes.

> CAST: *Shirley Temple* .... Girlfriend
> *Georgie Smith* .... Diaper Dampsy, boxer
> *Sidney Kilbrick* .... Thug

Directed by Charles Lamont; *Produced by* Jack Hays; *Written by* Jack Hays.

5. POLLY-TIX IN WASHINGTON, Educational Films Corp., 1932, 10 minutes.

    CAST: *Shirley Temple* .... Political gold-digger
              Georgie Smith .... Cowboy politician
              Gloria Ann Mack .... Other "woman"

Directed by Charles Lamont; *Produced by* Jack Hays.

6. KID'N' HOLLYWOOD, Educational Films Corp., 1932, 10 minutes.

    CAST: *Shirley Temple* .... Morelegs Sweetrick
              Georgie Smith .... Frightwig Von Stumblebum

Directed by Charles Lamont; *Produced by* Jack Hays.

7. KID'N' AFRICA, Educational Films Corp., 1932, 10 minutes.

    CAST: *Shirley Temple* .... Madame Cradlebait, Mrs. Diaperzan
              Danny Boone, Jr. .... Diaperzan

Directed by Charles Lamont; *Produced by* Jack Hays.

8. RED-HAIRED ALIBI, Tower Productions, Inc., 1932, 71 minutes.

    CAST: *Merna Kennedy* .... Lynn Monith
              Theodore Von Eltz .... Trent Travers
              Grant Withers .... Rob Shelton
              Purnell Pratt .... Regan
              Huntley Gordon .... Kente
              Fred Kelsey .... Corcoran
              John Vosburgh .... Morgan
              Marion Lessing .... Bee Lee
              Shirley Temple .... Gloria
              Paul Porcasi .... Margoli
              Arthur Hoyt .... Henri

Directed by Christy Cabanne; *Story by* Wilson Collison; *Screenplay by* Edward T. Lowe.

9. MERRILY YOURS, Educational Films Corp., 1932, 22 minutes.

    CAST: *Junior Coughlin* .... Sonny Rogers
              Shirley Temple .... Mary Lou Rogers

Kenneth Howell	Harry Vanderpool
Mary Blackford	Phyllis Dean
Sidney Miller	Harry's "stooge"
Harry Myers	Mr. Rogers
Helene Chadwick	Mrs. Rogers
Lloyd Ingraham	Mr. Dean
Thelma Hill	Betty
Isabel La Mal	Mrs. Vanderpool

Directed by Charles Lamont; *Written by* Charles Lamont; *Photographed by* Dwight Warren; *Recorded by* Western Electric Noiseless Recording.

10. GLAD RAGS TO RICHES, Educational Films Corp., 1933, 11 minutes.

CAST:	*Shirley Temple*	La Belle Diaperina, showgirl
	Eugene Butler	Her escort
	Marilyn Granas	Maid
	Georgie Smith	Director

NOTE: Marilyn Granas was later to become Shirley's first stand-in. *Directed by* Charles Lamont; *Produced by* Jack Hays.

11. OUT ALL NIGHT, Universal, 1933, 69 minutes.

CAST:	*Slim Summerville*	Ronald Colgate
	ZaSu Pitts	Bonny
	Laura Hope Crews	Mrs. Colgate
	Shirley Grey	Kate
	Alexander Carr	Rosemountain
	Rollo Lloyd	David Arnold
	Gene Lewis	Tracy
	Shirley Temple, *Billy Barty,* *Phillip Purdy*	Children
	Also: *Florence Enright, Dorothy Bay, Mae Busch, Paul Hurst*	

Directed by Sam Taylor; *Story by* Tim Whelan; *Screenplay by* William Anthony McGuire.

12. DORA'S DUNKIN' DOUGHNUTS, Educational Films Corp., 1933, 22 minutes.

CAST:	*Andy Clyde*	Andy
	Florence Gill	Dora
	Fern Emmett	Mrs. Zilch

Blanche Payson .... Mrs. Blotts
Georgia O'Dell .... Mrs. Ipswick
Shirley Temple .... Shirley
Also: The Meglin Kids Band, including *Sidney Miller*

Directed by Harry J. Edwards; *Produced by* Jack Hays; *Story and Dialogue by* Ernest Pagano and Ewart Adamson; *Musical Numbers by* Alfonse Corelli.

13. MANAGED MONEY, Educational Films Corp., 1933, 22 minutes.

CAST: *Frank (Junior) Coughlin* .. Sonny Rogers
Shirley Temple .... Mary Lou Rogers
Harry Myers .... Mr. Rogers
Helene Chadwick .... Mrs. Rogers

Directed by Charles Lamont; *Produced by* Jack Hays.

14. WHAT TO DO?, Educational Films Corp., 1933, 22 minutes.

CAST: *Frank (Junior)*
Coughlin .... Sonny Rogers
Shirley Temple .... Mary Lou Rogers
Harry Myers .... Mr. Rogers
Kenneth Howell .... Henry Vanderpool
Also: *Lila Leslie, Dorothy Ward, Broderick O'Farrell*

Directed by Charles Lamont; *Produced by* Jack Hays.

15. TO THE LAST MAN, Paramount, 1933, 60 minutes.

CAST: *Randolph Scott* .... Lynn Hayden
Esther Ralston .... Ellen Colby
Buster Crabbe .... Bill Hayden
Noah Beery .... Jed Colby
Jack LaRue .... Jim Daggs
Barton MacLane .... Neil Standing
Gail Patrick .... Ann Hayden Standing
(Shirley's mother)
Egon Brecher .... Mark Hayden
Fuzzy Knight .... Jeff Morley
James Engles .... Ely Bruce
Murial Kirkland .... Molly Hayden
Eugenie Besserer .... Granny Spelvin
Harlan Knight .... Grandpa Spelvin
John Peter Richmond .... Pete Garon
Harry Cording .... Harry Malone
Erville Alderson .... Judge

James Burke	Sheriff
Jay Ward	Lynn Hayden
Rosita Butler	Ann Hayden
Cullen Johnson	Bill Hayden
Russell Powell	Greaves
Delmar Watson	Tad Standing
Shirley Jane Temple	Mary Standing

Directed by Henry Hathway; *Screenplay by* Jack Cunningham, from the Zane Grey story; *Camera by* Ben Reynolds.

16. AS THE EARTH TURNS, Warner Brothers, 1933.

CAST:

Sarah Padden	Mrs. Janowski
Donald Woods	Stan Janowski
Egon Brecher	Janowski
David Durand	Manuel (12)
Cora Sue Collins	Maria (7)
Gloria Fisher	Louise (8)
David Landau	Mark Shaw
Clara Blandick	Cora Shaw
Jean Muir	Jen Shaw
Dorothy Appleby	Doris
Russell Hardie	Ed Shaw
William Janney	Ollie Shaw (18)
Dorothy Gray	Bunny Shaw (12)
Wally Albright	John Shaw (7)
Arthur Hohl	George Shaw
Dorothy Peterson	Mil Shaw
Emily Lowry	Margaret
Marilyn Knowlden	Esther Shaw (8)
George Billings	Junior Shaw (12)
Shirley Temple	Betty Shaw (6)
Joyce Kay	Sister

Directed by Alfred E. Green; *Produced by* Robert Lord; *Art Director,* Robert Haas; *Unit Manager,* Al Alborn; *Assistant Director,* William McGann; *Second Assistant Director,* Carol Sax; *Cameramen,* Byron Haskins, Carl Guthrie and Bob Burks; *Mixer,* E. A. Brown; *Gaffer,* C. Alexander; *Grip,* O. Compton; *Propman,* Emmett Emerson; *Wardrobe Man,* Bob Ramsen; *Wardrobe Woman,* Mary Deery; *Cutter,* Herbert Levy.

17. PARDON MY PUPS, Educational Films Corp., 1934, 22 minutes.

CAST:

Frank (Junior)	
Coughlin	Sonny Rogers

Shirley Temple .... Mary Lou Rogers
Kenneth Howell .... Henry Vanderpool
Harry Myers .... Mr. Rogers
Also: *Dorothy Ward, Virginia True Boardman* and *"Queenie" the spaniel*

Directed by Charles Lamont; *Suggested by the story "Mild Oats" by* Florence Ryerson and Colin Clements; *Adapted by* Ewart Adamson.

18. CAROLINA, Fox Film Corp., 1934, 63 minutes.

CAST: *Janet Gaynor* .... Joanna
Lionel Barrymore .... Bob Connelly
Robert Young .... Will Connelly
Henrietta Crosman .... Mrs. Connelly
Richard Cromwell .... Allen
Mona Barrie .... Virginia
Stepin Fetchit .... Scipio
Russell Simpson .... Richards
Ronnie Cosbey .... Harry
Jackie Cosbey .... Jackie
Almeda Fowler .... Geraldine
Alden Chase .... Jack Hampton
Roy Watson .... Jefferson Davis
John Elliott .... Gen. Robert E. Lee
John Webb Dillon .... Gen. "Stonewall" Jackson
J. C. Fowler .... Gen. Leonidas Polk
André Cheron .... Gen. Beauregard
(*Shirley Temple* received no film credit, although she did appear in a small role)

Directed by Henry King; *Based on The House of Connelly by* Paul Green; *Screenplay by* Reginald Berkeley; *Photography by* Hal Mohr.

19. NEW DEAL RHYTHM, Paramount, 1934.

CAST: *Charles "Buddy" Rogers,*
Marjorie Main
and *Shirley Temple*

20. MANDALAY, Warner Brothers–First National, 1934.

CAST: *Kay Francis* .... Tanya
Ricardo Cortez .... Tony Evans
Warner Oland .... Nick
Lyle Talbot .... Dr. Gregory Burton
Ruth Donnelly .... Mrs. Peters

Reginald Owen	Commissioner
David Torrence	Captain
Rafaela Ottiano	The Countess
Holliwell Hobbes	Col. Dawson Ames
Etienne Girardot	Mr. Abernathie
Lucien Littlefield	Mr. Peters
Bodil Rosing	Mrs. Kleinschmidt
Herman Bing	Mr. Kleinschmidt
Harry C. Bradley	Henry P. Warren
James B. Leong	Ram Singh
Shirley Temple	Betty Shaw
Lillian Harmer	Louisa Mae Harrington
Torben Meyer	Van Brinker

Directed by Michael Curtiz; *Screenplay by* Austin Parker and Charles Kenyon; *Story by* Park Harvey Fox.

21. STAND UP AND CHEER, Fox Film Corp., 1934, 80 minutes.

CAST:		
	Warner Baxter	Lawrence Cromwell
	Madge Evans	Mary Adams
	James Dunn	Jimmy Dugan
	Sylvia Froos	as herself
	John Boles	as himself
	Arthur Byron	John Harly
	Ralph Morgan	Secretary to the President
	Shirley Temple	Shirley Dugan
	Aunt Jemima (Tess Gardell)	as herself
	Mitchell & Durant	Senators Danforth and Short
	Dick Foran	as himself
	Nigel Bruce	Dinwiddie
	"Skins" Miller	Hillbilly
	Stepin Fetchit	as himself

Directed by Hamilton McFadden; *Produced by* Winfield Sheehan; *Story idea by* Will Rogers and Philip Klein; *Screenplay by* Lew Brown and Ralph Spence; *Songs by* Lew Brown and Jay Gorney; *Costumes by* Rita Kaufman; *Camera,* Ernest Palmer and L. W. O'Connell; *Musical Director,* Arthur Lange.

22. NOW I'LL TELL, Fox Film Corp., 1934, 75 minutes.

CAST:		
	Spencer Tracy	Murray Golden
	Helen Twelvetrees	Virginia

Alice Faye .... Peggy
Robert Gleckler .... Mositer
Henry O'Neill .... Doran
Hobart Cavanaugh .... Freddie
G. P. Huntley, Jr .... Hart
Shirley Temple .... Doran's Daughter
Ronald Cosbey .... Doran's Son
Ray Cooke .... Traylor
Frank Marlowe .... Curtis
Clarence Wilson .... Davis
Barbara Weeks.................. Wynne
Theodore Newton .... Joe
Vince Barnett .... Peppo
Jim Donlan .... Honey Smith

Directed by Edwin Burke; *Story by* Mrs. Arnold Rothstein; *Adapted and Dialogue by* Edwin Burke; *Photography by* Ernest Palmer.

23. CHANGE OF HEART, Fox Film Corp., 1934, 76 minutes.

CAST: Shirley Temple .... Shirley
Janet Gaynor .... Catherine Furness
Charles Farrell.................. Chris Thring
James Dunn...................... Mack McGowan
Ginger Rogers .... Madge Rountree
Beryl Mercer .... Harriett Hawkins
Gustav Von Seyffertitz........ Mr. Kreutzmann
Irene Franklin .... Greta Hailstrom
Fiske O'Hara .... T. P. McGowan
Drue Leyton...................... Mrs. Mockby, Jr.
Mary Carr .... Mrs. Rountree
Jane Darwell .... Mrs. McGowan
Kenneth Thomson.............. Howard Jackson
Nella Walker .... Mrs. Mockby
Barbara Barondess .... Phyllis Carmichael

Directed by John G. Blystone; *Story by* Kathleen Norris; *Screenplay by* Sonja Levien and James Gleason; *Additional Dialogue*, Samuel Hoffenstein; *Cameraman*, Hal Mohr; *Recording Engineer*, Joseph Aiken; *Editor*, Margaret Clancy.

24. LITTLE MISS MARKER, Paramount, 1934.

CAST: Shirley Temple .... Miss Marker
(Martha, Marky)

Adolphe Menjou	Sorrowful Jones
Dorothy Dell	Bangles Carson
Charles Bickford	Big Steve
Lynne Overman	Regret
Frank McGlynn, Sr	Doc Chesley
Jack Sheehan	Sun Rise
Gary Owen	Grinder
Willie Best	Sleep 'n' Eat, Dizzy Memphis
Puggy White	Eddie
Sam Hardy	Benny the Gouge
Tammany Young	Buggs
Edward Earle	Marky's father
John Kelly	Sore Toe
Warren Hymer	Canvas Back
Frank Conroy	Dr. Ingalls
James Burke	Reardon
Mildred Gover	Sarah
Lucille Ward	Mrs. Walsh
Craufurd Kent	Doctor
Nora Cecil	Head of Home Finding Society

Directed by Alexander Hall; *Produced by* B. P. Schulberg; *Story by* Damon Runyon, published in *Colliers*, 1932, *Adapted by* Gladys Lehman.

25. BABY, TAKE A BOW, Fox Film Corp., 1934.

CAST:		
	James Dunn	Eddie Ellison
	Claire Trevor	Kay Ellison
	Shirley Temple	Shirley
	Alan Dinehart	Welch
	Ray Walker	Larry Scott
	Dorothy Libaire	Jane
	Ralph Harolde	Trigger Stone
	James Flavin	Flannigan
	Richard Tucker	Mr. Carson
	Olive Tell	Mrs. Carson
	John Alexander	Rag Picker

Directed by Harry Lachman; *Produced by* John Stone; *Story by* Philip Klein and E. E. Paramore, Jr. (*from the play* Square Crooks *by* James P. Judge).

26. NOW AND FOREVER, Paramount, 1934.

CAST:
Gary Cooper	Jerry Day
Carole Lombard	Toni Carstairs
Shirley Temple	Pennie (Penelope Day)
Sir Guy Standing	Felix Evans
Charlotte Granville	Mrs. J.H.P. Crane
Gilbert Emery	James Higginson
Henry Kolker	Mr. Clark
André Cheron	Inspector
Tetsu Komai	Mr. Ling
Dog Buster	Daschund

Directed by Henry Hathaway (*Screenplay by* Vincent Lawrence and Sylvia Thalberg); *Story by* Jack Kirkland and Melville Baker; *Adapted by* Austin Parker.

27. BRIGHT EYES, Fox Film Corp, 1934, 84 minutes.

CAST:
Shirley Temple	Shirley Blake
James Dunn	Loop Merritt
Jane Darwell	Mrs. Higgins
Judith Allen	Adele Martin
Lois Wilson	Mary Blake (Shirley's mother)
Charles Sellon	Uncle Ned Smith
Walter Johnson	Thomas
Jane Withers	Joy Smythe
Theodore von Eltz	J. Wellington Smythe
Dorothy Christy	Anita Smythe
Brandon Hurst	Higgins
George Irving	Judge Thompson
David O'Brien	Airplane friend (later called "Tex")

Directed by David Butler; *Produced by* Sol Wurtzel; *Screenplay by* William Conselman; *Story by* David Butler, William Conselman and Edwin Burke; *Photography by* Arthur Miller.

28. THE LITTLE COLONEL, Fox Film Corp., 1935, 80 minutes.

CAST:
Shirley Temple	Lloyd Sherman (the Little Colonel)
Lionel Barrymore	Col. Lloyd
Evelyn Venable	Elizabeth Lloyd Sherman

John Lodge	Jack Sherman
Sidney Blackmer	Swazey
Alden Chase	Hull
William Burress	Dr. Scott
Hattie McDaniel	Mom Beck
Geneva Williams	Maria
Avonne Jackson	May Lily
Nyanza Potts, Jr.	Henry Clay
Frank Darien	Nebler
Bill Robinson	Walker

Directed by David Butler; *Produced by* B. G. De Sylva; *Story by* Annie Fellows Johnston; *Screenplay by* William Conselman; *Photography by* Arthur Miller; *Technicolor sequence photographed by* William Skall.

29. OUR LITTLE GIRL, Fox Film Corp., 1935, 63 minutes.

CAST:

Shirley Temple	Molly Middleton
Rosemary Ames	Elsa Middleton
Joel McCrea	Dr. Donald Middleton
Lyle Talbot	Rolfe Brent
Erin O'Brien-Moore	Sarah Boynton
Poodles Hanneford	Circus performer (clown, himself)
Margaret Armstrong	Amy
Rita Owin	Alice
Leonard Carey	Jackson
J. Farrell MacDonald	Mr. Tramp
Jack Baxley	Leyton

Directed by John Robertson; *Produced by* Edward Butcher; *Story by* Florence Leighton Pfalzgraf, *Heaven's Gate; Screenplay by* Stephen Avery, Allen Rivkin and Jack Yellen; *Photography by* John Seitz.

30. CURLY TOP, Fox Film Corp., 1935, 75 minutes.

CAST:

Shirley Temple	Elizabeth Blair (Betsy)
John Boles	Edward Morgan, orphanage trustee
Rochelle Hudson	Mary Blair, Betsy's sister
Jane Darwell	Mrs. Denham
Rafaela Ottiano	Mrs. Higgins
Esther Dale	Aunt Genevieve
Arthur Treacher	Morgan's butler
Etienne Giardot	Mr. Wyckoff
Maurice Murphy	Jimmie Rogers

Directed by Irving Cummings; *Produced by* Winfield Sheehan; *Story by* Jean Webster, *Daddy Long Legs; Adapted by* William Conselman; *Screenplay by* Patterson McNutt and Arthur Beckhard; *Music by* Ray Henderson; *Lyrics by* Ted Koehler, Edward Heyman and Irving Caesar; *Photography by* John Seitz; *Dances by* Jack Donohue; *Musical Director,* Oscar Bradley.

31. THE LITTLEST REBEL, Twentieth Century-Fox, 1935, 73 minutes.

CAST:
Shirley Temple	Virginia Houston Cary (Virgie)
John Boles	Confederate Captain Herbert Cary
Jack Holt	Union Colonel Morrison
Karen Morley	Mrs. Cary
Bill Robinson	Uncle Billy, Cary servant
Guinn Williams	Sergeant Dudley
Willie Best	James Henry
Frank McGlynn, Sr	President Lincoln
Bessie Lyle	Mammy
Hannah Washington	Sally Ann

Directed by David Butler; *Produced by* Darryl F. Zanuck; *Associate Producer,* B. G. De Sylva; *Screenplay by* Edwin Burke and Harry Tugend, based on Edward Peple's play *The Littlest Rebel; Photography by* John Seitz; *Sound by* S. C. Chapman

32. CAPTAIN JANUARY, Twentieth Century-Fox, 1936.

CAST:
Shirley Temple	Star
Guy Kibbee	Captain January
June Lang	Mary Marshall
Slim Summerville	Captain Nazro
Buddy Ebsen	Paul Rogers
Sara Haden	Agatha Morgan
Jane Darwell	Eliza Croft
Jerry Tucker	Cyril Morgan
Nella Walker	Mrs. John Mason
George Irving	John Mason
James Farley	Deputy Sheriff
Si Jenks	Old sailor
John Carradine	East Indian
Mary McLaren	Nurse at aunt's home
Billy Benedict	Messenger boy

Directed by David Butler; *Produced by* Darryl F. Zanuck; *Associate Producer,* B. G. De Sylva; *Story by* Laura E. Richards, *Captain January; Screenplay by* Sam Hellman, Gladys Lehman and Harry Tugend; *Photography by* John Seitz.

33. POOR LITTLE RICH GIRL, Twentieth Century-Fox, 1936, 72 minutes.

CAST:

Shirley Temple	Barbara Barry
Alice Faye	Jerry Dolan
Gloria Stuart	Margaret Allen
Jack Haley	Jimmy Dolan
Michael Whalen	Richard Barry (Shirley's father)
Sara Haden	Collins
Jane Darwell	Woodward
Claude Gillingwater	Simon Peck
Henry Armetta	Tony
Arthur Hoyt	Percival Gooch
John Wray	Flagin
Paul Stanton	George Hathaway
Charles Coleman	Stebbins
John Kelly	Ferguson
Tyler Brooke	Dan Ward
Mathilde Comont	Tony's wife
Leonard Kilbrick	Freckles
Dick Webster	Soloist
Bill Ray	Announcer
Gayne Whitman	Announcer (assumed)

Directed by Irving Cummings; *Produced by* Darryl F. Zanuck; *Associate Producer,* B. G. De Sylva; *Story suggested by* Eleanor Gates and Ralph Spence; *Screenplay by* Sam Hellman, Gladys Lehman and Harry Tugend; *Music and lyrics by* Mack Gordon and Harry Revel; *Photography by* John Seitz; *Dances staged by* Jack Haskell and Ralph Cooper; *Film Editing by* Jack Murray; *Art Directors,* William Darling and Rudolph Sternad.

34. DIMPLES, Twentieth Century-Fox, 1936.

CAST:

Shirley Temple	Sylvia Dolores Appleby (Dimples)
Frank Morgan	Professor Appleby
Helen Westley	Mrs. Caroline Drew

Robert Kent	Allen Drew
Delma Byron	Betty Loring
Astrid Allwyn	Cleo Marsh
Stepin Fetchit	Cicero
Berton Churchill	Colonel Loring
Paul Stanton	Mr. St. Clair
Julius Tannen	Hawkins
John Carradine	Richards
Herman Bing	Proprietor
Billy McClain	Rufus
Jack Clifford	Uncle Tom
Betty Jean Hainey	Topsy
Arthur Aylesworth	Pawnbroker
Greta Meyer	Proprietor's wife
Leonard Kilbrick, Warner Weidler, Walter Weidler, George Weidler	Children's Band
Jesse Scott, Thurman Black	The Two Black Dots
The Hall Johnson Choir	Choir

Directed by William A. Seiter; *Produced by* Darryl F. Zanuck; *Associate Producer,* Nunnally Johnson; *Screenplay by* Arthur Sheekman and Nat Perrin; *Dances staged by* Bill Robinson.

35. STOWAWAY, Twentieth Century-Fox release of a B. G. Sylva–Earl Carroll–Harold Wilson production, 1936, 87 minutes.

CAST:

Shirley Temple	Ching-Ching, daughter of missionaries
Robert Young	Tommy Randall
Alice Faye	Susan Parker
Eugene Pallette	The Colonel
Helen Westley	Mrs. Hope
Arthur Treacher	Atkins
J. Edward Bromberg	Judge Booth
Astrid Allwyn	Kay Swift
Allan Lane	Richard Hope
Robert Greig	Captain
Jayne Regan	Dora Day
Julius Tannen	First Mate
Willie Fung	Chang
Philip Ahn	Sun Lo
Paul McVey	Second Mate
Helen Jerome Eddy	Mrs. Kruikshank

William Stack	Alfred Kruikshank
Honorable Wu	Latchee Lee

Directed by William A. Seiter; *Produced by* Darryl F. Zanuck; *Associate Producers,* B. G. De Sylva, Earl Carroll and Harold Wilson; *Story by* Sam Engel; *Screenplay by* William Conselman, Arthur Sheekman and Nat Perrin.

36. WEE WILLIE WINKIE, Twentieth Century-Fox, 1937, 105 minutes.

CAST:		
Shirley Temple	Priscilla Williams
Victor McLaglen	Sergeant MacDuff
C. Aubrey Smith	Colonel Williams
June Lang	Joyce Williams
Michael Whalen	Lt. Brandes ("Coppy")
Cesar Romero	Khoda Khan
Constance Collier	Mrs. Allardyce
Douglas Scott	Private Mott
Gavin Muir	Capt. Bibberbeigh
Willie Fung	Mohammet Dihn
Brandon Hurst	Bagby
Lionel Pape	Major Allardyce
Clyde Cook	Pipe Major Sneath
Lauri Beatty	Elsie Allardyce
Lionel Braham	Major Gen. Hammond
Mary Forbes	Mrs. MacMonachie
Cyril McLaglen	Corporal Tummel
Jack Pennick	Soldier guard and Shirley's military instructor offstage
Pat Somerset	Officer
Hector Sarno	Driver

Directed by John Ford; *Produced by* Darryl F. Zanuck; *Associate Producer,* Gene Markey; *Story by* Rudyard Kipling; *Screenplay by* Ernest Pascal and Julien Josephson; *Photography by* Arthur Miller; *Musical Score by* Alfred Newman.

37. HEIDI, Twentieth Century-Fox, 1937, 87 minutes.

CAST:		
Shirley Temple	Heidi
Jean Hersholt	Adolph Kramer
Arthur Treacher	Andrews
Helen Westley	Blind Anna

Pauline Moore .... Elsa
Thomas Beck .... Pastor Schultz
Mary Nash .... Fräulein Rottenmeier
Sidney Blackmer .... Herr Sesemann
Mady Christians .... Aunt Dete
Sig Rumann .... Police Captain
Marcia Mae Jones .... Clara Sesemann
Delmar Watson .... Peter, the goat boy
Egon Brecher .... Innkeeper
Christian Rub .... Baker
George Mumbert................ Organ grinder

Directed by Allan Dwan; *Produced by* Darryl F. Zanuck; *Associate Producer,* Raymond Griffith; *Story by* Johanna Spyri; *Screenplay by* Walter Ferris and Julien Josephson.

38. REBECCA OF SUNNYBROOK FARM, Twentieth Century-Fox release of Raymond Griffith's production, 1938, 80 minutes.

CAST: Shirley Temple .... Rebecca Winstead
Randolph Scott .... Anthony Kent
Jack Haley .... Orville Smithers
Gloria Stuart .... Gwenn Warren
Phyllis Brooks .... Lola Lee
Helen Westley .... Aunt Miranda Wilkins
Slim Summerville .... Homer Busby
Bill Robinson .... Aloysius
Raymond Scott Quintet...... as themselves
Alan Dinehart .... Purvis
J. Edward Bromberg.......... Dr. Hill
Dixie Dunbar.................... Receptionist
Paul Hurst .... Mug
William Demarest............. Henry Kipper
Ruth Gillette .... Melba
Paul Harvey .... Cyrus Bartlett
Clarence Hummel
    Wilson ....Jake Singer
Sam Hayes, Gary Breckner,
    Carroll Nye .... Radio announcers
Franklin Pangborn........... Hamilton Montmarcy
William Wagner .... Reverend Turner
Elly Malyon .... Mrs. Turner
Mary McCarty................. Florabelle

Directed by Allan Dwan; *Produced by* Darryl F. Zanuck; *Associate Producer,* Raymond Griffith; *Story suggested by story by* Kate Douglas Wiggin; *Screen-*

play by Karl Tunberg and Don Ettlinger; *Cinematography by* Arthur Miller; *Songs by* Mack Gordon and Harry Revel, Lew Pollock and Sidney D. Mitchell, Sam Pokrass and Jack Yellen and Raymond Scott; *Dances by* Nick Castle and Geneva Sawyer; *Photography by* Arthur Miller; *Art Directors,* Bernard Herzbrun and Hans Peters; *Sets by* Thomas Little; *Edited by* Allen McNeil; *Musical Director,* Arthur Lange.

39. LITTLE MISS BROADWAY, Twentieth Century-Fox, 1938.

CAST:
Shirley Temple	Betsy Brown
George Murphy	Roger Wendling
Jimmy Durante	Jimmy Clayton
Phyllis Brooks	Barbara Shea
Edna Mae Oliver	Sarah Wendling
George Barbier	Fiske
Edward Ellis	Pop Shea
Jane Darwell	Miss Hutchins
El Brendel	Ole
Donald Meek	Willoughby Wendling
Patricia Wilder	Flossie
Claude Gillingwater, Sr.	Judge
George and Olive Brasno	as themselves
Charles Williams	Mike Brody
Charles Coleman	Simmons
Russell Hicks	Perry
Brian Sisters	as themselves for specialty number
Brewster Twins	Guests
Claire DuBrey	Detective
Robert Gleckler	Miles
C. Montague Shaw	Pool
Frank Dae	Scully
Eddie Collins, Syd Saylor, Jerry Colonna, Heinie Conklin	Members of the band
Ben Weldon	Taxi driver

Directed by Irving Cummings; *Produced by* Darryl F. Zanuck; *Original story by* Harry Tugend and Jack Yellen.

40. JUST AROUND THE CORNER, Twentieth Century-Fox, 1938, 80 minutes.

CAST:
Shirley Temple	Penny Hale
Charles Farrell	Jeff Hale

Joan Davis .... Kitty
Amanda Duff..................... Lola
Bill Robinson .... Corporal Jones
Bert Lahr .... Gus
Franklin Pangborn .... Waters
Cora Witherspoon.............. Aunt Julia Ramsby
Claude Gillingwater, Sr. .... Samuel G. Henshaw
Bennie Bartlett .... Milton Ramsby
Hal K. Dawson .... Reporter
Charles Williams .... Candid cameraman
Tony Hughes,
   Orville Caldwell .... Henshaw's assistants
Marilyn Knowlden .... Gwendolyn
Eddy Conrad .... French tutor

Directed by Irving Cummings; *Produced by* Darryl F. Zanuck; *Associate Producer,* David Hemptstead; *Screenplay by* Ethel Hill, J. P. McEvoy and Darrell Ware, *based on a story by* Paul Gerard Smith; *Music and lyrics by* Walter Bullock and Harold Spina; *Dances staged by* Nicholas Castle and Geneva Sawyer.

41. THE LITTLE PRINCESS, Twentieth Century-Fox, 1939, 94 minutes.

CAST: Shirley Temple .... Sara Crewe
        Richard Greene .... Geoffrey Hamilton
        Anita Louise .... Miss Rose
        Ian Hunter .... Capt. Crewe
        Cesar Romero .... Ran Dass
        Arthur Treacher .... Bertie
        Mary Nash .... Miss Minchin
        Sybil Jason .... Becky
        Miles Mander .... Lord Wickham
        Marcia Mae Jones .... Lavinia
        Beryl Mercer .... Queen Victoria
        Deidre Gale .... Jessie
        Ira Stevens .... Ermengarde
        E. E. Clive .... Mr. Barrows
        Keith Kenneth .... Bobbie
        Will Stanton,
          Harry Allen .... Grooms
        Holmes Herbert, Evan
          Thomas, Guy Bellis........ Doctors

> *Kenneth Hunter* .... General
> *Lionel Braham* .... Colonel

Directed by Walter Lang; *Produced by* Darryl F. Zanuck; *Associate Producer,* Gene Markey; *Screenplay by* Ethel Hill and Walter Ferris, *based on the story by* Frances Hodgson Burnett; *Photography by* Arthur Miller, A.S.C. and William Skall, A.S.C.

42. SUSANNAH OF THE MOUNTIES, Twentieth Century-Fox, 1939, 73 minutes.

CAST:

> *Shirley Temple* .... Susannah Sheldon
> *Randolph Scott* .... Monty (Inspector Angus Montague)
> *Margaret Lockwood* .... Vicky Standing
> *Martin Goodrider* .... Little Chief
> *J. Farrell MacDonald* .... Pat O'Hannegan
> *Maurice Moscovich* .... Chief Big Eagle
> *Moroni Olsen* .... Supt. Andrew Standing
> *Victor Jory* .... Wolf Pelt
> *Lester Matthews* .... Harlan Chambers
> *Leyland Hodgson* .... Randall
> *Herbert Evans* .... Doctor
> *Jack Luden* .... Williams
> *Charles Irwin* .... Sergeant McGregor
> *John Sutton* .... Corporal Piggot
> *Chief Big Tree* .... Chief

Directed by William A. Seiter; *Produced by* Kenneth Macgowan; *Story by* Fidel La Barba, *based on the book by* Muriel Denison; *Adapted by* Fidel La Barba and Walter Ferris; *Screenplay by* Robert Ellis and Helen Logan; *Photography by* Arthur Miller; *Edited by* Robert Bischoff; *Musical Direction by* Louis Silvers.

43. THE BLUE BIRD, Twentieth Century-Fox, 1940.

CAST:

> *Shirley Temple* .... Mytyl
> *Spring Byington* .... Mummy Tyl
> *Nigel Bruce* .... Mr. Luxury
> *Gale Sondergaard* .... Tylette the cat
> *Eddie Collins* .... Tylo the dog
> *Sybil Jason* .... Angela Berlingot
> *Jessie Ralph* .... Fairy Berylune
> *Helen Ericson* .... Light
> *Johnny Russell* .... Tyltyl

Laura Hope Crews .... Mrs. Luxury
Russell Hicks .... Daddy Tyl
Cecilia Loftus..................... Granny Tyl
Al Shean .... Grandpa Tyl
Gene Reynolds .... Studious boy
Leona Roberts .... Mrs. Berlingot
Stansey Andrews .... Wilheim
Dorothy Dearing .... Cypress
Frank Dawson .... Caller of Roll
Claire DuBrey .... Nurse
Sterling Holloway .... Wild Plum Tree
Thurston Hall .... Father Time
Edwin Maxwell .... Oak Tree
Herbert Evans and Brandon
   Hurst .... Footmen
Dewey Robinson .... Royal Forester
Keith Hitchcock .... Major Domo
Buster Phelps .... Boy Investor
Tommy Taker and Dorothy
   Joyce .... Lovers
Billy Cook .... Boy Chemist
Scotty Beckett, Juanita Quigley
   and Payne Johnson .... Children
Ann Todd .... Little sister
Diane Fisher .... Little girl

Directed by Walter Lang; *Produced by* Darryl F. Zanuck; *Associate Producer,* Gene Markey; *Based on the play by* Maurice Maeterlinck; *Screenplay by* Ernest Pascal; *Photography by* Arthur Miller and Ray Renahan; *Special Effects by* Fred Sersen.

44. YOUNG PEOPLE, Twentieth Century-Fox, 1941.

CAST: Shirley Temple .... Wendy
Jack Oakie .... Joe Ballantine
Charlotte Greenwood .... Kitty Ballantine
Arleen Whelan .... Marilyn
George Montgomery .... Mike Shea
Kathleen Howard .... Hester Appleby
Minor Watson .... Dakin
Frank Swann .... Fred Willard
Frank Sully .... Jeb
Sara Edwards .... Mrs. Stinchfield
Mae Marsh .... Marie Liggett

Irving Bacon	Otis
Arthur Aylsworth	Doorman
Olin Howland	Station Master
Billy Wayne	Stage Manager
Harry Tyler	Dave
Darryl Hickman	Tommy
Shirley Mills	Mary Ann
Diane Fisher	Susie
Bobby Anderson	Jerry Dakin
Ted North	Eddie

Directed by Allan Dwan; *Produced by* Harry Joe Brown; *Screenplay by* Edwin Blum and Don Ettlinger; *Director of Photography,* Edward Cronjager, A.S.C.

45. KATHLEEN, Metro-Goldwyn-Mayer, 1941, 85 minutes.

CAST:		
	Shirley Temple	Kathleen Davis
	Herbert Marshall	John Davis
	Laraine Day	Dr. A. Martha Kent
	Gail Patrick	Lorraine Bennett
	Felix Bressart	Mr. Schoner
	Nella Walker	Mrs. Farrell
	Lloyd Corrigan	Dr. Montague Foster
	Guy Bellis	Jarvis
	Fern Emmett	Miss Bewley
	Wade Boteler	Policeman
	Charles Judels	Manager
	Else Argal	Maid
	Margaret Bert	Margaret
	Joe Yule	Sign poster
	James Flavin;	
	Monty Collins	Moving men

Directed by Harold S. Bucquet; *Produced by* George Haight; *Based on the story by* Kay Van Riper; *Screenplay by* Mary C. McCall, Jr.; *Photography by* Sidney Wagner; *Edited by* Conrad A. Nervig.

46. MISS ANNIE ROONEY, United Artists, 1942, 85 minutes.

CAST:		
	Shirley Temple	Annie Rooney
	William Gargan	Tim Rooney
	Guy Kibbee	Grandpop
	Dickie Moore	Marty
	Peggy Ryan	Myrtle

Roland DuPree	Joey
Gloria Holden	Mrs. White
Jonathan Hale	Mr. White
Mary Field	Mrs. Metz
George Lloyd	Burns
Jan Buckingham	Madam Sylvia
Selmer Jackson	Mrs. Thomas
June Lockhart	Stella Bainbridge
Charles Coleman	Sidney
Edgar Dearing	Policeman
Virginia Sale	Myrtle's mother
Shirley Mills	Audrey Hollis

Directed by Edwin L. Marin; *Produced by* Edward Small; *Screenplay by* George Bruce; *Photography by* Lester White.

47. SINCE YOU WENT AWAY, United Artists, 1944, 172 minutes.

CAST:	*Claudette Colbert*	Anne Hilton
	Joseph Cotten	Lt. Anthony Willett
	Monty Woolley	Col. Smollet
	Jennifer Jones	Jane
	Shirley Temple	Bridget (Brig)
	Hattie McDaniel	Fidelia
	Jane Devlin	Gladys Brown
	Lloyd Corrigan	Mr. Mahoney
	Agnes Moorehead	Emily Hawkins
	Robert Walker	Corp. William G. Smollett, II
	Jackie Moran	Johnny Mahoney
	Guy Madison	Harold Smith, a sailor
	Lionel Barrymore	Clergyman
	Craig Stevens	Danny Williams
	Albert Basserman	Dr. Sigmund Gottlieb Golden
	Keenan Wynn	Lt. Solomon
	Nazimova	Zofia Kislowska, a welder

Directed by John Cromwell; *Produced by* David O. Selznick; *Based on the book by* Margaret Buell Wilder; *Screenplay by* David O. Selznick; *Production Designed by* William L. Pereira; *Photography by* Stanley Cortez, A.S.C., Lee Garmes, A.S.C.; *Music by* Max Steiner; *Settings by* Mark Lee Kirk; *Special Effects by* Jack Cosgrove; *Supervising Film Editor,* Hal C. Kern; *Sound Editor,* Charles L. Freeman; *Interior Decoration by* Victor A.

Gangelin; *Technical Adviser,* Lt. Col. J. G. Taylor, U.S. Army; *Cameras,* Edward P. Fitzgerald and Harry Webb; *Makeup by* Robert Stephanoff; *Hair Stylist,* Peggy Higgins; *Wardrobe Director,* Elmer Ellsworth.

48. I'LL BE SEEING YOU, United Artists, 1944, 82 minutes.

CAST:
Ginger Rogers	Mary Marshall
Joseph Cotten	Zachary Morgan
Shirley Temple	Barbara Marshall (Mary's cousin)
Spring Byington	Mrs. Marshall
Tom Tully	Mr. Marshall
Chill Wills	Swanson
Dare Harris	Lt. Bruce
Kenny Bowers	Sailor on the train
Olin Howland	Hawker
Dorothy Stone	Salesgirl
John James	Paratrooper
Eddie Hall	Charlie Hartman
Joe Haworth	Sailor in coffee shop
Jack Carr	Counterman
Bob Meredith	Soldier-father on train
Robert Dudley	YMCA hotel attendant
Margaret Bert	Mother of boys
Mickey Laughlin, Hank Tobias and Gary Gray	Boys outside theater
Earl W. Johnson	Dog owner

Directed by William Dieterle; *Produced by* Dore Schary; *Story by* Charles Martin; *Screenplay by* Marion Parsonnet, *based on the novel* Double Furlough *by* Charles Marton; *Cinematography by* Tony Gaudio; *Art Director,* Mark Lee Kirk; *Edited by* William H. Ziegler; *Music by* Daniele Amfitheatrof; *Song by* Irving Kahal and Sammy Fain.

49. KISS AND TELL, Columbia, 1945, 90 minutes.

CAST:
Shirley Temple	Corliss Archer
Jerome Courtland	Dexter Franklin
Walter Abel	Mr. Archer
Katharine Alexander	Mrs. Archer
Robert Benchley	Uncle George
Porter Hall	Mr. Franklin
Edna Holland	Mrs. Franklin
Virginia Welles	Mildred Pringle

Tom Tully .... Mr. Pringle
Mary Phillips .... Mrs. Pringle
Darryl Hickman .... Raymond Pringle
Scott McKay .... Private Jimmy Earhart
Scott Elliott .... Lenny Archer
Kathryn Card .... Louise

Directed by Richard Wallace; *Produced by* Sol C. Siegel; *Screenplay by* F. Hugh Herbert, based on his play of the same name.

50. HONEYMOON, RKO, 1947, 74 minutes.

CAST: Shirley Temple .... Barbara Olmstead
Franchot Tone .... David Flanner
Guy Madison .... Phil Vaughn
Lina Romay .... Raquel Mendoza
Gene Lockhart .... Prescott
Corinna Mura .... Señora Mendoza
Grant Mitchell .... Crenshaw
Julio Villareal .... Señor Mendoza
Manual Arvide .... Registrar
Jose R. Goula .... Dr. Diego

Directed by William Keighley; *Produced by* Warren Duff; *Based on the story by* Vicki Baum; *Screenplay by* Michael Kanin; *Director of Photography*, Edward Cronjager, A.S.C.; *Executive Producer*, Robert Sparks; *Art Direction by* Albert S. D'Agostino and Ralph Berger; *Music by* Leigh Harline; *Edited by* Ralph Dawson.

51. THE BACHELOR AND THE BOBBY-SOXER, RKO, 1947, 93 minutes.

CAST: Cary Grant .... Dick
Myrna Loy .... Margaret
Shirley Temple .... Susan
Rudy Vallee .... Tommy
Ray Collins .... Beemish
Harry Davenport .... Thaddeus
Johnny Sands .... Jerry
Don Beddoe .... Tony
Lillian Randolph .... Bessie
Veda Ann Borg .... Agnes Prescott
Dan Tobin .... Walters
Ransom Sherman .... Judge Treadwell
William Bakewell .... Winters

Irving Bacon .... Melvin
Ian Bernard .... Perry
Carol Hughes .... Florence
William Hall .... Anthony Herman
Gregory Gay .... Maître d'Hotel

Directed by Irving Reis; *Produced by* Dore Schary; *Story by* Sidney Sheldon; *Screenplay by* Sidney Sheldon; *Photographed by* Robert de Grasse, A.S.C. and Nicholas Musuraca, *Art Directors*, Albert S. D'Agostino, Carroll Clark; *Set Decorations*, Darrell Silvera, James Atwels; *Music by* Leigh Harline; *Edited by* Frederic Knudtson.

52. THAT HAGEN GIRL, Warner Bros.–First National, 1947, 83 minutes.

CAST: Shirley Temple .... Mary Hagen
Ronald Reagan .... Tom Bates
Dorothy Peterson .... Minta Hagen, mother
Charles Kemper .... Jim Hagen
Rory Calhoun .... Ken Freneau
Jean Porter .... Sharon Bailey
Nella Walker .... Molly Freneau
Winifred Harris .... Selma Delaney
Ruth Robinson .... Cora
Lois Maxwell .... Julia Kane
Conrad Janis .... Dewey Koons, Mary's dance
partner
Penny Edwards .... Christine Delaney
Harry Davenport .... Judge Merrivale

Directed by Peter Godfrey; *Produced by* Alex Gottlieb; *Based on the novel by* Edith Roberts; *Screenplay by* Charles Hoffman; *Photography by* Karl Freund; *Art Direction by* Stanley Fleischer; *Edited by* David Weisbart; *Sound by* Stanley Jones; *Set Decorations by* Lyle B. Reifsnider; *Special Effects by* William McGann; *Associate*, Weslie Anderson; *Music by* Franz Waxman; *Orchestral Arrangements by* Leonid Raab; *Musical Director*, Leo F. Forbstein; *Dialogue Director*, Herschel Daugherty; *Wardrobe by* Travilla; *Makeup by* Perc Westmore.

53. FORT APACHE, Argosy Pictures Production, RKO release, 1948, 127 minutes.

CAST: John Wayne .... Captain York
Henry Fonda .... Lt. Col. Owen Thursday
Shirley Temple .... Philadelphia Thursday

Pedro Armendariz	Sergeant Beaufort
Ward Bond	Sergeant O'Rourke
George O'Brien	Capt. Collingwood
John Agar	Lt. O'Rourke
Victor McLaglen	Sergeant Mulcahy
Anna Lee	Mrs. Collingwood
Irene Rich	Mrs. O'Rourke
Miguel Inclan	Chief Cochise
Dick Foran	Quincannon
Jack Pennick	Sergeant Shatuck
Guy Kibbee	Dr. Wilkins
Grant Withers	Silas Meacham
Mae March	Martha
Mary Gordon	Ma, the barmaid
Movita	Guadalupe
Hank Worden	Southern recruit
Ray Hyke	Recruit
Francis Ford	Fen, the stage guard
Cliff Clark	Stage driver
Fred Graham	Cavalry man
Mickey Simpson	Noncom officer
Frank Ferguson, William Forrest, Phillip Keiffer	Reporters

Directed by John Ford; *Produced by* John Ford and Merian C. Cooper; *Story by* James Warner Bellah, based on "Massacre" in *Saturday Evening Post; Screenplay by* Frank S. Nugent; *Cinematographer,* Archer Stout; *Edited by* Jack Murray; *Art Director,* James Basevi; *Musical Score by* Richard Hageman; *Sound by* Frank Webster and Joseph I. Kane; *Technical Advisers,* Major Phillip Kieffer, USA Rtd. and Katharine Spaatz; *Special Effects,* Dave Koehler; *Dance Sequences,* Kenny Williams; *Musical Arranger and Conductor,* Lucien Cailliet; *Set Dressings,* Joseph Kish; *Ladies Wardrobe,* Ann Peck; *Men's Wardrobe,* Michael Meyers; *Makeup,* Emile LaVicne.

54. ADVENTURE IN BALTIMORE, RKO, 1949, 89 minutes.

CAST:		
	Shirley Temple	Dinah Sheldon
	Robert Young	Dr. Sheldon
	John Agar	Tom Wade
	Albert Sharpe	Mr. Fletcher
	Josephine Hutchinson	Mrs. Sheldon
	Charles Kemper	Mr. Steuben
	Johnny Sands	Gene Sheldon
	John Miljan	Mr. Eckert

Norma Varden	H. H. Hamilton
Carol Brannan	Bernice Eckert
Patti Brady	Sis Sheldon
Gregory Marshall	Mark Sheldon
Patsy Creighton	Sally Wilson

Directed by Richard Wallace; *Produced by* Richard H. Berger; *Screenplay by* Lionel Houser; *Original Story by* Lesser Samuels and Christopher Isherwood; *Photography by* Robert de Grasse; *Art Direction by* Albert S. D'Agostino and Jack Okey; *Musical Score by* Frederick Hollander; *Musical Direction by* C. Bakaleinikoff; *Edited by* Robert Swink.

55. MR. BELVEDERE GOES TO COLLEGE, Twentieth Century-Fox, 1949, 82 minutes.

CAST:

Clifton Webb	Lynn Belvedere
Shirley Temple	Ellen Baker
Tom Drake	Bill Chase
Alan Young	Avery Brubaker
Jessie Royce Landis	Mrs. Chase
Kathleen Hughes	Kay Nelson
Taylor Holmes	Dr. Gibbs
Alvin Greenman	Corny Whittaker
Paul Harvey	Dr. Keating
Barry Kelly	Griggs
Bob Patten	Joe Fisher
Lee MacGregor	Hickey
Helen Westcott	Marian
Jeff Chandler	Pratt
Clancy Cooper	McCarthy
Evelynn Eaton	Sally
Judy Brubaker	Barbara
Kathleen Freeman	Babe
Lotte Stein	Marta
Peggy Call	Jean Auchincloss
Ruth Tobey	Nancy
Elaine Ryan	Peggy
Pattee Chapman	Isabelle
Joyce Otis	Fluffy
Lonnie Thomas	Davy
Reginald Sheffield	Prof. Ives
Katherine Lang	Miss Cadwaller
Isabel Withers	Mrs. Myrtle
Arthur Space	Instructor

Directed by Eliott Nugent; *Produced by* Samuel G. Engel; *Story by* Gwen Davenport, based on a character from *Sitting Pretty; Screenplay by* Richard Sale, Mary Loos and Mary McCall, Jr; *Music by* Alfred Newman; *Photography by* Lloyd Ahern; *Art Direction by* Lyle Wheeler, Richard Irvine; *Set Decorations by* Thomas Little; *Edited by* Harmon Jones; *Wardrobe Direction by* Charles Le Maire; *Costumes Designed by* Bonnie Cashin; *Orchestral Arrangements by* Edward Powell; *Makeup by* Ben Nye; *Special Effects by* Fred Sersen; *Sound by* E. Clayton Ward and Roger Heman.

56. A KISS FOR CORLISS, United Artists, independently produced by Enterprise Studios at General Service, 1949, 88 minutes.

CAST:
Shirley Temple .... Corliss Archer
David Niven .... Kenneth Marquis
Tom Tully .... Mr. Archer
Virginia Welles .... Mildred
Darryl Hickman .... Dexter Franklin
Robert Ellis .... Raymond Archer
Richard Craig .... Taylor

Directed by Richard Wallace; *Produced by* Colin Miller; *Associate Producer,* Marcus Lowe II; *Story based on character created by* F. Hugh Herbert; *Screenplay* by Howard Dimsdale; *Music by* Werner R. Reymann; *Production Manager,* Lewis J. Rachmil; *Photography by* Robert de Grasse; *Editor,* Frank Doyle; *Assistant Directors,* Robert Aldrich, Frank Baur; *Musical Director,* Rudolph Polk; *Set Decorations,* Edward G. Boyle; *Wardrobe by* Eloise Jenssen; *Dialog Director,* Anthony Jowitt; *Sound,* Frank Webster.

57. THE STORY OF SEABISCUIT, Warner Bros.–First National, 1949, 96 minutes.

CAST:
Shirley Temple .... Margaret O'Hara
Barry Fitzgerald .... Shawn O'Hara
Lon McCallister .... Ted Knowles
Rosemary De Camp .... Mrs. Charles S. Howard
Donald MacBride .... George Carson
Pierre Watkin .... Charles S. Howard
William Forrest .... Thomas Miltford
"Sugarfoot" Anderson ...... Murphy
Wm. J. Cartledge .... Jockey George Woolf
                Seabiscuit via genuine
                footage

Directed by David Butler; *Produced by* William Jacobs; *Screenplay by* John Taintor Foote; *Photography by* Wilfred M. Cline; *Technicolor color consultant,* Mitchell Kovaleski; *Music by* David Buttolph; *Edited by* Irene Morra.

TELEVISION CREDITS: SHIRLEY TEMPLE

1. January 12, 1958, to December 21, 1958, NBC, *Shirley Temple's Storybook*, hostess/narrator, Shirley Temple. Anthology series featuring entertaining adaptations of fairy tales and classic children's stories. Included stories (16): "Tom and Huck," "The Land of Oz," "Kim," "Little Men," "Beauty and the Beast," "Rapunzel," "The Sleeping Beauty," "Rip Van Winkle," "The Nightingale," "Dick Whittington and His Cat," "Hiawatha," "Charlotte's Web," "Son of Aladdin," "Rumpelstiltskin" and "Mother Goose." Shirley Temple appeared in "The Land of Oz," "Little Men" and (with her children) "Mother Goose." She also performed the theme song, "Dreams Are Made for Children." A special presentation of the regular series to mark her dramatic TV acting debut was telecast on NBC March 5, 1958, when she appeared in "The Legend of Sleepy Hollow." The series was shown again on ABC from January 12, 1959, to December 21, 1959.

2. September 18, 1960, to September 10, 1961, ABC, *Shirley Temple Theater*, hostess/narrator, Shirley Temple. She also performed the theme song, "The Enchanted Melody."

3. Pilot film for proposed series *Go Fight City Hall* (never released).

4. In addition to her own television programs, she appeared as a guest on other shows, including those of Red Skelton (April 1963), Mitch Miller (1964), Dinah Shore (1972) and Mike Douglas (1972).

393

NOTES

The abbreviation PI, used in the notes section, stands for Personal Interview.

Preface

Page

    5   "in mortal combat": Diana Serra Cary, PI.

        "larger-than-life": Ibid.

    6   "Little Shirley Temple": Windeler, p. 80.

Chapter 1

  18 "Our home in": letter from George F. Temple to Mrs. Robert Hetz, March 19, 1976.

       "driving through": Ibid

  20 "the cute little": *California*, p. 122.

  21 " 'Your child should": Cary, p. 93.

       "This was heady": Ibid.

  22 "Sometimes they did": Ibid.

       (fn) "My mother was": Windeler, pp. 16–17.

  23 "She looked like": *Parents Magazine*, undated article.

Chapter 2

  25 "remarkably sensitive": Perrett, *America in the Twenties*, p. 314.

       "urban provinciality": Ibid.

       "thanks to radio": Ibid.

  26 "When Mom and": Temple, *My Young Life*, p. 30.

  27 "America's Boy": Cooper, p..49.

  28 "She told him": *Parade*, December 7, 1986.

  29 "The place was": Cary, p. 201.

  31 "About Shirley Temple": Maltin and Bann, p. 17.

       "a virtual factory": Katz, p. 376.

  32 "There was a": Temple, *My Young Life*, p. 30.

       "exploitative, racist and": Mosley, p. 111.

       "And then the": Temple, *My Young Life*, p. 31.

       "I was walking": Columbia University Oral History Project.

33 "Mom gave my curls": Temple, *My Life and Times* (pages unnumbered).
    "Mr. Hays wanted": Ibid.
    "As soon as I": Ibid.
34 "All of us": Temple, *My Young Life*, p. 32.
35 "A movie lot": Ibid.
    "word for word,": Temple, *My Life and Times.*
    "cheap-jack comedy": Windeler, p. 111.
37 "[My father] said": Temple, *My Life and Times.*
38 "sufficiently bad": *Variety*, 10/25/32.
    "a wealthy": Temple, *My Life and Times.*
    "the incomparable": movie credits.
    "wearing lots of": Temple, *My Young Life*, p. 32.
    "really dreamy,": Ibid.
    "I was Jane": David, p. 38.
39 "Children were treated": Diana Serra Cary, PI.
40 "The picture lasted": *America Magazine*, circa 1934.
    "She kept whispering": Temple, *My Life and Times.*
    "about three hundred": Ibid.
42 "[Hays] came to": David, p. 40.
43 "The family lived": Moore, p. 72.
    "Many of us": Ibid.
    "He wore plaid": Ibid, p. 264.
    "I was seven": Delmar Watson, PI.
    "called for Shirley": David, p. 41.
44 "Pair of kids": *Variety*, September 8, 1933.
45 "Shirley was too": Robert Young, PI.

Chapter 3
50 "I stopped and": David, pp. 45–46.
51 "[Mr. Gorney] asked": Temple, *My Young Life*, p. 43.
    "If it wasn't": Ibid., p. 46.
52 "As we were": Ibid.
53 "was the start": Temple, *My Young Life*, p. 46.
    "I came in": Ibid.
    "I hadn't been": Ibid, p. 47.
54 "I almost fainted": Fox Films Studio biography.
    "The vista of": Ibid.
    "We took a taxi": Temple, *My Young Life*, p. 48.
55 "the same man": Allvine, p. 80.
56 "loved, feared and": Ibid.
    "He was a": Ibid, p. 81.
    "manufacturing new young": Ibid, p. 83.
    "dreamed up the": Ibid.
57 "Shirley Temple sparkles": *Variety*, May 25, 1934.
    "Mom remembered a": Temple, *My Young Life*, p. 48.
    "on the theory": Ibid.

58 "a three word": Ibid.
    "at long last": Ibid, p. 49.
    "Mom prayed": Ibid.
    "If nothing else,": *Variety*, April 24, 1934.
    "Although *Stand Up*": undated publicity release, circa 1934.
    "Despite the fact": Ibid.
59 "You must see": Ibid.

Chapter 4

61 DILLINGER FORCES DOCTOR: Wilson, p. 468.
62 "Shirley Temple, the": *LA Times*, May 25, 1934.
    "What took Mom": Temple, *My Young Life*, p. 67.
63 "I first met": Nancy Majors Voorheis, PI.
64 "for an hour": Ibid.
65 "a very handsome": Ibid.
    "Gertrude had a": David, p. 52.
    "monitored Shirley's entire": Ibid.
    "Shirley was the": Windeler, p. 38.
    "I wouldn't stand": *Parents Magazine*, undated article.
    "The mother was": David, p. 54.
66 "at the ease": *LA Times*, August 23, 1934.
    "hungrily eyeing": Harold Hefferman, *Detroit News*, April 13, 1949.
    "Gentlemen": Ibid.
67 "rather like an": *The Listener*, August 1931.
    "On the one side": Ibid.
    "Mom always went": Temple, *My Life and Times.*
68 "very anxious that": Temple, *My Young Life*, p. 69.
    "I couldn't even": Moore, p. 88.
69 "was on the set": Joseph LaShelle, PI.
    "I wanted desperately": Moore, p. 89.
    "Naturally, Shirley was": Ibid, p. 87.
    ". . . after *Bright Eyes*": Ibid, p. 88.
70 (fn) "Some writer started": Temple, *My Young Life*, p. 71.
    ("Well, I started": *Parade*, December 7, 1986.
    "I don't have": Moore, p. 83.
    "[Acting] was something": Ibid, p. 66.
71 "practically every agent": Cary, p. 210.
    "and walked up": Ibid, p. 209.
    "drawn into the": Ibid.

Chapter 5

73 "Darryl always thought": Mosley, p. 137.
74 "They didn't buy": *Detroit News*, April 13, 1949.
    "the first time": Mosley, p. 153.
    "bigger, richer, better": Ibid.
75 "like a lodestone": *Jump Cut Magazine*, July/August 1974.

"figures of cold": Ibid.

"She assaults, penetrates": Ibid.

76   "It is a splendid": FDR speech.

"[Shirley's] work entails": *Time,* circa 1935.

"Motion picture acting": *Jump Cut Magazine,* July/August 1974.

77   "on the dot": Temple, *My Young Life,* p. 88.

"as outside Hansel": Delmar Watson, PI.

"because our schedules": Temple, *My Young Life* p. 88.

78   "Lillian was not": Moore, p. 137.

"I remember once": Cary, p. 22.

"photographed her that": Ibid.

79   "You tend to": Ibid.

"To me [making": Temple, *My Young Life,* p. 69.

"carried a marvelous": Ibid, p. 70.

"handcuff people to": Ibid.

"whisked away": Alice Faye, PI.

"looking through the": Temple, *My Young Life,* p. 70.

"Sometimes he pretended": Ibid.

"a droop of": Ibid, p. 88.

80   "to have a complete": Ibid, p. 72.

"After the studio": Ibid.

"in grateful recognition": Academy of Motion Picture Arts and Sciences.

81   "I liked the": *Parade,* December 7, 1986.

"Mrs. Roosevelt was": *Good Housekeeping,* February 1981.

82   (fn) "I was being": *Current Biography,* 1941, Robinson, p. 720.

(fn) "until they are": Ibid.

"kissed each of": Windeler, p. 147

83   "a well-behaved, mannerly": Bogel, p. 48.

"Now, Honey, all": dialogue from film.

"cursed and cussed": Bogel, p. 48.

"who knew de ole": Ibid.

"tremendously proud of": *Current Biography,* 1941, Robinson, p. 719.

84   "During this period": Ibid, p. 36.

"The black low-lifers": Ibid, p. 46.

85   "Perfect Temple formula": University of Indiana Archives.

86   "Leave her here": dialogue from film.

"a modernist construction": *Photoplay,* March 1937.

87   "like a department": Ibid.

"They arrived": Nancy Majors Voorheis, PI.

88   "What a shame": Mosley, p. 162.

89   "a second father": Ibid.

"He hemmed and": Ibid, p. 163.

"[My father] was": Ibid, pp. 172–73.

"You know that Darryl": Ibid, p. 176.

90   "Darryl Zanuck was": Moore, p. 186.

"a health fanatic, worried": Mosley, p. 173.

"Then he was off": Ibid.

91 "Star, a waif": University of Indiana Archives, Bookman #15, p. 39.
"the arrival of": Ibid.
"a chase scene": Ibid.

92 "was not a normal": June Lang, PI.
"a small bit": Diana Serra Cary, PI.
"someone responsible for": Ibid.

93 "Shirley Temple acts": *The Spectator*, August 7, 1936.
"sentimental, a little": Ibid.

94 "earned fifteen times": Rosten, p. 343.

95 "who came all": David, p. 88.
"They were children": Ibid.
"I felt so darned": Ibid.
"I do not let": Windeler, pp. 34–35.
"Why don't you": Ibid., p. 38.

Chapter 6

97 "a psychological": Powdermaker, p. 229.

98 "We [child stars]": Moore, p. 67.
"We all knew": Ibid.
"When I came down": Ibid, p. 83.
"outgrew the other": Ibid, p. 86.
"rotten but nice": Katz, p. 409.

99 "A whole second": Temple, *My Young Life*, p. 153.
"Each dress would": Ibid.
"Seasonal stills always": Ibid.

100 "The hotel people": Ibid, p. 111.
"the police took": Ibid.
"two or three": Ibid.
"We all loved": Alice Faye, PI.

101 "nothing less than": *Variety*, May 28, 1936.
"The Shirley Temple": *NY Times*, January 10, 1936.
"The Golden Temple": Louella Parsons, October 2, 1936, syndicated
    column.
"No exhib[itor's] worrying": *Variety*, December 23, 1936.

102 "Whether or not": Ibid.
"a year-and-a-half": undated publicity release, Twentieth Century-Fox
    Archives, Academy of Motion Picture Arts and Sciences.

103 "whole-heartedly in": Gussow, p. 70.

104 "in all the innocence": Temple, *My Young Life*, p. 114.
"That Temple child": Anon., PI.
"One day Darryl": Gussow, p. 70.
"a quarrelsome": Ford, p. 134.
"Versailles Court": Ibid, p. 135.
"Zanuck's flunkies": Ibid.
"lacked artistic integrity": Ibid.

105 "I'd like to keep": Gussow, p. 70.

"Well we have": Ibid.

"When open warfare": *Variety*, June 30, 1937.

"Under John Ford's": *The New Yorker*, July 1937.

"I had not expected": *The Spectator*, May 24, 1938.

106   "I had accused": Greene, p. 2.

(fn) "Lesser was one": Diana Serra Cary, PI.

107   "Shirley hit her": Windeler, p. 187.

"Which one of": Delmar Watson, PI.

"Mrs. Temple had": Ibid.

108   "They're not being": Moore, p. 91.

"I do remember": Marcia Mae Jones, PI.

109   "The movie was made": Ibid.

110   "He was marvelous": Ibid.

"parked on the side": David, p. 86.

"Once, I was playing": Delmar Watson, PI.

"We talked and we": Marcia Mae Jones, PI.

111   "In *Heidi*, we had": David, p. 93.

"Since she obviously": Ibid, p. 94.

112   "He didn't like": Ibid.

"I don't know if": Marcia Mae Jones, PI.

"The first crowd": Cooper, p. 103.

113   "The national No. 1": *Variety*, March 8, 1938.

114   ". . . looks and acts": Mosley, p. 169.

"for Christ's sake keep": Ibid.

"the studio had a": Ibid.

"It couldn't have": Ibid.

"My secret ambition": publicity release, Twentieth Century-Fox chives, Academy of Motion Picture Arts and Sciences.

"There is a Shirley": Ibid.

Chapter 7

117   "He'll not get": *LA Times*, April 13, 1938.

"There never has": Ibid.

"efficiency man to": *LA Examiner*, April 13, 1938.

118   "The Temples naturally": Ibid, April 24, 1938.

119   "inserted in Shirley's": Ibid.

"The documents had": Cooper, p. 78.

120   "Looking at some": Mosley, p. 168.

"the mean old pumpkin": dialogue from *Little Miss Broadway*.

"a harassed": *LA Times*, November 3, 1938.

121   "Fee-fi-fo-film": *NY Times*, December 3, 1938.

"nothing so arch": Ibid.

(fn) "a sort of resident": Gussow, p. 77.

122   (fn) "Shirley's name was": Ibid.

"envious of her": Sybil Jason, PI.

"just in case": Ibid.

"It occurred to": Ibid.

123 "I remember that": Ibid.

"The scene I remember": Ibid.

"go on endlessly": Mosley, p. 176.

124 "Newspaper circulation": Perrett, *Days of Sadness*, p. 17.

125 (fn) "a flabby script": Halliwell, *Companion*, p. 167.

126 "Everyone kept an": Sybil Jason, PI.

"We rarely came": Sybil Jason, PI.

"In preproduction tests": Moore, p. 90.

127 "About one week": Sybil Jason, PI.

" 'My hands are": Moore, p. 90.

"The finished film": Sybil Jason, PI.

"Mrs. Temple had": Ibid.

"Shirley never realized": Moore, p. 91.

"The premiere was": Sybil Jason, PI.

"would not stand": Moore, p. 89.

128 "Zanuck didn't look": Ibid.

"presented her with": *Good Housekeeping*, February 1981.

Chapter 8

129 "Mom was sad": Temple, *My Young Life*, p. 208.

130 "Every morning the": Nancy Majors Voorheis, PI.

"I remember that": Ibid.

"Because I was": *Parade*, December 7, 1986.

"Westlake was a": Nancy Majors Voorheis, PI.

"We had chapel": Ibid.

131 "Miss Mills, our": Ibid.

"I remember the": Ibid.

"It seems to": Laraine Day, PI.

132 "I think it": Ibid.

133 "a Garlandesque": PI.

"boys! boys! boys!": Nancy Majors Voorheis, PI.

"Grif, Shirley's bodyguard": Ibid.

134 "Mom did more": Shirley Temple, *My Young Life*, p. 212.

"had no intention": letter of Swarts and Tannenbaum to Shirley Temple
   and George and Gertrude Temple, dated November 19, 1941, USC
   Archives, Edward Small Collection, Box 25.

135 "Photographers from every": Moore, pp. 63–64.

136 "I liked Gertrude": Ibid.

"was a terrible": Ibid., p. 89.

"not much, about": *The New Yorker*, June 13, 1942.

"Shirley is still": *Variety*, July 3, 1942.

137 "By her sophomore": Nancy Majors Voorheis, PI.

"first real dates": Temple, *My Young Life*, pp. 210–11.

"They didn't seem": Ibid.

"Great Hall": Ibid.

"dressed exquisitely": Nancy Majors Voorheis, PI.
138 "She was not": Ibid.
"My heart was": Temple, *My Young Life,* p. 208.
139 "that were young": Ibid., p. 227.
"Please be careful": Selznick, p. 327.
140 "Mrs. Temple was": Anon., PI.
141 "an O-Cedar mop": Shirley Temple, *My Young Life,* p. 228.
"He said that": Ibid.
"Selznick placed a": *Time,* July 17, 1944.
"Some of the MGM": Selznick, p. 292.
142 "He made": Ibid.
"Shirley is exceedingly": Ibid, p. 343.
144 "accorded the privilege": *NY Times,* January 21, 1945.
"in part too": Ibid.
"I've about decided": *LA Times,* October 20, 1945.
161 "In case you've": *Variety,* October 20, 1945.
"of course I'll": Windeler, p. 229.
"for garlic on": Ibid.
162 "What I wanted": *Seventeen,* October 1971.
163 "very pleasant": John Agar, PI.
"a fifteen-year": Ibid.
164 "[h]e was a": *LA Examiner,* December 25, 1945.
"infrequent": John Agar, PI.
"War reached down": Perrett, *Days of Sadness,* p. 368.
"Spelling lessons mixed": Ibid.
165 "You were married": *Photoplay,* February 1950.
"that eclipsed the": Perrett, *Days of Sadness,* p. 410.
"seized people's imaginations": Ibid.
"Please, for God's": Ibid.
166 "There I was": *Photoplay,* July 1945.
"Somehow, I wanted": Temple, *My Young Life* p. 235.
"Shirley and John": *LA Times,* April 9, 1945.
167 "sincerity": Ibid.
"the war interrupted": John Agar, PI.

Chapter 9
169 "I want an": *LA Examiner,* September 20, 1945.
"intimate": Ibid.
"closest friends": Ibid.
"the wedding of": Ibid.
"I gave my": Nancy Majors Voorheis, PI.
170 "Little Infanta": Ibid.
171 "with the deftness": *Hollywood Citizen-News,* September 20, 1945.
"a long, resounding kiss": Ibid.
"was longer than": Ibid.
"were tossed helter-skelter": Ibid.

172   "There seemed to": Nancy Majors Voorheis, PI.
      "particularly that the": Ibid.
173   "sparkling like a": *Hollywood Citizen-News*, September 20, 1945.
      "The first ride": *Photoplay*, June 1947.
174   "strong": John Agar, PI.
175   "Thank God, he": Anon., PI.
      DEAR DAVID: Warner Brothers Archives, University of Southern California.
176   "the most terrific": Selznick, p. 352.
      "more labored than": *Hollywood Reporter*, April 15, 1947.
177   "When Temple was": *PM* (N.Y. evening newspaper), May 21, 1947.
      "You can't boss": Anon., PI.
178   "Shirley Temple is": *Herald Tribune*, May 21, 1947.
      "The friends of": *NY Times*, May 21, 1947.
179   "What the veteran": *Fortune*, November 1947.
180   "Why shouldn't I?": *LA Times*, October 9, 1947.
      "He's good looking": Ibid.
      "Dore . . . convinced me": Loy, p. 204.
      "wild manipulations of": *The New Yorker*, August 2, 1947.
      "reasonably funny": Ibid.
181   "The 'fun' picture": Loy, p. 204.
      "trying to put one": Ibid.
      "I was taught": John Agar, PI.
183   "Johnny was inhibited": Anon., PI.
      "Jack Warner called": Alex Gottlieb, PI.
185   "I love to have": Warner Brothers publicity release, circa 1947.
      "Mrs. Temple maintained": Alex Gottlieb, PI.
      "To add to the": Edwards, p. 325.
      (fn) [HOW COULD YOU: Warner Brothers Archives, University of Southern California.
      "Shirley was ladylike": Alex Gottlieb, PI.
      "uninspired soap opera": *Hollywood Reporter*, October 22, 1947.
      "wooden . . . monotonous": *LA Times*, November 27, 1947.
      "a foamy dud": *NY Times*, November 28, 1947.
      "struggling valiantly in": *Variety*, October 22, 1947.
      "his level best": Ibid.
      "Balderdash isn't helped": Ibid.
      "Shirley's acting is": *Hollywood Reporter*, October 22, 1947.
      "Miss Temple smiles": *LA Times*, November 4, 1947.
186   "Mr. Ford knew": Ibid., December 11, 1947.
      "a romantic chronicler": Ford, p. 213.
      "it seemed to": Ibid., p. 214.
      "a spectacular region": Ibid., p. 125.
187   "brittle, his temper": Ibid., p. 217.
      "Well, you can": Ibid.
      "Every night the": Ibid, pp. 271–72.
188   "a vigorous, sweeping": *Hollywood Reporter*, March 10, 1948.

"Shirley Temple and": *LA Times,* May 28, 1948.

"In a picture": *New Yorker,* July 3, 1948.

"[John] began not": Divorce testimony, Shirley Temple Agar, December 5, 1949.

189 "I didn't drink": John Agar, PI.

"Shirley and John": *LA Times,* January 31, 1948.

190 "as confident and": Robert Young, PI.

"Young and Shirley": Anon., PI.

Chapter 10

191 "were engaged in": Perrett, *Dream of Greatness,* p. 13.

"—to outshine Greece": Ibid.

"the richest, the": Ibid.

"liberty in a": Ibid.

192 "ruled supreme": Gussow, p. 140.

"Every creative decision": Ibid.

"The studio couldn't": Harry Brand, archives, Academy of Motion Picture Arts and Sciences.

193 "Our main objective": Ibid.

"fast-paced; the": *NY Times,* April 19, 1949.

"Our hero, somewhat": Ibid.

195 "a little predatory": Anon., PI.

196 "spoiled-brat behavior": Niven, p. 313.

"could never think": *A Kiss for Corliss* screenplay.

197 "on Thursday for": Warner Archives, USC.

(fn) "right from time": Ibid.

(fn) "obliged to adopt": Ibid.

"rode the movie": Windeler, p. 249.

198 "found occasion to": Warner Archives, USC.

"With the mother": Warner Archives, USC, memo dated April 14, 1949.

"I always work": Ibid., publicity release, April 23, 1949.

"The weakest part": Ibid, memo dated August 8, 1949.

199 "Sometimes I think": *London Sunday Observer,* undated, circa 1949.

"When I was": Testimony of Shirley Temple Agar, divorce proceedings, December 5, 1949.

"After the baby": Ibid.

"very drunk and": Ibid.

200 "I feel I": Ibid.

"The Court views": Ibid.

"This court cannot": Ibid.

201 "As usual": AP release, December 5, 1949.

"reflects incorrectly our": Ibid.

"She had a": Anon., PI.

Chapter 11

205 "YOU CAN TAKE": Watson, p. 30.

"Hollywood [is a": Ibid, p. 73.

"I was tired": Selznick, p. 383.

206   "continued to produce": Ibid.

(fn) "While I was": Ibid, p. 383.

"to take her": Ibid.

"shouting, pushing persons": Ibid.

"roared a welcome": Ibid.

"the most enthusiastic": Ibid.

"I feel": *Photoplay*, November 1950.

207   "I really wasn't": *Saturday Evening Post*, June 5, 1965.

"It's corny, but": Ibid.

208   "When she fell": Anon., PI.

209   "was snagged": Ibid.

"I couldn't compete": *Saturday Evening Post*, June 5, 1965.

210   "Shirley wasn't a": Nancy Majors Voorheis, PI.

"The reason for": Ibid.

"At Westlake, Shirley": Ibid.

"Medicine, and especially": Ibid.

211   "I know now": *Photoplay*, November 1950.

"Charles was definitely": Nancy Majors Voorheis, PI.

"He's calm and conservative": Anon., PI.

212   "a snug red": *LA Times*, December 19, 1950.

"a mid-afternoon": Ibid.

(fn) "had bacon and": *LA Times*, December 19, 1950.

"Acting as though": Ibid.

"That's long enough": *Citizen News*, December 21, 1950.

213   "them even more": Perrett, *A Dream of Greatness*, p. 166.

"directed American": Ibid.

"turned the": Ibid.

"This will ruin": *LA Times*, July 21, 1951.

214   "Don't blame this": LA Court Record, July 20, 1951.

"on taking his": *LA Times*, July 21, 1951.

"God and religion": John Agar, PI.

215   "mute testimony that": Hedda Hopper, September 1952.

216   "General MacArthur is": *San Francisco Chronicle*, April 16, 1951.

"shocked indignation": Perrett, *A Dream of Greatness*, p. 166.

"Whereas, at one a.m.": Ibid.

"Louis Parsons": Anon., PI.

217   "During the two years": *LA Times*, August 9, 1968.

(fn) "We've just had": Wheeler-Bennett, p. 799.

(fn) "I'm so glad": Boothroyd, p. 148.

"They had me": *Saturday Evening Post*, June 5, 1965.

"I found her": *LA Examiner*, May 24, 1952.

218   "Adults do have": *American Weekly*, February 8, 1953.

"When discipline is": Ibid.

"intrigued by horses": Ibid.

"unimpressed": Ibid.

"very charmingly helped": *Washington Post*, December 7, 1952.

"apparently perfectly happy": Ibid., December 11, 1952.

"Shirley Temple's four-": Ibid., December 7, 1952.
219 "incensed": Ibid, December 11, 1952.
"My only desire": UP release, December 18, 1952.
"staggered": Ibid.
"baffled": Ibid.
"To me": Ibid.
220 "a human interest": Ibid.

Chapter 12
221 "even if it led": Perrett, *A Dream of Greatness*, p. 261.
"a restoration of the": Ibid.
"It has such": Mosley, p. 73.
"I was pregnant": Ibid.
222 "On [January 30]": John Agar, PI.
"When Shirley divorced": Ibid.
223 (fn) "From our divorce": John Agar, PI.
"an aggressively upwardly": *San Francisco Examiner*, July 15, 1983.
224 "The children love": *Movieland*, July 1958.
"I've been interested" Ibid.
"The funny thing is": *LA Daily News*, May 5, 1951.
"reddish-brown leather": Mosley, p. 74.
225 "I enjoy color": Ibid.
"Once I forgot the baby": *TV Guide*, December 3, 1958.
"a fearless conversationalist": Ibid.
"because of the reaction": Ibid.
"I accepted on": Ibid.
226 "Darling, only": Mosley, p. 73.
"It's senseless": Ida Zeitlin, syndicated col., November 1950.
"of the wealthy": *Life*, July 30, 1965.
"Somehow [among": Diana Serra Cary, PI.
227 "I think it comes down": Ibid.
"I inherit that from": Ida Zeitlin, syndicated col., November 1950.
228 "she couldn't resist": Anon., PI.
"I think she did it": Ibid.
"We had to memorize": Diana Serra Cary, PI.
229 "being a movie-star": *Photoplay*, March 1958.
"Yes, Lori is crazy": Ibid.
"After all": Mosley, p. 76.
230 "I had other TV offers": Ibid, p. 77.
"a pushover": Ibid.
"Does Mommy go to Hollywood": Ibid.
"I told Shirley": Ibid.
"she got out her typewriter": Ibid.
"I'm a lawyer": Ibid.
231 "did just about everything": *Movieland*, July 1958.
"Shirley felt that Beauty": *Time*, January 27, 1958.

232 "She had all the warmth": Ibid.
"There were unexplored": Ibid.
"I see him coming": Ibid.
"You've got to": Ibid.
"I'm getting tired": Ibid.
"You're the one": Ibid.
"a pathetic": Ibid.
233 "a stagehand said": Mosley, p. 78.
"It proved once again": Ibid.
"That was *my* deal": Ibid.
"She drives a hard bargain": Ibid.
234 "hysterical fans": *Publishers Weekly*, December 28, 1958.
"I think Shirley's hobby": Ibid.
"You only have to": Ibid.
"Quaker black and white": *Saturday Evening Post*, June 5, 1965.
"Right off": Ibid.
"You have to arrive": Anon., PI.
"We all talk": *Saturday Evening Post*, June 5, 1965.
"Even as a baby": Ibid.
"I have a mean eye": Ibid.
235 "Skelton held back": Moseley, p. 78.
"a hotbed of rest": *San Francisco Examiner*, July 7, 1983.
"haven of rolling hills": Ibid.
236 "more footage": *Saturday Evening Post*, June 5, 1965.
"with old friends": Ibid.
"If there had not been": Ibid.
"the party given": Ibid.
"[I could see": Ibid.

Chapter 13
239 " 'I'll have you kidnapped' ": *LA Times West*, November 1967.
240 "like phantoms": MacClean, p. 174.
241 "is the kind of husband": Mosley, p. 80.
"While Charles": Anon., PI.
242 "disastrous cycle": *Newsweek*, September 11, 1967.
"private will": Ibid.
"problems aren't solved": Ibid.
"God is the most important": Ibid.
"pornography for profit": *San Francisco Chronicle*, June 1966.
"they would appreciate": Ibid.
243 "representing every": Ibid.
244 "the odds-on favorite": Minott, p. 126.
"She is also": Ibid.
"one of the biggest": *LA Times*, August 30, 1967.
"Not all actors": Ibid.
"a pretty bad movie": Ibid.

"a lack of leadership": Ibid.
"We have to keep": Ibid.
"and less on": Ibid.
"and I am the mother": Ibid.

245 "little Shirley Temple": *Life,* November 3, 1967.
"half-mad": *LA Times,* August 30, 1967.

246 "Just a few days": Anon., PI.

247 "If he did encourage her": Minott, p. 126.
"She's trying to get": Ibid.
"was all for": Ibid, p. 127.
"a great honor": Minott, p. 127.
"General Eisenhower": *San Francisco Chronicle,* August 29, 1967.

248 "Well, here you had": Anon., PI.
"too awkward to make": Minott, p. 43.
"wound up as": Ibid.
"he continued to lead": Ibid, p. 52.
"daring initiative": Ibid.

249 "McCloskey put the balance": Ibid.
"a small-town lawyer": Ibid.
"McCloskey loved the law": Ibid, p. 54.
"handled no-fee cases": Ibid.
"devoted to the concept": Ibid, p. 61.

250 "In the few seconds": Ibid, p. 119.
"If Shirley Temple was": Ibid, p. 120.
"exploit the female": Ibid, p. 121.
"The female voter": Ibid.
"The image of" to "Finally, in all": Ibid, p. 121.

251 "depicted a glacial": Ibid, p. 152.
"lectured people on": Ibid.
"Mrs. Black of wanting": *LA Times,* November 12, 1967.
"I seek a meaningful": Ibid.
"Is rat control": *Look,* October 1967.
"Shirley Temple Black": *Look,* November 1967.
"The children in": Ibid.

253 "a basic indelicacy": Minott, p. 154.
"Charles pushed for": Ibid.
"a freshly registered": *Newsweek,* November 6, 1967.
"sidled up": Ibid.
"On the way in": Ibid.
"mellow, serious and sincere": Ibid.
"John Public": Ibid.
"the country ought": Ibid.

254 "Ideologically": Minott, p. 152.
"Whitaker and Baxter had": Ibid, p. 154.
"only a sweater": *Women's Wear Daily,* October 1967.
"too PTA": Ibid.

255 "It would only take": Minott, p. 157.

"hawk or dove": *LA Times*, November 4, 1967.

"I don't know": Minott, p. 185.

"Would not San Mateo": Ibid, p. 186.

"I think we shall draw": Ibid.

256 "Whitaker and Baxter": Ibid, p. 189.

257 "The number one issue": *San Francisco Chronicle*, November 13, 1967.

"off-limits, part-time": Ibid.

"How can you say": Ibid.

"You are timing": Ibid.

"the thing to do": Ibid.

"I feel Mrs. Black": Ibid.

"Sorry about that": Ibid.

258 "This is no rally": Mosley, p. 84.

"I don't know": Ibid.

"No one is experienced": Ibid.

"an honest, hard-working": Ibid.

"A radio was turned on": Minott, p. 218.

259 "Face drawn": Ibid.

"I will be": *NY Times*, November 15, 1967.

"I've always": *San Mateo Times*, February 2, 1968.

"Well, you certainly": Anon., PI.

"If I had had": Mosley, p. 85.

"truly desirous": Paul McCloskey, PI.

260 "a slaughter": Minott, p. 237.

"warm, interesting": Paul McCloskey, PI.

(fn) "She is far more": Ibid.

Chapter 14

261 "the cataclysm": Perrett, *A Dream of Greatness*, p. 172.

"I feel quite": Ibid.

"Congressman McCloskey": *San Mateo Times*, February 2, 1968.

262 "putting some": Johnson, p. 646.

"as an admission": Ibid.

"I call the Federation": Mosley, p. 85.

264 "A bleak stone wall": *McCall's*, January 1969.

"had been charmed": Ibid.

"just come from": Ibid.

265 "the shriek of a low-flying": Ibid.

"The American Embassy": Ibid.

266 "It reminded me": Ibid.

267 "It's the Czech": *San Francisco Chronicle*, August 27, 1968.

268 "There is no doubt": Anon., PI.

"but I'll take": *San Francisco Chronicle*, August 30, 1968.

"a great hope": Ibid.

269 "as a means of": Ibid.

"not aware": Ibid.

"a vivid red": Mosley, p. 86.

Chapter 15

271 "the lingering aftermath": Barclay Hotel pamphlet.

"genteel decline": Ibid.

"downright seedy": Ibid.

"took to be a": Mosley, p. 86.

273 "You know that old": *LA Times*, September 6, 1969.

"A certain faction": Kotsilibas-Davis, p. 239.

"[Shirley's] appointment": Ibid, p. 205.

274 "the spotlight at": *NY Times*, September 17, 1969.

"I'm all gooseflesh": Ibid.

"mingled on the floor": Ibid.

"generally [behaved]": Ibid.

"sailed unhurriedly": *Newsweek*, September 29, 1969.

"the opposite of": *NY Times*, September 17, 1969.

275 "advisably": Ibid.

"either sidetracked": Ibid.

"I am proud of": *Newsweek*, September 29, 1969.

"resolutions concerning": Dante B. Fascell, PI.

"One of the": Ibid.

"She had not": Ibid.

276 "a most clever": Anon., PI.

"The Beloved Lady Delegate": *LA Times*, September 6, 1969.

"appreciated her strong": Dante B. Fascell, PI.

"Everybody has the": *LA Times*, September 6, 1969.

277 "I had never seen": Ibid, December 19, 1969.

"and a kind of housewifely": Ibid.

"In Ancient Rome": UN Document A/63/613.

"a barrage of irate": *NY Times*, December 12, 1969.

278 "the guests": Ibid.

"telling stories": Ibid.

"Do you realize": *LA Times*, October 17, 1969.

"remarkably youthful": *NY Times*, December 12, 1969.

279 "that emphasized": Ibid.

"A party such as this": Ibid.

"I presented to him": Ibid.

"I started to": Ibid.

280 "a few faux pas": Ibid.

"the U.S.'s": Ibid.

"where personal impressions": Ibid.

"People were surprised": Ibid.

"In the autumn of": Official records, U.N. 24th General Assembly, A/ C2/SR/1289 pp. 308–9.

"an indictment": Ibid.

"deeply in social": Ibid.

281 "I'm not afraid": Mosley, p. 91.

"I'm sorry I'm": *Washington Post*, December 9, 1969.

"Cherokee Indian": Ibid.

"a down-to-earth": Ibid.

"refugees are people": Ibid.

"The American foreign": *Meet the Press*, December 14, 1969.

282 "As Apollo 12": Dept. of State Bulletin, January 26, 1970.

"From his perspective": Ibid.

"I'd like to come back": *NY Times*, December 20, 1969.

"My children told me": *LA Times*, March 22, 1970.

"Oh yes": Ibid.

283 "I note we have": Government transcript, 25th Anniversary of the UN,
pp. 167–75.

"I hope it doesn't": Ibid.

"wring our hands": Ibid.

"Mrs. Black, I want to": Ibid.

"Mr. Congressman": Ibid.

"Yes, you did": Ibid.

284 "I want to say": Ibid.

"Mr. Kazen, you will": Ibid.

285 "Mr. Chairman, if I could": Ibid.

Chapter 16

287 "I don't think": *LA Times*, March 22, 1970.

"It's very": Ibid.

288 "an overqualified": *Saturday Evening Post*, summer 1972.

"implement national": Ibid.

"to increase": Ibid.

"Shirley Temple Black, one-time": *NY Times*, November 15, 1970.

305 "Once at a White House dinner": *Saturday Evening Post*, summer 1972.

"If Shirley": Ibid.

"All of us who have": Department of State Publication, November 8,
1971.

"Imagine, only": *Washington Post*, January 26, 1972.

306 "Of course": Ibid.

"wise in the ways of": *NY Times*, June 18, 1972.

307 "the indiscriminate": Ibid, June 6, 1972.

"unequivocally proclaim": Ibid.

(fn)"We find it incomprehensible": Ibid.

"ugliest of all": Ibid.

"to work within the conference": Ibid.

"cry of the": Ibid, June 9, 1972.

"imperialistic superpowers": Ibid.

"Our conference should": Ibid, June 11, 1972.

308 "puffed to the platform": Ibid.

"that it needed a Thomas": Ibid, June 17, 1972.

"even a Jefferson": Ibid.

"the political squalls": Ibid, June 18, 1972.

"beneath the polemics": Ibid.

"the acknowledgment of": Mosley, p. 92.

309 "Some presidential aspirants": *San Mateo Times*, June 30, 1972.
"America's Little Sweetheart": Ibid.
"Has twenty-five years": Ibid.
"the law of the sea": *McCall's*, February 1973.

310 "There is no difference": UPI, September 21, 1972.
"[b]oth countries will": Ibid.
"Please do not refer": Ibid.

311 "I bet this isn't going": *McCall's*, February 1973.
"could not bring": Ibid.
"We discussed": Ibid.

312 "When I came": Ibid.
"signed a release": Ibid.
"I felt": Ibid.
"some intermittent": Ibid.
"adversity into some help": Ibid.
"to get it on the wires": *Redwood City Tribune*, November 8, 1972.

313 "a simple mastectomy": Ibid.
"Coming out of a hospital": *McCall's*, February 1972.
". . . as I look": Ibid.

Chapter 17

315 "as if they were party favors": Shannon, *NY Times*, September 16, 1974.
"contact a Dr.": Ibid.
"Well, you know": Ibid.

316 "President Ford": Ibid.
"Mr. Bush . . . knows as much": Ibid.
"I do not recall if": President Gerald R. Ford, PI.
"Mrs. Black to": *Washington Post*, September 13, 1974.

317 "was longstanding": Ibid.
"As a developing country": *Washington Post*, September 13, 1974.
"I think that proves": *NY Times*, November 30, 1974.
"a good deal of": Ibid.
"My mother put": *Peninsula*, April 1986.

318 "the largest canner": *LA Herald-Express*, September 11, 1974.
"In a big double feature": *Washington Post*, September 21, 1974.
"crash, brush-up": Mosley, p. 102.

319 "as a proof to": Lamb, p. 285.

320 "so much money": Ibid.
"Ghana had been stripped": Ibid.
"As the economic situation": Ibid.
"had talked about": David Lamb, p. 221.
"a consideration": Kenneth Bache, PI.
"Many foreigners": Ibid.

321 "The economy simply": Ibid.
"It's not much of an": Ibid.

"Every morning when we opened": Anon., PI.

"There's no country club": *Washington Post,* August 30, 1974.

322 "There was keen anticipation": Ralph Graner, PI.

(fn)"The cheap, obvious": *Washington Post,* February 9, 1975.

"I want to see the embassy": *LA Times* supplement, November 28, 1981.

"are all going": Ibid.

323 "The Embassy was": Kenneth Bache, PI.

"Ten minutes on": *LA Times* supplement, November 28, 1981.

"The downstairs looked": Ibid.

"Our first night": *Ladies' Home Journal,* October 1975.

"accepted their dusk": Ibid.

"every-Sunday ritual": Mosley, p. 10.

"a killer": *Peninsula,* April 1986.

324 "I asked the State": Ibid.

"I thought back": Ibid.

"My first impression": Kenneth Bache, PI.

325 "It was probably": Mosley, p. 103.

"Your Excellency": Ibid.

"dabbled in": *Peninsula,* April 1986.

"He was very fearful": Ibid.

326 "The presence of": Kenneth Bache, PI.

"It was an exciting": Mosley, p. 104.

327 "cheered, hugged": *Ebony,* March 1976.

"I can't imagine": Anon., PI.

"The event was": Kenneth Bache, PI.

"my deputy chief": *Peninsula,* April 1986.

328 "I had met": John Linehan, PI.

"Whenever I saw": Anon., PI.

"Four of them": Mosley, p. 105.

329 "She's got these people": *Ebony,* March 1976.

"You've got to give it": Ibid.

"She wasn't used to": Kenneth Bache, PI.

"She had a pretty good": William Rosner, PI.

330 "The embassy staff": Ibid.

"an imposing white": *Ladies' Home Journal,* October 1975.

331 "something really odd": William Rosner, PI.

332 "respected the professionalism": Ralph Graner, PI.

"do what is possible": *Ebony,* March 1976.

"of an economy": Ibid.

"I don't think black": *U.S. News and World Report,* November 8, 1976.

333 "When he arrived": Ibid.

"as being strongly": Ibid.

"One thing that upsets me": Ibid.

"women's liberation": *LA Herald-Examiner,* March 21, 1975.

"Liberation": *U.S. News and World Report,* November 8, 1976.

"he retained his love": *Ladies' Home Journal,* October 1975.

"The only thing": William Rosner, PI.

334 "the Ambassador's daughter": Ibid.
"I explained": Ibid.

335 (fn)"The choice Washington": Lamb, p. 178.
"[t]he Ghanaians": Craig Baxter, PI.
"The reason given": *NY Times*, April 28, 1976.
"the United States": Ibid.

336 "Obviously, the climactic": Kenneth Bache, PI.
(fn)"Action, action": Lamb, p. 285.
"for consultations": *NY Times*, April 28, 1976.
"and remarked rather": Kenneth Bache, PI.

337 "I vividly recall": Kenneth Bache, PI.
"Africa is calling": *U.S. News and World Report*, November 5, 1976.

Chapter 18

339 "made responsible for": Historical research project No. 767, U.S. Dept.
of State, Office of the Historian.
"about half of the": Ibid.

340 "which sounds more like": *Redwood City Tribune*, July 21, 1976.
"shaking up anything": *Washington Post*, June 24, 1976.
"They came back": *LA Times*, September 30, 1976.
"low budget eleven": *NY Times*, August 20, 1976.

341 "had a White House": *Redwood City Tribune*, July 21, 1976.
"We had won the": Carter, Rosalynn, p. 38.
"the only thing": *People*, September 13, 1976.
"They all need wives": *San Francisco Chronicle*, September 30, 1976.

342 "I have to be my own": Ibid.
"Indecision is the thing": Ibid.
"I'm durable": Ibid.
"in a bid to put together": Johnson, p. 672.
"Behind the orderly": Ibid.
"not only new formulas": Hill and Williams, p. 1.

343 "I don't think she liked": Anon., PI.

344 "We'll be putting them": *Redwood City Tribune*, December 24, 1976.
"Sometimes I feel": *NY Times*, December 26, 1976.
"I planned Jimmy Carter's": Syndicated Interview, Steve Berry, August
1982.

345 "I remembered the": Carter, Jimmy, p. 18.
"on the bunting": Ibid, p. 19.
"I went over to look": Berry, August 1982.
"All the ballrooms": Carter, Rosalynn, p. 148.
" 'Are you having": Ibid.

346 "At each party": Ibid.
"I'll tell you": Berry, August 1982.
"I like him": *The Country Almanac*, Woodside, spring, 1977.

347 "Well, we arrived": Nancy Majors Voorheis, PI.
"We talked and talked": Ibid.

"We had plenty": *San Mateo Times,* October 8, 1977.

"Conversation is": Ibid.

"I need not remind": Ibid.

348   "I've done all that": *LA Times,* February 7, 1978.

"When you start": Ibid.

349   "Success has never": *Variety,* December 13, 1978.

"I think the only": Ibid.

"Just wait": Ibid.

"There are no Democrats": Ibid.

"I liked it": Ibid.

350   "wearing a bright": Moore, p. 64.

"looked like the kind": Ibid.

"I don't have": Ibid, p. 184.

351   "Frankly, I don't": *Variety,* December 14, 1981.

"abhorrent practice": *Peninsula Times,* June 1, 1986.

352   "That's why": Academy of Motion Picture Arts and Sciences.

"This is really": Ibid.

BIBLIOGRAPHY

Books

Allvine, Glendon. *The Greatest Fox of Them All.* New York: Lyle Stuart, Inc., 1969.

APTER, DAVID. *Ghana in Transition.* New York: Atheneum, 1963.

BASINGER, JEANINE. *Shirley Temple.* New York: Pyramid Publications, 1975.

BEST, MARC. *Those Endearing Young Charms: Child Performers of the Screen.* New York: A.S. Barnes, 1971.

BICKFORD, CHARLES. *Bulls, Balls, Bicycles & Actors.* New York: Paul S. Eriksson, Inc., 1965.

BOGLE, DONALD. *Toms, Coons, Mulattoes, Mammies and Bucks.* New York: Viking Press, 1973.

BOOTHROYD, BASIL. *Philip: An Informal Biography.* Edinburgh, Scotland: T. & A. Constable Ltd., 1971.

BROWNLOW, KEVIN. *The Parade's Gone By.* New York: Alfred A. Knopf, 1969.

BURDICK, LORAINE. *The Shirley Temple Scrapbook.* Middle Village, NY: Jonathan David Publishers, 1975.

BUSH, SARAH (SALLY) L., AND GENEVIEVE MERRILL. *Atherton Lands.* Atherton, CA: Bush, 1979.

BUSIA, DR. KOFI. *The Challenge of Africa.* New York: Frederick A. Praeger, Inc., 1962.

————. *Africa In Search of Democracy.* New York: Frederick A. Praeger, Inc., 1967.

CARTER, JIMMY. *Keeping the Faith.* London: William Collins, 1982.

CARTER, ROSALYNN. *First Lady from Plains.* Boston: Houghton Mifflin, 1984.

CARY, DIANA SERRA. *Hollywood's Children.* Boston: Houghton Mifflin, 1979.

CHERICHETTI, DAVID. *Hollywood Director, The Career of Mitchell Leisen.* New York: Curtis Books, 1973.

COLEMAN, CHARLES M. *P. G. & E. of California.* New York: McGraw-Hill, 1953.

COOPER, JACKIE. *Please Don't Shoot My Dog.* New York: Berkley Books (pb), 1984.

CROWTHER, BOSLEY. *The Lion's Share.* New York: E. P. Dutton, 1957.

DAVID, LESTER, AND IRENE DAVID. *The Shirley Temple Story.* New York: G.P. Putnam's Sons, 1983.

DEMPSEY, DAVID, AND RAYMOND BALDWIN. *The Triumphs and Trials of Lotta Crabtree.* New York: William Morrow, 1968.

EBY, LOIS. *Shirley Temple.* Derby, CT: Monarch Books, Inc. (pb), 1962.

EDWARDS, ANNE. *Early Reagan,* New York: William Morrow, 1987.

FEDERAL WRITERS' PROJECT OF THE WORKS PROGRESS ADMINISTRATION FOR THE STATE OF CALIFORNIA. *California, A Guide to the Golden State.* New York: Hastings House Publishers, 1939.

FORD, DAN. *Pappy: The Life of John Ford.* Englewood Cliffs, NJ: Prentice-Hall, 1979.

GOODMAN, EZRA. *The 50 Year Decline and Fall of Hollywood.* New York: Simon and Schuster, 1961.

GREENE, GRAHAM. *Graham Greene on Film: Collected Film Criticism, 1935–1939,* 1972.

GUSSOW, MEL. *Don't Say Yes Until I Finish Talking: A Biography of Darryl Zanuck.* New York: Doubleday & Company, Inc., 1971.

HALLIWELL, LESLIE. *Halliwell's Filmgoer's Companion.* 7th ed., New York: Charles Scribner's Sons, 1983.

———. *Halliwell's Film Guide.* 4th ed., New York: Charles Scribner's Sons, 1985.

HILL, DILYS M., AND PHIL WILLIAMS. *The Carter Years.* London: Francis Pinter Publishers, 1980.

JAMES, C.L.R. *Nkrumah and the Ghana Revolt.* London: Allison & Busby, 1977.

JEWELL, RICHARD B., WITH VERNON HARBIN. *The RKO Story.* London: Octopus Books Limited, 1982.

JACOBS, LEWIS. *The Rise of the American Film.* New York: Harcourt Brace Jovanovich, 1968.

JOHNSON, PAUL. *Modern Times.* New York: Harper and Row, 1984.

KATZ, EPHRAIM. *The Film Encyclopedia.* New York: The Putnam Publishing Group, 1979.

KOTSILIBAS-DAVIS, JAMES, AND MYRNA LOY. *Myrna Loy, Being and Becoming.* New York: Alfred A. Knopf, 1987.

KLINGENDER, F. D., AND STUART LEGG. *Money Behind the Screen.* London: Lawrence and Wishart, 1937.

KNIGHT, ARTHUR. *The Liveliest Art.* New York: The MacMillan Company, 1957.

LAMB, DAVID. *The Africans.* London: Methuen, 1985.

LOCKWOOD, MARGARET. *Lucky Star.* London: Odhams Press Limited, 1955.

MACGOWAN, KENNETH. *Behind the Screen.* New York: Delacorte, 1965.

MALTIN, LEONARD, AND RICHARD W. BANN. *Our Gang: The Life and Times of the Little Rascals.* New York: Crown Publishers, 1977.

MAYO, MORROW. *Los Angeles.* New York: Alfred A. Knopf, 1932.

MINOTT, RODNEY G. *The Sinking of the Lollipop: Shirley Temple vs. Pete McCloskey.* San Francisco: Diablo Press Inc., 1968.

MOORE, DICK. *Twinkle, Twinkle, Little Star.* New York: Harper & Row, Publishers, 1984.

MOSLEY, LEONARD. *Zanuck.* Boston: Little, Brown, 1984.

NESTEBY, JAMES R. *Black Images in American Films, 1896–1954, The Interplay Between Civil Rights and Film Culture.* New York: University Press, 1982.

NIVEN, DAVID. *The Moon's a Balloon.* New York: G. P. Putnam's Sons, 1972.

NORRIS, BARBARA S., AND SALLY L. BUSH. *Atherton Recollections.* Atherton, CA: Town of Atherton, 1973.

NORRIS, KATHLEEN. *Manhattan Love Song.* New York: P. F. Collier, 1934.

PARRISH, ROBERT. *Growing Up in Hollywood.* New York: Harcourt Brace Jovanovich, 1976.

PERRETT, GEOFFREY. *A Dream of Greatness.* New York: Coward, McCann & Geoghegan, 1979.

———. *America in the Twenties.* New York: Simon and Schuster, 1982.

———. *Days of Sadness, Years of Triumph.* New York: Coward, McCann & Geoghegan, 1973.

PICKFORD, MARY. *Sunshine and Shadow.* Garden City, NY: Doubleday, 1955.

POWDERMAKER, HORTENSE. *Hollywood: The Dream Factory.* Boston: Little, Brown, 1950.

ROSTEN, LEO. *Hollywood: The Movie Colony, The Movie Makers.* New York: Harcourt Brace, 1941.

SELZNICK, DAVID. *Memo from David Selznick.* New York: Viking Press, 1972.

SMITH, PATRICIA R. *Shirley Temple Dolls and Collectibles.* Paducah, KY: Collector Books, 1977.

TEMPLE, SHIRLEY, as told to Max Trell. *My Life and Times*. Akron, OH: The Saalfield Publishing Company, 1936.

TEMPLE, SHIRLEY. *My Young Life*. Garden City, NY: Garden City Publishing Co., 1945.

TYLER, PARKER. *Magic and Myth of the Movies*. New York: Henry Holt, 1947.

WATSON, DELMAR. *Goin' Hollywood*, ed, Paul Arnold. Hollywood, CA: Delmar Watson Publisher, 1987.

WHEELER-BENNETT, JOHN. *King George VI*. London: Macmillan, 1958.

WILSON, EDMUND. *The Thirties*. New York: Farrar, Straus & Giroux, 1980.

WINDELER, ROBERT. *The Films of Shirley Temple*. Secaucus, NJ: Citadel Press, 1978.

ZIEROLD, NORMAN J. *The Child Stars*. New York: Coward-McCann, 1965.

————. *The Moguls*. New York: Coward-McCann, 1969.

Reference Books

Current Biography, Who's News and Why. New York: The H. W. Wilson Co., 1941.

Current Biography, Who's News and Why. New York: The H. W. Wilson Co., 1950.

Periodicals/Magazines

Films in Review. December 1976: "Shirley Temple," by R. Bowers, pp. 577–94.

Films in Review. May 1963: "Shirley Temple's Films" p. 318, letters.

Jump Cut. July–Aug., 1974, "Shirley Temple and the House of Rockefeller," by C. Eckert, pp. 1, 17–20.

Modern Screen. March 1945: "Life with Mother," by Cynthia Miller, p. 34.

Motion Picture Magazine. July 1936: "The Life and Loves of Shirley Temple," by Dorothy Spensley, p. 34.

————. September 1936: "What! No More Worlds for Shirley to Conquer?" p. 51.

Movieland. June 1944: "If You Were Shirley Temple," by Jane Reid, p. 52.

————. January 1945: "This Is Myself," Shirley Temple, p. 30.

————. May 1946: "Shirley Temple's Advice to Margaret O'Brien," as told to Dorothy O'Leary, p. 34.

————. November 1946: "First Year . . ." by Mickell Novak, p. 48.

————. September 1947: "2nd Wedding Anniversary," by David C. McClure, p. 44.

————. May 1948: "John and Shirl," by Helen Hover Weller, p. 20.

————. January 1950: "The Truth about Shirley and John," p. 28.

————. April 1953: "Shirley—Love Comes First?" p. 46.

Movieland and TV Time. July 1958: "Let's Visit Shirley Temple!" by Anne Dawson, p. 34.

Photoplay. April 1936: "The Amazing Temple Family," by Kirtley Baskette, p. 14.

————. March 1937: "Protecting the Future of the Greatest Little Star," by Michael Jackson, p. 26.

————. September 1937: "Myth Shirley Temple," by Jack Smalley, p. 36.

————. November 1937: "The Answer to Shirley Temple's Future," by Dixie Willson, p. 24.

————. May 1938: "A Goddess Grows Up," by Kirtley Baskette, p. 14.

————. January 1939: "Shirley Temple's Last Letter to Santa," , p. 9.

————. June 1944: "Shirley at the Turn of the Teens," by Louella O. Parsons, p. 32.

————. March 1945: "Shirley in Short," by Elsie Janis, p. 36.

————. July 1945: "The Love Story of Shirley and Her Sergeant," by Ruth Waterbury, p. 56.

————. April 1946: "Super Matron," by Maxine Arnold, p. 39.

————. September 1946: "Big Girl," by Cameron Shipp, p. 57.

————. October 1946: "Act As If You're Beautiful," by Anita Colby, p. 48.

————. June 1947: "Ten Rules for a Happy Honeymoon," by Shirley Temple Agar, p. 34.

————. March 1948: "For My Baby," by Shirley Temple, p. 44.

————. August 1948: "Temple Lullaby," by Louella O. Parsons, p. 33.

————. May 1949: "A Letter to My Daughter," by Shirley Temple, p. 69.

————. August 1949: "Breakfast in Hollywood," by Jack McElroy, p. 58.

————. December 1949: "What Happened to the Temple Marriage?" by Louella O. Parsons, p. 32.

————. February 1950: "This You Must Understand," by Elsa Maxwell, p. 34.

———. November 1950: "Living Is Fun!" by Ida Zeitlin, p. 39.

———. February 1951: "Hawaiian Love Song," by Roberta Ormiston, p. 33.

———. March 1951: "The House That Grew Up," by Lyle Wheeler, p. 56.

———. June 1951: "Try, Try Again," by Sheilah Graham, p. 52.

———. September 1952: "Shirley Won't Come Back!" by Hedda Hopper, p. 52.

———. March 1958: "Why Shirley Came Back," by L. Pollock, p. 57.

———. February 1960: "Mommy Did You Really Know Shirley Temple?" by Jane Ardmore, p. 44.

———. March 1962: "America Falls in Love Again!" by James Hoffman, p. 27.

———. February 1973: "How I Faced the Tragedy of Breast Cancer," by Pat Rogalla, p. 30.

Screen Facts, No. 12 (Vol. 2, No. 6), 1965: "Shirley Temple," by Gene Ringgold, p. 1, "Films of Shirley Temple," p. 38.

Screen Guide. May 1947: "Shirley Temple: Part-time Star," by Jon Leff, p. 60.

———. March 1948: "Shirley Temple—Young Mother," by Marva Peterson, p. 26.

———. November 1949: "Fun in Your Own Backyard," by Shirley Temple, p. 62.

Shadowplay. August 1934: p. 22.

Repositories

Academy of Motion Picture Arts and Sciences, Los Angeles, California

Bettmann Archive, New York

British Film Institute, London

George Eastman House, Rochester, New York

Government Documents Library, Seely G. Mudd Library, Yale University, New Haven, Connecticut

Museum of Broadcasting, New York

Radio Hutton Photographic Archive, London

Rex Features Photographic Archive, London

Twentieth Century-Fox Archives, University of Wisconsin, Madison, Wisconsin

United States Mission to the United Nations, New York

University of California at Los Angeles, Los Angeles, California
    Oral History Collections: Ralph Freud Collection: George
    Cukor, box 2; Roddy McDowall, box 16; Alfred Lunt and
    Lynn Fontanne, box 12. Nunnally Johnson, 304/11, 481 pp.
    Gene Fowler on Myron Selznick, 1600, 1944–1973.
    Twentieth Century-Fox Archives
Warner Brothers, Universal Studios, and RKO Studios Film
    Archives, University of Southern California, Los Angeles,
    California

INDEX

ABC-TV, 221
Abel, Walter, 144
"Abe Lincoln Dinner," 261
Academy of Motion Picture Arts and
  Sciences, 80, 351
Acheampong, Ignatius Kutu, 319–320,
  322n, 325, 334–335, 336n
Adam's Rib, 191
Addams Family, The, 118n
Adler, Jacob, 349n
Adrian, 137
Adventure in Baltimore, 189–190
Advisory Board on the Merchant Marine,
  208n
Africa in Search of Democracy (Busia), 319n
Agar, Frank, 163
Agar, James, 163, 169n
Agar, John (1st husband):
  in Army, 164, 165–166, 182–183
  arrests of, 213–214
  background of, 167, 182–183
  drinking problem of, 179, 181, 183,
    189–190, 194, 199–200, 206
  film career of, 179–180, 181, 183, 186,
    187, 188, 189–190, 193–194, 198, 201,
    213–214, 220
  personality of, 175, 179
  Shirley dated by, 161, 163–164
  Shirley's divorce from, 199–201, 206,
    210, 214, 222
  Shirley's marriage to, 166–167,
    169–183, 188–189, 194–195,
    199–201, 208, 214, 227, 245
Agar, John, III, 223n
Agar, John George, 163, 164
Agar, Joyce, 163, 169
Agar, Lillian Rogers, 147, 151, 174

Agar, Linda Susan, *see* Black, Linda Susan
Agar, Loretta Barnett Combs, 213, 214,
  223n
Agency for International Development,
  332
Agnew, Spiro, 262, 315
Ah, Wilderness, 104
Akuffo, Frederick W. K., 336n
Alexander, Katherine, 144
Alexander's Ragtime Band, 114
All About Eve, 191
Allen, Fred, 205
Allen, Gene, 352
Allied Arts Guild, 225
All the King's Men, 191
Allvine, Glendon, 56
Allwyn, Astrid, 101
"Alone with You," 113n
Ameche, Don, 98, 114
American Academy of Diplomacy, 351
American Cancer Society, 313
American Council on Environmental
  Quality, 309
American Medical Association, 254
Ampex Corporation, 227–228
Anderson, Hulda "Ande," 79
Anderson, Marion, 273
Andrews, Harry, 125n
Angel's Flight railway, 17
"Animal Crackers (in My Soup)," 82
Annenberg, Lenore, 351
Archibald, Roy, 257, 258, 259
Arliss, George, 74
Armetta, Henry, 100
Arrowhead Village, 110–111
Arthur, Jean, 177, 209
Asphalt Jungle, The, 191

Associated Federation of Television and
    Radio Artists (AFTRA), 229
Astaire, Fred, 48, 94, 101, 124, 349
As the Earth Turns, 44
"At the Codfish Ball," 91

Baah, Kwame, 330
Babes on Broadway, 131–132
Baby, Take a Bow, 63, 66, 67
"Baby, Take a Bow," 52, 53, 75
"Baby, Take a Bow" dress, 233
Baby Burlesk films, 31–40, 70
Baby Peggy, 21–22, 29, 39, 75, 91, 92–93,
    97, 106, 226–227, 228
Baby Peggy Corporation, 106
Bache, Kenneth, 320–321, 323–324, 326,
    327, 329, 336, 337
Bachelor and the Bobby Soxer, The, 84n,
    180–181
Bachelor Knight, 84n, 180–181
Bachelors' Dance, 209
Bait, 214n
Baldwin, Andrew, 257
Ball, Lucille, 214n
Bank of America, 318
Barclay Hotel, 269, 271–272, 305
Barkley, Lillian, 77–78
Barnes, Howard, 144
Baroody, Jamil, 278
Barrie, James, 209, 229
Barry, Robert, 243n
Barrymore, Lionel, 45–46, 81, 82, 83, 97,
    140, 162, 343
Bartholomew, Freddie, 98, 102, 104, 118
Basserman, Albert, 140
Batman, 140n
Baum, Vicki, 176
Baxley, Barbara, 209n
Baxter, Anne, 178, 184
Baxter, Craig, 335
Baxter, Warner, 49, 50, 52, 56, 75, 97
Beard, Mathew, 98
"beautiful baby" contests, 28
"Beauty and the Beast," 231
Beckett, Scotty, 127n
Beery, Wallace, 47, 48, 74, 97
Bel-Air Country Club, 131
Bellah, James Warner, 186
Bell's Palsy, 348
Benchley, Robert, 144
Bergman, Ingrid, 139, 143, 167
Bernstein, Arthur, 71, 117–118

Bernstein, Leonard, 209
Bernstein, Lillian Coogan, 117–118
Berthugh, Inc., 196
Best, Willie, 83, 84
Best Years of Our Lives, The, 184
Bickford, Charles, 62
Big Jake, 214n
Big Sleep, The, 37n
"biopics," 197
Bishop, Doc, 79, 80, 100
Black, Charles Alden, Jr. (son), 217, 218,
    225, 226, 231, 232–233, 241, 244, 262,
    287, 311, 318, 341
Black, Charles Alden, Sr. (2nd husband):
    ancestry of, 280, 281
    background of, 207–209, 210
    business career of, 207, 221, 223, 227,
        268, 269, 341
    as conservative, 209, 211, 216
    in Ghana, 318, 324, 330, 333, 337
    in Naval Reserve, 213, 215, 221
    pesonality of, 208, 210
    physical appearance of, 208, 279
    Shirley as viewed by, 305, 343, 351
    as Shirley's campaign manager, 246,
        251, 253, 254, 258, 259, 260
    Shirley's marriage to, 210, 211–212,
        226, 305, 343, 351
    in Soviet Union, 239–241
Black, James Byers (father-in-law), 207,
    208n, 225, 240, 241
Black, James Byers, Jr., 207–208
Black, Katharine McElrath, 207
Black, Kathryn, 207–208
Black, Linda Susan (daughter), 188, 206,
    213, 217, 225, 226, 232n, 262, 287, 305
    acting by, 218–220, 232n, 305
    adoption of, 223n, 241
    custody of, 199, 200, 201, 222, 223n
    in Ghana, 318, 330, 333–334, 337
    marriage of, 333–334, 350n
    Shirley's relationship with, 211,
        218–220, 221–223, 224
Black, Lori Alden (daughter), 223, 229,
    230, 231, 232n, 234, 241, 262, 269,
    287, 330, 341
Black, Shirley Temple, *see* Temple, Shirley
Black Panthers, 281
Blair House, 342, 344
Bloom, Claire, 231
Blue Bird, The (1940), 124, 125–127, 128,
    178

Blue Bird, The (1976), 125*n*
Bogart, Humphrey, 122*n*, 349
Bogle, Donald, 84
Boles, Janet, 129
Boles, John, 82, 85, 129, 162
Bond, Ward, 187, 188, 189
Bourne, William, 235
Bowen, Elizabeth, 106*n*
Bowery, The, 47, 74
Boys Town, 98
Bradbury, William C., 217, 223
Bradley Farms, 215
Brand, Harry, 192, 198
Brantingham, Louella, 170
Braslaw, Albert, 222*n*
Braun, Eva, 166
Breck shampoo, 231
Bright Eyes, 37*n*, 63, 65, 67–70, 75, 80, 94*n*,
    140, 197
Brinkley, David, 258
Brooks, Angie E., 274–275, 280, 317
Brooks, Phyllis, 120
"Brother, Can You Spare a Dime?," 52
Brown, Lew, 51–52
Bruce, George, 135
Bruce, Virginia and Howard, 220
Buchenwald concentration camp, 166
Buckner, Robert, 175
Buffum, William B., 269*n*
Bulldog Drummond Strikes Back, 74
Bunche, Ralph, 273
Burk, Joseph, 208*n*
Burke, J. Herbert, 283–284
Burnett, Carol, 245
Burnett, Hodgson, 87, 121
Bush, George, 260*n*, 315, 316, 351
Busia, Kofi A., 319, 328
Butler, David, 65, 68, 69, 80, 83, 92,
    197–198, 349
Buttram, Pat, 349
"By the Beautiful Sea," 235

Cabaret, 189*n*
Cagney, James, 56, 94
Calhoun, Rory, 184
California Bank, 20
California Museum of Science and
    Industry, 26*n*
California State Exposition Building, 224
Call of the Wild, 74
"calls," 40
Cantor, Eddie, 48, 101

Captain January (1924), 21, 39
Captain January (1936), 39*n*, 75, 91–93, 100,
    105, 122*n*, 197, 228
Captains Courageous, 104
Captain's Kid, The, 122*n*
Carnation milk, 36
Carolina, 45–46, 53
Carter, Jimmy, 341, 343–346
Carter, Lillian, 346
Carter, Rosalynn, 341, 345–346
Carthay Circle Theatre, 141
Cary, Diana Serra, 21–22, 29, 39, 75, 91,
    92–93, 97, 106, 226–227, 228
Caspary, Vera, 75
Catherine the Great, 48
Catto, Henry E., 340
Chadwick, Helene, 42
Challenge of Africa, The (Busia), 319*n*
Change of Heart, 37*n*, 57, 58, 140
Changing of the Guard, 122*n*
Chaplin, Charlie, 21, 125
Charlie Chan, 61
Chevalier, Maurice, 48
Chicago Tribune, 252
Chico (monkey), 87
child-labor laws, 34, 39
Children's Hour, The (Hellman), 109
child stars:
    appeal of, 97
    defense mechanisms of, 226–227
    earnings of, 117–120
    film contracts of, 34, 119–120
    guilt felt by, 98
    as juvenile leads, 132
    Oscars awarded to, 80
    public appearances of, 112–113
    publicity on, 21–22, 27–28
    scene stealing by, 44
    star system for, 97–98
    see also specific child stars
Ching-Ching (dog), 87, 102
Chisum, 214*n*
Choate, Mrs., 141
Christians, Mady, 106
Churchill, Winston, 5
Cinderella incident, 218–220
Cleopatra, 48
Clift, Montgomery, 194
Clive of India, 74
Clyde, Andy, 42
Cocoanut Grove, 166
Coe, Richard L., 218–219, 305, 306

Colbert, Claudette, 80, 139, 140
Collins, Cora Sue, 44
Colman, Ronald, 74
Columbia Pictures, 61
"Come Get Your Happiness," 113n
Comet over Broadway, 122
Commonwealth Club of California, 348
Connecticut Yankee, A, 57
Convention People's Party (CPP), 318
Coogan, Jackie, 21, 43, 57, 58, 71, 97, 106, 117–119
Coogan, John Henry, 106n, 117
"Coogan Act, The," 119
Coolidge, Calvin, 25
Cooper, Gary, 66, 97
Cooper, Grant, 199
Cooper, Jackie, 27, 28, 47, 48, 52, 57, 58, 74, 97, 112–113, 119–120, 226
Cooper, John Sherman, 318
Cooperman, Alvin, 230, 232
Corky (dog), 87
Corrigan, Lloyd, 140
Costello, Dolores, 109
Cotten, Joseph, 140, 141, 142
Coughlin, Junior, 42
Council on Foreign Relations, Inc., 348
Country Doctor, The, 102
Courtland, Jerome, 144, 350, 351
Covered Wagon, 34
"Crackly Grain Flakes," 113n
Crash (1929), 27, 31, 55
Crawford, Joan, 56
Crews, Laura Hope, 40
Cromwell, John, 141
Crosby, Bing, 48, 56, 189, 216, 253
Crouse, Russell, 175
Crowther, Bosley, 178
Cukor, George, 141
Cummings, Irving, 100, 120
Curley McDimple, 245
Curly Top, 75, 82–83, 91
Curtin, Bill, 133–134
Curtis, Tony, 62n
Curtiz, Michael, 175
Czechoslovakian Central Committee, 263

Daddy Long legs, 75
Dames, 48
Dandridge, Dorothy, 140
Darling of New York, The, 21
dash, 323
David, Mack, 231

David Copperfield, 98
David Harum, 57, 66
Davis, Bette, 56
Dawn Patrol, The, 125
Day, Laraine, 131, 132, 198
de Gaulle, Charles, 142
De Havilland, Olivia, 141
Dell, Dorothy, 62, 66n, 75
Del Monte area, 208
Del Monte Corporation, 318
Del Rio, Dolores, 33
Demarest, William, 113
DeMille, Cecil B., 28
Democratic National Convention (1924), 21
Dempsey, Jack, 38
Dennin, Joseph F., 341n
Department of Protocol, U.S., 339–340
Depression, 5, 47, 52, 84, 124, 191–192
detente, 306
Devil Is a Sissy, The, 104
Dewey, Thomas, 213n
Dietrich, Marlene, 38, 93
Dillinger, John, 61
Dimples, 84n, 101
Dimsdale, Howard, 196
Dinah Shore Show, The, 235
Dionne Quintuplets, 102
Diplomatic Corps, U.S., 341
"disclaimers," 196
Disney Corporation, 318
Disraeli, 73n
Dobelle, Evan, 346
Dole, James, 207
Donnelly, Ruth, 49n
Dora's Dunkin' Doughnuts, 41–42
Double Furlough, 141
Douglas, Kirk, 108n, 214n
Drake, Betsy, 198
Drake, Tom, 193
Draper, William H., III, 243n, 258, 259n
Dreamland Choochoo, 211
"Dreams Are Made for Children," 231
Dru, Joanne, 194
Drum, Dorothy, 66
Dubček, Alexander, 263, 264, 267n
Duel in the Sun, 167, 176, 183
Duke, Angier Biddle, 339
Duke, Patty, 226
Dunn, James "Jimmy," 53, 56, 57, 59, 66, 70
Dunne, Irene, 176, 273

Durante, Jimmy, 120
durbar, 327
Durbin, Deanna, 119, 132
Dwan, Allan, 65, 107, 108, 109, 111

Earhart, Amelia, 333
Earle, Edward, 61
Ebsen, Buddy, 91
Edens, Roger, 133
Educational Films, 28, 31–42, 44–45
Edward VIII, king of England, 5, 76
Edward Small Productions, 134–135
Eisenhower, Dwight D., 220, 221, 247,
    254, 344n
Elgin Watch Company, 15
Elizabeth II, queen of England, 5, 76, 217,
    324
Eltz, Theodore von, 37, 140
Elusive Pimpernel, The, 196
Engel, Samuel, 192, 193
Enterprise Films, 195
Ernest Belcher School of the Dance, 28
Esny, Reeves, 142
Ethel Meglin Studios, 28–31

Fairbanks, Douglas, 48
Falaschi, Roberto, 330, 350n, 333–34
Falaschi, Susan Black, *see* Black, Linda
    Susan
Falaschi, Theresa Lyn (granddaughter),
    350
Fallen Idol, The, 191, 205
Famous Meglin Kiddies, 29
Farkas, George, 316n
Farkas, Ruth, 315
Farrell, Charles, 56, 57, 120
Fascell, Dante B., 269, 275, 276, 284–285
Faye, Alice, 40n, 48, 56, 98, 100, 101, 102,
    103, 114, 349
Fellows, Edith, 78, 98, 118, 227
Ferguson, Katharine, 169n
Ferris, Walter, 106
Fetchit, Stepin, 84n
Fink, Hymie, 135
Firestone Tire and Rubber Company,
    326n
Fitzgerald, Barry, 197
Flake, Nancy, 18
Flanigan, Peter, 315, 316
Floor, Minerva, 133
Flynn, Errol, 94, 185n
Folger, James, 235

Folkets Hus, 307
Fonda, Henry, 186, 188
Fonda, Jane, 125n
Fong, Hiram, 268
Fontaine, Joan, 139, 143
Foote, John Taintor, 198
Ford, Betty, 312n
Ford, Dan, 187–188
Ford, Gerald R., 314, 315, 316, 317, 325,
    326, 336, 340–341, 342, 349
Ford, John, 104–105, 121n, 132, 186,
    187–188, 190, 193, 194
Foreign Correspondent, 132
Foreign Service, U.S., 341
Fort Apache, 37n, 121n, 186–188, 189, 190
Fortune, 179
Forty Pounds of Trouble, 62n
42nd Street, 49, 50, 73n
Fountainhead, The (Rand), 191
Fox, William, 54–55
Fox Pictures, *see* Twentieth Century-Fox
Fox Wilshire Theatre, 142
Francis, Kay, 49, 221
Franklin, Dexter, 144, 161
Freddie Martin's Orchestra, 166
Frelinghuysen, Felix, 283
"Frolics of Youth" series, 42, 45, 49
Frontier Gun, 214n
Front Page, The, 34
Funseth, Robert, 335
Furtseva, Eketerina, 310

Gable, Clark, 5, 56, 74, 80, 94, 97, 109, 189
Gallagher, Cornelius E., 283
Gallagher, Thomas, 169n
Gallery, Ann, 163
Gallup Poll, 142
Garbo, Greta, 5, 56, 94
Garden of Allah, The, 109
Gardner, Ava, 125n
Gargan, William, 135
Garland, Judy, 30, 118, 123, 124, 131, 132,
    349
Gay Divorcee, The, 48
Gaynor, Janet, 45, 46, 56, 57
General Service Studios, 195
George V, king of England, 5
George VI, king of England, 5, 217n
George White's Scandals, 40, 48, 51
German-Soviet Treaty of Friendship and
    Alliance (1939), 124
Ghost Mountain, 185n

Gill, Florence, 42
Gillette, William, 349n
Gillingwater, Claude, 121
Girls' Dormitory, 92
Glad Rags to Riches, 34, 36
Godfrey, Peter, 184
Go Fight City Hall, 235–236, 237
Goldwater, Barry, 237, 349
Goldwyn, Samuel, 196
Gone With the Wind, 84, 103, 139, 140, 141
Gone With the Wind (Mitchell), 86n, 103,
    125, 140
Good Housekeeping, 26
Gordon, Mack, 101
Gorney, Jay, 49–52, 53
Gottlieb, Alex, 183–184, 185
Goulding's Lodge, 186–187
Grable, Betty, 98, 118n
Granas, Marilyn, 77n
Graner, Ralph H., 322, 332
Grant, Cary, 180–181
Grapes of Wrath, The, 98, 121
Grayson, Kathryn, 195
Great Dictator, The, 125
Great Gatsby, The, 191
Great O'Malley, The, 122n
Great Society, 244
Great Western Power Company, 207
Greed, 41
Green, "Little Mitzie," 28
Green, Paul, 45
Greene, Graham, 93, 105–106, 240, 245
Greene, Richard, 122
Greer, Howard, 169
Greff, Ernest, 169n
Grey, Joel, 232n
Grey, Zane, 42
Griffith, John "Grif," 77, 79, 93, 100, 110,
    129, 133, 134, 137, 138, 139, 162
Gros, Richard R., 210
Grossman, George, 67
Guernsey, Otis L., 178
Guest in the House, 184
Gulf of Tonkin Agreement, 261
Gustav VI Adolph, king of Sweden, 306
Gwynn, Edmund, 176
Gypsy, 59

Hadsel, Fred Latimer, 320
Haldeman, Robert, 139
Hale, Jonathan, 135, 140
Haley, Jack, 100, 101

Hall, Al, 57
Hall, James Norman, 207
Hall, Porter, 144
Hamilton, Neil, 140
Hamlet, 191
Hammerstein, Oscar, 125
Hammons, Earl Woolridge, 31, 32–33, 34
"Hang Out the Washing on the Siegfried
    Line," 125
Hanneford, Poodles, 82
Happy Landing, 114
Harburg, E. Y. "Yip," 52
Hardie, Russell, 44
Harlow, Jean, 56
Harvard Business School, 175, 208
Harvey, Lilian, 67
Hathaway, Henry, 42, 43–44, 48, 57, 58
Hawaiian Pineapple Company, 207, 209
Hawaiian Pineapple Company Building,
    207
Hayakawa, S. I., 349
Hayes, Bill, 236
Hays, Jack, 31, 33, 34n, 38, 39, 41, 42, 45
Hearst, Phoebe, 129, 133, 162, 169n
Hearst, William Randolph, 129
Hecht, Ben, 34
Heidi, 65n, 103, 106–111, 123, 228
Heiress, The, 191
Hellman, Lillian, 109
Hellman, Sam, 91
Henie, Sonja, 98, 114
Hepburn, Katharine, 56
Herbert, F. Hugh, 143, 144, 196
Hereford, John, 169n
Here's My Heart, 48
Her First Beau, 132
Herndon, Roy L., 199, 200
Hersholt, Jean, 102, 106, 109–110
Herter, Christian A., Jr., 287, 308
Heston, Charlton, 231
Hetz, Mrs. Robert, 17n
Hickman, Darryl, 98, 144, 351
Highlife dance, 326
Hillcrest Memorial Hospital, 215
Hiller, Wendy, 123
Hills Brothers coffee, 231
Hoch, Winton C., 193n
Hoffman, Charles, 184
Holden, William, 190
Hollywood Reporter, 133n
Home of the Brave, 191
Honeymoon, 176–178

Honeywell Foundation School, 218–220
Hoover, Herbert, 25
Hope, Bob, 62n, 216
Hopper, Hedda, 126
Hotchkiss, Andrew D., 137, 141
Hotchkiss School, 208
Hotel Inter-Continental, 271n
Houck, Leo, 40, 51
House of Connolly, The (Green), 45
House of Rothschild, The, 74
Howell, Kenneth, 42
How Green Was My Valley, 132
Hudson, Rochelle, 82
Human Comedy, The, 36
Hunter, Ian, 122
Huntley, Chet, 258
Hurrell, George, 78–79

I Am a Camera (Van Druten), 189n
I Am a Fugitive from a Chain Gang, 73n
Ideal Toy Company, 233
"If I Had One Wish to Make," 113n
I Found Stella Parish, 122n
I'll Be Seeing You, 141, 143, 164
I Married a Communist, 198, 199
Informer, The, 104
Ingram, Reginald, 332
In Old Chicago, 114
"In Our Little Wooden Shoes," 107n
Intermezzo, 139
International Federation of Multiple
     Sclerosis Societies, 241n, 262, 263, 264
Isherwood, Christopher, 189
Islieb, Mary Lou, 64, 77, 79, 110, 136,
     169n, 192, 198, 229
It Happened One Night, 47–48, 80

Jackson, Anne, 209n
Jaffe, Henry, 229, 230–231, 232, 235
Jason, Anita, 122
Jason, Sybil, 122–123, 126–127, 178, 349,
     351
Javits, Jacob, 272
Jazz Singer, The, 73n
Jean, Gloria, 132
Jefferson, Thomas, 308
Jenkins, Jackie "Butch," 36
Jeritza, Maria, 55
Jiagge, Annie, 333
Johnny Reno, 214n
Johnson, Deane, 234
Johnson, Erskine, 205

Johnson, Lyndon, 241, 243, 244, 262
Johnson, Nunnally, 73–74
Johnson, Osa, 87
Johnson's Wax, 326n
Johnston, Johnny, 195
Joint Chiefs of Staff, U.S., 244
Joint Committee on Cooperation in the
     Field of Environmental Protection,
     309, 310
Jolson, Al, 48, 101, 122n
Jones, Carlisle, 198
Jones, Freda, 108
Jones, Jennifer, 139, 140, 143, 167, 176,
     183, 205
Jones, Marcia Mae, 106, 108–111, 112,
     123, 349, 351
Jorgensen, Harry G., 211
Josephson, Julien, 106
Journey for Margaret, A, 36, 132
Just Around the Corner, 84n, 120–121
"Just Around the Corner," 133
Justice Department, U.S., 55

Kahanamoku, Duke, 112
Kaiser Aluminum Corporation, 326n
Kalmbach, Herbert, 315
Kanin, Michael, 176
Kathleen, 131–133, 136
Katie (housekeeper), 63, 93
Kazen, Abraham, Jr., 284
Keating, Edward M., 257, 259n
Keaton, Buster, 31
Keeler, Ruby, 48, 49, 50
Keighley, William, 176–177
Kellogg's Corn Flakes, 36
Kelly, Grace, 220
Kennedy, Ethel, 266
Kennedy, John F., 220, 234, 248
Kennedy, Myrna, 37
Kennedy, Robert F., 263, 266
Kent, Robert, 101
Kern, Jerome, 125
Khrushchev, Nikita, 239, 240
Kibbee, Guy, 91, 122n, 135
Kid, The, 21, 97
Kid Millions, 48
Kid 'n' Hollywood, 38
Kid's Last Fight, 38, 39
Kimball, Dan, 216–217
King, Henry, 45, 46
King, Martin Luther, Jr., 263
King Kong (1976), 214n

Kinney, Abbot, 20
Kipling, Rudyard, 103
Kirillin, Vladimir, 310
Kirkland, Patricia, 143–144
Kiss and Tell, 143–144, 161, 190, 195
Kiss for Corliss, A, 195–197, 198–199
Kissinger, Henry, 305, 306, 318, 334–336, 342
Klampt, Frances "Klammie," 78, 79, 102, 236
Knight, Goodwin J., 254
Korean War, 212–213, 221
Krieger, Maude Elizabeth McGrath (grandmother), 15, 16, 19, 20
Krieger, Otto Julius (grandfather), 15–17
Krieger, Ralph (uncle), 15, 16, 19, 20, 24
Krieger's Jewelry Shop, 16–17
Kruschen, Jack, 236
KTTV, 209

La Barba, Fidel, 90
Lady for a Day, 61
Lahr, Bert, 120
Lail, Betty Jean, 169n
Lamb, David, 320
Lamont, Charles, 31, 32–34, 35, 36, 39, 45
Lanchester, Elsa, 232
Lang, June, 91–92, 105, 162
Lang, Walter, 123, 127
Langdon, Harry, 31
Lange, Jessica, 214n
LaShelle, Joseph, 69, 79
Last of the Mohicans, The, 134
"Last Time I Saw Paris, The," 125
Lauder, Harry, 99
Laughton, Charles, 74
Laurel, Kay, 55
Lawrence, Gertrude, 104
Lawrence, Peter, 209
League of Nations, 25
Lee, Dixie, 56
"Legend of Sleepy Hollow, The," 232
Lehman, Gladys, 91
Lehman Brothers, 208n
Leigh, Vivien, 139, 141, 143n
Leisen, Michael, 232
Lejeune, C. A., 199
Leonard, Audrey Ray, 33
LeRoy, Mervyn, 123
Lesser, Sol, 106
Lessing, Norman, 231

Life, 241
"Life Is Just a Bowl of Cherries," 24
Life of Emile Zola, The, 109
Life with Father, 175–176
Lincoln, Abraham, 84, 86, 229
Lindsay, Howard, 175
Lindsay, John, 272
Linehan, Jack, 327, 328, 329–330
Little Annie Rooney, 135
Little Bigshot, The, 122n
Little Caesar, 73n
Little Carnation (pony), 86
Little Colonel, The, 76, 77, 81–82, 83, 84n, 85, 91, 162, 197, 244n
Littlefield, Lucien, 49n
Little Miss Broadway, 120
Little Miss Marker (1934), 48, 57–58, 61–62, 66, 75, 80, 84n, 99, 102, 122n
Little Miss Marker (1980), 62n
Little Princess, The (1917), 20, 41
Little Princess, The (1939), 121–123, 124, 126, 127
Little Princess, The (Burnett), 87, 121
Littlest Rebel, The, 83, 85–86, 91, 105, 162, 197, 229, 283
Livingston, Jerry, 231
Lloyd, Harold, 130, 169
Lockhart, Gene and Kathleen, 129
Lockhart, June, 129
Lodge, John, 244n, 317n
Loew, Marcus, II, 195
Loew's, Inc., 55
Lombard, Gary, 66
London *Sunday Observer*, 199
Look, 252
Loos, Mary, 193
Loper, Don, 231
Los Angeles *Herald Tribune*, 21
Los Angeles Times, 59, 133n, 144, 188, 212n, 252
Louise, Anita, 122
Loy, Myrna, 180–181, 273, 276, 278
Lucky Penny (Smith), 120
Lyle, Bessie, 83, 84n

MacArthur, Charles, 34
MacArthur, Douglas, 213, 216, 244
McCall, Mary, Jr., 193
McCallister, Lon, 197
McCall's, 313
McCloskey, Paul N. "Pete":
    background of, 248–249

congressional campaign of, 243*n*,
  248–251, 252, 254–256, 258–262
McCormick, John, 99
McCracken, James, 209*n*
McCrea, Joel, 82
McDaniel, Hattie, 84*n*, 140
MacDonald, Jeanette, 48, 56
McDowell, Roddy, 132
MacFadden, Hamilton, 53
McFarland, Spanky, 28
McGovern, George, 309
Mack Sennett studio, 28, 31, 43
McKuen, Rod, 232*n*
McLaglen, Victor, 97, 104, 105, 162, 186,
  188, 189
McNamara, Robert S., 244
McNeill, John, 169*n*
Madison, Guy, 140, 176, 178
Madsen, Leonard John, 23
Maeterlinck, Maurice, 124
Magic Carpet, The, 214*n*
Main, Marjorie, 48
Maison de Rêves, La, 67
Majors, Cort, 64
Majors, Helen McCreary, 64, 171
Majors, Marion, 63, 64, 129, 130, 346–347
Majors, Nancy, *see* Voorheis, Nancy
  Majors
Majors family, 63–64, 87–88, 136, 162,
  229
Malele, 112
Malik, Yakov A., 279
Managed Money, 45
Mandalay, 49
Manhattan Club, 272
Man in the Iron Mask, The, 134
Mann, Thomas, 81
Mannequin, The, 109
Man Who Came to Dinner, The, 176
March, Fredric, 74
Margaret (housekeeper), 231
Margaret, princess of England, 5, 76, 327
Margie, 192*n*
Marin, Edwin, 135–136
Marine Development Associates
  (Mardela), 268
Market Women's Association, 326
Marshall, Herbert, 92*n*, 132
Martin, Graham, 281
Martin, Judith, 322*n*
Martin, Willsie, 169
Marwyck Farms, 198

Marx, Groucho, 349
Marx, Zeppo, 198
Mary Tyler Moore Show, 236
Masquers Club, 349–350
Massacre (Bellah), 186
Matthau, Walter, 62
Mayer, Louis B., 131, 133, 183
Meet the Press, 281
Meglin Kiddies Band, 42, 52*n*
Men, The, 191
Menjoy, Adolphe, 61
Merrily Yours, 41–42
Merry Widow, The, 48
Mesta, Perle, 271
Metro-Goldwyn-Mayer (MGM), 47, 56,
  61, 66, 73, 85, 94, 98, 102, 104,
  141–142
Michtom, B. F., 233
Milbak Productions, 195
Miller, Colin, 195–196
Mills, Carol, 129, 131, 138, 162
Minnie Mouse, 348
Miracle on 34th Street, 132
Misérables, Les, 74
Miss Annie Rooney, 135–137, 138, 351
Mississippi Flood (1927), 25
Mr. Belvedere Goes to College, 190, 192–193,
  194
"Mr. Clean," 214*n*
Mister Roberts, 121*n*
Mr. Smith Goes to Washington, 248
Mitchell, Margaret, 86*n*, 103, 125, 140
Mitchell, Sidney D., 107*n*
Mix, Tom, 67
Monaco, Daniel J., 257
Moneychangers, The, 108*n*
Montgomery, George, 349
Montgomery, Peggy, 21
Monument Valley, 186
Moore, Dickie, 43, 47, 98, 127*n*, 128,
  135–136, 350
Moorehead, Agnes, 140
Morgan, Frank, 97, 101
Morgenthau, Henry, 99
Morley, Karen, 162
Moscow Art Theatre, 349*n*
Mosher, John, 136
Mosley, Leonard, 90, 120
"Mother Goose," 232
Mother Was a Freshman, 192*n*
Motion Picture Patent Company, 54–55
Motion Picture Research Project, 94

Mountbatten, Edwina, 99
Mouthpiece, The, 73*n*
movies:
  "B," 67, 90
  comedy, 31, 35
  early period of, 19–20
  gangster, 61
  magazines about, 21
  music in, 48, 53
  production code for, 196
  sound in, 31
  two-reel, 48
  see also specific movies
Muni, Paul, 56
Murphy, George, 120, 237, 244*n*, 245, 250, 251, 253
musicals, 48, 53
Mussolini, Benito, 150
My Darling Clementine, 186
My Dog Buddy, 234
Myers, Harry, 42
My Gal Sunday, 26
Myrt and Marge, 26
My Son, My Son, 134
Nash, Mary, 107
National Committee on United
  States–China Relations, Inc., 348
National Conference on World Refugee
  Problems, 281
National Geographic, 325
National Labor Management Panel, 208*n*
National Multiple Sclerosis Society, 220,
  222, 225, 236, 239–241, 262, 263, 264,
  288, 343, 348
National Velvet, 132
NATO (North Atlantic Treaty
  Organization), 267*n*
Nazimova, Alla, 140
New Deal, 47
New Deal Rhythm, 48
New York Daily News, 56, 58
New Yorker, 105, 106*n*, 136, 188
New York Herald Tribune, 144, 178
New York *Journal,* 58
New York Times, 101, 121, 178, 252, 288,
  308, 316
New York World, 54
New York World's Fair Corporation, 208*n*
Night and Day, 105, 106*n*, 240
Night Games, 242, 252
Night Nurse, 109
Niven, David, 196

Nixon, Pat, 343
Nixon, Richard M.:
  China trip of, 306, 307–308
  Shirley and, 216, 220, 234, 239, 245,
    254, 262, 263, 268, 269, 281, 282, 287,
    288, 305, 316, 344*n*
  Watergate scandal and, 309, 313–314,
    315, 342
Nkrumah, Kwame, 318–319, 321, 325
Nob Hill area, 208
North American Company, 207
Northridge Farms, 198
Now and Forever, 63, 66, 75
Now I'll Tell, 57
Nugent, Frank, 101, 121, 186

Oberon, Merle, 279
obies, 224
O'Brien, Margaret, 36, 132
O'Brien, Pat, 122*n*
"Oh My Goodness," 101
"Oh, You Nasty Man," 30*n*, 40*n*
Oklahoma!, 209*n*
Olds, Glen, 280
Oliver, Edna May, 120
Oliver Twist, 47
Olivier, Laurence, 191, 349
O'Neill, Henry, 57
O'Neill Children, 29
One in a Million, 114
One Man's Family, 37*n*
"On the Good Ship *Lollipop,*" 70, 113*n*,
  243, 251, 259, 260, 322*n*, 334
On the Town, 191
Organization of American States, 344
Orsatti, Frank, 134
Osborne, Robert, 351
Our Gang series, 28, 31, 37, 98
Our Little Girl, 82, 91
Out All Night, 40–41, 42

Pacific style, 223–224
Padden, Sarah, 44
Palme, Olof, 306–307
"Parade of the Wooden Soldiers, The,"
  113
Paramount, 27, 47, 48, 49, 57–58, 61, 62,
  66
Pardon My Pups, 45
Parsons, Louella, 34, 62, 66, 101, 118–119
Parsons, Louis, 216
"Party for Shirley, A," 253

Pascal, Ernest, 125
Pawling Preparatory School, 164
Pearl Harbor attack, 165
Peck's Bad Boy, 47
Peduase Lodge, 330
People's Republic of China, 276, 306,
    307–308, 330, 347–348
Peple, Edward, 83
Perrett, Geoffrey, 148
Peter Pan (Barrie), 209, 229
Phelps, George, 222n
Phillipson, William, 229, 230
Photoplay, 26
Pickford, Mary, 20, 26, 41, 48, 65–66, 82,
    85, 100, 105, 113, 135, 271
Pie Covered Wagon, 34, 69n
Pigskin Parade, 132
Pinky, Champion, 191
Pitts, ZaSu, 40, 41, 42, 86, 163, 172–173,
    176
Pollack, Lew, 107n
Polly-Tix in Washington, 38, 39
"Pollywolly Doodle," 85
Polytechnic High School, 17
Ponselle, Rosa, 99
Poor Little Rich Girl, A (1917), 20
Poor Little Rich Girl, The (1936), 95,
    100–101
Pope, James, 332
Portrait of Jenny, 183
Powell, Dick, 48, 49
Powell, Jane, 98
Powell, William, 176
Power, Tyrone, 92n, 98, 109, 114
Pretty Baby, 198
Price, Robert, 321–322
Producers' Showcase, 229, 230
Prohibition, 47
Public Enemy, The, 73n
Pygmalion, 123

Queen of Bermuda, 104
Quiet Man, The, 121n
Quigley, Juanita, 127n

Ralston, Esther, 42
Ramparts, 257
Rand, Ayn, 191
Randolph, Lillian, 84n
Random House, 233
Rawlings, Jerry, 336n
Reagan, Nancy, 312n

Reagan, Ronald:
    film career of, 183, 184–185, 244n, 250,
        251, 253, 288
    political career of, 237, 242, 243, 244n,
        245, 247, 250, 251, 253, 351
Rebecca, 139
Rebecca of Sunnybrook Farm (1917), 20, 41
Rebecca of Sunnybrook Farm (1938), 84n, 113,
    114, 218, 228, 332–333
Red-Haired Alibi, 37–38
Red River, 194
Red Skelton Show, The, 235
Redwood City Tribune, 312
Reed, Carol, 191
Reis, Irving, 181
Republican National Committee, 262, 268
Revel, Harry, 101
Reynolds, Gene, 127n
Rin-Tin-Tin series, 73
RKO (Radio-Keith Orpheum), 47, 94,
    186
Roach, Hal, 30
Robards, Jason, 214n
Roberts, Edith, 184
Robinson, Bill "Bojangles," 76, 81–82, 85,
    86, 113, 120, 162
    racial prejudice and, 83–84, 332–333
Robinson, Edward G., 56
Rogers, Charles "Buddy," 48
Rogers, Ginger, 48, 57, 94, 102, 124, 141,
    142
Rogers, Will, 56, 57, 66, 74–75
Rogers, William P., 287
"Rogers family" series, 42, 45, 49
Rollins, Betty, 312n
Roman, Ruth, 140
Romay, Lina, 178
Romero, Cesar, 105, 122, 162, 349,
    351–352
Rooney, Mickey, 28, 98, 104, 131
Roosevelt, Eleanor, 81, 99, 333
Roosevelt, Franklin D., 5, 21, 47, 76, 81,
    84, 166, 339
Roosevelt, Selwa, 351
Roosevelt, Theodore, 249
Rosner, William K., 329–330, 331, 333,
    334
Rowdy (dog), 87
Runt Page, The, 34
Runyon, Damon, 48, 57, 61
Russell, Johnny, 125
Ryan, Robert, 198

"St. Louis Blues," 51
St. Valentine's Day Massacre, The, 214n
Sale, Richard, 193
Samuels, Lesser, 189
San Francisco Ballet Association, 208n
San Francisco Chronicle, 252
San Francisco Commonwealth Club, 347–348
San Francisco Film Festival Committee, 242
San Francisco Golden State International Exposition, 208n
San Francisco International Film Festival, 226
San Francisco Symphony Association, 208n
San Mateo County, Calif., 243, 245, 247n, 255–256
San Mateo Times, 261, 309
Santa Monica, Calif., 21, 22–23
Santa Monica Children's Little Theater, 87
Santa Monica Hospital, 23
Saroyan, William, 36
Saunders, Mary Jane, 62n
Schary, Dore, 141–142, 180, 181
Schenck, Joseph M., 63n, 66, 73, 74, 93, 119
Scheuer, Philip K., 144
Schilling, August, 235
Schrank, Joseph, 231
Schulz, Robert L., 247
Scott, Randolph, 42, 113, 124
Scott, Raymond, 113
Sealtest dairies, 231
Secret Service, 349n
Seiter, William, 102
Selznick, David O., Shirley's contract with, 103, 139, 141, 142, 143, 144, 166, 167, 171, 175–176, 179, 183, 184, 192, 195, 196–197, 205, 212, 225
Selznick, Irene Mayer, 183
Selznick International, 143, 197n, 205–206
Sevier, John, 280
Shannon, William, 316
Shearer, Norma, 56
Sheehan, Winfield, 52, 53–56, 66–67, 68, 74, 77, 83, 88, 119
Sheldon, Sidney, 180
"She's Only a Bird in a Gilded Cage," 34
She Wore a Yellow Ribbon, 121n, 190, 193–194

Shidler, Frederick P., 312
Shields, Arthur, 198
"Shirley Temple Amendment, The," 119
Shirley Temple dolls, 64, 233, 252, 334
Shirley Temple's Fairyland, 233n
Shirley Temple's Stories that Never Grow Old, 233n
Shirley Temple's Storybook, 230–233
Shirley Temple Storybook, The, 233n
"Shirley Temple Story Development," 75
Shirley Temple Theater, 235n, 246
Shultz, Dave, 312
"Side by Side," 235
Siegel, Sol, 143–144
Sierra Club, 225, 348
Simmonds, Roy, 106
Simon, Simone, 92n
Simpson, Wallace, 5
Sims, Gregory K., 243
Sinatra, Frank, 220
Since You Went Away, 37n, 84n, 139–141, 164, 176, 205, 208
Sinclair, Upton, 55
Singing Kid, The, 122n
Sitting Pretty, 190, 192
60 Minutes, 322
Skippy, 27, 28
Skolsky, Sidney, 65
Small, Edward, 134, 136–137
Smith, Alfred E., 21, 25–26
Smith, C. Aubrey, 104, 105
Smith, Georgie, 34, 37, 38
Smith, Paul Gerard, 120
soap operas, 26
Sondheim, Stephen, 59
Sorrowful Jones, 62n
Southern California Edison Company, 17, 19
Spectator, 93
Spellbound, 167
"Spelvin, George," 349n
Sperling, Milton, 89–90
Spring Valley Water Company, 235
Spunky (pony), 86, 87n
Spyri, Johanna, 103, 106
Stagecoach, 186
Stalin, Joseph, 221
Stand Up and Cheer, 50, 51–54, 57, 58–59, 67, 71, 75, 84n, 192
Stanford Children's Convalescent Hospital, 26n
Stanford Hospital, 225

Stanford Law School, 248
Stanford Research Institute, 223, 227
Stanford University, 208
Stanwyck, Barbara, 56, 109, 198
State Fair, 46, 57
Stevens, Craig, 140
Stevens, Roger, 209
Stewart, Jimmy, 97, 248
Stimson, Sara, 62
Story of Alexander Graham Bell, The, 114
Story of Seabiscuit, The, 197–199
Stowaway, 101–102, 190, 306
Strand Productions, 195–196
Strong, Maurice, 306
Stuart, Gloria, 100, 101, 113
studio lots, 35, 67
"Stymie," 98
Subcommittee on International
    Organizations and Movements,
    282–285
Sullivan, Walter, 308
Summerlin, George, 339
Summerville, Slim, 40, 92
Sunset Boulevard, 191
Susannah of the Mounties, 123–124
Swarts and Tannenbaum, 134*n*
Swedish National Day, 306
Swissair ad campaign, 272–273

Taft, Robert, 309
talent scouts, 30*n*, 31–32
talkies, comedy shorts and, 31
Tang Ka, 307
Taylor, Elizabeth, 125*n*, 132, 176, 225
Temple, Cynthia Yaeger (grandmother),
    18
Temple, Florence Bruce, 220
Temple, Francis (grandfather), 18
Temple, Francis, Jr. (uncle), 18, 19
Temple, George Francis (father):
    banking career of, 17, 19, 20, 21, 25, 26,
        27, 28, 63, 93, 94
    childhood of, 17–19
    death of, 350
    financial investments by, 71, 94–95,
        118–119, 128, 167, 175, 201, 228
    health of, 227
    personality of, 19, 65, 88
    physical appearance of, 19
    retirement of, 226
    Shirley's dependence on, 95, 112, 126,
        162, 169

Shirley's film career as viewed by,
    29–30, 32, 33, 34, 37, 39, 40, 49, 54,
    71, 89
Temple, George Francis, Jr. "Sonny"
    (brother), 15, 19, 22
    multiple sclerosis of, 220, 239–240, 262
    Shirley's relationship with, 23–24, 71,
        80, 88, 112, 138, 163, 169*n*, 180
Temple, Gertrude Amelia Krieger
    (mother):
    aloofness of, 41, 43, 69–70, 126
    ambition of, 41, 75
    childhood of, 15–17
    death of, 344
    doll collection of, 26, 87
    health of, 269, 311, 347, 348, 350
    marriage of, 15, 17, 19, 21, 22, 163, 182
    motion pictures watched by, 19, 20
    "normal" life desired by, 64, 76, 87, 226
    personality of, 43, 65, 88, 136, 174
    physical appearance of, 17, 19, 65
    romantic fantasies of, 15, 17, 21, 22, 30
    Shirley coached by, 23, 24, 35–36,
        62–63, 67–68, 69, 76–77, 79,
        102–103, 177–178, 185, 197–198,
        232–233, 234, 236
    Shirley's costumes designed by, 34–35
    Shirley's dependence on, 31, 35, 49,
        65–66, 78, 80, 95, 112, 134, 138, 139,
        161–163, 189, 201, 206, 226, 227, 228,
        246, 317, 344, 348
    Shirley's film career managed by,
        29–30, 32, 33, 34, 36, 37, 38, 40, 41,
        42, 54, 62, 71, 75, 85, 107–108, 114,
        121, 127–128, 129, 143, 352
    Shirley's first marriage as viewed by,
        166–167, 175, 194
    Zanuck and, 78, 107, 121, 128
Temple, Grace (aunt), 18–19
Temple, Herbert (uncle), 18, 19
Temple, John Stanley "Jack" (brother),
    15, 19, 22, 26, 39, 126, 175, 188, 215,
    227
    Shirley's relationship with, 23–24, 71,
        80, 88, 112, 138, 163, 169*n*, 180
Temple, Miriam Ellsworth "Mimsy," 138,
    169*n*, 175, 188, 215
Temple, Patricia Ruth, 220
Temple, Richard (nephew), 220
Temple, Shirley:
    acting of, 76–77, 98–99, 102–103, 184
    adolescence of, 5, 130, 131, 137

Temple, Shirley – *cont.*
  as adult star, 139, 161, 167, 177–178,
    184, 185
  advertisements filmed by, 36
  as ambassador to Ghana, 315–337, 341,
    342, 343, 347, 350, 351
  on American Council on Environmental
    Quality, 309
  ancestry of, 17–18
  as anti-communist, 269, 276
  appendicitis attack of, 215
  attire of, 273–274, 277, 278, 283, 285
  auditions by, 32–33, 40, 49
  in Baby Burlesk films, 31–40, 43, 49, 93
  Barrymore's confrontation with, 45–46,
    53
  "big break" for, 49–52
  birth of, 22, 23
  birth certificate of, 23*n*, 43*n*
  birthday parties for, 95, 198
  blacks in films of, 83–85, 332–333
  "bossiness" of, 93, 111
  box-office appeal of, 5, 82, 85, 99, 102,
    103, 111*n*, 113–114, 115, 121, 127,
    133, 136
  breast cancer of, 309–310, 311–313, 317
  Brentwood Heights home of, 86–87, 88,
    93
  bridal shower of, 169
  bungalow of, 67, 77, 78, 128
  business sense of, 230–231, 233–234
  Caesarian sections of, 217, 223
  camera appeal of, 36
  campaign contributions of, 317
  campaigning by, 251–258
  as career woman, 255, 333, 342
  as Carter inauguration, 343–346
  charm of, 48
  as chief of protocol, 339–346, 351
  childhood friends of, 39, 63–64, 79,
    87–88, 126
  as child star, 36–37, 39, 47, 57, 62, 88,
    98, 102, 104, 114, 123, 127–128, 138,
    161, 283, 324–325, 348–350
  in China, 347–348
  clippings and stills kept by, 224–225
  close-ups of, 57
  comebacks of, 141, 143, 167, 208, 225,
    226, 227–229, 230, 348
  competition of, 44, 68–70, 98–99, 102,
    114, 122, 126–127
  congressional race of, 5–6, 242–260,
    261–262
  as conservationist, 225, 276, 282,
    287–288, 305–309, 310, 311, 317, 343
  as conservative, 237, 255, 262, 276
  contracts of, 34, 37, 42, 43, 44, 54, 58,
    62–63, 78, 119, 128, 139, 190, 195,
    197, 205–206, 212, 230–231
  on corporate boards, 318, 348
  as corporation, 94, 95
  costumes of, 34–35, 52, 99, 137, 224
  critical reviews of, 93, 101, 102, 121,
    127, 133, 141, 144, 161, 177, 185–186,
    188, 199
  curls of, 35, 141
  in Czechoslovakia, 263–267
  daily routine of, 35–36, 70, 78, 79, 99
  as dancer, 23, 27, 28–31, 36, 48, 67–68,
    81–82, 135
  dancing lessons taken by, 28–31, 35, 48,
    50
  dangerous scenes filmed by, 38–39
  dating by, 130, 133, 137
  death threats against, 272, 324
  as debater, 254, 255–258, 260
  decline in career of, 97–99, 124–126,
    127–128, 129, 194, 195, 209, 212
  dental care of, 100
  determination of, 229
  as diplomat, 279–280, 288, 305, 315–337
  discovery of, 31–33
  divorce of, 199–201, 206, 210, 214, 222
  doll collection of, 26, 87, 136, 222, 224
  Doll House of, 136, 222
  drawings by, 126
  earnings of, 34, 49, 66–67, 85, 89,
    93–95, 114
  education of, 78, 79, 93, 102
  at Educational Films, 28, 31–42, 44–45
  engagement of, 166–167
  exploitation of, 41, 226
  fame of, 5, 63, 66, 71, 75, 80–81, 86,
    97–99, 100, 114, 131, 195, 234–235,
    245, 246–247, 251–252, 278
  family raised by, 226, 227, 229, 230, 241,
    303, 311, 312, 330
  famous visitors of, 81, 99
  fan mail of, 63, 66, 142–143
  father figures of, 88–89, 146
  feature films of, 35, 37–38, 40, 46, 47,
    49, 50*n*, 57, 63
  film credits of, 41, 42–43, 49
  film debut of, 33–34

finances of, 71, 94–95, 118–119, 128, 167, 175, 201, 228

first marriage of, 166–167, 169–183, 188–189, 194–195, 199–201, 208, 214, 227, 245

first screen kiss of, 135–136, 350

foreign affairs as viewed by, 272, 275–276, 281, 351

foreign voter registration drive of, 262, 263, 267–268

as former child star, 5–6, 74, 162, 218–220, 246, 250, 251, 273, 284–285, 287–288, 318, 329

frankness of, 280

French studied by, 318

as fund-raiser, 243, 253–254

golf played by, 225, 317

as goodwill ambassador, 288, 305

hair color of, 26, 215*n*

height of, 131

honeymoons of, 173–174, 212

as infant, 23

as interior decorator, 222, 223–225, 227, 235, 241

inventiveness of, 44

IQ of, 102

isolation of, 68–70, 79, 90, 110–111, 350

on Joint Committee on Cooperation in the Field of Environmental Protection, 309, 310

as juvenile lead, 131, 132–133

kidnapping as danger to, 80–81, 129, 324

leading men of, 161–162

lines memorized by, 35, 42, 45–46, 228, 232

as "Little Miss Fix-It," 75, 82

loan-outs of, 57–58, 143, 176, 183, 186, 196–197, 205

at Masquers Club ceremonies, 349–350

maturation of, 97–98, 101, 102, 104, 114–115

medicine as interest of, 210–211, 227

middle name of, 23*n*, 42–43, 247

as mimic, 24

moral values of, 233, 234, 242

as mother, 189, 211, 217–220, 225, 255

mumps contracted by, 225–226

naïveté of, 90, 103

in National Multiple Sclerosis Society, 220, 222, 225, 236, 239–241, 262, 263, 264, 288, 343, 348

Native American Indians as viewed by, 280, 281

nicknames of, 26, 36, 71, 89, 130

"normal" life needed by, 64, 76, 87, 226

official age of, 43, 58, 59, 102

Order of George Spelvin given to, 349

Oscar awarded to, 80, 352

perfect pitch of, 27

personality of, 43, 48, 68, 69, 88, 93, 137–138, 179, 181–182, 325, 333, 342

petulance of, 179

phonetic ability of, 306, 310

photographs of, 78–79, 80, 99

physical appearance of, 246, 253, 278–279, 347

piano owned by, 77, 128, 224

political opinions of, 216, 217, 234, 244, 259–260, 262, 272, 281

popular songs learned by, 48

preadolescence of, 98, 102, 104, 114, 123

precociousness of, 36, 59, 93

pregnancies of, 186, 187, 199

press coverage of, 5, 44, 57, 58–59, 62, 63, 244–245, 252, 256, 267–268, 276, 288, 310–311, 312–313, 316, 317, 332

press notices of, 44, 57, 58–59, 62, 63

as "princess," 5, 6, 76, 80, 86, 168, 194, 327

privacy valued by, 206

products with name of, 63, 64, 94, 99, 233, 252, 334

public appearances of, 86, 99–100, 112–113, 170, 171–172, 233–234, 255

publicity on, 5, 36, 102, 129, 139, 140, 142–143

as public speaker, 236–237, 241–242, 261, 262, 268, 273, 277–278, 280, 281–282, 308

radio as influence on, 26–27

rat-control issue and, 252–253, 255

rebellion of, 161–162, 174

recordings of, 211

refugee problem as viewed by, 281

rehearsing by, 35, 36

as religious, 347

as Republican, 25, 216, 236–237, 241, 245–246, 247, 259, 261–262, 273, 288, 343, 349

responsibilities of, 226–227

retirement of, 127–128, 129, 131

rhythmic sense of, 24

Temple, Shirley – *cont.*
  Rockingham Avenue home of, 210, 221,
    222
  in "Rogers Family" series, 42, 45, 49
  roles played by, 41, 42
  in Romania, 288
  Roosevelt and, 6
  Sarah Coventry "Woman of the Year"
    award given to, 281
  screen personality of, 75–76, 103–104,
    124, 135, 161–162
  screen tests of, 33
  as "screen veteran," 47
  scripts written for, 75–76, 85–86, 91,
    102, 124
  second marriage of, 210, 211–212, 226,
    305, 343, 351
  self-identity of, 138–139
  sexuality of, 93
  shooting schedules for, 78
  in short features, 48, 63
  sleeping habits of, 227
  at social affairs, 278, 279
  in Soviet Union, 239–241, 310–311
  "sparkle" of, 36, 37, 49, 102, 177, 198
  as storyteller, 232
  studio personnel for, 77–79
  before Subcommittee on International
    Organizations and Movements,
    282–285
  in Sweden, 306–308
  taxes paid by, 94, 128
  television pilot made by, 235–236, 237
  television series of, 229–233, 235n, 246
  on Third Committee, 276–278
  timing of, 36
  as tomboy, 104
  as Twentieth Century-Fox, 48, 50–58,
    62–63, 66–67, 74–75, 85, 88–89, 104,
    106, 115, 349
  in two-reelers, 48
  on United Nations Committee on
    Environment, 287, 288, 305–308
  at United Nations Conference on
    Human Environment, 305–308
  in United Nations Conference on
    Human Environment, 305–308
  in United Nations delegation, 268–285,
    316, 317, 343
  vacations of, 80, 99–100, 104, 112–113,
    206–207
  Vietnam War as viewed by, 242, 244,

  252, 253, 257, 259, 260, 261, 275, 276,
    305
  as viewed by other child actors, 43, 59,
    63–65, 68–70, 87–88, 128, 130,
    133–134, 137, 139, 169–170, 172, 210,
    346–347, 350
  voice of, 280, 324–325
  in Washington, D.C., 215–217, 221,
    228, 237
  wedding dress of, 169, 170–171
  weddings of, 169–173, 175, 211–212
  at Westlake School for Girls, 129–131,
    133–134, 137–139, 161, 162,
    164–165, 166, 182, 210, 226
  youth programs supported by, 276–277
"Temple blue," 170
Tennyson, Alfred, Lord, 61
terHorst, j. F., 316
Thant, U, 274
That Hagen Girl, 183–186, 197
Thaxter, Phyllis, 178
These Three, 109
Thin Ice, 114
Thin Man, The, 61
Third Committee, 276–278
Third Man, The, 191, 205
Thoroughbreds Don't Cry, 132
thriller serials, 20
Time, 76, 141
Todd, Ann, 127n
Tolbert, William R., 336
Tolstoy, Ilya, 99
Tom Sawyer, 28
Tone, Franchot, 178
To the Last Man, 42–44, 68
Touré, Sekou, 319
Tower Films, 37
"Toy Trumpet," 113
Tracy, Spencr, 57, 94, 98, 189
Train, Russell, 307, 308, 309
Treacher, Arthur, 83, 97, 110, 122
Treasure Island, 48
"Tribute to Shirley Temple, A,"
  351–352
Truman, Harry S., 166, 208, 212–213, 216,
  217n, 244, 254, 344n
Tully, Tom, 144
Twentieth Century-Fox:
  management of, 45, 50, 61, 73, 84,
    89–91, 92, 106, 120, 143, 192, 193,
    235–236
  Temple's career at, 48, 50–58, 62–63,

66–67, 74–75, 85, 88–89, 104, 106, 115, 349

Zanuck as head of, 66, 84, 88–91, 93, 104–105, 120, 192, 236

Twinkle, Twinkle, Little Star (Moore), 350

Two Men and a Girl, 176–178

two-reel featurettes, 48

Tyson, Cicely, 125n

Ugrin, Anthony, 99n

Uncle Tom's Cabin, 101

Undefeated, The, 214n

United Artists Corporation, 73, 74, 134, 195, 196

United Nations, 268–285, 316, 317, 343

United Nations Association, 279n, 348

United Nations Ball, 279

United Nations Committee on the Environment, 287, 288, 305–308

United Nations Conference on the Human Environment, 305–308

United Nations General Assembly, 274–275, 305

United Nations Security Council, 279, 305

United Press International, 310–311

Universal Studios, 45, 119

University of Nevada, 192

University of Pennsylvania, 18, 208n

Ustinov, Peter, 278

Vallee, Rudy, 24, 48, 51

Vanderbilt, Harold Stirling, 271

Van Druten, John, 189n

Vanguard Films, 197n

Vanity Fair, 26

Variety, 37, 44, 57, 58, 62, 101, 102, 114, 133n, 136, 161

Venable, Evelyn, 82, 162

Venice, Calif., 20

Vietnam War, 241, 242, 244, 252, 253, 257, 259, 260, 261, 262, 263, 275, 276, 305, 306–307, 345

Viva Villa!, 48

von Stroheim, Eric, 38, 41

Voorheis, Nancy Majors, 121, 129, 163, 173, 211

Shirley as remembered by, 59, 63–65, 87–88, 128, 130, 133–134, 137, 139, 169–170, 172, 210, 346–347

Voorheis, Philip, 210n

Wainwright, Carol, 87n

Waldheim, Kurt, 306, 307

Walker, Robert, 140, 143

Wallace, Richard, 190, 195

Wall Street Journal, 252

Walters, Frank, 169n

War Babies, 33–34, 36, 39–40

Warner, Clove, 200

Warner, Harry, 73

Warner, Jack, 122, 175, 183–185, 197

Warner Brothers Studios, 44, 47, 49, 56, 61, 66, 73, 74, 85, 94, 183–184, 196

Warren, Earl, 172, 254

Washbourne, Mona, 125n

Washbourne, Mona, 125n

Washington Post, 218–220, 305, 317, 318, 322n

Watergate scandal, 309, 313–314, 315, 342, 345

Watson, Bobs, 98

Watson, Coy, 43, 44, 57, 108

Watson, Delmar, 43, 68, 95, 98, 106, 107–108

Waugh, Evelyn, 106n

Wayne, John, 186, 187, 188, 189, 190, 193–194, 214n

Webb, Clifton, 190, 192, 193

Webb, Constance, 169n

Wee Willie Winkle, 103, 104–106, 111n, 122n, 162, 228, 328

Weidler, Virginia, 131–132

Weiner, Sanford, 250–251, 254, 256, 259

Welles, Virginia, 144

West, Mae, 349

Westlake School for Girls, 129–131, 133–134, 137–139, 161, 162, 164–165, 166, 182, 210, 226

Westley, Helen, 113

Whalen, Michael, 100

Whalley, J. Irvin, 269n

What Price Glory?, 33

What to Do?, 45, 49

"When I Grow Up," 83

Whitaker and Baxter, 254, 255, 256, 260

White, Pearl, 19–20

Whitmore, Earl B., 243n, 256

Wiggin, Kate Douglas, 113

Wilcox, Claire, 62n

Wilder, Margaret Buell, 140

Will Rogers Memorial Grounds, 86

Wilshire Methodist Church, 169, 170

Wilson, Edmund, 61

Wilson, Emerald "Speedo," 164

Wilson, Emmett H., 119
Wilson, Lois, 34, 69, 349
Wilson, Woodrow, 25
Withers, Grant, 37
Withers, Jane, 68–70, 75, 88, 90, 98, 132, 349, 351, 352
Wizard of Oz, The, 123, 124, 125, 231
Woman of the Year, 176
Women's Wear Daily, 254
Wonder Bar, 48
Wood, Natalie, 98, 132
Woods, Donald, 44
Woolley, Monty, 139, 140
Works Progress Administration (WPA), 84
World Affairs Council of Northern California, 348
"World Owes Me a Living, The," 66
World War II, 124–125, 164–165, 168
Wright, Loyd, 63, 71

Wright, Teresa, 178, 184
Wynn, Keenan, 140

Yost, Charles W., 269, 276, 283
Young, Loretta, 56, 74, 98, 103
Young, Robert, 45–46, 98, 102, 189, 190
Younger, Jean Arthur, 242–243, 247, 249
Young People, 127

Zanuck, Darryl F.:
    Gertrude Temple and, 78, 107, 121, 128
    as scriptwriter, 73–74, 85–86, 120
    Shirley and, 73–75, 85–86, 88–91, 95, 97–98, 100, 114–115, 119, 120, 124, 127–128, 170, 349
    as studio head, 66, 84, 88–91, 93, 104–105, 120, 192, 236
Zanuck, Richard, 89, 236
Ziegler, Ronald, 269